# Thinking About Clinical Legal Education



*Thinking About Clinical Legal Education* provides a range of philosophical and theoretical frameworks that can serve to enrich the teaching and practice of Clinical Legal Education (CLE). CLE has become an increasingly common feature of the curriculum in law schools across the globe. However, there has been relatively little attention paid to the theoretical and philosophical dimensions of this approach. This edited collection seeks to address this gap by bringing together contributions from the clinical community, to analyse their CLE practice using the framework of a clearly articulated philosophical or theoretical approach. Contributions include insights from a range of jurisdictions including: Brazil, Canada, Croatia, Ethiopia, Israel, Spain, UK and the US. This book will be of interest to CLE academics and clinic supervisors, practitioners and students.

**Omar Madhloom** is a Senior Lecturer and Solicitor at the University of Bristol Law School. His current research focuses on applying moral philosophy to clinical legal pedagogy.

**Hugh McFaul** is Director of the Open Justice Centre at The Open University and has research interests in the public understanding of law, knowledge exchange and technology enhanced learning.

## Emerging Legal Education

**Series Editors**:
Paul Maharg, *Osgoode Hall Law School, York University, ON, Canada,*
Elizabeth Mertz, *University of Wisconsin-Madison/American Bar Foundation, USA* and
Meera Deo, *Thomas Jefferson School of Law, San Diego, CA, USA*

Emerging Legal Education is a forum for analysing the discourse of legal education and creating innovative ways of learning the law. The series focuses on research, theory and practice within legal education, drawing attention to historical, interdisciplinary and international characteristics, and is based upon imaginative and sophisticated educational thinking. The series takes a broad view of theory and practice. Series books are written for an international audience and are sensitive to the diversity of contexts in which law is taught, learned and practised.

*Other titles in this series:*

**Affect and Legal Education**
Emotion in Learning and Teaching the Law
*Edited by Paul Maharg and Caroline Maughan*

**Imperatives for Legal Education Research**
Then, Now and Tomorrow
*Edited by Ben Golder, Marina Nehme, Alex Steel and Prue Vines*

**Better Law for a Better World**
New Approaches to Law Practice and Education
*Liz Curran*

**Public Legal Education**
The Role of Law Schools in Building a More Legally Literate Society
*Richard Grimes*

**Thinking About Clinical Legal Education**
*Omar Madhloom and Hugh McFaul*

https://www.routledge.com/Emerging-Legal-Education/book-series/ELE

"The past decade has seen a steady increase in the number of law schools in the UK offering a law clinic experience to their students. This book promises to make an important contribution to our understanding of the rich and varied experience that clinical legal education can bring to law schools. The global reach of the book and the application of pedagogical and legal theories to law clinic settings offers a rich and valuable resource that will be of interest, not only to the clinic legal community, but to all educators interested in transformative educational experiences grounded in social justice and community partnerships."

Lucy Yeatman, Director Liverpool Law Clinic, Co-Chair Clinical Legal Education Organisation.

**Lucy Yeatman**
Director Liverpool Law Clinic
Liverpool Law Clinic, School of Law and Social Justice

"*Thinking about Clinical Legal Education* provides the perfect opportunity to pause, reflect and reconsider. These essays beautifully articulate the natural entwinement of bustling student law clinics, and a wide spectrum of philosophical theories. An inspiring and essential read which rightfully challenges the reader to keep ethics at the forefront of legal education."

**Frances Ridout**
Director of the Legal Advice Centre (CLE) – Queen Mary University of London
Barrister and Senior Lecturer

"This is an exciting and innovative collection of essays that collectively represent a timely contribution to Clinical Legal Education literature (CLE). The philosophical and epistemological insights articulated by the authors underscore the value of CLE, salute its history, and provide a fresh, twenty-first century perspective on experiential learning, professionalism, and the challenges of contemporary legal practice. It's a 'must read' for every law teacher's bookshelf."

**Rachel Spencer**
Associate Professor
Director, Monash Law Clinics - Clayton & Melbourne
Monash University

"The editors are to be congratulated on drawing together such a team of all the talents to contribute to this timely collection of essays with its diverse global perspectives into clinical legal education. The future of this exciting and flexible form of learning through experience is guaranteed, despite the challenges of lockdown, by the innovative approaches of contributors, their evident passion for justice, and their ability to balance theory and practice."

**Professor Simon Lee**
Open University Law School

# Thinking About Clinical Legal Education

## Philosophical and Theoretical Perspectives

**Edited by**
**Omar Madhloom and Hugh McFaul**

Routledge
Taylor & Francis Group
LONDON AND NEW YORK

First published 2022
by Routledge
2 Park Square, Milton Park, Abingdon, Oxon OX14 4RN

and by Routledge
605 Third Avenue, New York, NY 10158

*Routledge is an imprint of the Taylor & Francis Group, an informa business*



*British Library Cataloguing-in-Publication Data*
A catalogue record for this book is available from the British Library

*Library of Congress Cataloging-in-Publication Data*
A catalog record has been requested for this book

ISBN: 978-0-367-27349-1 (hbk)
ISBN: 978-1-032-10131-6 (pbk)
ISBN: 978-0-429-29924-7 (ebk)

DOI: 10.4324/9780429299247

Typeset in Baskerville
by Taylor & Francis Books

*To Dr John Frederick Huntley (1949–2020)*
*(Omar Madhloom)*

*To Claudine, Maddie, Meri, Rupert and Sherbet*
*(Hugh McFaul)*

# Contents

# Table

# Foreword

At the International Journal of Clinical Legal Education ('IJCLE') conference at Comenius University in Bratislava,[1] Hugh McFaul called for those involved in Clinical Legal Education ('CLE') to engage in reflection that would be 'thicker, more grounded and more theoretical'. I wrote that down in my notebook, celebrating and thinking 'this is what I had hoped for in our network'. CLE is a lovely, active, collegial community, with a tradition of sharing the procedural specifics and local characteristics of clinical practice. When I took over as editor of the IJCLE[2] in 2014 I celebrated that tradition and pledged to preserve that vital space. It remains a strong theme in the journal, a source of rich descriptive data for interpretation as well as the basis for systematic review and pattern analysis.[3] I also knew that we could do different things, so I challenged my new colleagues to do more empirical work, more comparative studies and to engage more critically with theory. The first two challenges were taken up enthusiastically and in this strand of the conference, where I had been invited to act as Discussant, I saw the third coming to vibrant life.

What I thought – but did not write – was that this thick, grounded, theoretical reflection sounded difficult. I am a fan of theory and philosophy, though I should confess that this was a late-blooming preference (akin to olives, pickles and malt whisky) and I would like to apologise in print to my undergraduate philosophy tutor, who could not prise me away from my commitment to over-simplifying ideas. I still need to start somewhere: further down the page I wrote some key terms (with definitions where I thought I needed them) related to the goals of CLE, some temporary 'rough ground' in Wittgenstein's terms.[4] I was excited to see these concepts being introduced as tools we could work with and happy to work with my basic

1 Details of this conference, including papers and presentations can be found here <https://www.northumbria.ac.uk/about-us/news-events/events/2019/07/ijcle-2019/> accessed 03 March 2021.

2 An open access peer reviewed journal hosted here <https://www.northumbriajournals.co.uk/index.php/ijcle> accessed 03 March 2021.

3 See Tribe Mkwebu, 'A systematic review of literature on clinical legal education: a tool for researchers in responding to an explosion of clinical scholarship' IJCLE 22(3) (2015) 1; Tribe Mkwebu, 'Unpacking Clinical Scholarship: Why Clinics Start and How They Last' (2017) 4(1) Asian Journal of Legal Education 33.

4 Ludwig Wittgenstein, *Philosophical Investigations* (4th edn, John Wiley and Sons 2010).

understanding. Later I ventured onto the 'slippery ground' and added some marginal comments, wondering about the nature and potential of these concepts to become limiting or, preferably, to develop into epistemic tools.[5]

| | |
|---|---|
| *** | *Do these concepts mean what I think they mean?* |
| ***Eudaimonia – 'flourishing'*** | *Who gets to define them? Is excellence assessed? How?* |
| ****Arete – 'excellence'**** | *Are there multiple modes of being/professional or* |
| ***Phronesis/praxis*** | *practical wisdom/theorised practice? Probably yes.* |
| *** | *Are some privileged? Definitely yes.* |

The papers in that stream and the chapters in this book all contribute to both a plain text and a critical reading of these concepts-as-tools:[6] we are invited to explore the 'flourishing' of our students, our clients, our professional contexts and wider communities and to reflect on whether flourishing is supported by processes of streamlining or deliberation, of intervention or empowerment. The authors consider perspectives on excellence – pragmatic, virtuous, idealised – and what flows (and for whom) from accepting each perspective. Professional wisdom and theorised practice are used to represent, critique and promote specific modes of being as well as to open up discussions about alternatives. After participating in the conference and reading these chapters I am less sure that I know what eudaimonia is. I think that this is a good thing: my understanding is less certain and more complex, I am more open and curious. Eudaimonia and other tools remain in play as friendly partners: to be met each time with the expectation that I will learn more. Philosophical enquiry of this type deconstructs the 'scarcity model': multiple perspectives do not crowd each other out in the way that rigid definitions might and my experience with this book has been that I can approach conceptual tools from my own perspective and at my own pace, that changes to my understanding are both inevitable and create space for other voices. It is an exciting place to be: I am in dialogue with the theories and with my reflective practice, so that while I know less 'for sure', that is a more comfortable position than I might fear. I am very grateful to all the authors for their endeavours, for providing me with this enquiry space.

Forewords sometimes summarise content or direct you to particular spots, but I do not want, nor do I feel competent to do this. Instead, I commend this book to you as a philosophical escape: stay for as long as you like, enquire, learn new languages or new argot in familiar ones, make friends, argue fiercely, take snapshots of your understanding and return each time playful and curious.

Professor Elaine Hall
University of Northumbria

5 Karin Knorr Cetina, 'Objectual Practice' in Karin Knorr Cetina, Theodore R Schatzki and Eike von Savigny (eds), *The Practice Turn in Contemporary Theory* (Routledge 2001).

6 John Dewey, 'Logic, the theory of enquiry' in Jo Ann Boydston (ed), *The Later Works of John Dewey, Volume 12, 1925–1953: 1938, Logic: The Theory of Inquiry (Volume 12) (Collected Works of John Dewey)* (Southern Illinois University Press 2008).

# Acknowledgements

We are grateful for the patience and support of the authors and reviewers who have contributed to this volume and who have all worked hard to produce insightful essays under trying circumstances. We also acknowledge the support of the wider Clinical Legal Education community for its help in developing our own CLE programmes at the Open Justice Centre at The Open University and at the University of Bristol. In particular we would like to thank the organisers, presenters and participants of recent ENCLE and IJCLE conferences where the idea for the book was nurtured and where we hosted a stream on theoretical and philosophical approaches to CLE which helped refine many of the ideas presented in this volume. We are grateful for the financial support of The Open University in supporting this event. Particular thanks go to Andrew Gilbert for suggesting the title for the book and to our students for their commitment, energy and engagement. We are grateful to Irene Antonopoulos, Shreya Atrey, Arushi Garg and Michele Leering for introducing us to some of the authors in this collection.

Hugh would also like to thank Francine Ryan, Paul Catley, Jon-Paul Knight, Liz Hardie, Simon Lee and Keren Lloyd Bright for their work developing the Open Justice Centre and promoting CLE at The Open University. Omar would like to thank Folúkẹ́ Adébísí, Nicolette Butler, John Peake (Director of the University of Bristol Law Clinic), Basil Salman and Alan Uzelac.

# Contributors

**Omar Madhloom** is a Senior Lecturer and Solicitor at the University of Bristol Law School. He qualified in 2004 and practised as a commercial solicitor before joining the Ministry of Defence. He has been involved in teaching and developing clinical legal education since 2012. He was previously the director of two university law clinics and has published in international peer-reviewed journals. His current research focuses on applying moral philosophy to clinical legal pedagogy. Omar is Co-Chair of the Bristol Pro Bono Society and a trustee of CLEO (Clinical Legal Education Organisation), a UK-based charitable organisation aimed at promoting and developing Clinical Legal Education.

**Hugh McFaul** is Director of the Open Justice Centre at The Open University and a consultant for the United Nations Office on Drugs and Crime. He has research interests in the public understanding of law, legal ethics and technology enhanced learning. As Director of the Open Justice Centre he has developed a range of innovative community-based initiatives and is particularly interested in harnessing the potential of online technologies to support the work of civil society organisations.

**Miguel Angel Ramiro Avilés** is Associate Professor of Legal Philosophy at the Law School of University of Alcalá, Spain. He is also the Director of the HIV Legal Clinic of the Law School. Miguel is a member of both the Institutional Review Board of the University Hospital of Getafe and the 'Gregorio Peces-Barba' Human Rights Institute at Carlos III University, Madrid.

**Sarah Buhler** is an Associate Professor at the University of Saskatchewan College of Law, located in Saskatoon, Canada. She teaches and researches in the areas of clinical legal education, legal ethics and access to justice, and works closely with Community Legal Assistance Services for Saskatoon Inner City (CLASSIC), the award-winning community-based legal clinic that hosts the College of Law's intensive clinical law program.

**Scott L Cummings** is the Robert Henigson Professor of Legal Ethics and Professor of Law at the University of California, Los Angeles School of Law. He is faculty director of the Program on Legal Ethics and the Profession (LEAP), and a long-time member of the Epstein Program in Public Interest Law and Policy.

**Peter Čuroš** is a postdoctoral fellow at the Department of Private Law at the University of Oslo. In the project Judges Under Stress: The Breaking Point of the Judicial Institutions (financed by the FRIPRO program of the Norwegian Research Council and the University of Oslo (2019–2022) he focuses on structural changes in the judiciary in the Czech Republic and Slovakia. In 2016–2019, he was an assistant professor at the Pavol Jozef Šafárik University in Košice, Faculty of Law. The academic year 2015–2016 he spent as a visiting scholar at the Washington and Lee University School of Law, with the research areas of Professional Ethics and Professional Responsibility.

**Andrés Gascón-Cuenca** is Co-Director of the Legal Clinic for Social Justice, Faculty of Law, University of Valencia, a researcher at the Human Rights Institute and a Professor at the Department of Philosophy of Law and Politics. His main fields of research are: human rights protections and globalisation, hate speech regulations, anti-discrimination law, racial profiling, right to health, access to justice and legal clinics. He was appointed a member of the Board of Directors of the Global Alliance for Justice in Education (GAJE) in 2017.

**Andrew Gilbert** is a Senior Lecturer in The Open University's Law School. His interest in Clinical Legal Education stems from his earlier experience as a family law solicitor. Andrew's work explores how legal education generally, and Clinical Legal Education in particular, can develop social and cultural capital, promote social justice and enhance student employability. He has also taught and researched in family law and policy, publishing British Conservatism and the Legal Regulation of Intimate Relationship with Hart in 2018.

**Christopher F Gray** is a PhD candidate and teacher at the University of Bristol Law School. He was previously a Visiting Lecturer at the University of The Gambia, Faculty of Law, where he also coordinated the law clinic. His research relates to human rights and fair trial procedure in international, comparative and pluralist perspective.

**Fernanda Lapa** is Coordinator of the Human Rights Clinic at the University of the Region of Joinville and UNESCO Chair on Citizenship Education and Human Rights. She is also the Executive Coordinator of the Institute for Development and Human Rights, an NGO whose main work is to promote social justice and human rights education in Brazil. A lawyer, with a J.D and Master's in Law, she holds a PhD in Education and is the current President of the Legal Education Commission at the local Bar Association.

**Tobore O Okah-avae** is a Lecturer in Law at Leicester Law School, De Montfort University. His research focuses on issues relating to corporate governance and the broad concept of corporate citizenship. He was admitted as a Barrister and Solicitor of the Supreme Court of Nigeria in 2009 and obtained a Doctorate from

Lancaster University in May 2019. His thesis was titled High Executive Compensation: Are Current Pay Levels Evidence of Avarice or Just Reward for Performance? and considered the justice of high executive pay, utilising the contrasting justice theories of Robert Nozick and John Rawls in making his arguments.

**Richard Owen** began his teaching career at the Cayman Islands Law School. Returning to the United Kingdom he was the Clinic Director at the University of Essex before joining Swansea University as Director of the Swansea Law Clinic in January 2017.

A former Chair of the Association of Law Teachers, Richard was also a member of the Law Commission's Wales Advisory Committee. He has been a visiting professor to Fudan University, People's Republic of China, and a reviewer for the Quality Assurance Agency. Currently, Richard is a member of the Law Society's Access to Justice Committee. Richard is a member of the Editorial Board of The Law Teacher.

**Ben Perdue** is the Director of International Programmes at Street Law, Inc., a US-based non-profit organisation dedicated to advancing justice and improving individuals' legal and civic knowledge, skills and confidence. He has trained hundreds of law faculty, law students and legal professionals around the world and has supported the development and implementation of dozens of public legal education programs. He is a graduate of Colorado College (BA in Sociology) and University College London Institute of Education (MA in Educational Planning, Economics, and International Development).

**Barbara Preložnjak** is an Assistant Professor at the Department of General Theory of State and Law. In 2003 she graduated from the University of Zagreb Faculty of Law, and then proceeded to complete her MA in 2009 and receive her PhD in 2013 after successfully defending her doctoral thesis entitled Liberal Theories of Justice and Legal Aid Schemes. She worked as a trainee at the Municipal and County Court in Zagreb (2003–2005) and passed the bar exam in 2007. Since 2010, she has been working as the Assistant Director of the Legal Clinic at the University of Zagreb Faculty of Law. During her doctoral studies, she used her ERASMUS program scholarship to conduct a part of her research at the University of Ljubljana Faculty of Law. Her fields of research and teaching interests include the theory of law, philosophy of law, civil procedure law and family law.

**Horácio Rodrigues** is a retired Professor of Law from the Federal University of Santa Catarina and currently a Coordinator and Professor of Law at Centro Universitário Euripides de Marilia. He holds a Master's and a PhD in Law and has research interests in philosophy and education. He is author of several articles and books on legal education in Brazil.

**Roni Rothler** is Co-Director of the Disability Rights Clinic, Faculty of Law, Bar Ilan University (Israel), and is the Chairperson of the Advisory Committee to the Commissioner of Equal Rights for Persons with Disabilities in the Ministry of Justice. Roni is currently a PhD candidate at Bar Ilan University. Her doctoral research focuses on the subject of dispute system design in parenthood legal proceedings involving parents with disabilities.

**Rachel Stalker** is the Clinical Legal Education Programme Leader in the School of Law at Liverpool John Moores University. She read Jurisprudence at Christ Church, Oxford, qualifying as a solicitor in 2005. After seven years as a commercial litigator in private practice in Liverpool and Manchester, she joined LJMU in 2013 where she coordinates the School of Law's pro bono activities, establishing the award-winning Legal Advice Centre in April 2014.

**Getachew Assefa Woldemariam** is an Associate Professor of Law at Addis Ababa University. He has published research articles on national and foreign refereed journals. His most recent publication is: Legal Pluralism in Ethiopia: actors, challenges and solutions (2020, with Susanne Epple). His areas of interest include Ethiopian and comparative constitutional law, federalism and local governance, human rights law, African Constitutionalism and traditional (informal) justice systems. He has served as the chairman of the Democratic Institutions' Working Group established in 2018 by the Ethiopian Government to undertake legal and institutional reform of Ethiopia's democratic institutions. He obtained a PhD from the University of Melbourne, Australia.

# Introduction

*Omar Madhloom and Hugh McFaul*

Authors of the chapters in this collection are legal academics from around the world who are interested in Clinical Legal Education ('CLE') as a methodology.[1] Contributors were invited to generate fresh insights into CLE by thinking about their work from a particular theoretical or philosophical perspective.[2] Although CLE does not have a universally accepted definition, we have adopted the wording posited by the European Network of Clinical Legal Education (ENCLE) which emphasises the practical and experiential approach to legal education:

> Clinical legal education is a legal teaching method based on experiential learning, which fosters the growth of knowledge, personal skills and values as well as promoting social justice at the same time. As a broad term, it encompasses varieties of formal, non-formal and informal educational programs and projects, which use practical-oriented, student-centered, problem-based, interactive learning methods, including, but not limited to, the practical work of students on real cases and social issues supervised by academics and professionals. These educational activities aim to develop professional attitudes and foster the growth of the practical skills of students with regard to the modern understanding of the role of the socially oriented professional in promoting the rule of law, providing access to justice and peaceful conflict resolutions, and solving social problems.[3]

The intention of this volume is not to obscure or eclipse the practical and experiential by focusing on theory, but to invite the reader to consider whether the practice of CLE can be enhanced by paying more explicit attention to its theoretical underpinnings. Although the growth and influence of the CLE

1 Garry Bellow, 'On Teaching the Teachers: Some Preliminary Reflections on Clinical Education as Methodology' (1973) in *Council on Legal Education for Professional Responsibility, Clinical Education for the Law Student: Legal Education in a Service Setting*, 381.
2 Hugh McFaul, 'Does Clinical Legal Education Need Theory?' [2020] Asian Journal of Legal Education 152.
3 European Network of Clinical Legal Education, *Definition of a Legal Clinic* <http://encle.org/about-encle/definition-of-a-legal-clinic> accessed 18 January 2021.

DOI: 10.4324/9780429299247-1

movement has been well documented,[4] there has been relatively little attention paid to the theoretical and philosophical dimensions of CLE outside of the United States.[5] The aim of this volume, therefore, is to provide a range of philosophical and theoretical frameworks that can serve to enrich the teaching and practice of CLE, which has become an increasingly common feature of the curriculum in law schools across the globe[6] and which provides an alternative to the dominant doctrinal method.[7]

The doctrinal approach has been criticised for being too narrow and giving students the false impression that law 'is autonomous and disconnected from the social forces that animate it'.[8] One of the consequences of the doctrinal method is that:

> Lawyers are trained to solve routine problems within routine procedures. They are not trained to reflect creatively on the emergence and stabilization of the complex institutions that lawyering silently presupposes.[9]

This echoes Donald Schön's critique of the professions, including law, for overemphasising substantive knowledge of a profession, which he defines as 'technical rationality':

> [P]ractitioners are instrumental problem solvers, who select technical means best suited to particular purposes. Rigorous professional practitioners solve well-formed instrumental problems by applying theory and technique derived from systematic preferably scientific knowledge.[10]

4 Frank S Bloch, *The Global Clinical Movement: Educating Lawyers for Social Justice* (Oxford University Press 2010); Emma Jones, Hugh McFaul and Francine Ryan, 'Clinical Legal Education in the United Kingdom: Origins, Growth and the Technological Innovations and Challenges of Its Future' (2017) 4 German Journal of Legal Education 107; Orla Drummond and Gráinne McKeever, *Access to Justice through University Law Clinics* (Ulster University Law School 2015).

5 Richard J Wilson, *The Global Evolution of Clinical Legal Education: More than a Method* (Cambridge University Press 2017), 137.

6 Frank S Bloch, *The global clinical movement: educating lawyers for social justice* (Oxford University Press 2011); Alberto Alemanno and Lamin Khadar (eds), *Reinventing legal education: how clinical education is reforming the teaching and practice of law in Europe* (Cambridge University Press 2018); Linden Thomas et al., *Reimagining clinical legal education* (Hart Publishing 2018); Richard J Wilson, *The Global Evolution of Clinical Legal Education: More Than a Method* (Cambridge University Press 2018).

7 Doctrinal analysis is concerns with the substance of the law, its rules, and procedures.

8 Margaret Thornton, 'The Law School, the Market and the New Knowledge Economy' (2007) 17 (1&2) Leg Ed Rev 1 <http://www5.austlii.edu.au/au/journals/LegEdRev/2007/2.html> accessed 01 February 2021.

9 Stephen Holmes, 'Can Foreign Aid Promote the Rule of Law' (1999) 8 E Eur Const Rev 68, 71.

10 Donald Schön, *Educating the Reflective Practitioner* (Jossey-Bass 1987), 3–4.

Schön recommends searching for an epistemology of practice that attends to the knowledge professionals generate through reflection in and reflection on professional practice.[11] This collection aims to support this reflective approach. The theoretical approaches, adopted by the authors in this volume, collectively attempt to address the limitations of technical rationality identified by Schön and to provide CLE educators and students with different methods of addressing the complexities and uncertainties encountered in practice. The themes of the chapters are varied and have been applied to a wide variety of clinical contexts from across various jurisdictions. We hope that this theoretical, geographical, and disciplinary diversity will provide the reader with interesting insights and point to potential synergies between approaches. A brief summary of the approaches adopted by the authors is provided below.

The first chapter in this collection, by **Rachel Stalker** and **Sarah Buhler**, posits that clinicians should examine and make more explicit the links between CLE and place-based education. Bringing together these two disparate strands of literature and practice enriches both. The authors explore the generative dimensions of place in CLE by discussing two very differently located clinical law programmes: the Legal Advice Centre at the School of Law at Liverpool John Moores University (England), and the University of Saskatchewan College of Law's clinical law program at Community Legal Assistance Services for Saskatoon Inner City (Canada).

**Roni Rothler** applies Therapeutic Justice (TJ) in order to maximise the effectiveness of legal aid in Israel. Her chapter describes four main aspects of TJ, focusing primarily on the work of the disability rights clinic at Bar-Ilan University: students' training; handling the legal case; client–lawyer–student interaction; and dealing with the emotional aspects of the legal work. Through her work in the Disability Clinic, Rothler develops CLE by demonstrating how TJ can aid practitioners in enhancing the well-being of their clients.

**Andrew Gilbert's** chapter draws on insights from the work of French sociologist, Pierre Bourdieu, to consider the extent to which CLE can function as an engine of social justice and mobility for students through the development of their social and cultural capital. **Fernanda Lapa** and **Horácio Rodrigues** select some theoretical insights from the pedagogy of Paulo Freire and point out how Freire's philosophy can contribute to CLE. They draw on their experience of developing legal clinics in Brazil and argue that Freire's theoretical and methodological framework can serve to enrich and inform the key principles of clinical legal education both in Brazil and in other jurisdictions.

**Andrés Gascón-Cuenca** reflects on his experience of developing legal clinics in Spain, particularly in light of the structural changes to university education implemented by the Bologna Process. He uses the insights offered by the Italian philosopher and legal theorist Luigi Ferrajoli's discussion of fundamental rights and their importance for constitutional democracies. He argues that scholars can utilise Ferraojli's theory through CLE in order to implement new learning

11 Donald Schön, *Educating the Reflective Practitioner* (Jossey-Bass 1983), 49.

techniques which counter the negative impacts of the Bologna process; an approach that prioritises critical thinking, social justice and the study of fundamental and human rights in legal studies.

**Omar Madhloom** and **Barbara Preložnjak's** chapter addresses the limitations of the doctrinal method in the Croatian context, by arguing for developing student reflection on social institutions in the Republic of Croatia and the distribution of primary social goods. The authors apply John Rawls' theory of justice to CLE in a way that allows for the critique of social institutions involved in the provision of legal aid. The authors' aim is to develop reflective practice beyond the dominant lawyer–client model where students act as 'hired guns' to resolve their clients' issues. The authors conclude their chapter by outlining the limitations of Rawls' theory of justice.

One of the criticisms levelled against Rawls' theory from authors utilising the capability approach is that, as an ideal theory, it pays too little attention to the practical task of mitigating and preventing injustice in the real world. The capability approach to social justice is explored in **Hugh McFaul's** chapter, which considers how the framework pioneered by Amartya Sen and Martha Nussbaum can inform and enrich the practice of CLE. McFaul draws on recent literature which has applied their work to the promotion of civic virtue in the university-level education of professionals. In light of this discussion, he maps out three areas where the capability approach can enrich clinical legal education: by illuminating the social justice dimensions of clinical work; by providing a reasoned foundation for reflective practice, and through situating the ethical dimensions of clinical practice within a wider philosophical framework.

**Ben Perdue's** chapter examines the growth of a particular aspect of CLE in the context of neoliberalism. He asks how it is that a communitarian and socially focused educational initiative has grown and thrived in a higher education system that has increasingly become individualistic and market-oriented? Using Street Law as a case study, Purdue argues that Street Law's success is at least in part due to the fact that it simultaneously subverts neoliberal ideals in its community-centred approach while still achieving outcomes that fit within the neoliberal value-system. These market-oriented and individualistic outcomes have allowed Street Law not only to be accepted, but to flourish within a neoliberal higher education system. **Peter Čuroš** also uses his chapter to consider the impact of wider political forces on legal education and discusses his experience of teaching legal ethics in the context of a post-communist state. He advocates using an institutional approach to teaching, drawing on Pierre Bourdieu's conception of habitus to address the flaws in the formalistic approach to legal education prevalent within Slovakian and other higher education systems in Central and Eastern Europe.

**Getachew Assefa Woldemariam** considers his experience of CLE in Ethiopia through the lens of legal pluralism. His discussion applies insights from the Ethiopian legal system, characterised by plural normative orderings, where various levels of formal (state) laws interact, compete and cooperate with non-state (customary) laws of more than 80 ethno-linguistic communities. Woldemariam's discussion focuses on the efforts being made by CLE programmes in law schools in

Ethiopia to realise access to justice by tapping into this normative pluralism. This chapter is followed by **Christopher Gray's** which considers the nature of human rights as a means of promoting access to justice, in the Gambia, through CLE programmes. This chapter reflects on how duties in relation to human rights might be instilled and fulfilled by law clinics. The author concludes that a solidarity-community understanding of a human right to access to justice better manages to conceptualise how clinics can promote a duty held by individuals and communities to improving access to justice. The subject of human rights is also discussed in **Miguel Avilés** and **Omar Madhloom's** chapter which considers how human rights issues can enhance reflective practice. The authors develop reflective practice in CLE through the work carried out in the law clinic at the University of Alcalá, which is primarily focused on assisting HIV-positive migrants. This chapter argues that human rights discourse develops reflective practice by providing students with a conceptual framework that allows them to challenge settled law and reflect on the impact of law and policy on vulnerable clients. This in turn provides students with the opportunity to challenge the status quo and argue for reform.

**Tobore Okah-avae** examines the role of business-focused law clinics and their role in positioning corporate entities as organisations which exist for the common good. Okah-avae offers two approaches whereby CLE can challenge the existing orthodoxy on the role of business in society: first, they could help instil progressive values in a participating student body, who would undoubtedly form the next generation of leaders in business, government, academia, and the judiciary. Secondly, by advising businesses in their infancy, clinics are able to encourage companies to formulate policies that prioritise the needs of employees and their host communities as a whole.

**Richard Owen's** chapter considers how CLE can prepare students for the myriad of sustainability challenges they will face in their careers. He examines the intersection of sustainability, the provision of legal services and clinical legal education from the perspective of rebellious lawyer theory. He discusses recent developments in human rights litigation and activism and examines the role of strategic litigation in a rebellious lawyer's toolkit. **Scott L Cummings** considers the impact of social activism on his clinical practice by reflecting on the impact of the Black Lives Matter movement on his work in California. He argues in favour of three steps, firstly to invest in building communities of students connected to movements of social change, secondly to support these movements by example and not just exhortation, and thirdly channel experience gained from working with such movements back into academic teaching and scholarship.

The chapters in this collection demonstrate that CLE encompasses a varied and vibrant approach to legal education which, given its focus on the practical and experiential, often operates on the fringes of the mainstream university law curriculum.[12] The authors in this collection demonstrate that the insights derived

12 Steven Vaughan, Linden Thomas and Bharat Malkani, 'Clinical Legal Education Reimagined' in Linden Thomas et al. (eds), *Reimagining Clinical Legal Education* (Hart Publishing 2018), 19.

from applying theoretical and philosophical approaches to CLE provide new pathways for a reflective, critical, and socially engaged approach to legal education. In this way the chapters resonate with the origins of the CLE movement, which are routinely traced to Jerome Frank's 1933 paper 'Why Not a Clinical Lawyer-School'[13] where Frank used his own theoretical insights to argue for a more socially engaged approach to the teaching of law, an approach that would challenge the dominance of the case method then used throughout law schools in USA.

It is not our intention to promote or prioritise one particular theoretical position to the exclusion of another; rather it is to invite and encourage readers to draw on the insights and ideas offered by the various theoretical positions presented in this volume and think about how they can be applied to their own CLE programme. In this way, we hope the volume will have succeeded in its core aim of having an illuminating and energising effect on CLE practice.

13 Jerome Frank, 'Why Not a Clinical Lawyer-School?' (1933) 81 University of Pennsylvania Law Review and American Law Register 907.

# 1 Place-based education: Clinical Legal Education and ethics

*Sarah Buhler and Rachel Stalker*

This chapter explores the generative dimensions of place in CLE by discussing two very differently located clinical law programmes: the Legal Advice Centre ('LAC') at the School of Law at Liverpool John Moores University, and the University of Saskatchewan College of Law's clinical law programme at Community Legal Assistance Services for Saskatoon Inner City ('CLASSIC').[1] A comparative approach helps illuminate the relationships between place and CLE, demonstrating the centrality and complexities of local places when it comes to clinical pedagogies and practices.[2]

## PBE and its relationship with CLE – definitions and synergies

PBE has developed principally in the USA, in an attempt to reorient primary and secondary education from what has been described as the 'dehumanizing and colonizing implications of the banking model … of education which is the preferred delivery method for schools trying to improve their standardized test scores'.[3] As David Gruenewald has written of dominant pedagogies:

> [i]n place of actual experience with the phenomenal world, educators are handed, and largely accept, the mandates of a standardized, 'placeless'

1 See Elizabeth Mertz, 'Teaching Lawyers the Language of Law: Legal and Anthropological Translations' (2000) 34 J Marshall L Rev 91, 99. In Canada, David Sandomierski's recent detailed and nuanced study of contract law teaching tends to support the proposition that consideration of context becomes marginalised in the actual practice of teaching in Canadian law school classrooms. See David Sandomierski, Aspiration and Reality in Legal Education (University of Toronto Press 2020), 24–25.

2 For more on comparative approaches in socio-legal research, see Annelise Riles, 'Comparative Law and Socio-Legal Studies' in Mathias Reimann and Reinhard Zimmerman (eds), *The Oxford Handbook of Comparative Law* (OUP 2006), 775.

3 S Anthony Deringer, 'Mindful Place Based Education: Mapping the Literature' (2017) 40(4) Journal of Experiential Education 333, 334, citing Paolo Freire, *Pedagogy of the Oppressed* (Continuum 1970). Deringer's article is a useful, recent overview of literature on PBE as well as mindfulness.

DOI: 10.4324/9780429299247-2

> curriculum … what is most striking about the classroom as a learning technology is how much it limits, devalues, and distorts local geographical experience.[4]

In contrast, PBE is 'concerned with context and the value of learning from and nurturing specific places, communities, or regions'.[5] For Sobel, PBE requires 'hands-on, real-world learning experiences', which leads to better academic achievement and strengthened community and civic connections.[6]

Bringing together critical pedagogy and PBE, scholars such as Gruenewald have proposed that 'critical PBE' must concern itself with 'the contextual, geographical conditions that shape people and the actions people take to shape these conditions'.[7] Critical PBE is concerned also with the ways that power operates in and across places. For Gruenewald, 'place' is always political, and therefore PBE must 'identify and confront the ways that power works through places to limit the possibilities for human and non-human others'.[8]

Any clinical practitioner will immediately feel a shock of recognition at descriptions such as these, even if coming to PBE for the first time. Putting aside the references to non-law curricula and applying these ideas to CLE, the synergies are immediately obvious. Both educational methods depart from, and implicitly critique, conventional pedagogical techniques by incorporating experiential learning into what can be a monolithic, static curriculum, whether in terms of content or delivery. Both embody a critique of 'placeless' and acontextual approaches to knowledge and practice; both emphasise that education can and should be concerned with addressing injustices and inequities in the real world.

These critiques apply to traditional law school pedagogies. Certainly, classroom-based legal education has aimed to produce better citizens, and not merely technicians able to navigate the complexities of the legal system. However, numerous studies attest to the negative effect that the study of the law can have on law student wellbeing, the suggestion being that there is a distinctly unethical undercurrent to the messages imparted by legal education's 'hidden curriculum'.[9]

4 David A Gruenewald, 'The Best of Both Worlds: A Critical Pedagogy of Place' (2003) 32(4) Educational Researcher 3, 8.
5 Ibid. 3.
6 David Sobel, *Place-based Education: Connecting Classroom and Community* (The Orion Society 2004), 4.
7 Gruenewald (n4) 4.
8 Ibid. 7.
9 For two excellent overviews, see Kennon M Sheldon and Lawrence S Krieger, 'Does Legal Education Have Undermining Effects on Law Students? Evaluating Changes in Motivation, Values, and Well-Being' 22(2) Behavioral Sciences and the Law 261 and Colin James, 'Lawyers' Wellbeing and Professional Legal Education' (2008) 42(1) The Law Teacher 85. For a discussion of the hidden curriculum and Clinical Legal Education, see Caroline Gibby, 'Clinical Legal Education and the Hidden Curriculum in the Neoliberal University in England and Wales' in Caroline Strevens and Rachael Field (eds), *Educating for Well-being in Law: Positive Professional Identities and Practice* (Routledge 2020).

One factor among others for these negative outcomes is legal education's disavowal of social context, which Granfield has referred to as a 'self-alienating ideology associated with legal consciousness.'[10] Elizabeth Mertz argues that when law is conceptualised as being separated from social context, legal decision-making and practice can become alienated from ethics.[11] In other words, the dominant pedagogies in law schools have tended to embrace an acontextual and 'placeless' view of law: what Elizabeth MacDowell refers to as 'point-of-viewlessness'.[12] In this model, law is presented as neutral and not connected to place or the local, as existing purely in a conceptual space and with little attention to the emplaced, material contexts in which law operates and is interpreted.[13]

In contrast to these approaches in law school classrooms, the educational richness of a student engaging with a paradigm problem-based learning scenario in a clinical setting – in the guise of meeting a client with an undigested and often urgent legal question – has been widely discussed.[14] As Sameer Ashar argues, it is hard to 'replicate the experience of an immersive confrontation with an intractable social problem and close work with clients … on that problem'.[15] CLE necessarily happens outside of the classroom – in place and 'in context' – through students' experiences of working directly with clients, hearing clients' stories, and determining how the law may or may not promise solutions or justice for clients. Donald Schön refers to this material, lived, world of practice as the 'swampy lowlands', where problems are 'messy and confusing and incapable of technical solution'.[16] According to Deobrah Curran:

> We learn differently when we change the physical context. To experience law in action in a place … creates opportunities for deep learning that listening to someone tell you about the law cannot provide.[17]

10 Robert Granfield, *Making Elite Lawyers: Visions of Law at Harvard and Beyond* (Routledge 1992), 53.
11 Elizabeth Mertz, *The Language of Law School: Learning to 'Think Like a Lawyer'* (OUP 2007), 220.
12 Elizabeth L MacDowell, 'Law on the Street: Legal Narrative and the Street Law Classroom' (2007) 9(2) Rutgers Race and Law Review 285, 317.
13 See discussion in Nicholas K Blomley and Joel C Bakan, 'Spacing Out: Towards a Critical Geography of Law' (1992) 30(3) Osgoode Hall Law Journal 661, 663–664.
14 See John Dewey, *Experience and Education* (Touchstone 1997); Donald A Schön, *The Reflective Practitioner: How Professionals Think in Action* (Routledge 1991). For a more recent example, see Fran Quigley, 'Seizing the Disorienting Moment: Adult Learning Theory and the Teaching of Social Justice in Law School Clinics' (1995) 2(1) Clinical Law Review 37.
15 Sameer Ashar, 'Deep Critique and Democratic Lawyering in Clinical Practice' (2016) 104(1) California Law Review 201, 219.
16 Donald A Schön, *Educating the Reflective Practitioner: Toward a New Design for Teaching and Learning in the Professions* (Jossey-Bass 1987), 3.
17 Quoted in John Borrows, 'Outsider Education; Indigenous Law and Land-Based Learning' (2016) 33(1) Windsor Yearbook on Access to Justice 1, 9.

One final point of note is that PBE scholars have been more assiduous at quantifying measurable improvements in student skills and/or educational attainment than CLE,[18] with some exceptions.[19] As CLE continues to become more widespread, this is something clinicians should emulate in order to analyse, evaluate and improve clinical methods.

## Lessons from PBE for CLE

Both CLE and PBE seek to equip students with a critical sensibility by immersing them in places and experiences that may be unfamiliar.[20] For PBE, the settings for these immersions is often a rural one, focused on 'local, ecological

18 Gerald A Lieberman and Linda L Hoody, 'Closing the Achievement Gap, Using the Environment as an Integrating Context for Learning', State Education and Environmental Roundtable, San Diego, CA, 1998, available at <https://digitalcommons.unomaha.edu/slcek12/64> accessed 26 February 2021. This report made clear that PBE can have a demonstrably positive effect on test scores, attendance and self-expression, among other things. More recently, other positive effects have been considered in Yafuz Akbas and Safiye Çakmak, 'The Effect of Place-Based Education Integrated Project Studies on Students' Problem-Solving and Social Skills' (2019) 5(1) Asian Journal of Education and Training 183; and Murni Sianturi et al., 'Impact of a Place-Based Education Curriculum on Indigenous Teacher and Students' (2018) 11 (1) International Journal of Instruction 311.

19 We anticipate that most, if not all, clinical teachers can attest anecdotally to the positive impact of CLE on their students, whether on their legal skills, exam results, 'soft' skills, or simply their confidence. However, quantitative research in CLE has tended to focus on student attitudes to pro bono rather than specific academic or professional achievements: see Paul McKeown, 'Law student attitudes towards pro bono and voluntary work: The experience at Northumbria University' (2015) 22(1) International Journal of Clinical Legal Education 1. Ann Thanaraj's phenomenographic examination of student skills development is also instructive: Ann Thanaraj 'Understanding how a law clinic can contribute towards students' development of professional responsibility' (2016) 23(4) International Journal of Clinical Legal Education 89. Further afield, the results of an initial, 2001 study suggested – but did not confirm – the assumption that CLE makes some difference to the attitudes that lawyers hold: Adrian Evans, 'Lawyers' Perceptions of Their Values: An Empirical Assessment of Monash University Graduates in Law 1980–1998' Legal Education Review (Australia) 12 (2) 209. A subsequent large scale survey of law graduates demonstrated 'some evidence of the impact of participating in a clinical placement program in particular, and weaker evidence in relation to the effects of having completed an ethics course. There is also a third, tentative indication, particularly evident among women in their eventual decisions about pro bono work, that the effects on ethical consciousness of any tertiary legal education experience dissipate over time and in the face of the (powerful and male-controlled) law firm environment': see Adrian Evans and Josephine Palermo, 'Almost there: Climbing the Hill Towards Lawyers Professionalism' (2008) 17(1) Griffith Law Review 323.

20 This is true for many, but not all students. For a powerful discussion of the importance of law students who are connected to and come from marginalised communities, see Julia Hernandez, 'Lawyering Close to Home' (2020) 27(1) Clinical Law Review 131.

experience'.[21] We note that there are some examples of PBE in land-based legal education focused on Indigenous laws. Gainsford and Robertson's vivid description of Australian final-year law undergraduates 'yarning' with Wiradyuri Elders at a residential school is a striking account of how experiencing a physical environment with the guidance of Indigenous teachers can fuel unique and transformative student insights, not to mention fostering vital cultural competence.[22] There are similar examples of land-based education about Indigenous laws in Canadian law schools.[23] Writing about land-based Indigenous legal education, John Borrows writes that Indigenous laws are contained within, and must be learned through, the land, requiring a 'literacy' that cannot be learned in the classroom, but on and through the land itself.[24] However, these examples of land-based learning in law school are far from the norm in law schools, which, as previously stated, continue to prioritise classroom-based, acontextual approaches to law and learning.

Despite the original emphasis in PBE on rural and ecological places, critical PBE has also embraced place-based education in urban settings,[25] and this is where its connections with CLE are perhaps the clearest. Streetlaw projects, conducted on the home territory of specific community groups, are internationally popular in CLE,[26] and because not all university law clinics are based on-campus.[27] Indeed, CLASSIC, the clinic associated with the University of Saskatchewan College of Law's clinical programme (and which is discussed below), is physically located in a neighbourhood where many of its clients live. In CLE, then, the location of the clinical activity is sometimes (though by no means always) dictated by where those in need of legal information or advice might be located, whereas in PBE *the place itself* serves a didactic function.

Drawing on geographical scholarship, critical PBE scholars argue that urban places are social constructions that reflect ideologies and power relations. That is to say, physical places are not simply neutral containers where things are situated or located.[28] Rather, place both produces and is produced by these power relations. Stephan Haymes writes that attention to the dynamics of urban place can

21 Gruenewald (n4) 4.
22 Annette Gainsford and Su Robertson, 'Yarning Shares Knowledge: Wiradyuri storytelling, cultural immersion and video reflection' (2019) 53(1) The Law Teacher 500.
23 See Borrows (n17).
24 Ibid. 62.
25 Gruenewald (n4) 5.
26 Richard Grimes et al., 'Streetlaw and Social Justice Education', in Frank S Bloch (ed), *The Global Clinical Movement: Educating Lawyers for Social Justice* (OUP 2010).
27 CLASSIC in Saskatoon, discussed in detail below, is one such example. In the UK, Huddersfield University runs a law clinic from a unit at the Packhorse Shopping Centre: University of Huddersfield, 'About the Legal Advice Clinic' (University of Huddersfield Legal Advice Clinic, 2021) <https://www.hud.ac.uk/about/schools/huddersfield-business-school/legal-advice-clinic/> accessed 26 February 2021.
28 Sharene H Razack, 'Introduction: When Place Becomes Race', in Sharene H Razack (ed), *Race, Space, and the Law: Unmapping a White Settler Society* (Between the Lines Press 2002) 1, 7.

help members of marginalised urban communities reflect on their experiences and identify means to transform oppression.[29] CLE can build on these insights by paying closer attention to the ways that law and legal processes and institutions shape the places and communities where clients live. Andreas Philippopoulos-Mihalopoulos points out that the physical world can itself be spoken of not only in terms of *landscapes*, but also *lawscapes,* 'Everything is a matter of spatial positioning … and every spatial positioning is potentially or actually controlled by the law'.[30]

Certainly, some clinicians and scholars of access to justice have studied the significance of place and geography in various ways. One example is the work that has been conducted in relation to 'mapping' legal need.[31] Richard Owen argues that this place-specific knowledge is key to enable clinics to meet the needs of the communities they serve.[32] Furthermore, as discussed in more detail below, the work of some critical lawyering scholars already highlights the significance of place and the disparate impact of law on differently located communities. We argue that CLE can draw on PBE to centre and deepen this attention to place.

Spatial thinking also means that new reasoning processes can be used to help with problem solving. The classic example is directing someone to where they need to go[33] – demonstrating obvious parallels with the signposting services many clinics offer, especially in England and Wales where only a quarter of clinics offer casework and ongoing representation, rather than just one-off advice, and around a third of all enquirers cannot be assisted.[34]

Thinking about place and its importance for clinical practice and pedagogy is perhaps especially meaningful during the current era of the COVID-19 global pandemic and the switch by law schools to online learning. Although online learning technologies create 'spaces' for students to engage with ideas and with each other, the Internet is not really a 'place' in the sense described by PBE practitioners; for them, 'place' is material and experienced through embodied,

29 See Stephen Nathan Haymes, *Race, Culture, and the City: A Pedagogy for Black Urban Struggle* (State University of New York Press 1995).

30 Andreas Philippopoulos-Mihalopoulos, *Spatial Justice: Body, Lawscape, Atmosphere* (Routledge 2015), 175. The concept of the 'lawscape', as defined here, could even be thought of as a cousin to psychogeography: the layering of history, culture and place and the consequent impact on the behaviour and emotions of individuals described by Guy Debord in his 'Introduction to a Critique of Urban Geography', in Harald Bauder and Salvatore Engel-Di Mauro (eds), *Critical Geographies: A Collection of Readings* (Praxis (e) Press 2008), 23–27.

31 See for example Laura Goodwin and Vivek Maru, 'What do we know about Legal Empowerment? Mapping the Evidence' (2017) 9(1) Hague Journal on the Rule of Law 1.

32 Richard Owen, 'Lawzone: Mapping unmet legal need' (2017) 24(2) International Journal of Clinical Legal Education 3.

33 Douglas Llewellyn, 'Thinking Spatially: Taking observation, classification, and communication skills to a higher level of reasoning' (2009) 32(6) Science Scope 69.

34 LawWorks, 'Activities and Impact Report 2018–19' (January 2020) <https://www.lawworks.org.uk/sites/default/files/files/LawWorksImpactReport2019%E2%80%93Web.pdf> accessed 26 February 2021.

physical presence. That said, critical Internet geographers theorise the overlapping and mutually constitutive relationship between place and the Internet. Matthew Zook writes that cyberspace and the Internet 'is changing geography; it is warping space, shrinking distance, and modifying our sense of place'.[35]

Yet, Zook also argues that the Internet has also reconnected us to place.[36] Zook's observations, although made in 2007, ring true in the midst of the pandemic, where people are living and working online, yet are required by public health measures to remain 'in place' in their homes and cities, leaving us hyper aware of our physical location in place and our interconnectedness with our neighbours. Meanwhile, the COVID-19 pandemic itself has laid bare and exacerbated the pre-existing inequalities in our societies, and has been more devastating in some places that in others.[37] PBE reminds us to keep paying attention to place and the experiences of living, breathing human beings whose location in place impacts their access to health and justice, even in a world where so much has moved online.

## The concept of place – a tale of two cities

The authors operate from opposite side of the Atlantic and are involved with very different clinical activities.[38] This section gives a short overview of those places and activities, to illustrate how PLE is already an undercurrent in CLE, and to provide an example of how a comparative approach can bring up useful subjects for critical analysis, clinic design, internationalisation, and discussion.

### *Saskatoon and CLASSIC*

Saskatoon is a growing mid-sized city located on the banks of the South Saskatchewan river in the province of Saskatchewan, in the middle of the Canadian prairies. Indigenous people have lived on the territory where Saskatoon is now located for over 11,000 years. In the 1880s, Methodist settlers moved to what is now Saskatoon seeking to create a 'Temperance colony'.[39] The City of Saskatoon was officially founded in 1906, with its population growing to about 250,000 by 2016.[40] Today, Saskatoon is the largest city in the Province of Saskatchewan,

35 Matthew Zook, 'The Geographies of the Internet' (2007) 40(1) Annual Review of Information Science and Technology 53, 56.
36 Ibid. 69.
37 See Reuben Rose-Redwood et al., 'Geographies of the Covid-19 Pandemic' (2020) 10 (2) Dialogues in Human Geography 97.
38 Ironically, the authors began writing this chapter during a time their physical access to their own cities was constrained by public health regulations due to the COVID-19 pandemic.
39 City of Saskatoon History and Archives, 'History' (City of Saskatoon, 2021) <www.saskatoon.ca/community-culture-heritage/saskatoon-history-archives/history> accessed 26 February 2021.
40 Statistics Canada, 'Census Profile Saskatoon, City' (2016) <www12.statcan.gc.ca/census-recensement/2016/dp-pd/prof/details/page.cfm?Lang=E&Geo1=CSD&Code1=

serving as an economic, educational, and healthcare hub. Ten per cent of its population identify as Indigenous (First Nations and Metis), and the remaining population is comprised of the descendants of white European settlers, and more recent 'arrivants' from around the world.[41]

As mentioned above, CLASSIC is a community-based legal clinic that hosts the University of Saskatchewan's Intensive Clinical Law programme. CLASSIC's vision is 'a just society that is supported by a fair legal system.[42] Its mission is to 'work towards social justice with low-income, marginalized Saskatchewan residents, with a commitment to Indigenous peoples, through a legal clinic that is guided by the needs of the community'.[43] The clinical programme places upper year law students from the University of Saskatchewan College of Law at CLASSIC for a full semester, for which they receive academic credit. Under lawyer supervision, students assist clients in a wide variety of legal areas, including housing law, social assistance appeals, prison law, criminal law, human rights, and immigration and refugee law.

CLASSIC is located in the Riversdale neighbourhood – an area with a strong sense of history and vibrant social networks.[44] With a high Indigenous population, this part of the city has also been constructed as racialised space. People living in the neighbourhood have been subjected to both over- and under-policing, as well as disruptive and often harmful institutional interventions. Peters and Lafond found that for many Indigenous people in Saskatoon, public space is not safe or hospitable and the threat of police harassment is ubiquitous.[45]

The neighbourhood has also been the site of recent residential and commercial development which has often been accompanied by an implicit or explicit narrative about the neighbourhood as being 'degenerate' and in need of revitalisation. As Ben Fawcett writes, the 'the racialization of neighbourhoods such as Riversdale works to justify the increasing occupation (or 'revitalization') of such

4711066&Geo2=PR&Code2=01&Data=Count&SearchText=4711066&SearchType=Begins&SearchPR=01&B1=All&Custom=&TABID=3> accessed 26 February 2021.

41 Ibid. The term 'arrivants' was used by poet Edward Kamau Brathwaite in *The Arrivants: A New World Trilogy* (OUP 1981) and taken up more recently by Jodi A Byrd in *The Transit of Empire: Indigenous Critiques of Colonialism* (University of Minnesota Press 2011) to refer to 'those people forced into the Americas through the violence of European and Anglo-American colonialism and imperialism around the globe', xix.

42 See CLASSIC Law, 'What we do' (2021) <www.classiclaw.ca> accessed 26 February 2021.

43 Ibid.

44 See Laura Woodward, '"It's Ignorance about Language": Riversdale website removes posts after complaints about language' (CTV News, August 17, 2018) <https://saskatoon.ctvnews.ca/it-s-ignorance-about-language-riversdale-website-removes-post-after-complaints-1.4057999> accessed 26 February 2021.

45 Evelyn Peters and Carol Lafond, '"I Basically Stick with my own Kind": First Nations Appropriation of Urban Space in Saskatoon' in Evelyn Peters and Chris Anderson (eds), *Indigenous in the City: Contemporary Identities and Cultural Innovation* (UBC Press 2013), 93.

neighbourhoods and the displacement of Indigenous peoples'.[46] As urbanist scholar Edward Soja writes, the racialisation of space justifies 'locational discrimination'.[47]

### *Liverpool and the LAC*

Liverpool's city centre population is growing faster than any other city in the UK, increasing by 181 per cent (9,100 to 25,600 people) between 2002 and 2015.[48] Liverpool officially came into existence as a place in 1207, when King John named it as an official town in his Royal Charter, but it spent the next four centuries as little more than a fishing village, not becoming a city until 1880. The 18th century started a cycle of extreme boom and bust which continues to this day. Liverpool's infrastructure benefited significantly from the influx of wealth earned in the slave trade in the late 1700s[49] with the biggest population jump coming in the middle of the 19th century, reaching 300,000 by 1851.

The Legal Advice Centre ('LAC') based in the School of Law at Liverpool John Moores University gives free verbal and written advice in a city which is now the fourth most deprived in the UK[50] and where more than a quarter of children live in poverty.[51] At the time of writing, a combination of austerity

46 Ben Fawcett, 'Ben on Gentrification and Urban Change' (Wahkohtowin Justice Map, 2021) <www.arcgis.com/apps/MapTour/index.html?appid=b83485f7347e4edc991fca28fb52cc05#> accessed 26 February 2021.

47 Edward Soja, 'The City and Spatial Justice' (*Spatial Justice*, September 2009) <https://www.jssj.org/wp-content/uploads/2012/12/JSSJ1-1en4.pdf> accessed 26 February 2021.

48 Office for National Statistics, 'Population estimates by output areas, electoral, health and other geographies, England and Wales' (2015) <https://www.ons.gov.uk/peoplepopulationandcommunity/populationandmigration/populationestimates/bulletins/annualsmallareapopulationestimates/mid2015> accessed 26 February 2021.

49 Liverpool Museums, 'European Traders' (2021) <https://www.liverpoolmuseums.org.uk/history-of-slavery/europe> accessed 26 February 2021. The recent Black Lives Matter protests in the UK have given fresh impetus for this element of British history to be articulated more strongly in our public spaces. In Liverpool, the city council has backed a motion in favour of public notices to educate passers-by about the links between city sites and streets, and the beneficiaries of the slave trade who funded their construction and/or after whom they are named: Veronique Dupont, 'Liverpool addresses its slave trade past' (*International Business Times*, 7 October 2020) <https://www.ibtimes.com/liverpool-addresses-its-slave-trade-past-3009388> accessed 26 February 2021. Criticism of Liverpool's involvement in the 'Triangular Trade' was made throughout the 18th and 19th centuries; in one widely reported incident, actor George Frederick Cooke (1756–1812) responded to boos from his audience whilst performing while the worse for drink at Liverpool's Theatre Royal by declaring, 'I have not come here to be insulted by a set of wretches, every brick in whose infernal town is cemented with an African's blood': see Gomer Williams, *History of the Liverpool Privateers and Letters of Marque, with an account of the Liverpool Slave Trade* (CUP 2010), 430–462.

50 Ministry of Housing, Communities and Local Government, 'English Indices of Deprivation 2019' (*National Statistics*, 26 September 2019) <https://www.gov.uk/government/statistics/english-indices-of-deprivation-2019> accessed 26 February 2021.

51 Liverpool City Region Child Poverty and Life Chances Commission, 'Child Poverty and Life Chances Strategy 2015–2018' (Knowsley Council, 2015) <https://www.

policies and funding cuts due to the COVID-19 pandemic has put the city on the brink of bankruptcy.[52] Simultaneously, public funding for legal advice was decimated across England and Wales by the Legal Aid, Sentencing and Punishment of Offenders Act 2012[53] when it came into force in 2013. The direct consequence of this is a sharp increase in the number of litigants unable to afford representation for reasons of cost alone.[54]

As such, whilst the LAC now advises on a wide range of matters, it was initially established to advise for free on the areas of law for which Legal Aid is now scarce or not available at all (family and employment). The LAC does not means test its clients, but they regularly report not being able to pay for legal advice or representation at any stage of their case. Others have started their case with representation, but have since run out of money. Clients' cases often disclose multiple social issues, with housing, family and employment matters regularly clustering in the same case.

## A brief comparison

The modern populations of both Saskatoon and Liverpool were built on immigration; but as will be discussed below, in the case of Saskatoon, European immigrants settled and took possession of Indigenous land.[55] Liverpool has always been a diverse city: by way of example, it has the oldest Chinese population in Europe.

Areas such as Scotland Road in Liverpool were historically gathering points for Irish and Scottish immigrants, and the North Liverpool area remains economically deprived.[56] The Irish influence on the city was fundamental, making Liverpool the only English city to have ever had an Irish nationalist Member of Parliament.[57] The 1851 census reported that 22 per cent of the population were Irish – believed to be the largest single Irish population at that time outside Dublin and New York. Some 1.5 million Irish came through Liverpool during the years of the famine (1847–1854), many of whom evidently stayed. Around 5.2

knowsley.gov.uk/knowsleycouncil/media/Documents/liverpool-city-region-child-poverty-and-life-chances-strategy-refresh-2015-18.pdf> accessed 26 February 2021.

52 'Coronavirus: Liverpool Mayor warns virus crisis could "bankrupt" city' (*BBC News*, 30 April 2020) <https://www.bbc.co.uk/news/uk-england-merseyside-52494414> accessed 26 February 2021.

53 The forerunner to Legal Aid originated in Liverpool, with the work of philanthropist and Member of Parliament Eleanor Rathbone (1872–1946), who established the Poor Man's Lawyer Society in 1920.

54 Liz Trinder et al., 'Litigants in person in private family law cases', Ministry of Justice Analytical Series, 2014.

55 For a discussion of this history, see Bill Waiser, *A World We Have Lost: Saskatchewan Before 1905* (Fifth House 2016); James Daschuk, *Clearing the Plains: Disease, Politics, and the Loss of Indigenous Life* (University of Regina Press 2019).

56 Liverpool City Council, 'Ward profile: Kirkdale' (2018) <https://liverpool.gov.uk/media/9955/kirkdale.pdf> accessed 26 February 2021.

57 TP O'Connor, MP for the Scotland Road area (1885–1929).

million Catholics live in England and Wales, or around 9.6 per cent of the national population.[58] In the North West this rises to as around 20 per cent, with a population of 441,000 Catholics to be found within the Archdiocese of Liverpool.[59] This has an impact on politics at both local and national level,[60] with Liverpool a traditionally left-wing city. The economic decline of the city led to the marginalisation of many communities, and tensions with authority. The Toxteth riots – or, as local terminology puts it, 'uprising'[61] – of the 1980s arose in part from long-standing tension between the black community and the police, whose 'strategy for Toxteth at the time placed greater emphasis upon coercion than upon policing by consent'.[62] The effects of these incidents continue to be felt to this day.[63]

In Saskatoon, settler colonialism is woven into the fabric of the city and its institutions. As Indigenous scholars have pointed out, settler colonialism is always about access to land. Glen Sean Coulthard writes that while its methods have changed over time, the ends of settler colonialism remain the same: 'to shore up continued access to indigenous peoples' territories for the purposes of state formation, settlement, and capitalist development'.[64] Law and legal institutions are key tools of settler colonialism, creating the frameworks for property ownership and ongoing dispossession. Scholars have documented the ways that colonialism operates through various systems including the criminal justice, healthcare, child welfare, and educational systems.[65] As Audra Simpson states, 'in law, settler colonialism maintains itself'.[66]

58 Reuters Staff, 'Factbox: Catholicism in Britain' (*Reuters World News*, 13 September 2010) <https://www.reuters.com/article/us-pope-britain-catholics/factbox-catholicism-in-britain-idUSTRE68C1R420100913> accessed 26 February 2021.

59 'Archdiocese of Liverpool' (*Catholic Directory England and Wales*, 2018) <https://directory.cbcew.org.uk/search.php?pageType=groupView&ID=14> accessed 26 February 2021. The Archdiocese covers an area geographically larger than the city of Liverpool itself, but this figure illustrates the relative prevalence of a minority religion.

60 'The Catholic Vote in Britain helped Carry Blair to Victory' (*IPSOS Mori Public Sector*, 23 May 2005) <https://www.ipsos.com/ipsos-mori/en-uk/catholic-vote-britain-helped-carry-blair-victory> accessed 26 February 2021.

61 Alice Butler, 'Toxic Toxteth: Understanding Press Stigmatization of Toxteth during the 1981 uprising' (2019) 21(4) Journalism 541.

62 Paul Cooper, 'Competing Explanations of the Merseyside Riots of 1981' (1985) 25(1) The British Journal of Criminology 60.

63 Simon Parker and Rowland Atkinson, 'Disorderly cities and the policy-making field: the 1981 English riots and the management of urban decline' (2020) 15(1) British Politics 160–177.

64 Glen Sean Coulthard, *Red Skin, White Masks: Rejecting the Colonial Politics of Recognition* (University of Minnesota Press 2014), 125.

65 See for example: Samir Shaheen-Hussain, *Fighting for a Hand to Hold: Confronting Medical Colonialism against Indigenous Children in Canada* (McGill-Queens University Press 2020); Raymond Mason, *Spirit of the Grassroots People: Seeking Justice for Indigenous Survivors of Canada's Colonial Education System* (McGill-Queen's University Press 2020); Lisa Monchalin, *The Colonial Problem: An Indigenous Perspective on Crime and Injustice in Canada* (University of Toronto Press 2016).

66 Audra Simpson, 'Subjects of Sovereignty: Indigeneity, the Revenue Rule, and Juridics of Failed Consent' (2008) 71(3) Law and Contemporary Problems 191, 214.

Both clinics under discussion were established with a clear view of the community and unmet need of the places where they are based. Framing a comparison of their services in a place-based context immediately highlights commonalities and differences. This stimulates examinations of what we mean by phrases such as social justice and access to justice; identifies racial, economic, and social difference as key to discussions of hierarchies of power and law; and gives a longitudinal perspective to current social problems which allows for a fuller understanding of the current unmet legal needs of the respective communities. However, even more than this, a place-based understanding of individual clinics fosters a deeper understanding of the ethics of clinic service delivery, and CLE more broadly.

## *Ethics, place and clinic*

In Canada, all law students must take a mandatory course in legal ethics and professionalism.[67] In UK law schools, undergraduate ethics education is not compulsory and there is a limited nature of compulsory postgraduate ethics education. However, some have gone so far as to suggest that, regardless of the topic of law being taught, law teachers are transmitting their view of ethics and what it means to be a 'good lawyer'.[68]

CLE allows clinicians to be innovative in their teaching, and the teaching of ethics in particular. The potential for CLE to enhance ethical education is widely recognised. It has been suggested that ethics education without clinic is artificial, and clinic without ethics education is sterile;[69] without an express consideration of ethical principles CLE cannot achieve its aim of re-humanising legal education and concepts of professional duty and identity.[70] In recognition of this, from 2020 all LJMU undergraduate LLB Law students will study a compulsory Law in Society module during their first year of study, which teaches legal ethics and professional conduct along with carefully supervised and controlled experiential work in the LAC.

For many students, CLE will be their first experience of legal practice. Uniquely, CLE allows students not only to engage in decision-making processes about what advice a client with a particular problem should receive, but also observe, discuss and potentially take action on a number of ethical issues which may arise during the course of the case (for example, conflicts of interest, client confidentiality, and access to justice). These in turn can expose and even

67 See Federation of Law Societies of Canada, 'National Requirement' (2015) <http://docs.flsc.ca/National-Requirement-ENG.pdf> accessed 26 February 2021.

68 Carrie J Menkel-Meadow, 'Can a Law Teacher Avoid Teaching Legal Ethics?' (1991) 41(1) Journal of Legal Education 3–10.

69 Kevin Kerrigan, '"How do you feel about this client?" A commentary on the clinical model as a vehicle for teaching ethics to law students' (2007) 9(1) International Journal of Clinical Legal Education 7.

70 For a fascinating discussion, see Julian Webb 'Being a Lawyer/Being a Human Being' (2002) 5(1) Legal Ethics 130.

challenge existing hierarchies within the law that may not be immediately visible.[71] Furthermore, students' clinical encounters with clients and the ways in which clinicians teach students to handle those encounters can serve to illustrate more fundamental, philosophical aspects of ethics and morality, as well as encouraging them to identify the nature of their clinics as their own distinct place. Throughout, attention to place in clinical pedagogy can help students reflect on their own positionality and situatedness in relation to their clients; and also reveal important insights about the geographies of law and justice.

At this point it is instructive to examine key ethical theories and the ways in which they may inform, or challenge, the ideas of place illustrated above.

### *Deontology*

Deontological and consequentialist theory have dominated the modern era from the Enlightenment onwards, checked only by the late 20th century resurgence in virtue ethics. Here we briefly consider both deontology (with a focus on Immanuel Kant) and virtue ethics to illuminate their links with ideas of community and place.

Many students taking part in CLE wish to progress into legal practice, which will confer upon them a number of professional duties. The study of deontological theories, with their emphasis on binding duties, therefore provides a vital ethical toolkit to would-be lawyers. Deontology is a broad church, so for the purposes of our discussion we take the theories of Kant as our focus. Kant's philosophy takes an approach encompassing agent-centred, patient-centred, and contractualist positions; avoids the structural pitfalls in later deontological theories such as Fried's,[72] or the Judeo-Christian locus of Donagan;[73] and is becoming recognised as of particular value to clinical lawyers.[74]

Kant's Formula of Humanity requires one to '[a]ct so that you treat humanity, whether in your own person or in that of any other, never simply as a means, but always at the same time as an end'.[75] Kant's emphasis on the individual and respect for human autonomy might, on a first reading, appear to run counter to the features of a 'community' that PBE might bring to light. Kantian ethics certainly contrasts with the outcomes-focused, consequentialist format of the Solicitors Regulation Authority ('SRA') Code of Conduct for Solicitors, RELs (Registered Eruopean Lawyers) and RFLs (Registered Foreign Lawyers), and

71 Sarah Buhler, 'Painful Injustices: Encountering Social Suffering in Clinical Legal Education' (2013) 19(1) Clinical Law Review 405.

72 Charles Fried, *Right and Wrong* (Harvard University Press 1978); see also Stephen R Munzer, 'Persons and Consequences: Observations on Fried's Right and Wrong' (1979) 77(3) Michigan Law Review 421.

73 Alan Donagan, *The Theory of Morality* (University of Chicago Press 1977).

74 For a discussion of the benefits of Kantian ethics for CLE, see Omar Madhloom, 'A normative approach to developing reflective legal practitioners: Kant and Clinical Legal Education' (2019) 53(4) The Law Teacher 416.

75 Immanuel Kant, *Groundwork of the Metaphysics of Morals* (CUP 2012).

Code of Conduct for Firms, which govern Solicitors in England and Wales, as well as provincial professional Codes of Conduct in Canada. Kantian ethics' focus on individual autonomy is also entirely distinct from consequentialism, not to mention Millian utilitarianism, whose Greatest Happiness Principle requires that one ought always to act in such a way as to produce the greatest balance of happiness over unhappiness for as many people as possible.[76] It is worth remembering that Kant believed the natural consequence of rational individuals employing his methods would be 'a systematic connection … that is, a Kingdom of Ends';[77] but this community is expressly envisaged as taking no account of individuals' personal differences. This makes it more aspirational in nature than reflective of the communities in which we live and work.

Our view is that, in fact, having a good understanding of the *place* where a client comes from – in alignment with the key aims of PBE – is an essential part of understanding a client's needs in a clinical setting. It is a common experience for clinical students to act for a client from a socio-economic background, and with life experiences, completely different to those of the student.[78] A Kantian focus on client humanity, combined perhaps with a PBE-style comprehension of the client's place of origin could be argued to support students in having appropriate empathy for someone very different for themselves. This in turn will inform the students' understanding of the client's best interests and consequently the advice and/or practical assistance they provide in the clinical setting.

Some might object that a focus on place might encourage stereotyping. By way of example, Liverpool caricatures abound in British popular culture and imagination, ranging from more or less kind-hearted comedy depicting poverty-stricken 'scallies' and 'Scousers'[79] with an ambivalent attitude to law-breaking and a distinctive (and much-mimicked) local accent;[80] through to nebulous, classist ideas about standards of living;[81] all the way up to offensive attacks on the whole psyche of the city's 'tribal' inhabitants.[82] Across the Atlantic, racist attitudes are

76 John Stuart Mill, *Utilitarianism* (OUP 1998).

77 Kant (n75).

78 Federation of Law Societies of Canada (n67).

79 The local dish is lobskaus or 'Scouse', the taste (and recipe) for which was supposedly imported by Norwegian sailors during the 19th century.

80 Another legacy of the Irish influence on the city, and the influx of other immigrants, is its unique regional accent. For a full guide see Tony Crowley, *The Liverpool English Dictionary: A Record of the Language of Liverpool 1850–2015* (Liverpool University Press 2017).

81 *R. Stalker*: During my first week at Oxford University in 1999, I was asked by more than one person and in a spirit of apparently genuine anthropological curiosity whether, coming from Liverpool, I had an indoor or outdoor lavatory at home.

82 'Liverpool is a handsome city with a tribal sense of community. A combination of economic … and an excessive predilection for welfarism have created a peculiar, and deeply unattractive, psyche among many Liverpudlians. They see themselves whenever possible as victims, and resent their victim status; yet at the same time they wallow in it. Part of this flawed psychological state is that they cannot accept that they might have made any contribution to their misfortunes, but seek rather to blame someone else for it, thereby deepening their sense of shared tribal grievance against

pervasive towards Indigenous people in Saskatoon, and in some cases Saskatoon's relatively high Indigenous population has been used by Canadian media to cast Saskatoon as a 'dangerous' city.[83] It is notable that in both cities it is the most marginalised sectors of the population which form the source and bear the brunt of outsiders' perceptions of each place. Students arriving at our institutions from other places may have internalised, and brought with them, such schema about the cities where they will study – and, by extension, clients they may meet in our clinics, since there is likely to be considerable overlap between marginalised communities and those in need of free legal assistance.

However, whilst concerns about stereotyping are understandable, it is our belief as well as our experience that a well-informed understanding of place can be used to myth-bust common misconceptions about individuals within certain groups; highlight for students the unfounded assumptions on which such misconceptions are based; bring to light hitherto-unchallenged unconscious biases, and unpack ideas of privilege. In other words, a combination of PBE and CLE can ensure that clients are understood and treated *as autonomous human beings* in the way that Kant's Formula of Humanity envisages. This in turn can frame and enrich discussions about the meaning of such concepts as a client's 'best interests',[84] client autonomy, professionalism, and empathy.

It must be mentioned at this point that Kant has been criticised for his views about non-white and Indigenous persons, in terms of both race and space.[85]

the rest of society.' Editorial Team, 'Bigley's Fate' (*The Spectator*, 16 October 2004) <www.spectator.co.uk/article/bigley-s-fate> The aim of this (the Spectator) article was to deride a 'mawkish' silence held in Liverpool to commemorate Kenneth Bigley, a civil engineer from the city who was beheaded by extremists in Iraq in October 2004. The article also repeated slurs about Liverpool Football Club fans having been responsible for the Hillsborough Stadium disaster of 15 April 1989. Inquests eventually held between 2014 and 2016 ruled that the 96 fans who died in the disaster were not in any way responsible, but were in fact unlawfully killed: Home Office and the Rt. Hon. Theresa May, 'Determinations and Findings of the Hillsborough inquests' (27 April 2016) <https://www.gov.uk/government/speeches/determinations-and-findings-of-the-hillsborough-inquests> accessed 26 February 2021. Given this chapter's focus on CLE, it is worth noting that many of the Hillsborough victims' families were represented at the inquests by lawyers acting on a pro bono basis (some for many years). The then-editor of *The Spectator*, Boris Johnson, apologised in 2004 for publishing 'Bigley's Fate', and again in 2012 after the report of the Hillsborough Independent Panel was published, but the apology was rejected by the Hillsborough Families Support Group: 'Hillsborough Papers: Boris Johnson apologises over article' (*BBC News*, 13 September 2012) <www.bbc.co.uk/news/uk/england/19589039> accessed 26 February 2021.

83 See for example Ken MacQueen, 'The Rankings: Canada's most dangerous cities' (MacLeans, 5 March 2009) <https://www.macleans.ca/news/canada/the-most-dangerous-cities-in-canada/> accessed 26 February 2021.

84 Solicitors Regulation Authority, 'Principles', (30 May 2018), Principle 7 <https://www.sra.org.uk/solicitors/standards-regulations/principles> accessed 26 February 2021.

85 See, for example, Lucy Allais, 'Kant's Racism' (2006) 45(1–2) Philosophical Papers 1–36 and Stuart Elden 'Reassessing Kant's geography' (2009) 35(1) Journal of Historical Geography 3.

Whilst he appears to advocate against colonialism in his *Toward Perpetual Peace* (1795), some have questioned whether this may have been more of a criticism of colonial conflict than anything else.[86] This specific topic is beyond the scope of this chapter and will no doubt be the subject of much continued discussion and scrutiny. However, we make mention of this issue here since PBE and CLE are valuable tools to assist us in decolonising our curricula. This may on occasion require us, as teachers, to subject not only the theories of the authors we are teaching, but also the authors themselves, to critical scrutiny.[87]

### *Virtue ethics*

Virtue ethics has, perhaps, a more problematic place in CLE. This earliest of moral theories has had something of a resurgence in the 20th century via the scholarship of writers such as Alasdair Macintyre and Rosalind Hursthouse. Its insistence on the idea that goodness stems from character virtues has been criticised for failing to provide clear instructions on how to act in specific circumstances. However, the Principles in accordance with which solicitors in England and Wales must act include acting with honesty and integrity[88] and these behaviours are judged to an extremely high standard.[89] In Canadian Codes, integrity and honesty are similarly framed.[90] A practitioner must furthermore demonstrate satisfactory character and suitability to be admitted to the Roll of Solicitors in England and Wales; Canadian provinces also all utilise some version of a 'good character' requirement.[91] These standards must by extension be observed by students working in university law clinics, so a discussion of virtue is not out of place.

It might seem problematic to extend discussions of virtue beyond students and supervisors to clinic clients. After all, such an approach might go against the consequentialist grain of the Code, as discussed above, not to mention risking that students make unwarranted and arrogant judgements about client character.[92] However, one striking feature of classical virtue ethics for proponents of both CLE and PBE to note is that it is strongly rooted in the concept of the polis:

86 Ines Valdez 'It's Not about Race: Good Wars, Bad Wars, and the Origins of Kant's Anti-Colonialism' (2017) 111(4) American Political Science Review 819.

87 See for example Foluke Adebisi, 'Decolonising the law school: presences, absences, silences … and hope' (2020) 54(4) The Law Teacher 471.

88 Solicitors Regulation Authority Principles (n84), Principles 4 and 5.

89 For a recent example, see *Wingate & Anor v The Solicitors Regulation Authority* [2018] EWCA Civ 366.

90 See Federation of Law Societies of Canada, 'Model Code of Professional Conduct' (October 2019), Rule 2.1 <https://flsc.ca/wp-content/uploads/2019/11/Model-Code-October-2019.pdf> accessed 26 February 2021.

91 See Alice Woolley, 'Tending the Bar: The Good Character Requirement for Bar Admission' (2007) 30(1) Dalhousie Law Journal 27.

92 Thomas L Shaffer elegantly examines this dichotomy in 'Legal Ethics and the Good Client' (1987) 26(2) Catholic University Law Review 319.

'Aristotle's account of the virtues presupposes the now-long-vanished context of the social relationships of the ancient city state'.[93]

MacIntyre's rejection of modern liberalism posits that place and ethics are, in fact, inextricably linked:

> We all approach our own circumstances as bearers of a particular social identity … *I am a citizen of this or that city* … I belong to this clan, that tribe, this nation. Hence what is good for me has to be the good for one who inhabits these roles. As such, I inherit from the past of my family, my city, my tribe, my nation a variety of debts, inheritances, rightful expectations and obligations. These constitute the given of my life, *my moral starting point.* This is in part which gives my life its own moral particularity.[94]

MacIntyre's analysis is compelling, but its focus on community is not without its problems. For example, it ignores the fact that citizens rely on states for the safeguarding of everyday freedoms, such that their lives are constructively informed by national constitutions and legislature and communities are not only (in fact seldom) voluntary but also geographic territories to which people belong more so by birth than disposition.[95]

However, even this brief discussion demonstrates, once more, that using place as a common link between CLE and ethics can stimulate discussion and encourage students to think in a more interdisciplinary manner. Interdisciplinarity in CLE is often discussed in the context of clinical work which combines legal and non-legal expertise to create the best possible solution for clients.[96] We believe that CLE, when aligned with key principles of PBE, can also foster academic interdisciplinarity in both legal education and CLE.

## *Ethics and the community*

Proponents of 'community lawyering' approaches to CLE have advocated that lawyers should move closer to the communities that they serve, seeking invitations by the community.[97] Community lawyering is: 'an approach to the practice of law and to clinical legal education that centres on building and sustaining

93 Alasdair MacIntyre, *After Virtue: a study in moral theory* (Duckworth 1981), 152.
94 Ibid. 205. Emphasis added.
95 Keith Breen, 'The state, compartmentalization and the turn to local community: A critique of the political thought of Alasdair MacIntyre' (2005) 10(5) The European Legacy 485, 494.
96 For a US example, see Paula Galowitz, 'The Opportunities and Challenges of an Interdisciplinary Clinic' (2014) 18(1) International Journal of Clinical Legal Education 165–180 in the context of the USA, and for a Continental one, Cecilia Blengino, 'Interdisciplinarity and Clinical Legal Education: How synergies can improve access to rights in prison' (2018) 25(1) International Journal of Clinical Legal Education 210.
97 See Lucie White, 'The Transformative Potential of Clinical Legal Education' (1997) 35(3) Osgoode Hall Law Journal 603, 604.

relationships with clients, over time, in context, as a part of and in conjunction with communities'.[98]

It seeks to frame clients as 'protagonists in framing and resolving their concerns'.[99] Thus, learning in place with the communities that we serve demystifies the realities to how law operates 'on the ground' in marginalised communities. This can act as a strong antidote to what Shin Imai calls 'epistemological imperialism' – the process of 'invading, subjugating and transforming other peoples' realities into forms and concepts that [make] sense in the world of law'.[100] If we listen and learn from our clients and their communities, we learn about how law and legal institutions too often intervene in ways that are harm/oppress individuals. We learn about structural violence – the uneven distribution of risk and harm across places.[101]

This approach to pedagogy is in fact in line with the original mandate of CLE: William Pincus, an early American proponent of CLE, wrote that the purpose of CLE is for students to learn to: 'recognize what is wrong with the society around them – particularly what is wrong with the machinery of justice in which they are participating and for which they have a special responsibility'.[102]

This approach insists that as lawyers and law students, we must 'enter as learners as well as teachers'. As Mary McNeal argues, relationship-building must be central: 'the goal is the building of relationships between outsider lawyers and those in their new communities of practice, which requires empathy and connection over time'.[103]

Attention to place here is key. If we understand that law does not operate neutrally across space but is actually imbricated in the production of power relations in place, we can start seeing relationships between and across client experiences. This, in turn, can lead to insights about individual advocacy and larger law reform or systemic advocacy campaigns. As Blomley and Bakan write:

> Space, like law, is not an empty or objective category, but has a direct bearing on the way power is deployed and social life constituted. The geographies of law are neither passive backdrops in the legal process, nor of random import; they can, in combination with their implied claims concerning social life, be problematic and even oppressive.[104]

98 Karen Tokarz et al., 'Conversations on "Community Lawyering": The Newest (Oldest) Wave in Clinical Legal Education' (2008) 28 Washington University Journal of Law and Policy 359, 364.

99 Ibid. 364–365.

100 Shin Imai, 'A Counter-pedagogy for Social Justice: Core Skills for Community Lawyering' (2002) 9(1) Clinical Law Review 195, 197.

101 See Susannah Taylor, 'Structural Violence, Oppression, and the Place-Based Marginality of Homelessness' (2013) 30(2) Canadian Social Work Review 255.

102 William Pincus, *Educational Values in Clinical Experience for Law Students* (Council on Legal Education for Professional Responsibility 1980).

103 Mary Helen McNeal, 'Slow Down, People Breathing: Lawyering, Culture, and Place' (2011) 18(1) Clinical Law Review 183, 236.

104 Blomley and Bakan (n13) 669–670.

A refusal by lawyers to acknowledge context has repercussions and results in a blinkered focus on individual solutions for clients. This is highlighted by Janet Mosher who contends that '[b]roadening the context to question whether others share a similar problem, or to include an assessment of social, economic, or political structures is beyond the reach of most lawyering'.[105]

The above is a cursory overview of some of the more obvious ways in which geographical place plays a role in moral theory. Nevertheless, even this brief interlude demonstrates that PBE can illuminate not only CLE but also the teaching, whether implicit or explicit, of ethics in a clinical setting.

## Clinic as a distinct place

PBE also encourages us to see our clinics, not only as services responding to particular characteristics of their geographical settings, but as *their special, distinct places with their own characteristics*. Many clinicians will be familiar with the client who makes an appointment but does not turn up, with one of the possible reasons being that the unfamiliar university environment where a clinic is located is too alien or too intimidating to be trusted. Mayoun Lim points out that people:

> [D]raw upon their place identity to assess and make sense of whether the place is a good fit or not. When the place is compatible with one's place identity, the place can offer satisfying and meaningful experiences for the person that in return reinforce the person's place identity. However, when the place is in conflict with the person's place identity, the place can act to limit the person's meaningful and satisfying place experiences.[106]

It is easy in a busy clinic environment, focused on delivering quality advice service with often limited resources, to dismiss the fact that the clinic is not simply a process but a place. Our students' assessment of a clinic as a place is therefore vital for teachers of CLE to identify and articulate. Even more crucial is taking into consideration clients' assessment, in the design or re-design of our clinics. It is instructive to recognise that clients may associate clinics with the larger legal system which, as discussed earlier, has all too often been a hostile terrain for them. PBE in the context of the clinic environment can assist us develop strategies for improving clients' relationship to those spaces and what happens in them, promoting an ethic of care in our treatment of clients. Nancy Cook's suggestion that clinics seek out invitation from and relationship with the community is important in this context.[107] In arguing that lawyers should focus on the importance of place, Cook states:

105 Janet Mosher, 'Legal Education: Nemesis or Ally of Social Movements?' (1997) 35(3) Osgoode Hall Law Journal 613, 617.

106 Mertz (n11).

107 Nancy Cook, 'Looking for Justice on a Two-Way Street' (2006) 20(1) Washington University Journal of Law and Policy 169, 188.

> Community belongs to those who reside there … Those who live outside the community, however great their expertise and however pure their intentions, need the support of residents to put their skills to use. Thus, a grounding in community space, with increasing familiarity over time, is essential to a community-centered approach.[108]

The value of this kind of approach has only been thrown into relief by the COVID-19 pandemic, where clinics have either suspended their activities or opted to operate virtually, in response to national lockdowns. For many of us, our clinics will be 'located' on the digital plane to a greater or lesser degree at least for so long as social distancing measures are required for the protection of public health.

The need to consider the ethical implications of these new locations is pressing. Anecdotal evidence from some UK clinics suggests that when clients have been offered 're-located' remote advice services, when the lockdown in the UK initially came into force, only around one-third took up the opportunity. The ethical treatment of clients, and the digital features and identities of these new environments, must be at the forefront of designing and running such places. Considerations of digital exclusion and capability among our local populations are also pertinent. Furthermore, clinical teachers and students will need to carefully consider the ethics of our digital selves even more urgently than we have had to in the past:

> Ought we possess one, unified identity that coherently integrates the various aspects of our lives, or, incarnate deeply distinct selves suited to different occasions and contexts? At bottom, are we one, or many? The question is not only palpable today, but also urgent because if a decision is not made by us, the forces of big data and surveillance capitalism will make it for us by compelling unity.[109]

The impact of the pandemic on CLE will no doubt be the subject of a great deal of literature in coming years. The discussion as to which digital innovations help, and which harm, access to legal advice, and the reasons why, will no doubt in many cases discuss issues around digital exclusion and socio-economic deprivation. Inevitably, some form of analysis of the places where clinics and/or other legal advice services are needed and/or located will be required.

From the academic side of CLE, clinics have recently had the opportunity to use place as a starting point for comparing legal responses to the pandemic. Whilst it is both unfortunate and disquieting to have witnessed how a natural disaster can impact every country in the world, simultaneously the pandemic

108 Ibid. 192.

109 See James Brusseau, 'Ethics of Identity in the time of big data' (2019) 24 (5) First Monday, available at <https://firstmonday.org/ojs/index.php/fm/article/view/9624> accessed 26 February 2021.

presents a real-time window into how different legal systems react to such circumstances and a real-time opportunity for internationalised clinical initiatives.[110]

## Conclusions

PBE teaches us that CLE can connect students more closely with their local communities, as well as their fellow clinic students abroad. PBE has the potential to give clinic training or curricula an additional, valuable dimension which allows for a deeper and broader exploration and understanding of ethical practice and theory. Crucially, approaches drawing on PBE can help CLE to achieve its core aim of developing students' critical faculties in relation to the legal system they are seeing in operation in their immediate locality as well as in the classroom.

The essence of CLE is to connect theory to practice, often using reflection as method of both teaching and assessment. In that spirit, we have chosen to close our chapter, not only with a brief conclusion of the usual kind, but also with some reflective questions for anyone working or studying in a clinic to consider.

We acknowledge that addressing some of these questions may be aspirational, given the labour-intensive nature of CLE and the myriad insurance and financial constraints which necessarily apply to educational institutions and regulated practitioners working with the public. However, we hope these questions will nevertheless lead to some real-world, small-scale steps towards incorporating PBE principles into your clinical practices.

- How much do you understand about the place where your clinic operates? What is the most important information for you to know connected with this, which will help you to better understand clients' needs?
- How does law operate in the place where your clinic is located and/or the places where your clients live? What is the allocation of resources to advice and administrative resources (such as law centres or courts) like?
- What data does your clinic collect about its local community, from its own work or the work of other agencies? How could this be put to use to better understand the needs of that community? How could this be communicated to those who volunteer and/or study in your clinic?
- Does the demographic of your client base reflect the demographic of the place where your clinic is situated? What might differences between the two tell you about local access to justice and legal empowerment?
- How much is your clinical activity dictated by the curriculum, and how much by local need? What measures might you put in place to check whether these are in balance, and what would that balance look like for you? How could this exercise be undertaken by both staff and students?

110 In May 2021, a consortium of 31 law clinics around the world coordinated by Professor Yehia Mattar of the University of Law, Qatar was due to publish its report of the impact of the pandemic on legal issues such as Human rights, contract law, free movement and healthcare.

- Is a discussion of the concept of place, and place-based thinking, incorporated into the clinic training, or academic curriculum?
- Are there local community challenges which illustrate wider systemic problems in the legal system where you operate, or which illuminate power imbalances that might not be obvious based on classwork alone?
- If your training/curriculum includes an ethics topic or module, what dimension might a concept of place add to discussions of ethical issues?
- How can you raise consciousness of your clinic as a distinct place, and articulate your views about it? How might clients be encouraged to freely express their honest views on the same matter? How could these two viewpoints be compared and contrasted, and points of divergence addressed?
- If your clinic is located on campus, does all your clinical activity have to be on campus? Is there a point of mutually supportive co-location which might demystify your service and make it more approachable, and/or reach clients who would not traditionally be able to reach your physical space?
- Can your campus clinic space be usefully opened to other community groups or services, again making a point of co-location?

# 2 Clinical Legal Education and Therapeutic Jurisprudence in the Disability Rights Clinic

*Roni Rothler*[1]

Although the chapter acknowledges the problematic aspects of dealing with therapeutic content in the legal clinic, it claims that to maximise the effectiveness of legal aid, clinical supervisors might find it helpful to apply therapeutic tools and aspire for therapeutic goals, using Therapeutic Jurisprudence. The chapter describes four main aspects, focusing primarily on the work of the disability rights clinic: 1) students' training; 2) handling the legal case; 3) client–lawyer–student interaction; and 4) dealing with the emotional aspects of the legal work.

## Introduction

During my years in the Disability Rights Clinic ('DRC'), I have always been attracted to the connection between law and therapy. Most of the legal cases, if not all of them, call for therapeutic tools as well as legal ones. Even in the simplest disability pension cases, one needs to understand the disease and its psychological implications; to know how to read in and between the lines of medical opinions; and to understand how the students' presence in the medical appeal committee will affect the client. The link between law and therapy is usually even stronger in cases involving legal capacity or family relationships that mainly address matters of care, desires, needs, and vulnerability. Representing people with disabilities in their battle to fulfil their rights – in disability pension, labour, accessibility, education, legal capacity, and parenting – often presents an opportunity to explore the relationship between law and therapy. In this chapter I

1 Co-Director of the DRC, Faculty of Law, Bar Ilan University, PhD candidate at Bar Ilan University, and the chairperson of the Advisory Committee to the Commissioner of Equal Rights for Persons with Disabilities in the Ministry of Justice. I thank Susan Brooks, Michal Alberstein, David Wexler, Philip Genty, David Chavkin, and the editors of this book – Omar Madhloom and Hugh McFaul – for their excellent comments and thoughts. I thank Gideon Sapir and Maya Gaffan for insightful conversations and for their encouragement to write this chapter. I also wish to thank Inbar Cohen, Yehoshua Weiss, Silvana Hakier, Adva Mesilati, Tal Refaeli, Shifra Mescheloff, Keren Tzafrir, Shiri Regev-Messalem and Tamar Luster for our ongoing discussions and practice of psycho-legal collaboration and therapeutic jurisprudence.

DOI: 10.4324/9780429299247-3

attempt to describe my own experience with this dyad and share my insights regarding their overlap and boundaries in the DRC.

One of the main educational goals of almost every clinical supervisor is to teach the students that clients are not to be reduced to their legal problems: that they are persons of flesh and blood, that we encounter in the clinic at a critical point of their lives and should, therefore, be treated in a holistic manner, taking into consideration, alongside the legal aspects, aspects of psychological welfare, respect for autonomy, family ties, and community. Moreover, having in mind their vulnerable state, it is a widely held belief that clients need to be treated with empathy, patience, and understanding during the legal proceedings and sometimes even after their conclusion. My first years as a clinical supervisor in the DRC were based on that belief. I knew that I did not hold therapeutic training and skills (such as reflection, exploring clients' pasts and their problems, intervention, and empowerment), but in fact, my actions, driven by my emotions and feelings, were very much to the contrary. I felt that as a public interest lawyer, a compassionate person, and a holder of a bachelor's degree in Psychology, I could, and even should, solve the clients' distress as well as their legal problems, and that their emotional wellbeing, as well as the results of their legal case, depended on me.

A course of action that demanded multi-dimensional help and empathy came with a high personal and professional price tag, including my own sense of despair, impatience toward both clients and students, and self-flagellation. Conversations I held with my colleagues over the years have taught me that these feelings are shared by many clinical supervisors and lawyers who work with underprivileged communities, lawyers who are not satisfied by merely winning the case but want to change society and the lives of vulnerable individuals and groups. Although legal and therapeutic professions might sometimes share similar goals, as they do many times in the clinic, they differ greatly in their practice.[2] This difference is under-appreciated by most lawyers, causing a misinterpretation of the way legal and therapeutic content can and should co-exist. Therefore, in this article I wish to focus on the recognition that while therapeutic content is critical to the clinic's work, lawyers should generally look to mental health professionals for this expertise where possible, limit themselves when they try to implement it, and strive to find the balance that can allow clinical supervisors to use therapeutic tools and still maintain professional boundaries.

I will recommend some ground rules and suggestions for a positive and meaningful collaborative implementation of legal and therapeutic content using a Therapeutic Jurisprudence ('TJ') approach. TJ deals with the law's role as a therapeutic agent and focuses on the impact of the law on the psychological

2 See for example: Maryann Zavez, 'The Ethical and Moral Considerations Presented by Lawyer/Social Worker Interdisciplinary Collaborations' (2005) 5 Whittier J Child & Fam Advoc 191; Jada Fehn, 'What to Expect at the Intersection of Law and Social Work' (2015) Mitchell Hamline open access faculty scholarship, Paper 300, http://open.mitchellhamline.edu/facsch/300.

wellbeing of individuals, and on the emotional aspect of the law and the legal proceedings.[3] TJ is often connected to courts' conduct,[4] but it can also be an effective tool outside the court: In this article I discuss a 'lawyer's TJ': the implementation of therapeutic and social work content in the legal clinic, content that holds the potential to enrich the legal services, while keeping the necessary boundaries. I use examples from the DRC, a classic confluence of legal and therapeutic content.[5] Finally, I discuss the critical need for collaboration with therapeutic professionals and suggest that the academic and pedagogical aspects of the clinic make it an ideal platform for TJ.

## The clinics' multiple purposes and modes of action

Worldwide, most clinics are driven by a socio-legal reform ideology, which is based on social justice and social, political and economic change.[6] To implement this ideology, clinics use a variety of legal tools: individual and group legal aid provided to vulnerable communities or minority groups, class actions, legislative reforms, awareness raising through lectures and conferences, and so on.[7] Unlike other legal non-government organisations ('NGOs'), all of the clinics in Israel operate from within law faculties in public universities or private colleges and, therefore, they also have a pedagogical purpose.[8] They are usually the only practical course taken by students, where they have a chance to learn the ins and outs of the legal profession and best practices, and also are exposed to underprivileged groups in society, groups they may well not meet further along in their professional lives. In clinics, students are supposed to learn to be critical legal agents, in the hope that they will carry this knowledge with them and use it in the future. In addition, many clinics also serve as 'legal labs', utilising their vast

3 Michal Alberstein, 'Therapeutic Keys of Law: Reflections on Paradigmatic Shifts and the Limits and Potential of Reform Movements' (Book Review: Bruck J. Winick and David B. Wexler (eds) *Judging in a Therapeutic Key: Therapeutic Jurisprudence and the Courts* (CAP 2003)) (2006) 39(1) Isr Law Rev 1, 9.

4 Bruce J Winick and David B Wexler (eds) *Judging in a Therapeutic Key: Therapeutic Jurisprudence and the Courts* (CAP 2003).

5 See also: Roni Rothler, 'Sense and Sensibility: Difficulties and Advantages in Implementing Therapeutic Contents in the Legal Clinic' (2012) 17(1) HaMishpat 209 [Hebrew].

6 Donald Nicholson, '"Our Roots Began in (South) Africa": Modelling Law Clinics to Maximize Social Justice Ends' (2016) 23(3) Int J Clin Leg Educ 87.

7 For more reading regarding public-interest lawyering, its clients and special challenges, see: Lucy E White, 'Subordination, Rhetorical Survival Skills, and Sunday Shoes: Notes on the Hearing of Mrs. G.' (1990) 38(1) Buf L Rev 1; Gerald P Lopéz, 'The Work We Know So Little About' (1989) 42(1) Stan L Rev 1; Gerald P Lopéz, 'Training Future Lawyers to Work with the Politically and Socially Subordinated: Anti-Generic Legal Education' (1989) 91(2) W Va L Rev 305.

8 For further reading regarding clinics in Israel, see: Yael Efron, 'Clinical Legal Education in Israel' in Shuvro Prosun Sarker (ed.), *Clinical Legal Education in Asia: Accessing Justice for the Underprivileged* (2015) 91.

knowledge regarding the field, combined with theoretical tools and aspirations for policy reforms that are inherent in academia.[9]

To serve all these purposes, in Israel, each clinic typically focuses on a specific legal field, such as disability rights, poverty, elderly rights, or criminal defence. In addition, some clinics promote a certain practice approach or goal, such as mediation, environmental justice, cyber rights issues, or fair international trade and investments. Clinics vary greatly in their character and mode of action as a result of the legal field they operate in and the personal preferences of the clinical supervisors.[10] And yet, almost all of them share two main aspects: they serve clients (either individuals or organisations), and they care about advancement of general interests.[11] This latter goal differentiates clinics from 'regular' legal advocacy that perceives the client's interest as the case's sole goal.

In most of the academic institutions in Israel, clinics are an elective course. In Bar Ilan Faculty of Law it is mandatory for every third-year student to participate in either a clinic or an externship, such as in the offices of the Attorney General, the Public Defender, or in the Ministry of Justice's Department of Consultancy and Legislation. The placement is usually based on each student's preference. The clinic's work is assessed by the Faculty regularly upon its work products (such as lawsuits filed, reports submitted, and students' evaluation). Unlike other academic activities, the clinics are not regulated or funded by the Ministry of Education (through the Planning and Budgeting Committee working within the Council for Higher Education). Therefore, the clinics in Israel are financially supported in various ways, according to each institution's means and preferences: through the universities' or the Law Faculties' general budgets, research funds,

9 In Israel, clinics exist in each and every law school and are an inherent part of the legal social reform NGOs, but they do not receive financial support from the state or the bar. The American Bar Association (ABA), on the other hand, has set rules based on a report that dealt with the basic values and skills of the legal profession, including promotion of justice, fairness and consciousness, and the clinics' important role in educating law students. Rule 301(a) of the ABA 'Standards for Approval of Law Schools' (2011–2012) states that faculties should prepare students both for the bar exam and for an effective and responsible participation in the legal profession. These rules were drafted as a result of the 'McCrate Report' ('Building the Educational Continuum', 1993), a report that examined the American legal education and its implications on the professional development of lawyers. The report criticised the existing theory-based teaching method and called for a more practical approach, through teaching of basic skills and values in the faculties, internships, and experienced lawyers. The lack of an equivalent recognition by the Israeli Bar can be attributed, at least in part, to the fact that in Israel, unlike the US, all law students must complete 12 or 18 months of internship after they finish their legal studies, before they take the bar exams.

10 Jayashri Srikantiah and Jennifer Lee Koh, 'Teaching Individual Representation Alongside Institutional Advocacy: Pedagogical Implications of a Combined Advocacy Clinic' (2010) 16 Clinical L Rev 451.

11 For further reading regarding global clinical legal education see: Philip Genty, 'Reflections on US Involvement in the Promotion of Clinical Legal Education in Europe' in Alberto Alemanno and Lamin Khadar (eds), *Reinventing Legal Education: How Clinical Education Is Reforming the Teaching and Practice of Law in Europe* (Cambridge University Press 2018).

philanthropic foundations, or private donors. In regard of the students, the clinics' participation requirements are both practical-professional – dealing with the clinic's cases and projects under the supervision of the clinical supervisor; and theoretical – attending weekly lectures. Both practical and theoretical aspects take place throughout the entire academic year. As for students' representation, unlike some places (the United States as a main example) where students are allowed to represent clients in court while being closely supervised by clinical supervisors. In Israel, the Bar Association forbids students from providing legal representation. Therefore, clinical supervisors try to involve students in the case in other ways, such as meeting with clients, legal research, and document drafting, all under close supervision.

The clinic I will focus on in this article is the DRC at Bar Ilan University.[12] In Israel, like in many other places, persons with disabilities (physical, sensory, cognitive and mental) make up about 20 per cent of the population, and are discriminated against in many social and legal fields,[13] such as accessibility to places and services, labour, education, health, legal capacity, and parenting. Therefore, the clinic, motivated by the Equal Rights of Persons with Disabilities Law 5758–1998, is dedicated to promoting accommodations in all fields of life.

## Therapeutic and social work aspects in the clinic

Most, if not all, of the clinic's clients, in Bar Ilan and Israel, bring to the clinic a variety of problems, many of which have therapeutic and social work aspects alongside their legal case. This is due, at least in part, to their belonging to vulnerable communities, and is, many times, invited by some of the clinical supervisor's character, which encourages, even unconsciously, an atmosphere of help and openness. It is common to say that many of our interactions have 'social work character' and require social work skills,[14] and that the emotional capabilities which are required in order to handle a case and cope with its implications on our clients are many times greater than the legal or rational ones.[15] This does not mean that we should act like social workers, but rather that we can learn from the

12 The Clinic is co-directed by Dr Maya Gaffan and by me, and is academically supervised by Prof. Gideon Sapir. The clinic was formerly co-directed by Karine Elharrar, who is now a member of the Israeli Parliament.

13 The Israeli Commission on the rights of persons with disabilities (Ministry of Justice) website: https://www.justice.gov.il/En/UNITS/COMMISSIONEQUALRIGHTSPERSONSDISABILITIES/Pages/About-the-Commission-for-Equal-Rights-of-Persons-With-Disablities.aspx.

14 Jane H Aiken and Stephen Wizner, 'Law as Social Work' (2003) 11 Wash U J L & Pol'y 63; Susan L Brooks, 'Using Therapeutic Jurisprudence to Build Effective Relationships with Students, Clients and Communities' (2006) 13 Clinical L Rev 213; Susan L Brooks, 'Practicing (and Teaching) Therapeutic Jurisprudence: Importing Social Work Principles and Techniques into Clinical Legal Education' (2005) 17 St Thomas L Rev 513.

15 Ann Juergens, 'Practicing What We Teach: The Importance of Emotion and Community Connection in Law Work and Law Teaching' (2005) 11 Clinical L Rev 413.

education, values, and practice of social workers, such as focusing not only on the client but also on the client's surroundings, and considering aspects of minority groups.[16]

This idea of legal clinics learning from the field of social work makes a lot of sense when we think about the theoretical underpinnings of the clinics: their goals, like those of social workers, and opposed to 'regular' law firms, are based on values of social justice, legal aid, and social reform. These goals focus not only on the individual client but also on her surroundings, family, and community. They consider aspects of minority groups such as gender and ethnicity, and they acknowledge the ways in which governmental institutions and bureaucratic procedures affect their clients, many times for the worst. Similar to social workers, clinical supervisors should consider not only the specific legal case but the limiting surroundings that generated the legal problem, take part in initiating legislative reform instead of merely implementing the existing laws, see themselves as one of client's resources and not as the administrator of her life, and take into account that a certain legal action might not serve the client's or the group's interests in a broad sense and for the long term.

Through conversations I held with my students over the years I learnt that at least some of them chose to study law out of justice-related motivations, since they felt that power gaps leave some people or communities in a disadvantageous position, which could be corrected through legal means. For those students, the actual studies which emphasise rationality and formal rules do not satisfy this need. Moreover, the theoretical studies include very little information regarding practical lawyering values and skills,[17] and sometimes, their emphasis on formal rules, facts, and evidence are even contrary to those practical and value-driven concerns.[18] It is even claimed that the way legal studies are conducted and perceived, as rational and emotionless, leads to personal distress and professional dissatisfaction.[19] Therapeutic professional students (such as psychology or social work students), on the other hand, are required, throughout their studies, to engage in field work, which is closely supervised by therapeutic experts. This way they have a chance to experience the practical sides of the profession very early on while receiving the necessary emotional guidance and support.[20]

The clinics, being practical in nature, have a potential to fill in this gap. But, although the clinics share many social work ideologies, usually, the formal

16 Fehn (n 2).

17 This is (or is supposed to be) somewhat different in the US, where law studies sometime include aspects of relationship. See Marjorie A Silver, 'Introduction' in Marjorie A Silver (ed.), *The Affective Assistance of Council: Practicing Law as a Healing Profession* (CAP 2007).

18 Kristin B Gerdy, 'Clients, Empathy and Compassion: Introducing First Year Students to the "Heart" of Lawyering' (2008) 87 Nebraska L Rev 1.

19 Juergens (n 15).

20 Stephanie K Boys, Carrie A Hagan, and Valerie Voland, 'Lawyers are Counselors, Too: Social Workers can Train Lawyers to More Effectively Counsel Clients' (2011) 12 Adv Soc Work 241.

training that students go through does not include systematic study of the human factor of the cases. This is usually learnt during the case-by-case practical work and is subject to the clinical supervisor's discretion in terms of which aspects of the case-related work they choose to emphasise. Also, it is rare to find permanent therapeutic consultation in the clinic – for students, lawyers, or clients. Therefore, when we deal with therapeutic aspects in the clinic, we need to do so carefully, knowing that we do not necessarily know how to act therapeutically, let alone teach therapeutic content and practice.

## Therapeutic Jurisprudence

As mentioned above, dealing with therapeutic aspects in the clinic is complicated. Nevertheless, it is still desirable and sometimes even crucial to implement therapeutic theory and practice in the clinic's work, not just for the sake of the clients' wellbeing, but also in order to win cases and achieve the broader goals that the clinics usually set. TJ can be the most suitable platform to achieve all these outcomes.

TJ deals with the law as a therapeutic agent. It focuses on the emotional life and psychological wellbeing of the individual, and on the human and emotional side of the law and the legal process. According to TJ, the law can be much more than a set of rules with limited functions, such as dispute resolution, resource distribution, and conduct directing.[21] TJ emerged out of concerns related to intersection of law and mental health[22] and since then has developed in different fields, such as criminal law,[23] family law, and children's rights.[24] TJ views the law as a social force that can yield behaviours and consequences that can be either therapeutic or anti-therapeutic. Its basic premise is that the law should promote not only justice and other normative legal values, but also outcomes connected to improved wellbeing for the persons involved.[25]

TJ seeks to raise legal agents' awareness to these concerns in order to try and implement the law in more therapeutic ways, while other central values, such as justice and due process, are fully respected.[26] TJ does not place therapeutic goals above other primary goals of legal processes; rather, it strives to enrich and broaden the law's impact. It promotes consideration of factors that in the past generally were not considered part of the legal process, such as the potential for

21 Winick and Wexler (n 4).

22 Michael L Perlin, *International Human Rights and Mental Disability Law: When the Silenced are Heard* (OUP 2012).

23 Winick and Wexler (n 4).

24 Susan L Brooks, 'The Case for Adoption Alternatives' (2001) 39 Fam Court Rev 43; Susan L Brooks, 'Therapeutic Jurisprudence and Preventive Law in Child Welfare Proceedings: A Family Systems Approach' (1999) 5 Psychol Pub Pol'y & L 951.

25 Winick and Wexler (n 4); Inbar Cohen, 'Standing at a Crossroad – the Crossroad between Therapy and Law as Manifested in the Testimony of Mental Health Professionals' (2016) 23 Hamishpat 139 [Hebrew].

26 Winick and Wexler (n 4).

broader impact, rehabilitation, preventing future disputes, long-term dispute resolution, and protection of the individual's rights and psychological wellbeing.[27] These can be achieved through broadening the scope of the goals to be considered by judges, courts, and lawyers, as well as through the collaboration with therapeutic professionals. Overall, TJ focuses on improving the psychological functioning and the mental health of the client while handling her legal case.[28] Also, through TJ, therapeutic principles such as empowerment and self-determination can be integrated into the legal advocacy and support provided to people who are usually not legally represented.[29]

It is not easy to implement TJ in the classic legal world, which is based on a dichotomy of legal success or failure, that usually does not leave room for broader considerations. Therefore, implementing TJ in private practice is left to each lawyer's discretion. Nevertheless, from a TJ point of view, the client's overall wellbeing should be one of the lawyer's goals or considerations, even if only just to serve for a better and more effective legal representation and legal outcome.[30] In contrast to 'classic lawyering', the legal clinics can be an ideal field for TJ, since they deal not only with individual cases and their final outcomes, but also with ideas and goals of overall wellbeing of individual clients and underprivileged groups.[31] Also, clinics do not depend financially on their clients' legal problems, and therefore they usually find space for activities that are not solely legal.[32] Still, as mentioned above, law students usually do not receive enough theoretical education or practical training regarding the lawyer–client relationship (such as the psychological implications of client representation, or listening and counselling skills), even though such education and training would help them practice TJ in their work in the clinic and as future lawyers. In the next section I will outline TJ implementation in the work of the DRC.

## Implementing TJ in the DRC

TJ does not dictate a certain way of conduct. It merely seeks carefully to consider aspects of psychology, psychiatry, behavioural science, criminology, and social work in order to see if knowledge from these fields can be implemented or

27 Brooks, 'Using Therapeutic Jurisprudence' (n 14).

28 For further reading regarding counselling duties and opportunities for lawyers see: David A Binder, Paul B Bergman, Paul R Tremblay, and Ian S Weinstein, *Lawyers as Counselors, A Client-Centered Approach* (4th Addition, West Academic Publishing, 2019).

29 Rose Voyvodc and Mary Medcalf, 'Advancing Social Justice Through an Interdisciplinary Approach to Clinical Legal Education: The Case of Legal Assistance of Windsor' (2004) 14 Wash U J L & Pol'y 101.

30 Michal Alberstein, 'Preface' (2010) 21 Mehkarey Mishpat 351, 361–62 [Hebrew].

31 Voyvodc and Medcalf (n 29).

32 Mary Berkheiser, 'Frasier Meets CLEA: Therapeutic Jurisprudence and Law School Clinics' (1999) 5 Psychol Pub Pol'y & L 1147; Bruce J Winnick and David B Wexler, 'The Use of Therapeutic Jurisprudence in Law School Clinical Education: Transforming the Criminal Law Clinic' (2006) 13 Clinical L Rev 605.

integrated into the legal system or legal case, to lead to more therapeutic processes and outcomes.[33] Given that orientation, TJ could be implemented in various ways, according to each legal field's characteristics. In the DRC, I have found that the most effective way to implement TJ is through importing social work's values, theories, and skills[34] as detailed below. This approach is based on the shared focus of social work and TJ on advancing the individual's wellbeing, which is linked to social work's and the clinic's shared commitment to social justice and welfare. Thus, wellbeing contemplates respecting the client's dignity, culture, and voice, to ensure that the lawyer's work is responsive to the client's self-identified needs and interests. As mentioned above, implementing social work values in the clinic doesn't turn the clinic's work into social work, nor the clinical supervisor and students to social workers. It means simply that the legal representation includes therapeutic considerations.[35] Implementing social work elements in the clinic, through TJ, helps us deal better with the 'psycho-legal soft spots', which are the legal situations most likely to cause, or to shed light on psychological problems.[36]

Disability rights practice can be a natural field for TJ.[37] This is because disabilities usually have psychological and therapeutic aspects that cannot and should not be overlooked,[38] and also because the clinic's aspiration is not merely to win the case but also to enhance the client's wellbeing, as well as the wellbeing of people with disabilities in general. Therefore, expanding knowledge regarding theories, principles, and practices of social work, like the ones I will elaborate on during the next sections, would help the clinical supervisor and the students, and supply them with a sophisticated toolbox that will help both their clients and them. Based on these notions, the following are some social work-related concepts that should be implemented in the clinic. This guidance is disability rights oriented, but most of them can be implemented in any clinic. The discussion will involve four aspects: students' training, legal case handling, client–lawyer–student interaction, and the influence of the work on the clinical supervisors and the students.

33 Winick and Wexler (n 4).

34 Brooks, 'Practicing (and Teaching) Therapeutic Jurisprudence' (n 14). Naturally, this calls for incorporating basic knowledge of these fields in the course of the legal studies, and the collaboration with therapeutic professionals, as mentioned further in this chapter.

35 Ibid.

36 David B Wexler, 'Practicing Therapeutic Jurisprudence: Psycholegal Soft Spots and Strategies' (1998) 67 Rev Jur UPR 317.

37 It should be noted that Disability Rights and certain practices of TJ can also contradict. See: Anna Arstein-Kerslake and Jennifer Black, 'Right to Legal Capacity in Therapeutic Jurisprudence: Insights from Critical Disability Theory and the Convention on the Rights of Persons with Disabilities' (2020) 68 Int J Law Psychiatry 1.

38 Michael L Perlin, Keri K Gould, and Deborah A Dorfman, 'Therapeutic Jurisprudence and the Civil Rights of Institutionalized Mentally Disabled Persons: Hopeless Oxymoron or Path to Redemption?' (1995) 1 Psychol Pub Pol'y & L 80.

## *Students' training: basic understanding of disability studies and social work*

### *Cultural aspects and cultural knowledge*

One of the cornerstones of social work is 'cultural ability': acquiring knowledge regarding different cultures and traditions, developing sensitivity and understanding of variety, and an awareness of the existing prejudice and structured premises that result from the therapist's own cultural belonging.[39] These competencies are needed so the therapist and client are able to cooperate and the therapist does not impose her decisions and can help the client find the best solution for her, while being sensitive to her needs and surroundings.[40] When considering the disability field, both individual and theoretical-ideological cultural aspects need to be taken into account. In Israel, persons with disabilities make up 20 per cent of the population, and they are discriminated against in almost every aspect.[41]

At the theoretical-ideological level, it is therefore very important to hold knowledge regarding disability studies, and especially the shift from the *individual* and *bio-medical approach*, which dominated the disability field up until the 1980s, and defined disability mainly as an organic deficit that requires fixing, rehabilitation, or treatment in segregation,[42] into the *social approach*, which affected the right's based legislation regarding disability today, and perceives disability mainly as a result of an inaccessible social structure.[43]

On the individual level, it is important to hold knowledge regarding different kinds of disabilities and their psychological ramifications for the individual and her surroundings. The clinic's work involves health rights, labour, disability pensions, education, community living, legal capacity, parenting, and so on, and therefore it is important to contemplate how achieving, or not achieving those rights will affect clients' lives. While understanding the needs of persons with physical and sensory disabilities is fairly simple (ramps, clear speech, etc.), understanding the implications of intellectual and psychological disabilities is more complex. For example, clients with autism or psychological disabilities might be

39 Carwina Weng, 'Multicultural Lawyering: Teaching Psychology to Develop Cultural Self Awareness' (2005) 11 Clinical L Rev 369.

40 Juergens (n 15); Boys, Hagan, and Voland (n 20).

41 See 'Summary of Findings' in Doron Dorfman, Yossi Hasson, Karin Sandel, and Eran Halperin, *The Municipal Accessibility Index in Israel* (2019) 6–8.

42 Michael Oliver, *Understanding Disability: From Theory to Practice* (Palgrave MacMillan 1996) 30–33.

43 In fact, the individual and bio-medical approaches still effect the disability legislation and policy. For further information see: Arie Rimmerman, Michal Soffer, Dana David, Tsilly Dagan, Roni Rothler, and Lior Mishali, 'Mapping the Terrain of Disability Legslation: The Case of Israel' (2014) 30(1) Disabil Soc 46; for more reading regarding disability studies and the different models for disability see: Carol Thomas, 'How is Disability Understood? An Examination of Sociological Approaches' (2004) 19 Disabil Soc 569.

perceived as annoying, exhausting or even threatening. Understanding the disability and holding basic knowledge regarding typical behaviours might diminish aversive feelings. For example, a clinical supervisor or a student who holds disability culture knowledge would not initiate physical contact with a client with autism, such as a handshake, and would not be confused if the client does not make eye contact; they would wait patiently for clients with various disabilities to talk, and not address the people who escorted them, instead; they would agree to meet clients in their homes when they have physical or mental difficulties that prevent them from going outside. Clinical supervisors and students who meet people with many kinds of disabilities can find it easier to overcome communication differences, and therefore can give a more effective legal aid.

### *Systems theory*

Systems theory is a theoretical model that has heavily influenced a number of disciplines, including social work. It explains the connections between different systems in the client's life: community and family systems as well as government and bureaucratic systems. As clinical supervisors, we can give better service to our clients if we understand the ways different systems affect their lives, and the possible outcomes of laws and legal acts, given those systems. For example, it is important to know that if you help a person to remove restrictions on her legal capacity, so she can act autonomically regarding personal or economical aspects of her life, it will likely affect her relationship with former guardians, or that a child's entitlement to disability benefits might affect decisions regarding their education in the future.

### *The abilities approach*

Legal cases frequently focus on deficits and its compensation through legal actions. In contrast, therapeutic approaches call for processes that emphasise abilities and strengths.[44] Research has shown that clients who feel strong are more likely to help themselves.[45] Even though the lawyer–client relationship is usually based on the professional strength of the lawyers, sometimes, the clinic can help by strengthening the client. Such a process happened in our clinic 'by proxy', at a time when many children with autism lost their disability pensions. There were so many similar incidents that we decided to draft templates for the parents to modify and file by themselves. The feedback we received from our clients taught us that the clients' successes had a double positive impact – they won the case while strengthening their self-esteem and belief in their abilities to help their children.

44 This inherent difference cannot always be settled. Many cases. such as disability pension, require emphasising weaknesses as an inherent strategy, since the disability pension system does not reward abilities and strengths.

45 Boys, Hagan, and Voland (n 20).

### ***Handling the legal case***

*Attention and listening skills*

Listening is one of the main pillars of legal-therapeutic aid.[46] Sometimes, clients thank us or our students just for listening, even if we couldn't help them at all. There are two critical elements for productive listening. One of them is *time*: we must conduct meetings and conversations when we have enough time to do so. The second is the *stress* that we often feel, out of our commitment and desire to provide immediate legal help to every client. In order to deal with this stress, we must remind ourselves that not every conversation or every meeting has to have specific results. We listen better if we do not try to think of solutions while listening, and the counselling and advice can and frequently must be postponed to the next meeting. This kind of listening usually enables us to see the 'big picture' and capture implicit messages, like the client's tone of voice, the nature of the client's relationships, and the client's emotional state. This is one reason it is critically important to tell our students that listening is not only a means to get information, but a goal in itself.[47]

*Working together with the client – 'Nothing about us without us'*

'Nothing about us without us' is a phrase used to express the idea that group members should be involved in constructing policies that affect their particular group and is a leading principle in the disability rights field. This notion fits social work principles of the client's agency and responsibility regarding the process of decision making that needs to be adopted by clinical supervisors. Clinical supervisors should appreciate and honour clients' expertise over their own and understand that their time in the clinic is only temporary – they will have to carry on living and interacting with family and institutions after the case is done. Such was the case with one of the clinic's clients, who initially looked for help with his disability benefits case. During the legal process he became a leading member of the autistic community, and eventually we co-authored an article, describing legal and social aspects of autism and disability rights.[48]

Drawing from therapeutic values and perceptions, focusing on the individual's subjective experience rather than the search for the ultimate truth,[49] will assist clinical supervisors to appreciate that each client's case might have a different suitable solution, even if objectively there could be a 'better' legal one. When we

46 Leonard L Riskin, 'Awareness in Lawyering: A Primer on Paying Attention', in Marjorie A Silver (ed.), *The Affective Assistance of Council: Practicing Law as a Healing Profession* (CAP 2007) 447.

47 Brooks, 'Using Therapeutic Jurisprudence' (n 14).

48 Roni Rothler and Ronen Gil, 'On the Spectrum and Beyond It: Representing Autistic Persons – Diversity, Abilities, Rights, and What Lies in Between' (2010) 3 Law and Social Change 83 [Hebrew].

49 Susan L Brooks and Robert G. Madden, 'Relationship-Centered Lawyering: Social Science Theory for Transforming Legal Practice' (2009) 78 Revista Juridica UPR 23.

think only about legal facts, we might overlook other important aspects that affect our clients, their wishes, and their experience. This legalistic lens might lead us to miss opportunities for reconciliation, or draft contracts that do not suit our clients' wishes and needs.[50] As lawyers, collaborating with clients in the process of decision making is far from simple or intuitive, yet it needs to an aspiration and a goal of clinical supervisors' work. Typical examples from the DRC include legal capacity cases, in which we have to consult with our clients regarding the construction of an alternative plan that would enable them to achieve full legal capacity; education cases, where we must listen to the wishes and needs of the children and their parents regarding the desired education institute; and cases that involve people or institutions that have an ongoing connection with the client, such as employers or municipalities.

*Clients who do not do what we expect them to do*

One of the most common experiences in therapy is the patient's unwillingness to act according to the therapeutic plan.[51] These incidents are also quite common in the clinic, when we make a certain plan for the client to achieve their rights and find out that the client did not do his part, or acted in a way that contradicts the achievement of the legal goals, whether by giving partial and missing information, failing to supply documents, or simply disappearing.[52] This conduct, of course, is a great source of frustration for the clinical supervisor and students, who wish to achieve the best possible legal outcome for their clients and don't understand why clients who initially turned to the clinic and asked for its help fail to cooperate. Social workers learn to respect this aspect of the process, work with it and recognise the 'undoing' of the client as a valid choice.[53] Following this understanding, the clinical supervisor should explain the students that there is no point in making the client act in a certain way, nor should they act on his behalf, but rather make sure that the client receives all the relevant information, and keep the communication channels open, in case he changes his mind.

*Accessible language*

Accessibility is one of the main pillars of disability rights.[54] The 'legal language' is not always accessible for people with no legal background, let alone for persons with intellectual disabilities. Clients might not follow our advice merely because they did not understand it, and therefore, clinical supervisors must try to make the legal language accessible by using simpler terms whenever possible.

50 Juergens (n 15).
51 Brooks, 'Using Therapeutic Jurisprudence' (n 14).
52 Neta Ziv, 'Lawyers Talking Rights and Clients Breaking Rules: Between Legal Positivism and Distributive Justice in Israeli Poverty Lawyering' (2004) 10(1) Clinical L Rev 209.
53 Brooks, 'Practicing (and Teaching) Therapeutic Jurisprudence' (n 14).
54 Sagit Mor, 'With Access and Justice for All' (2017) 39 Cardozo L Rev 611.

### *Client–lawyer–student interaction*

#### *Transference and counter-transference*

Transference and counter-transference are psychological concepts that describe the patient's reaction to the therapist, which includes the projection from his other significant relationships, and the therapist's reaction to this reaction.[55] These themes are complex, too complex to be dealt with directly within the legal clinic. Nevertheless, it is important to be aware of common contents of counter-transference, and particularly the emotions of the clinical supervisor and the students toward the clients and their disabilities. One should not ignore the fact the certain disabilities might evoke negative feelings, such as fear or restraint. Such feelings are usually derived from lack of knowledge about or acquaintance with persons with disabilities, which leads to a lack of day-to-day interaction, on the one hand, and on the other hand, enhances existing prejudice and stigma.[56]

In the DRC, we try to touch upon these concerns during the orientation days, through exercises and simulations that strive to surface feelings and prejudices the students hold regarding disabilities. These exercises and simulations include meetings with persons with disabilities and discussing the emotions that these encounters sometimes spur, such as fear, pity, or even disgust; and simulations of consultation to clients with different disabilities, such as clients in a state of depression, in order to help students detect depression signs and discuss their implications on the legal case. Throughout the academic year, we also dedicate classes to communication skills. The unsurprising finding is that students are usually intimidated by disabilities with which they are unfamiliar. Accordingly, once they have had some kind of interaction with a person with a certain disability, most of the time the intimidation diminishes. This finding has encouraged us to give them more information about certain disabilities and raise their awareness to the fact that if they can overcome their initial fear and get acquainted with the client, the intimidation will diminish or even disappear.

Alongside the clinic's aspiration for the students' feelings of intimidation and prejudice to diminish over the course of the academic year, we also recognise that ignoring them or considering them illegitimate would of course be harmful. Therefore, we must encourage our students to express their feelings toward certain clients and try to address issues whenever they arise. It is important that students know they will not have to deal with such feelings on their own, and that they are feel free to discuss these difficult issues with the clinical supervisor. Having said that, the clinic might not be the most suitable place to deal with deep negative emotions, and therefore sometimes the most suitable solution, for all parties – clinical supervisor, student, and client – would be to let the student handle a different case.

55 Brooks, 'Using Therapeutic Jurisprudence (n 14).
56 Michal Soffer, 'Culture, Causal Attributions to Visual Impairments, and Stigma: A Mediation Model' (2019) 12(3) Disabil Health J 437.

*Maintaining boundaries*

One of the most indispensable skills in the clinic is to maintain professional boundaries, especially since boundaries tend to blur when we implement aspects of social work, such as creating trust, empathy, active listening, and expression of emotions. Therefore, it is important to talk with students about boundaries and make informed decisions regarding matters such as providing cellular/mobile phone numbers to clients, sharing aspects of their personal lives, accompanying the clients to social or therapeutic meetings, and counselling them regarding non-legal matters. It is important to remember that most of the time students have direct contact with clients, and that we usually encourage them to be involved in the case, very early in their professional lives. Therefore, it is the clinical supervisor's duty to be involved in the student–client relationship, to get updates on their conversations, to approve meetings, and be aware of the contents of all those in order to make sure that the students are keeping the legal-professional boundaries. Doing this provides the clinical supervisors with an excellent opportunity to analyse the situation with the students and teach them to better recognise these boundaries. Consequently, the clinical supervisor must stop or moderate the relationship when it goes too far.

*Dealing with depression and suicidal emotions*

Clients who experience clinical depression are a common phenomenon in the DRC. These are cases where we should make sure the boundaries are not crossed and ensure that the clients' metal health situation is dealt with by therapeutic professionals.[57] These are also cases that call for professional ethical consideration. For example, one day, on a phone conversation, a client asked for the clinic's formal address. She told me she wanted to send her computer to us, since 'in the place where I'm going there is no need for such a thing'. I was very worried when she ended the call. I knew that she does not have any contact with her relatives, and I called the social services providers in her town and asked them to help her. From a letter she sent me later, I learnt that she did receive help and was content with it. Still, I was not sure if I had acted ethically, and later, when I received the clinics' Ethics Committee response, I was told that I should have asked her for permission to do it first, and only call the social services if she did not actively object to it. This guidance, like other advice, is usually easier said than done, and even in retrospect, I do not know if I could have acted in a different manner.

## The influence of the legal work on the clinical supervisors and the students

*Negative feelings and secondary trauma*

Negative feelings and secondary or vicarious trauma (also referred to as compassion fatigue), which is defined as indirect exposure to trauma through a first-hand

57 Paula Galowitz, 'Collaboration Between Lawyers and Social Workers: Re-examining the Nature and Potential of the Relationship' (1999) 67(5) Fordham L Rev 2123.

account or narrative of a traumatic event, resulting in cognitive or emotional representation,[58] can be the outcome of dealing with clients' problems, and can be manifested in students' or clinical supervisors' feelings of hopelessness, the inability to feel pleasure, stress, anxiety, depression, and a decrease in compassion. It can result in lack of willingness to work with the client or, on the other hand, over-identification with the client – both resulting in negative implications such as paralysis or over-controlling behaviour.[59] Negative feelings and secondary trauma can be intensified due to the fact the during law studies, unlike therapeutic-oriented studies, students are not exposed to the notion of secondary trauma, let alone the ways to deal with it.

Enjoying one's work is an important key for professional success, endurance and 'anti-burnout' over time. Many of the clinic's cases are based on social injustice and can spur negative feelings or even despair within the clinical supervisor and students. Some feelings, such as anger, can sometimes serve us as 'fuel', but this fuel usually runs out and does not allow a high level of satisfaction over time.[60]

It is therefore important to be aware of the fact that we could experience negative feelings or secondary trauma in the course of our work, and sometimes the awareness itself can be part of the solution. In addition, it is important to attend to the symptoms of secondary trauma professionally, both those that occur in clinical supervisors and students. Preferably, this will be done by a therapeutic professional who is a part of the clinic's staff or who is collaborating with it. It is also important to identify the causes of the trauma and try to control the number of cases with traumatic potential. For example, if we detect some kind of vulnerability in a student, we could let that student attend to cases which are more research-oriented, or work with organisations that are focused on empowerment.

### *Time and workload*

It is impossible to implement all these TJ aspects such as attention, cultural sensitivity, collaboration, empowerment, and dealing with negative contents, without making enough space and time within the clinic's day-to-day work. In this respect, I found it helpful to remind myself that the clinic's location at the Faculty of Law should help us remain conscious and aware of our main educational goal, a goal that sometimes conflicts with the urge to take too many cases. In order to have enough time to teach students best practices, we have to choose cases (in

58 Charles R. Figley (ed.), *Compassion Fatigue: Coping with Secondary Traumatic Stress Disorder in Those who Treat the Traumatized* (Brunner-Routledge 1995).

59 Mary Ann Dutton and Francine L. Rubinstein, 'Working with People with PTSD: Research Implications', in Charles R. Figley (ed.), *Compassion Fatigue: Coping with Secondary Traumatic Stress Disorder in Those Who Treat the Traumatized* (1995) 82; for a deeper discussion regarding lawyers' and law students' wellbeing see: Caroline Stevens and Rachael Field (eds), *Educating for Well-Being in Law: Positive Professional Identities and Practice* (Routledge 2019).

60 Juergens (n 15).

nature and number) that allow us to devote time for experiential teaching. Such teaching cannot take place in an atmosphere of constant pressure and urgency. We should also strive for full time clinical jobs and a low number of students per clinical supervisor. This idea brings me to the last section of this article, in which I claim that the clinic can be an ideal place for implementing TJ.

## The clinic as an ideal platform for TJ

Legal clinics can be an ideal field for TJ, as they deal not only with individual cases and their final outcomes, but also with ideas and goals of overall wellbeing of the clients and their underprivileged groups. Also, they do not depend financially on their clients' legal problems, and therefore they usually find space for activities that are not solely legal. Yet, implementing TJ in the clinic in all the ways and aspects mentioned above, while helpful, is not a 'one-time decision' but rather an ongoing effort.

### *Contextualising TJ in the legal clinic*

#### *Collaboration with therapeutic professionals*

My main resolution regarding TJ, one which is shared by other writers,[61] is that in order to implement most of the therapeutic contents while handling a legal case, the lawyer must collaborate with and consult therapeutic professionals (for example, to help the client cope with the stress that the legal case entails, to assist clients follow court orders, or in order to help the client form plans for the future that should be presented to the court). This type of assistance will help the clinic provide its clients with a more comprehensive legal aid, while maintaining the wellbeing of the students, the clients, and the clinical supervisors.

One efficient way to collaborate with therapeutic professionals, one that does not call for special resources, is to collaborate with therapeutic professionals that are already taking part in our clients' lives, so that legal aid is provided while fully collaborating and sharing information with those professionals. It is crucial that this information-sharing is done with the full consent of the client. Such collaboration can be highly effective as long as the therapeutic help that is provided is human rights-oriented and not over-protective or based on outdated notions regarding persons with disabilities or members of other vulnerable groups.

The clinic's 'academic position' can be very helpful regarding this type of collaboration, because in addition to representing clients, it can also engage in academic activities such as holding conferences, seminars, and lectures, and therefore has the opportunity to communicate with therapeutic and other professionals at many levels. For the DRC, such has been the situation with our expertise around

61 Galowitz (n 57); Karen Tokarz, Nancy L Cook, Susan Brooks, and Branda Bratton Blom, 'Conversations on "Community Lawyering": The Newest (Oldest) Wave in Clinical Legal Education' (2008) 28 Wash U J L & Pol'y 359.

legal capacity: in this field the clinic represents clients that want to gain back their legal capacity, and it has also engaged in legislation reform in this field in Israel,[62] and has held conferences and lectures on this topic. These activities have led to situations where the government's social workers[63] in charge of issuing reports to the court regarding our clients have attended our conferences and lectures and have, therefore, been much keener to accept and implement the reforms we have advocated for in their reports. Also, since the clinic is perceived as having its own agenda apart from merely representing clients, we have found that most social workers are more inclined to collaborate with us. For instance, they have permitted us to participate in meetings that are considered 'therapeutic', unlike our private lawyer colleagues. The clinic's special location, within the academic institution, can also make it easier to contact therapeutic professionals and academics, and develop practical and theoretical collaborations, both within the university as well as within other academic institutions which take interest in this kind of collaboration.

Another kind of socio-legal collaboration can happen within a certain clinic that hires therapeutic professionals, mainly social workers, as clinical supervisors. As an illustration, our clinical programme included over the years social worker clinical supervisors[64] in the clinic for elderly people and holocaust survivors, in the clinic for social and economic affairs, and in the DRC. This kind of collaboration enables the clinic to give some social work services to its clients, and social work-oriented education to its students[65] (an education that can also be provided by outside professionals, if necessary), while developing complex and comprehensive resolutions regarding professional collaborations, such as common goals, methods, differences, and hierarchies, which are beyond the scope of this chapter.[66] Another interesting aspect of this kind of inter-clinic collaboration is the ethical one, since the ethical duties and responsibilities of lawyers and social workers (including competency, mandatory reporting, role, and confidentiality) are different and can sometimes contradict.[67]

62 The 2016 amendment to the Legal Capacity and Guardianship Law, 5722–1962.
63 In Israel, the relevant official is the municipality's social worker.
64 The social worker clinical supervisors are part of the clinical staff in the faculty. They are supervising the students and provide social work-oriented services to the clients alongside the legal clinical staff.
65 Ian Gallacher, 'Thinking Like Non-Lawyers: Why Empathy Is a Core Lawyering Skill and Why Legal Education Should Change to Reflect Its Importance' (2012) College of Law Faculty – Scholarship 6; Marjorie A Silver, 'Supporting Attorney's Personal Skills' (2009) 78 Revista Juridica UPR, 147.
66 In our clinical programmes we are holding an ongoing process regarding the scope and definitions of the social worker and lawyer as clinical supervisors. The process is led by Dr Maya Gaffan, and includes clinical supervisors from Bar Ilan University, Tel Aviv University, the College of management, Sapir Academic College, and Ono Academic College.
67 Zavez (n 2); Alexis Anderson et al., 'Professional Ethics in Interdisciplinary Collaboratives: Zeal, Paternalism, and Mandated Reporting' (2007) 13 Clinical L Rev 659; Stacy Brustin, 'Legal Services Provision Through Multidisciplinary Practice –

The types and modes of socio-legal clinical collaboration of this sort can vary, according to each clinic's subject matter and the supervisor's personal inclinations. For example, in some clinics all of the cases are handled together by the lawyer and social worker (pending on each client's consent to acquire this kind of dual service), while in others there can be a separation between 'legal cases' and 'social work cases'.[68] Usually, the social workers will co-teach the classes and co-conduct supervision sessions with the students, and many times they will also be involved in the student's well-being issues and not only the client's.

Involving therapeutic professionals in the clinic, whether in-house or outsourcing, can also provide the clinical staff and the students with on-going counselling and supervision regarding the emotional aspects of cases and their individual implications, thus diminishing the negative feelings that are sometimes inherent to the public interest lawyering profession.[69]

### *Student-related TJ advantages*

Another important aspect regarding the integration of TJ in the clinic regards the role of the students. While usually the main aspect of the clinical supervisor–student relationship regards a one-direction pedagogic duty, the student can also help the clinical supervisor deal with some of the emotional burden that the public interest lawyering work entails, thus impacting on the cost of delivering a clinical programme. This possible reciprocity is due to the clinic's goals, which are broader than merely providing legal aid, and include pedagogical aspects. This broader agenda provides us with the privilege of selecting 'pedagogic-oriented' cases, ones that the students can learn the most from, and particularly avoiding cases that require urgent responses. Another pedagogical issue regards heavy caseloads, which do not leave much room for education. Therefore, our pedagogical mission should prevent us from taking too many cases and dealing with too heavy a workload, thus helping us to relieve some work-related stress.

Another student-related advantage derives from that nature of the student–client connection. Because the clinic's goal is to allow students to experience the legal world first hand, it is important to let them have as much contact as possible with clients, rather than second-hand contact through the clinical supervisor. In this sense, a unique student–clinical supervisor entity is formed, an entity that is better positioned to provide TJ-oriented response to clients while maintaining each individual's psychological welfare and balance and preventing burnout. When clinical supervisors share contact with clients with their students, they are less prone to be negatively involved with the client's legal and social issues and might find it easier to have a broader view of the case, give relevant advice, and

Encouraging Holistic Advocacy While Protecting Ethical Interests' (Summer 2002) 73 U Colo L Rev 787, 794.

68 At least one clinic in Israel is supervised only by a social worker – the socio-legal clinic for youth at risk in the College for Management.

69 Nomi Levenkron, 'Gently Weeping: The Emotional Price Paid by Public Interest Lawyers' (2014) 6 Law and Social Change 13 [Hebrew].

'take care' of students who might cross the boundaries from effective socio-legal aid into harmful emotional involvement.

In addition, the students might hold characteristics and personal skills that help them implement therapeutic content even better than lawyers: they are just beginning to become acquainted with the legal profession and are not yet fixated on 'acceptable' legal modes of thinking and legal roles. Therefore, they may be much more open to therapeutic content. In addition, since they are only in the clinic for one or two semesters and are closely supervised, they are unlikely to suffer from burnout or other negative aspects of the work. In addition, in our clinical programme, resembling many clinical programmes around the world, most students must work in pairs or groups, a fact that enables them to share the workload as well as the emotional load, and support each other.[70] Another aspect in the student's work is their cognition that at the end of the day, the professional responsibility for the case is the lawyer's. This awareness usually also diminishes the stress and negative emotions, realising that they are always supervised, and can be 'saved' by the clinical supervisor.

## Summary

In this chapter I have outlined the reasons clinical supervisors usually want to solve problems that are not necessarily legal connected to the clinic's multiple purposes, and the reasons they should not always do so, especially regarding therapeutic content. I have suggested the notion of TJ as a mean to deal with therapeutic and social work contents in the clinic, in four different aspects: students' training, handling the legal case, client–lawyer–student interaction, and the influence of the legal work on the clinical supervisors and students. In these respects, I have written about the importance of boundaries between the legal and the therapeutic professions, as well as the importance of collaborating with therapeutic professionals.

I have also suggested that the clinic might be the ideal platform to practice TJ, especially because of its academic-oriented activities alongside the practical ones, its proximity to therapeutic professionals, its pedagogical goals, and the unified 'student–clinical supervisor' entity that is formed in the clinic. Naturally, there are many ways to implement TJ in the clinic, depending on the clinic's field of expertise, the clinical supervisor's inclinations, the availability of therapeutic professionals in the academic institution, and of course, the clinic's resources. All of these issues should be taken under consideration when planning the therapeutic aspects of the legal activity.

70 David F Chavkin, 'Matchmaker, Matchmaker: Student Collaboration in Clinical Programs' (1994) 1 Clin L Rev 199.

# 3 Capitalising on Clinical Legal Education: Insights from Bourdieu

*Andrew Gilbert*

## Introduction

We already expect a lot – maybe too much – from Clinical Legal Education (CLE). It provides access to justice, trains students in practical lawyering skills and knowledge of the law in action, raises the profile of universities in their communities, builds links between law schools and legal professionals, serves as a useful marketing tool to attract new students, and so on. In this chapter I draw on insights from the work of Pierre Bourdieu to consider a further addition to the list: CLE as an engine of social justice and mobility for student participants through the development of their social and cultural capital.

Generally I seek to locate this work in the literature on the purpose of legal education, and specifically this chapter joins others which have argued for 'the transformative potential of clinical legal education'.[1] However, even where legal writers have considered CLE's transformative potential, particularly its potential to transform the lives of student participants, it has been limited to student 'career goals' and 'professional self-conceptions',[2] or to opening the eyes of students to the imperfections and uneven protection of the law, or possibly presenting them 'alternative career paths and opportunities'.[3] I wonder if we could go still further …? My research question echoes that of A. V. Dicey in an early contribution to the debate around the purpose of legal education in his inaugural lecture, 'Can English Law be taught at the universities?',[4] asking instead: Can social and cultural capital be developed through clinical legal education? And if so, how might we do that?

1 Lucie White, 'The Transformative Potential of Clinical Legal Education' (1997) 35 Osgoode Hall Law Journal 603.
2 Ibid. 606. To be fair to White, though, her essay is mainly a more radical call to reconsider the entire notion of 'transformation' and the lawyers' place in effecting it.
3 Frank Bloch and Mary Anne Noone, 'Legal Aid Origins of Clinical Legal Education' in Frank Bloch (ed.), *The Global Clinical Movement: Educating Lawyers for Social Justice* (OUP 2011) 164.
4 Albert Venn Dicey, 'Can English Law be Taught in the Universities', Inaugural Lecture at All Souls College, Oxford, 21 April 1883. The then recently appointed Vinerian Professor of English Law at Oxford wisely concluded that it could be.

DOI: 10.4324/9780429299247-4

Before going further, I set out a working understanding of the term 'Clinical Legal Education' drawn from the work of Grimes:

> It is a process by which students study legal and related knowledge, skills and/or values through exposure to real or realistic legal cases or scenarios and are required to critically reflect on that experience as a structured part of their study.[5]

CLE is characterised by a student-centred pedagogy of active participation and reflective learning,[6] which suits it particularly to the formation of professional identities and potentially as a site for developing social and cultural capital. My discussion starts by exploring the aims and claims of CLE, contending that its social justice remit can be more broadly understood. I then go on to introduce key concepts in Bourdieu's work and survey aspects of the literature on CLE and employability. Finally, Bourdieu's ideas are deployed to argue for, again, a broader understanding of CLE's role in enhancing employability to promote social justice and social mobility.

## CLE: aims and claims

The primary driver for the 'first wave of modern clinical legal education' in the United States in the 1960s and in Australia and Canada in the 1970s was not to remedy deficiencies in legal education but to address a lack of access to justice for the poor.[7] Clinics in the US, India, South Africa and elsewhere often began as community legal aid services, with the education aspect being an 'offshoot'.[8] In contrast, the objectives of the first English law clinic, established by the University of Kent in 1973, were:

> to bring students into contact with practical problems which illuminate their study of law and make it, in that overworked word, 'relevant.' Additional advantages are the increase in contact and communication between practitioners, intending lawyers, and academics, and increases in collaboration

5 Richard Grimes, 'Experiential Learning and Legal Education – the Role of the Clinic in UK Law Schools' in Emma Jones and Fiona Cownie (eds), *Key Directions in Legal Education* (Routledge 2020) 95.

6 Emma Jones, Hugh McFaul and Francine Ryan, 'Clinical Legal Education in the United Kingdom: Origins, Growth and the Technological Innovations and Challenges of its Future' (2017) 4 German Journal of Legal Education 107, 111.

7 Jeff Giddings, Roger Burridge, Shelley Gavigan and Catherine Klein, 'The first wave of modern Clinical Legal Education: The United States, Britain, Canada, and Australia' in Frank S. Bloch (ed.), *The Global Clinical Movement: Educating Lawyers for Social Justice* (OUP 2011) 3–5; Judith Dickson, 'Clinical Legal Education in the 21st Century: Still Educating for Service?' (2000) 33 (1) International Journal of Clinical Legal Education 33.

8 Bloch and Noone (n 3) 157.

> which could lead to research on the legal profession and the problems encountered in practice.[9]

Rees observes that even the intention behind clinic-related vacation placements was that students should be 'of practical use' to the organisations they attended, i. e. it was more about benefits to third parties rather than to students themselves.[10] Indeed, nowhere in his evaluation of the Kent experience does Rees consider that CLE might be useful to students in obtaining employment. The University of Warwick established a clinic in 1975, primarily to enhance the educational experience of law students,[11] although Grimes claims that it was not always the case that the pedagogic value of CLE was assumed and that this was a site of opposition in the early days of its development.[12]

More recently, the growth of CLE provision in UK law schools has been driven by the neoliberal dyad of the widespread withdrawal of legal aid provision and the marketisation of higher education.[13] In contrast to many clinics founded in the last quarter of the twentieth century, university law clinics founded in recent years are perhaps more, or at least as, likely to view the provision of legal services to the community as the context for the educational experience, rather than necessarily a clinic's primary purpose. However, founding motives are wide-ranging. When discussing how to develop a business case for establishing a new university law clinic, *The Clinical Legal Education Handbook* claims the following benefits: development of student skills and awareness; professional insight; community engagement; student wellbeing; student recruitment; possibly providing qualifying work experience for those seeking to qualify as solicitors; providing a site for research; and various benefits to external stakeholders.[14] To this list can be added CLE as an expression of a university's civic mission, supporting employability initiatives, and to encourage co-construction of knowledge.[15] At its core CLE has three elements: professional skills training, experiential learning, and educating for public responsibility and

9 William Rees, 'Clinical Legal Education: An Analysis of the University of Kent Model' (1975) 9 The Law Teacher 125, 131, quoting from a University of Kent document.

10 Ibid. 127.

11 Giddings et al. (n 7) 6.

12 Richard Grimes, Joel Klaff and Colleen Smith, 'Legal Skills and Clinical Legal Education – a Survey of Undergraduate Law School Practice' (1996) 30 The Law Teacher 44, 56.

13 Hugh McFaul, 'Does Clinical Legal Education Need Theory?' (2020) 7 (2) Asian Journal of Legal Education 152, 152–153

14 Linden Thomas and Nick Johnson (eds), *The Clinical Legal Education Handbook* (University of London Press 2020) 13–15.

15 Emma Jones, Hugh McFaul and Francine Ryan, 'Clinical Legal Education in the United Kingdom: Origins, Growth and the Technological Innovations and Challenges of its Future' (2017) 4 German Journal of Legal Education 107, 121: 'Law students should be encouraged to think of new ways to be the producers of knowledge in a digital age to help address legal problems'.

social justice.[16] The scope of these claims places a considerable weight of expectation on law clinics. Unsurprisingly, given the increased marketisation of higher education in many countries, there is growing emphasis on using CLE to develop skills to enhance employability.[17] Mkwebu's recent literature review revealed a widespread view that CLE exists, in part, to equip law students with 'the required employability skills' to enable to them to be effective in the work environment.[18] I return to employability below and use insights from Bourdieu to contend that CLE holds potential to go beyond skills development to effect transformations which address some of the structural disadvantage faced by students from less privileged backgrounds.

## *CLE and social justice*

McFaul identifies there is space for further engagement around discussions of social justice and CLE,[19] and in this section I suggest an idea to fill some of that space. It has been noted above that a social justice imperative sits at the bedrock of CLE. However, my reading of the literature reveals that this imperative is nearly always articulated from the perspective of enabling access to justice for those seeking legal advice and assistance, i.e. an externally directed clinic objective. For example, 'many law school clinical programs around the world have at the center of their educational mission exposing students to social issues and *the role that the legal system can play in improving social justice*'.[20] Moreover, social justice often really means something narrower when mentioned in a clinical context: access to justice.[21]

On fewer occasions, where discussion of social justice and student volunteers intersect in the literature, it is regarding developing those students as the next

16 Frank Bloch, 'Access to Justice and the Global Clinical Movement' (2008) 28 Washington University of Law and Policy 111, 121. Grimes sets out his own 11-point list of benefits of CLE in Grimes (n 5) 96.

17 Tribe Mkwebu, 'Research on Clinical Legal Education: Unpacking the Evidence' in Linden Thomas and Nick Johnson (eds), *The Clinical Legal Education Handbook* (University of London Press 2020) 280.

18 Ibid. 287.

19 McFaul (n 13) 162. For a consideration of meanings of social justice in a higher education context, see Andy Furlong and Fred Cartmel, *Higher Education and Social Justice* (Open University Press 2009) especially 3–7.

20 Frank Bloch and Mary Anne Noone, 'Legal Aid Origins of Clinical Legal Education' in Frank Bloch (ed.), *The Global Clinical Movement: Educating Lawyers for Social Justice* (OUP 2011) 158 (emphasis added). See also Shuvro Prosun Sarker, 'Empowering the Underprivileged: The Social Justice Mission for Clinical Legal Education in India' (2013) 19 International Journal of Clinical Legal Education 321; Jeff Giddings and Jennifer Lyman, 'Bridging Different Interests: The Contributions of Clinics to Legal Education' in Frank Bloch (ed.), *The Global Clinical Movement: Educating Lawyers for Social Justice* (OUP 2011) 305; and Adrian Evans, Anna Cody, Anna Copeland, Jeff Giddings, Peter Joy, Mary Anne Noone and Simon Rice, *Australian Clinical Legal Education* (ANU Press 2017) chapter 5.

21 Evans et al. (n 20) 99.

generation of lawyers with a strong social justice ethos and a commitment to pursue pro bono work once they enter practice.[22] Sarker argues that there are two aspects to this: '[CLE] introduces law students to ideas of public service responsibility or pro-bono work … [and] creates an understanding of the relationship between law and social justice among the law students.'[23] Through its focus on assisting the less wealthy, CLE provides a powerful corrective to the classist concerns of much of the law school curriculum and exposes students to perspectives which they might not experience anywhere else on their course. For example, contract law, land law, trust law, and even much of family law focus on arguments over property, one way or another – whereas housing, social welfare and immigration law are much less likely to be encountered.

Those sympathetic to the cause of CLE are unlikely to find anything to disagree with in what I have just written, but they will also not find in the literature referred to an argument for an *internally directed* – i.e. student-directed – social justice clinic objective. In addition to the literature referred to in the above paragraph, I have not been able to find any reference to a student-directed social justice objective in Mkwebu's literature review, nor in Bloch's edited volume, nor in a chapter on social justice in an Australian context.[24] Therefore, I argue that we should broaden our understanding of the social justice remit of CLE to explicitly include the student's educational experience as a site for the operation of social justice. This social justice argument is evident in the mission statements of open access institutions like The Open University, 'We promote educational opportunity and social justice by providing high-quality university education to all who wish to realise their ambitions and fulfil their potential'.[25] This is social justice as social mobility; education providing equality of opportunity and a shot at equality of outcomes through unlocking latent talent. Admittedly, the social mobility aspect of social justice will not be a core mission of some universities, but even elite institutions are committed to widening access and participation and many have diverse student bodies including some students with relatively low levels of social and cultural capital. Before looking in more detail at how CLE could be deployed as an agent of social mobility, I turn to consider the theoretical foundation on which that later discussion is based.

22 For example, Donald Nicolson, '"Our Roots Began in (South) Africa": Modelling Law Clinics to Maximise Social Justice Ends' (2016) 23 (3) International Journal of Clinical Legal Education 87, 92.

23 Sarker (n 20) 324.

24 Respectively, Tribe Mkwebu, 'Research on Clinical Legal Education: Unpacking the Evidence' in Linden Thomas and Nick Johnson (eds), *The Clinical Legal Education Handbook* (University of London Press 2020) 282–285; Frank Bloch (ed.), *The Global Clinical Movement: Educating Lawyers for Social Justice* (OUP 2011); Adrian Evans, Anna Cody, Anna Copeland, Jeff Giddings, Peter Joy, Mary Anne Noone and Simon Rice, *Australian Clinical Legal Education* (ANU Press 2017) chapter 5.

25 See <http://www.open.ac.uk/about/main/strategy-and-policies/mission> accessed 19 October 2020.

## Bourdieu: introduction and key concepts

Pierre Bourdieu was a French sociologist, anthropologist and philosopher who lived from 1930 to 2002. Not insignificantly, given his study of the mechanisms of cultural and social reproduction and his views on social mobility, he rose from working-class origins to become Professor of Sociology at the highly prestigious Collége de France. Despite his work demanding attention due to its importance in contemporary sociology,[26] reading Bourdieu is rarely easy. Even though it has been rendered into English from the original French, at times it can feel like the translation has not helped much in increasing the reader's understanding. But the reader's perseverance is rewarded because, as Bourdieu wrote a lot about class and a lot about education, he is useful to think about in the context of CLE and social mobility. He also considered the generation and transmission of social advantage through families and education, as well as writing about his ideas in a legal context.[27]

One way to unlock Bourdieu is to start with an appreciation of where he was seeking to situate his thinking about individuals in society, and specifically the interplay between notions of structure and agency.[28] His two counterpoints are structuralism (understanding social phenomena in terms of structures and relations within and between structures) and phenomenology (the study of structures of experience from a first-person perspective): the opposition between objectivism and subjectivism; or perhaps, to put it another way, how much we are shaped by the world and how much the world is shaped by us. The former – in Bourdieu's view – leans too much towards the determining effects of structures at the expense of agency, and vice versa in respect of the latter. Bourdieu's ontology maps out a third way, 'part reaction and part compromise':[29] a form of structured agency which credits the individual with some freedom to pursue their vision of the good life, but constrained by structures of history, society, culture, politics, law, family, and so on. He rejects structuralism in his early work, *Outline of a Theory of Practice*, 'It is necessary to abandon all theories which explicitly or implicitly treat practice as a mechanical reaction, directly determined by the antecedent conditions and entirely reducible to the mechanical functioning of pre-established assemblies, "models" or "roles"'.[30] And in his following sentence he dispatches the claims of phenomenology, stating that we should not 'reduce the objective intentions and

26 From Tony Bennett's introduction to Pierre Bourdieu, *Distinction* (Routledge 1984) xvii.

27 Pierre Bourdieu, 'The Force of Law: Toward a Sociology of the Juridical Field' (1987) 38 Hastings Law Journal 814.

28 Ciaran Burke, Jenny Thatcher, Nicola Ingram and Jessie Abrahams, 'Introduction: The Development of Bourdieu's Intellectual Heritage in UK Sociology' in Jenny Thatcher, Nicola Ingram, Ciaran Burke and Jessie Abrahams (eds), *Bourdieu: The Next Generation* (Routledge 2016) 2–3.

29 Ciaran Burke, 'Bourdieu's Theory of Practice: Maintaining the role of capital' in Jenny Thatcher, Nicola Ingram, Ciaran Burke and Jessie Abrahams (eds), *Bourdieu: The Next Generation* (Routledge 2016) 8.

30 Pierre Bourdieu, *Outline of a Theory of Practice* (Cambridge University Press 1977) 73.

constituted significations of actions and works to the conscious and deliberate intentions of their authors'.[31] So it can be seen that structuralism, according to Bourdieu, cannot account adequately for social change, whereas phenomenology downplays the power of structures to reproduce social status.

### *Field*

The central organising concepts Bourdieu deploys are field, habitus and capital. The word *field* could be understood in neutral terms, merely as a physical space, or in the sense of a cultivated field (where plants grow and flourish) or a sports or battlefield, which are sites of rivalry, victory and loss. It is this latter sense that best corresponds to Bourdieu's view of field as a locus of contest between the dominant and the dominated, both attempting to marshal their resources to their optimal advantage in a competition to secure and reproduce (in the case of the dominant class) or advance (for the dominated class) their social positions. According to Bourdieu, individuals do not move about randomly within fields, but their trajectories are 'subject to'[32] forces which structure the field and partly because individuals are disposed – through their habitus and capital – to resist such forces. This arrangement results in the individual's life course having a 'field of the possibles',[33] being a range of potentialities arising from the quantum of an individual's capital. The field, then, is 'an active and dynamic site in which habitus and capital interact'.[34] Further, Bourdieu expressed the relationship between field, habitus and capital in this way: [(habitus) (capital)] + field = practice.[35] The use of mathematical notation is not helpful, but it does at least explain that 'practice' (i.e. human action) is the result of the interpenetrative relationship between habitus, capital and field, and it also denotes Bourdieu's bridge between structure and agency: studies of this relationship can be found in Bourdieu's *Outline of a Theory of Practice* (examining the practice of the Kabyle people); *Reproduction in Education, Society and Culture* (the practice of the French education system); and *Distinction* (the practice of aesthetic choices).

The utility of Bourdieu's theories is demonstrated through the many and diverse fields in which his ideas have been explored and applied, ranging from law to medicine and acting to computing.[36] For the purposes of this chapter, the

31 Ibid.
32 Pierre Bourdieu, *Distinction* (Routledge 1984) 104.
33 Ibid.
34 Burke et al. (n 28) 2–3.
35 Bourdieu (n 32) 95.
36 Examples include Louise Ashley and Laura Empson, 'Differentiation and Discrimination: Understanding Social Class and Social Exclusion in the UK's Leading Law Firms' (2012) 66 (2) Human Relations 219; Ola Lindberg, 'Gatekeepers of a Profession? Employability as Capital in the Recruitment of Medical Interns' (2013) 26 (4) Journal of Education and Work 431; Sam Friedman and Daniel Laurison, *The Class Ceiling: Why it Pays to be Privileged* (Policy Press 2020); Sally Smith, Ella Taylor-Smith, Liz Bacon and Lachlan Mackinnon, 'Equality of Opportunity for Work

field under consideration is professional work, including access points to professions such as internships and other work experience undertaken during undergraduate studies, especially in law. The chapter specifically examines whether CLE might grow the stock of a student's capital and thereby transform the habitus to improve the student's prospects of successfully entering the field of graduate-level employment. In order to operate successfully in a professional field such as law, it is necessary for an individual to possess both a suitable habitus and a strategic understanding of that field.[37]

## Habitus

The habitus is 'a system of dispositions',[38] more specifically 'a system of schemes of thought, perception, appreciation and action'.[39] These dispositions generate 'meaningful practices and meaning-giving perceptions':[40]

> The word *disposition* seems particularly appropriate to express what is covered by the concept of habitus (defined as a system of dispositions): it expresses, first, the *result of an organising action*, with a meaning very close to that of words such as 'structure'; it can also denote a manner of being, a habitual state (especially of the body), and, in particular, a *predisposition*, tendency, *propensity* or *inclination*. [41]

The habitus functions as a type of immanent law, shaped by past experiences, in turn shaping present and future behaviour: 'history turned into nature'.[42] Elsewhere Bourdieu describes the habitus as 'the site of the internalization of externality and the externalization of internality'.[43] The habitus is the individual's incarnation of those external influences which have acted, and continue to act, on the formation of those dispositions. Bourdieu's notion of habitus is also integral to his understanding of class; to him the habitus is 'embodied class'.[44] He avoids classifications such as working, middle, and upper class, although he does refer to the 'dominant' and 'dominated' classes, and to the 'bourgeoisie'. Essentially, though, for Bourdieu a person's class corresponds to their location within the field, determined by how much capital (economic, social, cultural – see below)

Experience? Computing Students at Two Universities "Play the Game"' (2019) 40 (3) British Journal of Sociology of Education 324.

37 Hilary Sommerlad, 'Researching and Theorizing the Processes of Professional Identity Formation' (2007) 34 (2) Journal of Law and Society 190, 200.

38 Pierre Bourdieu and Jean-Claude Passeron, *Reproduction in Education, Society and Culture* (2nd edn, Sage Publications 1990) 67; also Bourdieu (n 32) xxix.

39 Bourdieu and Passeron ibid. 40.

40 Bourdieu (n 32) 166.

41 Bourdieu and Passeron (n 38) 67 (original authors' emphasis).

42 Pierre Bourdieu, *Outline of a Theory of Practice* (Cambridge University Press 1977) 78, 82.

43 Bourdieu and Passeron (n 38) 205.

44 Pierre Bourdieu, *Distinction* (Routledge 1984) 438.

they possess and by the composition of that capital.[45] An individual's actions within a given field will be constrained unless they possess a habitus suited to successful navigation of the field.[46]

Primary formation of the habitus occurs in families and, just as parents bequeath to their children a bundle of genetic predispositions, so 'the habitus is the analogue of genetic capital'.[47] Physical traits are passed on through biological reproduction and dispositional traits are transmitted through social practices occurring in domains such as home and school. The habitus follows a developmental course, with its development in infancy shaping the habitus through early years education, which in turn structures the experience of secondary and tertiary education, forming the bundle of dispositions which structure an individual's entry into employment.[48] Much early habitus formation occurs through simple imitation by the child of adult behaviour: gestures, deportment, accent, etc. are acquired without conscious effort but can be converted into different levels of cultural capital in later life.[49] It is significant to observe, in light of the discussion below about the transformative potential of CLE, that a student's habitus will have been shaped by – at least – almost two decades of highly formative practices even before starting university.

As this chapter argues that CLE has potential to transform students' employability prospects, to what extent does Bourdieu's conception of the habitus permit such transformation? Is it fixed or can it develop over the life course? If the former then no amount of education will make a difference. In short, the habitus is durable[50] but not immutable.[51] And while it directs an individual's behaviour in society to a significant extent, 'agents are not completely defined by [it]'.[52] This is what has made it probably the most contested of Bourdieu's concepts because of the implications of different readings of it for human agency. He does, however, state than an individual could 'quasi-consciously' make a 'strategic calculation' to act in a way contrary to the weighted bias of the habitus.[53] So while we are not necessarily completely defined by our histories, the heavy drag of past experiences is not easily overcome by the incentive of new opportunities because our pasts stretch for longer than our momentary presents. Social mobility also depends on capital acquisition, and as capital often remains within a fixed range – with dominant classes attempting to reproduce their dominance through

45 Ibid. 439; see also Lucille Jewel, 'Bourdieu and American Legal Education: How Law Schools Reproduce Social Stratification and Class Hierarchy' (2008) 56 Buffalo Law Review 1155, 1159–1161.

46 Andrew Francis, 'Legal Education, Social Mobility, and Employability: Possible Selves, Curriculum Intervention, and the Role of Legal Work Experience' (2015) 42 Journal of Law and Society 173, 179.

47 Bourdieu and Passeron (n 38) 32.

48 Bourdieu (n 42) 87.

49 Ibid.

50 Pierre Bourdieu (n 42) 72; Bourdieu and Passeron (n 38) 31.

51 Bourdieu and Passeron (n 43) 33, 44.

52 Bourdieu (n 44) 103.

53 Bourdieu (n 42) 76.

structural advantage – so most class members will remain within a given trajectory, with a fraction deviating from it.[54]

### *Capital*

Bourdieu uses the example of roulette to provide a counterpoint to his understanding of capital. The random nature of the roulette wheel holds the possibility that a player's number might come up, changing the course of their life in an instant, an outcome purely determined by chance and not by anything in the player's history or character 'so that at each moment anyone can become anything'.[55] By contrast, an individual's accumulated capital acts like their GPS locator in social space, at which point – unlike roulette – all futures are not equally possible. Capital is one of Bourdieu's most useful thinking tools, and throughout his oeuvre he seeks to develop the idea of capital beyond its Marxian economic confines, whereby other asset types can be converted into value. He argues that it is impossible to understand society without extending the idea of capital beyond economics into the structures and relationships of the social world.[56] Most importantly, capital is seminal to Bourdieu's understanding of class, which is determined by 'the structure of relations between all the pertinent properties [which include capitals but also cover factors such as age, sex, ethnic origin] which gives its specific value to each of them and to the effects they exert on practices.'[57]

However, there is a second aspect to Bourdieu's conception of capital which is as a means of exchange for things of value.[58] The value of the capital is determined by the level of competition for the goods sought by the possessors of capital, i.e. it relates to the relative scarcity of the goods in the market.[59] So, for example, if the 'good' is a position as a trainee lawyer in a leading law firm – a relatively scarce provision – then this can only be appropriated with high value capital. Some have argued that there is a distinction between possessing capital and activating capital,[60] but understanding 'capital' to mean 'resources' is to fall into error: 'From a Bourdieusian perspective, goods and resources are not capitals if they do not produce gains in the dominant market.'[61] This means that an

54 Bourdieu (n 44) 105.

55 Pierre Bourdieu, 'The Forms of Capital' in John Richardson, *Handbook of Theory and Research for the Sociology of Education* (Greenwood 1986) 241.

56 Ibid. 242.

57 Bourdieu (n 44) 100.

58 Ciaran Burke, 'Bourdieu's Theory of Practice: Maintaining the Role of Capital' in Jenny Thatcher, Nicola Ingram, Ciaran Burke and Jessie Abrahams (eds), *Bourdieu: The Next Generation* (Routledge 2016) 2.

59 Bourdieu (n 55) 246.

60 See discussion in Caroline Sarojini Hart, 'Education, Inequality and Social Justice: A Critical Analysis Applying the Sen-Bourdieu Analytical Framework' (2019) 17 (5) Policy Futures in Education 582, 590.

61 Derron Wallace, 'Cultural Capital as Whiteness? Examining Logics of Ethno-racial Representation and Resistance' (2018) 39 (4) British Journal of Sociology of Education 466, 470–471.

individual must not only possess capital but needs 'savviness'[62] to deploy it effectively in order to secure social advantage.

There are different types of capital, although the term is commonly understood in narrow economic terms to include, for example, real estate, shareholdings or cash. To economic capital Bourdieu would add social and cultural capital, which are often 'transubstantiated' forms of economic capital.[63] For example, economic capital might be used to increase cultural capital through fee-paying elite education or visits to cultural venues such as theatres or art galleries; whereas social capital could be increased through using economic capital to cover living costs to enable a student to undertake an unpaid internship and develop useful professional connections.

### *Social capital*

According to Bourdieu, 'social capital is the aggregate of the actual or potential resources which are linked to possession of a durable network of more or less institutionalized relationships of mutual acquaintance and recognition.'[64] Our initial stock of capital arises from the families in which we are born and raised. Bourdieu goes on to explain that:

> The volume of the social capital possessed by a given agent thus depends on the size of the network of connections he can effectively mobilize and on the volume of the capital (economic, cultural or symbolic) possessed in his own right by each of those to whom he is connected.[65]

But it is not just how many people one knows that counts. The status of someone's contacts (i.e. their own social and cultural capital) and the individual's willingness and ability to use those contacts are also essential as part of a strategy to increase their life chances.[66]

Attending an elite fee-paying school or a high-ranking university could increase an individual's social capital through the development of useful networks, e.g. to facilitate informal internships. There is evidence that social capital obtained through such educational experiences plays an important part in enabling access to the elite professions in Britain. The Sutton Trust studied the school and

62 Allison Hurst, 'Classed Outcomes: How Class Differentiates the Careers of Liberal Arts College Graduates in the US' (2018) 39 (8) British Journal of Sociology of Education 1075, 1082.

63 Rob Moore, 'Capital' in Michael Grenfell (ed.), *Pierre Bourdieu* (2nd edn, Routledge 2012) 98–99.

64 Bourdieu (n 55) 248.

65 Ibid.

66 Sam Friedman, 'The Limits of Capital Gains: Using Bourdieu to Understand Social Mobility into Elite Occupations' in Jenny Thatcher, Nicola Ingram, Ciaran Burke and Jessie Abrahams (eds), *Bourdieu: The Next Generation* (Routledge 2016); Jessie Abrahams, 'Honourable Mobility or Shameless Entitlement? Habitus and Graduate Employment' (2017) 38 (5) British Journal of Sociology of Education 625.

university backgrounds of senior judges, barristers and partners at leading law firms and found that around 70 per cent of judges and barristers, and around 60 per cent of partners attended fee-paying schools, with attendance at 'top' universities accounting for at least 90 per cent of judges and barristers (mostly Oxford and Cambridge) and 80 per cent of partners, with some modest declines in those proportions between 1988 and 2004.[67] More recent evidence confirms this slow downward trajectory of elite educational dominance amongst Britain's leading people but it remains that around two-fifths attended a fee-paying school (the national average is 7 per cent).[68] We know too that this is not a simple correlative effect – i.e. top law firms want bright people, bright people go to top universities,[69] therefore top law firms hire people from top universities – but that some firms target their recruitment activities at reputationally advantaged universities[70] and some studies claim to have found 'significant bias' against 'new university' students.[71]

### ***Cultural capital***

Cultural capital has been described as 'cultural competency',[72] and Bourdieu understood its existence in three forms: embodied ('long-lasting dispositions of the mind and body'); objectified (e.g. through possession and use of books, pictures, music and other cultural artefacts); and institutionalised (most significantly in the form of academic and professional credentials).[73] Scholastic achievement is the hard currency of cultural capital; or as Bourdieu puts it: 'academic qualifications are to cultural capital what money is to economic capital'.[74] The certification of a student's achievement by an academic institution is similar to a state or central bank standing behind the value of its currency: its value does not need to be constantly proved but can be taken as read. Importantly, Bourdieu does not

67 Sutton Trust, *The Educational Backgrounds of the UK's Top Solicitors, Barristers and Judges* (Sutton Trust 2005).

68 Sutton Trust and Social Mobility Commission, *Elitist Britain 2019: The Educational Backgrounds of Britain's Leading People* (Sutton Trust and Social Mobility Commission 2019) 4.

69 It is worth pointing out, of course, that not all bright people go to top universities, and some don't go to university at all.

70 Andrew Francis, 'Legal Education, Social Mobility, and Employability: Possible Selves, Curriculum Intervention, and the Role of Legal Work Experience' (2015) 42 Journal of Law and Society 173, 196.

71 Hilary Sommerlad, 'Researching and Theorizing the Processes of Professional Identity Formation' (2007) 34 (2) Journal of Law and Society 190, 204. In the UK, 'new universities' tends to refer to a group of institutions which became universities after 1992. Hence why they are also sometimes referred to as 'post-1992' universities.

72 Ciaran Burke and Sarah Hannaford-Simpson, '"Investing in Your Future": The Role of Capitals in Graduate Employment Pathways' in Ciaran Burke and Fiona Christie (eds), *Graduate Careers in Context: Research, Policy and Practice* (Routledge 2019) 20.

73 Pierre Bourdieu, 'The Forms of Capital' in John Richardson, *Handbook of Theory and Research for the Sociology of Education* (Greenwood 1986) 243.

74 Pierre Bourdieu, *Outline of a Theory of Practice* (Cambridge University Press 1977) 187.

accept that academic success or failure is solely determined by natural talent, but it is linked to a person's level of cultural capital developed from birth within the family.[75]

Social and cultural capital are often linked, and their interconnected, relational nature can be seen in the following example. A former student of mine, who was a talented cricketer, got his first job at a top law firm partly because he clicked with a partner over a shared love of the sport (and he went on to play for the firm's team). The student's cultural capital had value because of an affinity with someone with similar cultural capital and also with significant social capital who had power to advance the student's career. This example also demonstrates the place of homophily (i.e. we like people like us), or 'fit', when it comes to cashing in cultural capital.[76] The idea of 'fit' entails cultural indicators serving as proxies for demonstrable competence in a subconscious thought process which runs something like this: I don't know you but I know me; I know I am a good lawyer; I like you because you are like me, therefore I suspect you will also be a good lawyer. 'Taste is a match-maker', according to Bourdieu.[77] The sense of affinity produced by fit, or why fit feels like fit, is because: 'When habitus encounters a social world of which it is the product, it is like "a fish in water": It does not feel the weight of the water and it takes the world about itself for granted'.[78] However, the very act of designating something as 'cultural capital' privileges those experiences and traits and, in a self-reinforcing process, preserves the interests of possessors of power. Crucially, Bourdieu argues that this designation is arbitrary in that it is purely a matter of taste. It perhaps cannot be argued that cricket is intrinsically superior to football, but the point is that cricket might be preferred to football in order to make a class distinction. In order to preserve a position of power, the arbitrariness of this distinction must remain hidden, or 'misrecognised' in Bourdieu's taxonomy.[79] I consider below some of the challenges these matters pose to aspiring lawyers.

One area where I start to part company with Bourdieu is that he tends to view education as a site for the reproduction of class advantage, rather than as a means of social mobility.[80] While he certainly does not argue that this *should* be the case, nor does he discount the upwardly mobilising effects of education (it would be illogical for him to do so as a child of working-class parents), anyone looking in his work for an impassioned, systematic argument for the emancipatory potential

75 Bourdieu (n 73) 243.
76 Sam Friedman and Daniel Laurison, *The Class Ceiling: Why it Pays to be Privileged* (Policy Press 2020) 111.
77 Pierre Bourdieu, *Distinction* (Routledge 1984) 239.
78 Pierre Bourdieu and Loic Wacquant, *An Invitation to Reflexive Sociology* (University of Chicago Press 1992) 127.
79 Pierre Bourdieu and Jean-Claude Passeron, *Reproduction in Education, Society and Culture* (2nd edn, Sage Publications 1990) 210; Bourdieu (n 77) 388.
80 Hart agrees, see Caroline Sarojini Hart, 'Education, Inequality and Social Justice: A Critical Analysis Applying the Sen-Bourdieu Analytical Framework' (2019) 17 (5) Policy Futures in Education 582, 594.

of education will be disappointed. This highlights how it can be useful to think with Bourdieu, rather than attempt to deploy his theoretical framework wholesale. With this in mind, I turn next to how Bourdieu might help us to think differently about clinical legal education.

## CLE, employability and Bourdieu

In the early 1980s Bourdieu identified the market mechanism that would give rise to the sectoral emphasis on employability in the opening decades of the new millennium: increased demand for academic credentials produces inflationary effects which result in a devaluation of those credentials.[81] Individuals must therefore find other ways to maintain a competitive edge in the market (i.e. to be an employable, and ultimately employed, graduate). Although its antecedents stretch back through much of the last century, the concept of 'employability' has been central to labour market policy since the emergence of the Third Way politics of the late 1990s (and to some extent in the neoliberal politics of the 1980s) and it has appeared in high-level policymaking at national, European Union and United Nations levels.[82] While the focus of the term in this chapter will be in the context of CLE, its use cuts across the whole spectrum of economic, political and social aspects of labour market policy. Definitions of the term shift around differing emphases on the role of the individual, employers and the state, and around demand- or supply-side factors. It can be understood in the narrow sense of defining an individual's employability skills (although this suffers from some circularity) or in a broader sense incorporating, for example, an individual's personal circumstances and wider economic factors regulating the availability of employment.[83] One issue is that someone can be highly employable, but actually unemployed due to issues with the supply of jobs or personal factors such as caring responsibilities or geographical restrictions, and this issue ('the mismanagement of talent' as Brown and Hesketh put it)[84] relates back to Bourdieu's above point about credential devaluation.

I do not seek here to fix on one definitive understanding of employability, but in the context of my discussion, I take it to be the contribution CLE can make to student competitiveness for graduate-level employment in general, and legal professional employment in particular through 'supporting students to develop a range of knowledge, skills, behaviours, attributes and attitudes which will enable them to be successful not just in employment but in life'.[85] This inevitably results in a predominantly supply-side focus on employability, i.e. on the role of the

81 Bourdieu (n 77) 127–129.

82 Ronald McQuaid and Colin Lindsay, 'The Concept of Employability' (2005) 42 (2) Urban Studies 197, 198, 200–201.

83 For a useful selection of definitions and models, see Doug Cole and Maureen Tibby, *Defining and Developing Your Approach to Employability: A Framework for Higher Education Institutions* (The Higher Education Academy 2013) 6–9.

84 Phillip Brown and Anthony Hesketh, *The Mismanagement of Talent* (OUP 2004).

85 Cole and Tibby (n 83) 5.

individual and the university in preparing the student for employment, although some of the arguments in this chapter are aimed at enabling the individual to navigate the structural, demand-side, aspects of gaining work.

## *CLE and employability*

The claim that CLE is good for students educationally and vocationally is discernible from the outset, even from when Jerome Frank dreamt of a 'clinical-lawyer school'.[86] However, despite the hopes placed by some (not least by university managers) in CLE to bestow blessings of employability on participants, and anecdotally a widespread sense that CLE is doing our students good,[87] there is surprisingly little research to back it up. Cantatore,[88] and more recently Tam,[89] both observe the gap in the literature around the (long-term) effects of CLE on graduate careers, with Tam commenting: 'Despite extensive literature on the aims and theories of CLE, sparse empirical research has been done on the attitudes and experiences of students towards CLE.'[90] Of course, there are some studies which have evaluated students' experience of clinic. For example, Cantatore's work involved two groups of about 30 students (one group was a control and the other had attended a pro bono teaching clinic for one semester) completing a survey to rate progress in their level of competence in 14 graduate employability indicators. The CLE students reported higher perceptions of an increase in competence, although the robustness of these findings will necessarily be limited by the highly subjective nature of the dataset and the inherent risk of confirmation bias. Similarly, McKeown's earlier work examining whether there is a relationship between student participation in pro bono work at university and intended engagement in pro bono after graduation (it seems not), also considered student *perceptions* of the value of CLE.[91] Elsewhere, Francine Ryan evaluated the student experience of a virtual law clinic at The Open University.[92] While this research sheds valuable light on an innovative form of CLE – which has become more salient following the COVID-19 pandemic – it is based on a small sample of five students and the focus was more on the students' experience of an online

86 Jerome Frank, 'Why Not a Clinical-Lawyer School?' (1933) 81 University of Pennsylvania Law Review and American Law Register 907.

87 Francina Cantatore, 'The Impact of Pro Bono Law Clinics on Employability and Work Readiness in Law Students' (2018) 25 International Journal of Clinical Legal Education 147, 168–169.

88 Ibid.

89 Claudia Man-yiu Tam, 'Measuring Law Students' Attitudes Towards and Experiences of Clinical Legal Education at the University Of Hong Kong' (2020) 27 (1) International Journal of Clinical Legal Education 47.

90 Ibid. 63; see also Cantatore (n 87) 169–170.

91 Paul McKeown, 'Pro Bono: What's in It for Law Students? The Students' Perspective' (2017) 24 (2) International Journal of Clinical Legal Education 43.

92 Francine Ryan, 'A Virtual Law Clinic: A Realist Evaluation of What Works for Whom, Why, How and in What Circumstances?' (2020) 54 (2) The Law Teacher 237.

clinic rather than on the clinic's employability impact. Other work has found little evidence that students were motivated to do CLE because of the difference it might make to their employment prospects. Although just over half of students in Tam's research agreed with the statement that 'clinical work assists me in obtaining employment',[93] this agreement seems to be voiced speculatively and not following students having actually obtained employment. So, the evidence, or lack of it, suggests that Tam is right in saying that current understanding of student experiences of CLE is sparse. To that I would add that there is also a dearth of scholarship of a longitudinal nature which tests for signs of a causative relationship between CLE and graduate career trajectories. What we currently know tends to be based on student subjectivities which, while not lacking validity per se, should be triangulated with evidence of actual career success and the views of employers.

### *Going further – capitalising on CLE*

Employability programmes tend to focus above all on developing students' skills.[94] It can be seen from the discussion above that, while this focus falls under the umbrella of social and cultural capital, it certainly does not exhaust the meaning of those terms. I contend therefore that there is more CLE might do to capitalise on its employability potential. The pedagogy of CLE, being focussed on what the student does (rather than what the tutor does), makes it a setting in which it is more likely for capital to be developed than in more traditional didactic forms of education; but how much more might be done?

One factor in whether, and to what extent, CLE develops capital might be how intensive and immersive the CLE experience is for students. Although not in the context of CLE, there is evidence of habitus transformation in students whilst at university, but for some it depended on immersion in the social life of the institution,[95] although others also spoke about how their studies brought about an intellectual change, making them more open to different cultures, ideas and generally embracing diversity.[96] When students start CLE they will already have experienced around two decades or more of habitus formation up to that point. It must therefore be questioned what degree of change can be brought about through engagement in CLE which might be measured in weeks or months. In any event, it is unclear to what extent the relationship between immersion in university life and habitus change is causative or correlative. This also poses important questions, worthy of future investigation, around the differential experience of students. Possible parallels might be found in the literature on

93 Tam (n 89) 74.

94 Andrew Francis, 'Legal Education, Social Mobility, and Employability: Possible Selves, Curriculum Intervention, and the Role of Legal Work Experience' (2015) 42 Journal of Law and Society 173, 177.

95 Wolfgang Lehmann, 'Habitus Transformation and Hidden Injuries: Successful Working-Class University Students' (2013) 87 (1) Sociology of Education 1, 7.

96 Ibid. 8.

extra-curricular activities (ECA) which shows that there is significant variation between students in the types of ECA they engage in and the extent with which they do so. Non-traditional students often experience less freedom of choice because of other responsibilities (e.g. jobs, family) or personal factors (e.g. living off campus, age, ethnicity),[97] and mature students leverage less advantage in the labour market from their ECA.[98]

Even though change appears possible it might require the student to start out the transition by 'faking it' before a more authentic expression of the self is arrived at.[99] While there is evidence for the success of this strategy, I expect that most CLE tutors would be uncomfortable being upfront with students and encouraging them to mimic dominant class behaviours, even if this is effectively what is going on in advocacy training, for example. Maybe, though, change can occur without highly intensive instruction. Lucinda Ferguson, drawing on her research of undergraduate law students at Oxford, argues for a programme of 'targeted micro-adjustments' or 'nudges' to develop the social and cultural capital of disadvantaged students.[100] To get some students to engage in capital-building behaviour it will be enough to simply tell them what former students have done who have gone on to enjoy professional success.[101] But what is also needed, Ferguson argues, is support for students to internalise, rather than merely simulate, the sensibilities of the dominant class habitus.[102]

CLE presents opportunities to develop social capital. Although it probably cannot compensate for having a close relative in the aspired-to profession, CLE can be a means of students developing their networks and training them how to do so. Evidence shows that even weak ties could be useful (e.g. through LinkedIn) but strong ties might produce more benefit.[103] While being conscious that lawyers are already giving their time for clinic activities, some might also be willing to mentor students (particularly where the lawyer and student have similar backgrounds), advise on covering letters and CVs, and provide a competitive paid internship (perhaps tied to the best mark in a CLE module). The same points apply to making use of one of the most valuable employability resources of any university: its alumni. Tapping into the social capital of former students could

97 Mary Stuart, Catherine Lido, Jessica Morgan, Lucy Solomon and Steve May, 'The Impact of Engagement with Extracurricular Activities on the Student Experience and Graduate Outcomes for Widening Participation Populations' (2011) 12 (3) Active Learning in Higher Education 203.

98 Zsuzsa Blasko, John Brennan, Brenda Little and Tarla Shah, *Access to What: Analysis of Factors Determining Graduate Employability* (HEFCE 2002).

99 Robert Granfield, 'Making it by Faking it: Working-Class Students in an Elite Academic Environment' (1991) 20 (3) Journal of Contemporary Ethnography 331.

100 Lucinda Ferguson, 'Complicating the "Holy Grail", Simplifying the Search: A Critique of the Conventional Problematisation of Social Immobility in Elite Legal Education and the Profession' (2017) The Law Teacher 51 (4) 377, 390–399.

101 Ibid. 396–397.

102 Ibid. 398.

103 Sam Friedman and Daniel Laurison, *The Class Ceiling: Why it Pays to be Privileged* (Policy Press 2020) 110.

provide current students with a host of benefits, not least expanding student vistas of 'the field of the possibles'. Law students could also be active in groups such as (in England and Wales) the Black Solicitors Network; the Law Society's Lawyers with Disabilities Division; the Society of Asian Lawyers; and the Association of Women Barristers, all of which provide opportunities for mentoring, support and networking.

Some of the above measures might also be useful in developing the cultural capital required for entry into professional roles. Legal knowledge is essential for those roles but not sufficient: 'it's not just *what* you know that matters, but *who* you are and *how* you present yourself'.[104] This embodied cultural capital often presents as 'polish' and it serves as a proxy for competence in advisory roles where it is difficult for consumers to assess the ability of the advisor in advance,[105] unlike, say, an artist who can show examples of her work. Even an emphasis on merit in recruitment and promotion criteria does not offset the advantage which flows from privilege: merit itself contains elements – for example, of a performative nature – which derive from elevated levels of cultural capital.[106] In the legal professions, some styles of dress, accents of speech and types of behaviour possess higher cultural capital than others even though there is nothing intrinsically superior about them. For some, giving elocution advice to students as part of CLE might be going too far, but perhaps the same result could be achieved by simply making the tacit explicit by getting students to reflect on the observed behaviour of the lawyers they work with in clinic and then assisting them to decode those cultures. However, Francis suggests that much of this sort of employability development should be done in a way which does not draw attention to itself. His point is that explicit employability initiatives, e.g. through being awarded credit, could be self-defeating as they risk being seen by leading firms as compensatory, attempting to make up for a student's capital deficit and the low reputational capital of the institution.[107] Even if credentialed cultural capital is of limited worth,[108] there is a role for CLE to train students to maximise its value and to stand out by articulating clearly how their experiences have developed the skills and competencies for job roles and signal potential cultural fit with an organisation.[109] Much professional etiquette can be taught, but other aspects are more likely to be caught, i.e. picked up through exposure to others' behaviour in much the same way that early cultural capital is acquired in the family. This is where CLE can play a role, whether through university-based clinic, internships or externships, and even micro-adjustments could provide at least marginal gains.

104 Ibid. 133, their emphasis.
105 Ibid.
106 Ibid. 212–214.
107 Francis (n 94) 196.
108 Francis (n 94) 201.
109 Stuart et al. (n 97) 211.

## Concluding thoughts

While the aim of using CLE to enhance the social and cultural capital of students from disadvantaged groups may be well intentioned, it is not immune to criticism. One criticism is that it is based on a deficit model, attempting to make up for deficiencies in an individual's upbringing,[110] which does not actually change the dominant position: lower status individuals who progress socially are accepted by assimilation, not belonging. Individuals who make the class transition may benefit from their enhanced status, but the existing order is maintained, although it leaves open the possibility that wider transformation could occur if those lower status individuals who accessed the elite professions in this way were willing to try to change the system from within. The term 'social mobility' arguably reinforces this idea that mobility is a property of an individual within ossified societal structures. Harnessing the transformative potential of CLE does not necessarily engage with how the existing system reproduces class advantage, but instead is directed at symptomatic relief rather than curing causes.[111]

A further criticism is that this approach risks pathologising working-class identities and behaviours. Sommerlad found that success in the legal profession for working-class people only follows when the signifiers of working-class identify are 'internalized in terms of lack'.[112] The period of habitus transformation may also produce an inauthentic self, where the individual 'fakes it to make it', as Granfield found in his study of working-class law students at Harvard.[113] Other studies have observed a sense of disintegration of the self and of social dislocation which can result when individuals move between working- and middle-class identities, or straddle the two, feeling a loss of connection to old friends and family while also of being imposters in their new environment.[114] This leaves some in a precarious position, having burnt their working-class bridges yet unsure how much social capital they might be able to trade in their new middle-class field, or if they will be accepted there at all.[115] Social progress might prove precarious where low levels of capital are quickly exhausted and an individual reverts to the pre-existing habitus: the so-called 'Pygmalion Dilemma'.[116]

110 Caroline Sarojini Hart, 'Education, Inequality and Social Justice: A Critical Analysis Applying the Sen-Bourdieu Analytical Framework' (2019) 17 (5) Policy Futures in Education 582, 587.

111 Lucille Jewel, 'Bourdieu and American Legal Education: How Law Schools Reproduce Social Stratification and Class Hierarchy' (2008) 56 Buffalo Law Review 1155, 1158.

112 Hilary Sommerlad, 'Researching and Theorizing the Processes of Professional Identity Formation' (2007) 34 (2) Journal of Law and Society 190, 215.

113 Robert Granfield, 'Making it by Faking it: Working-Class Students in an Elite Academic Environment' (1991) 20 (3) Journal of Contemporary Ethnography 331.

114 Sam Friedman and Daniel Laurison, *The Class Ceiling: Why it Pays to be Privileged* (Policy Press 2020) 177–183; Granfield (n 113) 343.

115 Wolfgang Lehmann, 'Habitus Transformation and Hidden Injuries: Successful Working-class University Students' (2013) 87 (1) Sociology of Education 1, 12.

116 Ciaran Burke, 'Bourdieu's Theory of Practice: Maintaining the role of capital' in Jenny Thatcher, Nicola Ingram, Ciaran Burke and Jessie Abrahams (eds), *Bourdieu: The Next Generation* (Routledge 2016) 20.

I return to the question posed in the introduction: can social and cultural capital be developed through clinical legal education? I contend that they can be but there is a sense in which this question can only be addressed through well-designed longitudinal studies because capital is only verified as capital when it is converted into money or money's worth. A study would need to show 'capital gains' in order to demonstrate the efficacy of CLE to assist entry into, and also perhaps progress through, a professional career. We also need to know more about how employers view CLE and how students use it as part of a narrative of employability when seeking work. Perhaps more than anything then, this paper is a call for more research about the lasting impacts of CLE on graduate careers.

Those who work in CLE witness its transformative effects on a regular basis. They see the difference it makes to service-users and to students, and the sense of fulfilment it gives to the professionals involved. But CLE on its own, like work experience, is unlikely to increase social mobility.[117] And while its role as an engine of social justice through social mobility might be challenged, its broader social justice mission stands firm. The irony is that the more effective CLE becomes at developing social and cultural capital across a generation of students, the less advantage it will give them in securing higher-level employment. It then comes back to finding other ways to play the game.

117 Andrew Francis, 'Legal Education, Social Mobility, and Employability: Possible Selves, Curriculum Intervention, and the Role of Legal Work Experience' (2015) 42 Journal of Law and Society 173, 199.

# 4 Clinical Legal Education in Brazil: Insights from Paulo Freire's pedagogy

*Fernanda Lapa and Horácio Rodrigues*

After presenting the life trajectory of Paulo Freire, in order to highlight some of his important theoretical concepts, we will introduce the emergence of legal clinics in Brazil and argue that Freire's theoretical and methodological framework can serve to enrich and inform the key principles of Clinical Legal Education.

## Introduction

It is important to state at the outset that the goal of this chapter is not a proposal to repeat or transpose Paulo Freire's theory onto Clinical Legal Education (CLE). The aim of this article is to outline Freire's philosophy so that CLE educators are provided with a platform for reflecting and implementing more humane and creative pedagogical approaches to CLE. As noted by Gadotti:

> Being faithful to Paulo Freire's educational proposal does not consist in *repeating it* mechanically, by reproducing it uncritically. Paulo Freire abhors the mechanism, the attitude of submissive and obedient disciples. Being faithful to Paulo Freire means, first and foremost, *to reinvent him* and to reinvent yourself, like he did. This, in fact, is the translation of *striving* in dialectics: it is neither a copy nor the negation of the past, of the path already trailed by others. It is his *transformation* and, at the same time, the *conservation* of what he has that is fundamental and original, and the *development* of a new qualitative synthesis.[1]

This chapter will begin by summarising aspects of Freire's life and work to highlight some of the key theoretical concepts he has developed which are of most relevance to CLE. It will then discuss the emergence of legal clinics in Brazil before arguing that Freire's thought can enrich and inform CLE.

1 Moacir Gadotti, *Pensamento Pedagógico Brasileiro* (6th ed., Ática, 1995) 38.

DOI: 10.4324/9780429299247-5

## The philosophy of Paulo Freire

The development and expression of Freire's pedagogy can best be understood in the context of his lived experience, so this section will present his key philosophical ideas in relation to important biographical events in his life. Our aim isn't to produce a biography per se, but to highlight moments of his adult, personal and professional life, which were essential in the construction of his theory. As Freire said: 'In this effort to recall moments of my experience that, necessarily, no matter when they happened, they were the sources of my theoretical reflections'.[2]

The central life event that significantly informed the development of his work and theory was exile. Therefore, we will describe his life trajectory divided into three phases of his adult life: one before the exile, another during the exile and, finally, the return from exile until his death. We will then highlight the manner in which some of his pedagogical insights can enrich and inform the development of CLE.

### *Life trajectory*

#### *Before the exile (1947–1964)*

Freire was a professor of Portuguese when he studied law, between 1943 and 1947, in the Faculty of Law of Recife, in the northeast of Brazil. Having practised law for a short time after graduation, he took on a position in the newly created *Serviço Social da Indústria* (SESI – Social Service of Industry), the institution that promotes the social welfare of industrial workers in Brazil. His role, on the board of education and culture, was to bridge and connect the relations between teachers, workers and their children, which today would be called popular education.[3]

This period was important for Freire's teaching method because he began to experiment with participatory decision-making, collective and democratic processes, such as ensuring the agenda of meetings was proposed by the participants and their families, and not imposed by the team; listening to the workers' life stories to inform his development of an education strategy. Freire maintains that the foundation of his pedagogy was formed by his experience at SESI.[4] The experience of listening carefully to the workers was the foundation that made him aware of the importance, not only of the adaptation of language in the learning process, but to go deeper, getting to know about the life of the workers and the way they interpreted the world: 'The educational process should necessarily

2 Paulo Freire, *Pedagogia da Esperança* 'Pedagogy of Hope' (16th ed., Paz e Terra, 2009) 20.

3 Sergio Haddad, *O Educador: o perfil de Paulo Freire* – 'The Educator: a profile of Paulo Freire' (Todavia, 2019) 451.

4 Department of Arts and Faculty of Education of Unicamp, Interview with Paulo Freire, (Video File TV Unicamp, 1985) <https://www.youtube.com/watch?v=5yRyAXPXHmA>.

originate from the experience of reality and interpretation that the workers made of it'.[5]

In addition to the experience with the workers, another that greatly influenced Freire was his participation in pastoral activities, like the Catholic Action movement. As an active Christian, he became responsible for the education sector of his parish and he led a programme to support the education and training of teachers and parents. 'This form of exercising Christianity – with a strong community outreach –, [...] would also be expressed in the formation of groups of followers with diverse social composition, combining popular sectors with the middle class in social projects'.[6]

This practical work informed his academic work as professor of history and philosophy of education at the Faculty of Fine Arts of the University of Recife. His 1959 doctoral thesis, *Education and Brazilian Actuality*, [7] gained national attention in the field of Brazilian education, but also brought his ideas to the attention of conservative political groups. These groups were concerned by his critique of the antidemocratic tradition of Brazilian schools, lacking a spirit of solidarity with the lived experience of students and also his arguments for a programme of education specifically aimed at the proportion of the population below the poverty line.[8]

From the 1960s, Freire's ideas influenced public policy and was the subject of public attention, especially the literacy campaigns in Angicos, a poor city in the hinterland of northeast of Brazil.[9] In this instance, more than 400 illiterate people learned to read and write in 40 hours. This success led to him being invited to work in the Ministry of Education and Culture with the aim of extending the project to the whole of Brazil. Having accepted the invitation of President João Goulart, he started teacher training to implement a National Literacy Programme (PNA, in Portuguese), which would be launched in May 1964, and aimed to teach literacy skills to an average of five million people, between 15 and 45 years of age, who did not know how to read or write.[10]

However, a military coup in Brazil in April 1964 resulted in the PNA being extinguished before it was launched. At that time, the military, pressured by social conservatives, was hostile to Freire's work, seeing it as being subversive, contrary to the interests of the nation, and an attempt to implant communism in Brazil.[11]

5 Haddad (n 3) 451.

6 Ibid. 546.

7 Paulo Freire, *Educação e Atualidade Brasileira* – 'Education and Actuality Brazilian' (Cortez, Paulo Freire Institute/IPF, 2001).

8 Ibid. 591.

9 See also the documentary made with the former students about the experience in Angicos: <https://www.youtube.com/watch?v=PkN97kOriJc>.

10 Haddad (n 3) 894.

11 It is important to highlight that illiterate people could not vote in Brazil at this time and, therefore, the possibility of teaching people to read and write in the interior of Brazil, in 40 hours, became strategically interesting for the political classes. 'The number of voters with the PNA would increase about 40% in the country'. Freire was

The climate of intimidation in Brazil was growing, especially in universities and other institutions of public education. According to the historian Elio Gaspari:

> The right-wing led Brazil into dictatorship because they built a regime that, if it had the strength needed to demobilize the society intervening in unions, retiring teachers and magistrates, imprisoning, censuring and torturing, it had no strength to discipline the barracks that ensured the demobilization … Torture was practiced as a form of interrogation in several military garrisons. Installed as an effective means to combat 'corruption and subversion', the government committed itself to the megalomaniac task of ending up with both of them.[12]

In June 1964, Freire was arrested and interrogated about his teaching methods. He was released after being incarcerated for more than 70 days and later sought exile, first in Bolivia and then in Chile.

### *In exile (1964–1979)*

In Chile he developed his theoretical position in light of his work developing education amongst peasants and low-skilled workers, which became known in Chile as the psychosocial method. This method aimed to facilitate peasants to gain an understanding of their own economic and social situation, by debating their own life situation in small 'culture circles', where they could identify problems and plan to transform their situation. During this period, he published two major works: *Education as a Practice of Freedom* (1967)[13] *and Pedagogy of the Oppressed* (1968),[14] where he systematises his philosophy of education and presents the method used in Angicos and in the PNA, which became known as 'the Paulo Freire Method'.

The experience of the coup in Brazil and his subsequent exile clearly influenced Freire's academic work. Without abandoning his previous philosophy of education and his Christian vision of the human being as an agent of change, he starts using terms such as 'oppressor' and 'oppressed' and 'denounce the class struggle', as is evident in his work *Pedagogy of the Oppressed.*

alerted after the visibility in Angicos, of the subversive vision of his method among the more conservative classes. Haddad (n 3) 853.

12 Elio Gaspari, *A Ditadura Envergonhada* – 'The Ashamed Dictatorship' (2nd ed., Intrínseca, 2014) 143 and 136.

13 Paulo Freire, *Educação como Prática da Liberdade* – 'Education as a Practice of Freedom' (1967).

14 The manuscripts of the book are dated from 1964 to 1968, during Freire's exile in Chile. *Pedagogy of the Oppressed* is his most famous book, published in more than 40 languages, first in English (1970) and in 1975 in Portuguese. Cf. Beiseigel, Celso de Rui, *Prefácio para a reedição de Pedagogia do oprimido, de Paulo Freire* (2018) Estudos Avançados, *32*(93), 13–24. <https://dx.doi.org/10.5935/0103-4014.20180027>.

*After exile (1979–1997)*

Although the Brazilian dictatorship ended in 1985, the regime began a process of liberalisation which facilitated Freire's return in 1980, after 15 years of exile. During this period he became Secretary of Education for the city of São Paolo, and responsible for the improvement of education in São Paolo, then the second largest city in Latin America, with nearly ten million inhabitants. At that time, despite criticism, he implemented one of the pillars of his teaching theory: the democratisation of content and syllabi, the implantation of student councils, school vegetable gardens and sexual education.[15]

In 1991, the Paulo Freire Institute (IPF, in Portuguese) was created, which remains an institute that aims to 'gather people and institutions who, moved by the same dreams of a humanizing and transformative education, could deepen their reflections, improve their practices and strengthen the fight for the construction of "another possible world"'.[16]

Given his professional role, his later work focused on teacher training and include *Politics and Education* (1993)[17] and *Education in the City* (1991).[18] His final works, *Pedagogy of Hope: A reunion with the pedagogy of the oppressed* [19] and *Pedagogy of Autonomy: Knowledge needed for educational practice*, [20] provide a reflection and restatement of his fundamental ideas.

## Theoretical concepts of Freire's education system

*The autonomy and the concept of 'being more'*

For Freire, it is not possible to make a reflection on what education is without reflecting on man himself.[21] Man, different from animals, can reflect on himself; he is a being constantly seeking at 'being more' and, as he can practise self-reflection, he may find he is an unfinished being that is engaged in a constant search. 'Education is possible for man, because he is unfinished, known to be unfinished. […] Man must be the subject of education itself. He cannot be the object of it. Therefore, nobody can educate anyone.'[22]

15 Dalva Franco, 'A gestão de Paulo Freire à frente da Secretaria Municipal de São Paulo (1989–1991) e suas consequências' (2014) v. 25 n. 3 (75) Rev. Pro-Posições, 103–121.

16 See also in the Institute of Paulo Freire website <www.paulofreire.org>.

17 Paulo Freire, *Política e Educação* – 'Politics and Education' (Cortez, 1993).

18 Paulo Freire, *A Educação na cidade* – 'The Education in the City' (Cortez, 1991). This book Freire wrote after his position as Secretary in Sao Paulo describing his experience.

19 Cf. (n 2).

20 Paulo Freire, *Pedagogia da Autonomia: Saberes necessários à Prática Educativa* – 'Pedagogy of Autonomy: Knowledge Needed for Educational Practice' (37th ed., Paz e Terra, 2008).

21 Paulo Freire, *Educação e Mudança* – 'Education and Change' (32nd ed., Paz e Terra, 2010) 27.

22 Ibid. 28.

For Freire, the human being has an ontological vocation of 'being more' and has an unlimited capacity to learn and teach. People are unfinished inconclusive beings constantly seeking for improvement and become subjects in their path towards humanisation. Freire argues that education should be the path to the constitution of the subject's autonomy and, with this, ensures the process of 'becoming':

> Autonomy, as the maturing of the being himself is a process, it means becoming. It does not happen on a specific date. It is in this sense that pedagogy of autonomy has to be focused on stimulating experiences of decision and responsibility, especially, on experiences that respect freedom.[23]

The Freirean concept of 'being more' has had influence beyond education, as can be seen by the way the contemporary Inter-American Court of Human Rights (IACHR) has conceptualised 'the project of life'. In the case Loayza Tamayo v. Peru, the Court presents, for the first time, the concept of damage to the project of life:

> The project of life is associated to the concept of personal fulfillment, which in turn is based on the options that the subject may have to live their life and reach the destination they have proposed. Strictly speaking, the options are the expression and guarantee of freedom. It is difficult to say that a person is truly free if they lack options to advance their existence and live it to its natural culmination. These options have in themselves a high existential value. Therefore, its cancellation or depreciation implies in the objective reduction of freedom and the loss of a value that cannot be discarded from the observation of this Court.[24]

For Freire, this existential path for social realisation and project of life is also a right for all people, but that must be done through a humanising and liberating education. The subject has their dignity respected when they are allowed to humanise in the process of seeking to 'be more', , because 'the respect for the autonomy and dignity of each one is an ethical imperative and not a favor that we may or may not grant to each other'.[25]

This Freirean view of human nature resonates with Article 26 of the Universal Declaration of Human Rights (UDHR), the human right to education envisages the full development of the human personality and the strengthening of respect for human rights and fundamental freedoms. In his theory Freire ends up corroborating this statement of the UDHR on sustaining that it is the right of people to seek full development and to 'being more', to have autonomy and freedom as a condition of seeking their project(s) of life.

23 Paulo Freire (n 20) 107.
24 Loayza Tamayo v Peru (27/11/1998), the Inter-American Court of Human Rights, (Reparations and Costs) para. 148.
25 Paulo Freire (n 20) 59.

*Praxis and context*

> if men are beings of 'what is to be done' it is exactly because 'what they do' is action and reflection. It is praxis. It is the transformation of the world. And, in the reason itself of 'what is to be done' is praxis, all the doing of 'what is to be done' must have theory and practice. It is reflection and action.[26]

A key aspect of Freire's theory is praxis, where theory and practice come together in a concrete action. Freire argues that

> man is a being of praxis; action and reflection. In these relations with the world, through his action on it, man is marked by the results of his own action. Acting, transforms; transforming, creates a reality which, in turn, involves it, and conditions the way he acts.[27]

Freire argues that theory and practice act symbiotically, each providing feedback to the other. In his vision, 'theory without practice becomes "verbalism", likewise practice without theory, becomes activism. However, when practice and theory are joined there is praxis, the creative and modifying action of reality.'[28]

According to Freire, school is a privileged place for the transformation of reality and for the emancipation of subjects through a liberating education that is provided as

> a process by which the educator invites learners to recognize and unveil the reality critically; there are no subjects liberating and objects that are liberated, since there is no dichotomy between subject and object. The liberating is dialogical.[29]

Thus, all the teaching-learning process must be based on topics of interest of the students themselves, of their reality and context. For education to be humanised, it must be centred on the reality of the student. This reality is a consequence of actions of men and women during the historical process; it is not something natural, but created socially and culturally and, therefore, it must always be contextualised in the educational process. The concept of context (knowledge, language, power relations) is important for Freire's teaching theory, as Giroux affirms:

> Contexts mattered to Paulo; he was concerned how they mapped in distinctive ways the relationships among knowledge, language, everyday life, and the machineries of power. Any pedagogy that calls itself Freirean must

26 Ibid. 121.
27 Paulo Freire, *Pedagogia da Esperança* – 'Pedagogy of Hope' (Paz e Terra, 1992) 28.
28 Paulo Freire, *Educação: a prática para a liberdade* – 'Education: the practice of freedom' (Paz e Terra, 1989) 67.
29 Paulo Freire, *The Politics of Education* (Bergin & Garvey, 1985) 125.

acknowledge this key principle that our current knowledge is contingent on particular historical contexts and political forces. For example, each classroom will be affected by the different experiences students bring to the class, the resources made available for classroom use, the relations of governance bearing down on teacher-student relations, the authority exercised by administrations regarding the boundaries of teacher autonomy, and the theoretical and political discourses used by teachers to read and frame their responses to the diverse historical, economic, and cultural forces informing classroom dialogue.[30]

*Dialogue and the critical thinking*

> Dialogue is the encounter between men, mediatized by the world, to designate it. On saying their words, on raising awareness on the world, men transform it, dialogue is imposed as the path by which men find their meaning as men; dialogue is, therefore, an existential need.[31]

Dialogue plays a structuring role in the thinking of Paulo Freire, because it enables the search for the realisation of the ontological vocation of 'being more'. If there is dialogue, there is no imposition. The imposition of a discourse is a practice of the mechanisms of domination, which inhibits, rather than facilitates the process of humanisation.

> Self-sufficiency is not compatible with dialogue. The men who do not have humility or lose it, cannot get closer to the people. They cannot be their companions of *pronunciation* of the world. If someone is not able to know and feel they are as much a man as the others, it means they still have a long way to go, to get to the gathering place with them. In this gathering place, there is no absolutely [sic] ignorance, nor absolute knowledge among them: there are men in fellowship seeking to learn more.[32]

Dialogue is the only means capable of producing real thinking and Freire noticed that, in the education system, democratic spaces and open-minded educators were almost non-existent. Basically, every pedagogical action adopted and defended by Freire occurs through fellowship between people with participatory, dialogical and horizontal methodologies. For Freire, education as a practice of freedom can only be achieved through critical thinking, where the learner will 'read' the world critically. In Freire's concept of education, 'reading the world' is one of the central theoretical-methodological elements. It is loaded with

30 Henry Giroux, 'Critical Pedagogy, Paulo Freire and the courage to be political' (2016) v14 n1 Revista e-Curriculum 303.
31 Paulo Freire, *Conscientização* – 'Awareness' (Paz e Terra, 1980) 42.
32 Paulo Freire, *Pedagogia do Oprimido* – 'Pedagogy of the Oppressed' (18th ed, Paz e Terra, 1987) 46.

significance for all those involved in the educational process: it is a specific type of relationship between the human being and the world.

> Critical thinking is a historic commitment … it implies that men assume their role of subjects who make and remake the world. It requires men to create their existence with the material that life offers them … it is based on the awareness of man's relationship with the world.[33]

To foster social change, it is necessary to be aware of social reality, leave the initial awareness and adopt critical awareness. Freire warned that 'in our schools very naive awareness is emphasized', where 'only mediocre individuals are formed, because there is no incentive for creation'.[34] Now the role of emancipatory education, according to him, is not only to allow the construction of critical awareness, but through it, enable people to create and transform the world: 'awareness cannot stop at the stage of unveiling of reality. Its authenticity is when the practice of unveiling reality is a dynamic and dialectic unity with the practice of transformation'.[35] As Giroux highlights, for Freire, critical pedagogy is always related to present conditions, dialogue with history and means 'imagining literacy as not simply the mastering of specific skills but also as a mode of intervention, a way of learning about and reading the word as a basis for intervening in the world'.[36]

### *Problem-solving education vs. banking education*

Paulo Freire defends the existence of two opposing concepts of education: the banking and the problem-solving. Banking is where the educator valorises what he knows and believes, while students are mere objects. In contrast, the problem-solving concept is based precisely on the dialogic/dialectic relationship between educator and learner – both learn together, both are emancipated.

Freire outlines the banking concept in ten points:

1 The teacher is the one who teaches; students are the ones taught;
2 The teacher is the one who knows everything; students are the ones who are ignorant;
3 The teacher is the one who thinks; students are the ones thought about;
4 The teacher is the one who narrates; students are the ones who listen passively;
5 The teacher is the one who disciplines; students are disciplined;
6 The teacher is the one who chooses and decides; students comply with the decision;

33 Paulo Freire, *Extensão ou Comunicação?* – 'Extension or Communication?' (Paz e Terra, 1980) 26.
34 Paulo Freire (n 21) 38.
35 Paulo Freire, *Cultural Action for Freedom* (Paz e Terra, 1981) 117.
36 Henry Giroux (n 30) 299.

7 The teacher is the one who acts; students have the illusion they are acting, but they are merely observing the teacher;
8 The teacher chooses the curriculum; students never have a say on this choice, they adapt to it;
9 The teacher claims to have authority of knowledge due to their position of authority, which precludes antagonistically the freedom of students; they must adapt to the teacher's determinations;
10 The teacher, finally, is the subject of the process; students are mere objects.[37]

Thus, in the banking concept didactic relations predominate, education becomes an act of depositing (as in banks); knowledge is a donation from those who think they are wise to those who know nothing.[38] Banking education aims to maintain the division between those who know and those who do not know, between the oppressed and oppressors.

## Legal clinics in Brazil and the philosophy of Freire

The previous discussion demonstrates that Freire's philosophy discusses challenges that are common to higher education in general, and in particular for the teaching of law, even though Freire is better known in Brazil and in the world by his method of adult literacy and popular education. However, we believe that his philosophy can influence the pedagogical theory of any educator, including CLE professors in universities.

Just as Richard Wilson argues that 'CLE is a vital and necessary tool for legal education everywhere, a tool that has been and must be continued to be deployed as part of an effective curriculum designed to prepare lawyers for the practice of law',[39] we also believe that, specifically in the law curriculum, which has a tradition of theoretical, authoritative, narrative teaching that can be far removed from the lived experience of students, engagement with Freire can provide transformative insights which will facilitate innovative and transformative practice.

### *The teaching of law in Brazil and the legal clinics*

Legal education in Brazil has a relatively recent history. The first legal courses in the country began in the first half of the 19th century, shortly after the country's independence in 1827, when the Academy of Law of São Paulo and the faculty of Law of Olinda in the northeast of Brazil were established.[40] These first two

37 Paulo Freire (n 32) 34.
38 Ibid. 67.
39 Richard J. Wilson, *The Global Evolution of Clinical Legal Education – More than a Method* (Cambridge University Press, 2018) 12.
40 The Brazilian legal system was constituted based on the European tradition, chiefly a result of Portuguese colonisation. Thus, since its first constitution, enacted back in the imperial era in 1824, the country has had its legal tradition follow the precepts of

courses were created with the aim of both educating the local Brazilian elite and to provide professionals to fill the country's administrative positions.[41]

The main pedagogical changes in the legal courses only occurred in the second half of the 20th century. Between the 1980s and 1990s, after the process of re-democratisation of the country, there were three major reforms to the legal curricula (1994, 2004 and 2018).[42] The main changes had four key aims: to better integrate the legal theory to professional practice; encourage interdisciplinarity and participatory methodologies; improve the learning of personal and professional skills; and also train future professionals with a greater commitment to social justice.[43]

Legal clinics began to be implemented in Brazilian universities in the first decade of the 21st century. The clinical movement in Brazil was driven by human rights clinics led by teachers who had experience in international clinics and who envisioned the potentiality of this pedagogy for the country, the first of which appeared in 2007 at the University in the Joinville Region (Univille).[44]

From then on, this movement of clinics has become more widely established. Currently, it is estimated that there are approximately 50 legal clinics throughout Brazil, and the vast majority (70 per cent) continues with a focus on human rights

Civil Law. This model of law organisation in society comes from the Roman and Germanic traditions of Western Europe. One of Civil Law's main characteristics is the focus on norms described in laws and codes. When reviewing individual actions, judges use the general rules to apply them to particular cases. However, the 1988 Constitution incorporated elements of the legal tradition practised in the United States, which relies on the Common Law system, originally conceived in England. The core precept of Common Law is the reliance on previous rulings by the courts as the basis to guide the conduct of judges in similar cases. Recognition of rights is based on customs. Such is the case of Brazil's *súmulas* (precedents) and *súmulas vinculantes* (binding precedents), which are judicial decisions that serve as models for other cases. Brazil has not broken with the tradition of Civil Law, in the sense that it privileges the law as the main source of rights. However, there is progress in realising that precedents are sources of decisions. Cf. <http://www.brazil.gov.br/about-brazil/news/2018/11/civil-law-tradition-guides-rights-in-brazil-but-common-law-is-also-present> Accessed 20 May 2020.

41 Fábio C. M. de Sá e Silva. *Legal Education* (Fabris Ed., 2007) 57.

42 Decree 1.886/1994; CNE/CES Resolution no. 9/2004; CNE/CES Resolution no. 5/2018.

43 For more information about the reforms the co-author Horacio Wanderlei Rodrigues has written recent articles and books about the main changes in these reforms: *Cursos de Direito no Brasil: diretrizes curriculares e projeto pedagógico* (Habitus, 2020); *Novas Diretrizes Curriculares Nacionais dos Cursos de Direito: análise crítica da Resolução CNE/CES n.o 5/2018.* In: ROCHA, Maria Vital da; BARROSO, Felipe dos Reis. Educação Jurídica e didática no ensino do Direito: estudos em homenagem à professora Cecilia Caballero Lois (Habitus, 2020) 199–232; RODRIGUES, Horácio Wanderlei (org.). *Educação Jurídica no Século XXI: novas Diretrizes Curriculares Nacionais do Curso de Direito – limites e possibilidades* (Habitus, 2019).

44 The co-author Fernanda Lapa was the founder of the first human rights clinic in Brazil: Fernanda Lapa, *Human Rights Clinic – a methodological proposal for legal education in Brazil* (Ed. Lumen Juris, 2014), 116–138.

issues.[45] There are two networks of main cooperation: the Amazon Network of Clinics of Human Rights, created in 2012, composed of eight older human rights clinics in the country; and the National Forum of Legal clinics, created in 2017, with approximately 30 legal clinics.[46]

## ***Principles of legal clinics and Freire's pedagogical theory***

We will describe some principles that we uphold as important for the deployment of a legal clinic in Brazil[47] and we will demonstrate how they relate to Freire's pedagogical theory by considering the following points: the commitment to social justice; student autonomy; participatory methodology; theory and practice integration; and interdisciplinarity.[48]

In CLE, unlike traditional classroom teaching, students, with the guidance of supervisors, acquire theoretical and practical skills at the same time. As Huerta states,[49] clinical education is not meant to replace the traditional method of teaching at all, but rather seeks to be the link between theory and practice to develop certain skills in students and to provide them with socially responsible training.

There is a persistent tension in clinical legal education between theory and practice in the legal academy and in law practice, as Richard Wilson points out:

> Critics of legal education among the legal profession suggest law training is too theoretical and doctrinal, and thus it does not prepare students for practice. Critics of practice suggest that it does not rely sufficiently on theory in that it approaches each new case in piecemeal fashion, without reference to universal principles.[50]

45 B. Enzo; F. Lucas, 'Human Rights Clinics in Brazil: a study on the implementation process and functioning in practice and in the teaching of Law' (2018) 10.2 RECHTD 173.

46 Ibid. 174.

47 In the first doctoral thesis defended in Brazil on the theme of legal clinics, in 2014, the co-author Fernanda Lapa defends seven principles for the inclusion of human rights clinics in Brazilian universities: i) Commitment with Social Justice; ii) Participatory Methodology; iii) Articulation of Theory and Practice – Praxis; iv) Integration between teaching, research and outreach activities; v) Interdisciplinarity; vi) Formal Recognition in the university; vii) Public Target (students and communities). LAPA, F.B. 2014. *Human rights clinics: An alternative for training in human rights for legal courses in Brazil.* São Paulo, SP. Doctoral thesis. Pontifícia Universidade Católica de São Paulo, 185.

48 Fernanda Lapa, *Human Rights Clinic – a methodological proposal for legal education in Brazil* (Ed. Lumen Juris, 2014), 116–138.

49 Huerta, G. *Enseñanza Clinica del Derecho – una alternativa a los métodos tradicionales de formación de abogados* (Clinical Teaching Law – an alternative to traditional methods of training lawyers) (ITAM/México, 2007) 5, 6.

50 Wilson (n 39) 125.

By learning through experience, students experience what Paulo Freire would call *praxis*, which for him is the ontological condition of any human being: 'If men are beings of what to do, it is precisely because their doing is action and reflection. It is *praxis*. It is transformation of the world.'[51] As Buhler and others maintain, the concept of Freirean *praxis* is central to Clinical Legal Education, where students form their professional identities and develop approaches to practice guided by their peers, supervisors, clients, their readings, theories and other ways of being and knowing. The authors argue that:

> once exposed to clinical work, it is difficult to see the world in the same way. This learning experience can be profoundly disorienting for students who must shift certain ideas about what they thought they knew about law, society or themselves: the ability to reflect on these experiences is therefore a crucial component of clinical pedagogy.[52]

Importantly, we do not argue that clinical pedagogy brings only or primarily the practical component for students. Clinical pedagogy is innovative because law students are able to relate to theory and practice at the same time. It also provokes critical and strategic thinking for solutions to real and complex problems.

There are several experiential learning[53] facets being used in legal education, inside and outside Brazil, which aim to boost the critical thinking and a direct student participation. Many of these methodologies can also be employed within clinics because the philosophy of clinical pedagogy is learning by doing.[54] For this to happen, it is a condition that the student has *autonomy* to think, reflect, express themselves, make decisions and, also, assume the consequences for their actions (always under teacher supervision).[55]

51 Paulo Freire, *Pedagogia do Oprimido* (Paz e Terra, 2005) 121.

52 Sarah Buhler, Sarah Marsden and Gemma Smith, *Clinical Law – practice, theory and social justice advocacy* (Emond/Canada, 2016) 36.

53 According to Richard Wilson: 'Experiential learning is more than a method; it is a way of seeing, learning and caring grounded in live[d] experience. Moreover, while experiential learning may have a cultural dimension, learning and teaching through experience provides a universally accepted educational gateway for law students and guided appropriately, to rigorous intellectual inquiry as well as an enhanced sense of professional responsibility and true commitment to the highest values of legal profession.' Wilson (n 39) 127.

54 This idea of doing by experience was inspired by the New School or Progressive Education, known in the United States from John Dewey. Paulo Freire was not inspired directly by John Dewey but from the famous Brazilian educator Anísio Teixeira, who was very impressed and inspired by Dewey's model of teach-learning. Anísio Teixeira wrote the first book in Brazil organising Dewey's ideas (Anísio Teixeira, *Aspectos Americanos da Educação*, Tip, 1928). There is a virtual library Anísio Teixeira (*Biblioteca Virtual Anísio Teixeira*) where you can find all his books: <http://www.bvanisioteixeira.ufba.br/delivro.htm>.

55 Fernanda Lapa, *Novas Diretrizes Curriculares Nacionais do Curso de Direito: a inclusão das clínicas na educação jurídica brasileira* (In: Rodrigues. Educação Jurídica do Século XXI. Habitus, 2019) 215, 216.

Richard Wilson extracted five points about experiential learning, expounded in the thinking of John Dewey, to give support to CLE theory:

- Learning happens through experience, by doing something on one's own rather than thinking about it or memorising; (the student and learning, not the teacher and teaching, is where the educational focus lies);
- Experience is immersed in life, and life is messy. Thus, there are social, political and moral dimensions to learning;
- Learning must take place in a collective context, the individual needs society to learn (social dimension);
- The moral dimension brings a reflection on poverty and exclusion;
- Learning is not an end in itself, but a process.[56]

All these points can be identified in Freire's theoretical concepts of education. For Freire, the problem-based education, the opposite of banking education, is the path to give a person a chance for 'being more', to be emancipated and have critical thinking about his or her context and reality. Learning through his or her experience and in communion, in relation with others, the students will experience the social, political and moral dimensions of the topic.

Inspired by Freire himself, Wilson states that clinical legal education offers an effective alternative that motivates learning, as it is more student-centred than teacher-centred. Thus, he argues that this autonomy not only allow the student to put himself in the role that he must play, but also that he seeks his self-determination:

> Clinical legal education offers an effective alternative that motivates learning because it is more student-centered than teacher-centered. Drawing from the work of contemporary Brazilian educational theorist Paulo Freire, clinical legal education is a form of awareness, or 'the deepening of the attitude of awareness characteristics of all emergence', because is not only puts the student in to the role but 'enrolls them in the search for self-affirmation'.[57]

This autonomy is an important principle for Freire's theory, where, through a dialogic interaction, educator, learner and client are emancipated together. There is a teacher–student–client/partner relationship in CLE that can benefit with Freire's participatory approach, once all of them have an active voice to propose ideas and new solutions for the problems and challenges presented.

There are different types of legal clinics established in Brazil. The legal human rights clinic we run within the University of the Region of Joinville (UNIVILLE), since 2004, develops teaching, research and outreach activities fostering this active voice from students and clients/partners. Usually the projects are divided into three steps: a) academic seminars (teaching-learning of human rights law

56 Wilson (n 39) 129.
57 Ibid. 18.

related to the context); b) investigation of the facts (research and the elaboration of a fact-finding report); and c) practical intervention (an outreach or extension action). Regardless of the topic and of the target audience, we believe that all legal clinics must have a commitment to social change and social justice.

To demonstrate these CLE principles in practice with Freire's theory, we will share one example of one of our projects and a table relating them. During 2018–2019, our clinic worked in partnership with a Brazilian NGO called Institute for Development and Human Rights (IDDH) at a project with (not for) incarcerated pregnant women, or those who have children under 12 years old, in preventive detention, and affected by the criminal justice system in the province of Santa Catarina. This project had at least four main objectives: a) study the legislation and decisions which benefit women in this situation and try to understand why the Supreme Federal Court's (STF) decision was not being implemented in our province (seminars and research); b) organise and attend human rights trainings with sexual and reproductive rights experts at the women's prison and dialogue with these women to understand their challenges and expectations (outreach); c) give legal aid to those women who could and want to benefit from the STF's decision and go under house arrest; and d) coordinate a public hearing at the State Legislative House to raise awareness on these cases.[58]

*Table 4.1* Comparison of CLE principles with Freire's pedagogy

| *Principles for CLE* | *Freire's pedagogical theory* |
|---|---|
| 1. Commitment to social justice | • Context and the social-historical reality<br>• Transformation: intervention of reality<br>• Education is always political |
| 2. Theory and practice integration<br>– Learning by doing<br>– Experiential learning | • Praxis<br>• Liberating practice |
| 3. Autonomy of the learner | • Concept of being more<br>• Critical thinking vs. naive awareness<br>• Subject vs. object<br>• Reading of the world |
| 4. Dialogic and participatory methodology | • Problem-solving concept vs. banking concept<br>• Dialogue and emancipation<br>• Narrative education vs. active education |
| 5. Interdisciplinarity | • Culture and world<br>• Generating themes |

58 The results of this project are available at: <https://mulheresnocarcere.iddh.org.br/>. Moreover, information regarding the situation of women under house arrest in Latin America is available at: <https://www.wola.org/wp-content/uploads/2020/07/Imprisoned-at-Home.pdf>.

Critical pedagogy, for Freire, meant imagining literacy as not simply the mastering of specific skills but also as a mode of intervention, a way of learning about and reading the word as a basis for intervening in the world. Critical thinking was not reducible to an object lesson in test-taking or the task of memorising so-called facts, decontextualised and unrelated to present conditions. To the contrary, it was about offering a way of thinking beyond the seeming naturalness or inevitability of the current state of things, challenging assumptions validated by 'common sense', soaring beyond the immediate confines of one's experiences, entering into a dialogue with history, and imagining a future that would not merely reproduce the present.

## Conclusion

Considering that the emergence of legal clinics is a recent phenomenon in Brazil, they are still the subject of some resistance by some educators and legal professionals. These critics often ignore the positive impact that clinics can have in increasing access to justice for underprivileged people and groups in Brazil. They are more concerned with questions about students' skills development, rather the social change which are happening at the same time.

There is, so far, no consensus on these questions amongst educational experts and policy makers in Brazil: should legal clinics exist to broaden skills development or to provoke social change? In this chapter we have argued that a clinical pedagogy, informed by some theoretical concepts of educator Paulo Freire, are capable of developing both: broaden competences for law students and, moreover, foster individual and social transformation in teachers, students and communities. It allows educators not to give undue focus to cognitive learning (theoretical knowledge) over the development of others' competences such as personal (empathy), instrumental (know-how) and ethical/relational (reflected action).

In addition, we argued that the role of a law school is also to train critically minded citizens who are able to creatively develop new responses to societal problems. To this end, legal clinics use more interactive and action-based teaching, which, in our assessment, significantly complements the personal and professional education of law students.

Freire's contribution, in our view, is unquestionable for CLE. His pedagogical proposal raises questions about the relationship between local conditions and wider political, economic and social forces which necessarily provokes a critical reflection on the impacts and role of the law. Our traditional legal education system in Brazil still prioritises a 'depositing' of knowledge, where students usually memorise the content and are assessed, most of the time, in theoretical exams, disconnected with the real challenges of our society.

Moreover, taking into consideration the inequalities and the continental dimension of Brazil, our legal education system should consider the context and the reality of our students, respecting the diversity of our regions. This is why Freire maintained that politics is always part of education; social, economic, racial and moral considerations cannot be ignored. Therefore, clinics can be an opportunity to foster these reflections and debates, in Freire's terms, through praxis and the path to 'being more', not only for students, but also for clients and partners. In doing so, this will facilitate autonomy and critical thinking in partners and clients and also improve students' learning by challenging them to think about their own role in using law for social justice.

# 5 Luigi Ferrajoli's theory of fundamental rights and Clinical Legal Education

*Andrés Gascón-Cuenca*

## Introduction

Universities have been traditionally considered as places where freedom of thought and critical thinking are enhanced and fostered. In Spain, since the 1960s,[1] the university community and the labour movement were active in fighting for the recognition of political, civil, economic, social and cultural rights during Franco's dictatorship. The lack of freedom imposed by the regime and the subsequent absence of opportunities became the cause for students, professors and workers to develop a strong oppositional culture, to the extent that the Spanish 'university became the guinea pig of democracy'.[2] Nevertheless, this active role as a crucible for the discussion and development of counter-hegemonic ideas is currently at risk for several reasons, not least due to the reforms of the university curricula introduced by the Bologna Process.[3] As pointed out by Boaventura Sousa Santos,[4] universities are currently facing big changes that shape the central role they play in society. These changes introduce ontological questions about the epistemic

1 Rubén Díez García, 'De Berkeley a Madrid: las protestas estudiantiles en la década de los 60' *TheConversation* (Madrid, 11 June 2019).

2 Alberto Carrillo-Linares, 'Movimiento estudiantil antifranquista, cultura política y transición a la democracia' (2006) 5 Pasado y Memoria. Revista de Historia Contemporánea 149, 170.

3 The Bologna Process started in 1999 and introduced important changes in the university curricula of the member states of the European Higher Education Area (EHEA). Succinctly, it entails a homogenisation across member states in the structure of the degrees, the recognition of qualifications and learning periods abroad completed in other EHEA countries, and the implementation of a system of quality assurance, to strengthen the quality and relevance of learning and teaching. More information: <http://www.ehea.info>.

4 Boaventura de Sosa Santos, 'The University at a Crossroads' in Ramón Grosfoguel et al. (eds), *Decolonizing the Westernized University* (Lexington Books 2016); Boaventura de Sosa Santos, 'La Universidad en el siglo XII. Para una reforma democrática y emancipadora de la universidad', in René Ramírez (ed.), Transformar la universidad para transformar la sociedad, (2nd edn, Secretaria Nacional de Educación Superior 2012).

DOI: 10.4324/9780429299247-6

objectives universities must enhance when designing the curriculum of their degrees.[5]

This chapter will seek to analyse the challenges discussed by Sousa Santos in three ways. Firstly, it will examine the changes the Bologna Process brought to legal curricula in Spanish universities and consider how they impacted on the overall quality of the education law students received; secondly, it considers philosopher Luigi Ferrajoli's conception of fundamental rights and their protection within constitutional democracies;[6] and finally, it will explore how scholars can develop Ferraojli's theory through Clinical Legal Education (CLE) in their courses to implement new learning techniques which resist the general degradation of the quality of law curricula resulting from changes imposed by the Bologna Process; an approach that prioritises critical thinking, social justice and the study of fundamental and human rights in legal studies. This final section will be informed by the author's practical experience as a legal clinic mentor and co-director of the Legal Clinic for Social Justice at the University of Valencia.[7]

## The modification of legal studies introduced by the Bologna Process

In Spain, a great number of scholars[8] opposed the implementation of the Bologna Process, especially in relation to law programmes, because of the deep concerns they had about the consequences of the restructure it proposed.[9] Many changes were introduced, but for reasons of space, this chapter will analyse three of the main characteristics of this reform. Firstly, the reduction of the law degree from five to four years, secondly, the promotion of formal training over reflexive and critical thinking, and lastly, the use of the Human Capital Theory[10] in the design of the learning goals of the new curricula in law. In conclusion, it will be

5 Changes that may jeopardise the 'epistemic justice' public institutions must cultivate. Elizabeth Anderson, 'Epistemic Justice as a Virtue of Social Institutions' (2012) Social Epistemology 26:2, 163.

6 Luigi Ferrajoli, *Principia iuris: teoría del derecho y de la democracia* (v.1 and v.2, Trotta 2011); Luigi Ferrajoli, *Derechos y Garantías: la ley del más débil* (Trotta, 2016).

7 Website: <Uv.es/clinica>.

8 More than 300 law professors participated in a declaration against the implementation of the Bologna Process in the law programmes. See: Andrés Boix Palop, 'Saquemos los estudios de Derecho del proceso de Bolonia' (*No se trata de hacer*, 2 June 2009) <http://www.lapaginadefinitiva.com/aboix/?p=206> accessed 7 May 2020.

9 Eduardo García de Enterría et al., 'Saquemos los estudios de derecho del proceso de Bolonia' (2009) 6 El Cronista del estado social y democrático de derecho 4; Manuel Atienza, 'Reformatio in Peius' (2009) 26 El Notario.

10 Human Capital is defined as a theory that uses the standard neo-classical model to describe human behaviour. 'People are seen as calculating individuals seeking maximisation of their personal economic utility – the model of "egoistic rationality" […]. In this view of the universe the only acknowledged benefits of education are economic benefits […] all educational benefits of any kind – including those understood as aesthetic, intellectual or spiritual – are seen as reducible to economic values, dollar amounts of consumption or investment benefit'. Simon Marginson, *Human capital*

argued that this process has led to an erosion of the overall quality of university-level legal studies by perceiving legal experts[11] as mere technicians whose task is to perform their professional function whilst remaining uncritical of the status quo and inattentive to the substantive protection of fundamental rights.

The criteria that drove the transition from five- to four-year duration of the degree in law were flawed, as the compression and consequent elimination of subjects led to a disagreement between different departments within the faculties of law. The reform was criticised for being implemented without sufficient reflection on the central question of 'what kind of jurist we want to train',[12] and its results were a product of the bargaining powers of the departments, which were different from faculty to faculty. This process led to a 'degradation of the legal professions and the belittling of the contribution of jurists to the organization of the coexistence and the structure of the Spanish society'.[13]

Consequently, curricula were not designed with the holistic understanding of the training needs of future legal professionals. Their modification was not based on the necessity students have of a 'solid knowledge of the structure of the legal system, and a deep command of the categories, disciplines and institutions that construct the cornerstones of the legal profession',[14] but rather thinking about them as merely legal technicians. Accordingly, this homogenisation gave paramount importance to purely formal requirements, disregarding the importance that critical thinking[15] and a social justice orientation have in the training of legal experts, individuals whose fundamental role should embrace the protection of individual rights and freedoms and the promotion of democracy.

This reality paved the way to a disproportionate emphasis on the promotion of *practical skills*, intended to promote *employability*, a development which was served to undermine the quality and depth of legal studies. This focus on practical skills replacing the promotion of scientific knowledge and critical thinking is identified by Donald Schön as the promotion of Technical Rationality,[16] which serves to

*theory and education policy* (University of New South Wales, discussion paper No. 3, 1989), 2.

11 References to legal experts should be understood as alluding to any person whose work is to interpret or to apply the law or defend a person before a court of justice like judges, prosecutors, public defenders, lawyers, among others.

12 Atienza (n 9).

13 García de Enterría (n 9) 4; Vicente A Sanjurjo Rivo, 'El nuevo espacio europeo de educación superior: desafíos e incertidumbres' (2012) 10 Revista de Derecho UNED 585, 607.

14 García de Enterría (n 9) 5.

15 According to Dewey, 'the essence of critical thinking is suspended judgment; and the essence of this suspense is inquiry to determine the nature of the problem before proceeding to attempts at its solution'. John Dewey *How We Think* (D. C. Heath & Co 1910) 74. Cf. Andrés Gascón-Cuenca; C Ghitti and F Malzani 'Acknowledging the relevance of empathy in clinical legal education. Some proposals from the experience of the University of Brescia (IT) and Valencia (ESP)' (2018) 26–2 International Journal of Clinical Legal Education 218.

16 Schön defines Technical Rationality as the 'professional activity [that] consists in instrumental problems solving made rigorous by the application of scientific theory

disregard the holistic reflection legal experts must engage in as professionals.[17] University is now no longer the place where law students become equipped with the expertise, knowledge and intellectual capacity that enables them to challenge accepted norms of the legal system such as the neoliberal concept of formal equality[18] (often used to secure the status quo of the privileged), or to unveil the relations of power inside of societies. A disproportionate focus on *employability* prevents this, because the task of future legal professionals is not to dispute the system or to care about its substantial aspects, but to formally learn the positive law and apply it without further reflection.[19]

As such, the Bologna Process promoted an instrumental tendency in university education, 'a mechanism to obtain a "product": the young "employable"'.[20] This brought *Human Capital Theory* (HCT) to the centre of new curricula design. HCT 'refers to knowledge, attitudes, and skills that are developed and valued primarily for their economically productive potential'.[21] Much has been discussed about the

and technique. [...] The systematic knowledge base of a profession is thought to have four essential properties. It is specialized, firmly bounded, scientific, and standardized. This last point is particularly important, because it bears on the paradigmatic relationship which holds, according to Technical Rationality, between a profession's knowledge base and its practice'. Donald Schön, 'From Technical Rationality to reflection-in-action' in Roger Harrison et al. (eds), *Supporting Lifelong Learning. Volumen 1 Perspectives on Learning* (RoutledgeFalmer 2002), 21–24, 40; cf. Elisabeth Anne Kinsella, 'The art of reflective practice in health and social care: reflections on the legacy of Donal Schön' (2010) 11:4 Reflective Practice 565. Kinsella introduces important reflections about Schön's theory that are useful in the area of health and social care education that might be exported to juridical sciences.

17 Schön (n 16) 50.

18 Catherine Barnard and Bob Hepple, 'Substantive Equality' (2000) 59–3 *Cambridge Law Journal*, 562, 562–564.

19 As Nussbaum says, 'thirsty for national profit, nations, and their systems of education, are heedlessly discarding skills that are needed to keep democracies alive. If this trend continues, nations all over the world will soon be producing generations of useful machines, rather than complete citizens who can think for themselves, criticize tradition, and understand the significance of another person's sufferings and achievements'. Martha C Nussbaum, *Not for Profit. Why Democracy Need the Humanities* (Princeton University Press 2010) 2. Luis Lloredo Álix, 'Derechos y democracia: juntos pero no revueltos' in Oscar Pérez de la Fuente and et al. (eds), *Democracia: perspectivas políticas e institucionales* (Editorial B de F 2019) 8.

20 Francisco J Laporta San Miguel, 'Bologna Process and the Spanish Law Schools' (2010) 10 Revista de Estudios Jurídicos 1, 4; cf. Rebeca Moreno, 'De la declaración de Bolonia a la estrategia 2015: el proyecto europeo neolibreal de mercatilización de la universidad' in Luis Alegre and Victor Moreno (eds), *Bolonia no existe. La destrucción de la universidad europea* (Hiru 2009) 32.

21 Ian Baptiste, 'Educating Lone Wolves: Pedagogical Implications of Human Capital Theory' (2000) 51 (3) Adult Education Quarterly 184, 185; cf. D A Olaniyan and T Okemakinde 'Human Capital Theory: Implications for Educational Development' (2008) 5 (5) Pakistan Journal of Social Sciences 479. This is not only happening in Spain, as 'the pressure for economic growth has led many political leaders in Europe to recast the entirety of university education – both reaching and research – along growth-oriented lines, asking about the contribution of each discipline and each researcher to the economy'. Nusssbaum (n 19) 127.

implications of HCT in higher education.[22] Private corporations are the ones entitled to identify the skills and the professional competencies (learning outcomes) that are productive,[23] so university curricula have to focus on them. However, the promotion of these private interests may not be in the interests of wider society.[24] HCT 'treats humans as lone wolves: radically isolated hedonists, creatures of habit (not intentions) who temper their avarice with economic rationality'[25] bringing the most basic and plain characteristics of the globalised neoliberal ideology to university degrees.[26] Moreover, HCT fosters patters of structural discrimination within societies, as it associates social inequality with different interests when someone invests in his or her own training and employment opportunities.[27] During the Bologna Process, Spanish law faculties embraced HCT as it drove the design of the new degrees in law. It implied that private corporations and interests led the discussion about learning outcomes,[28] and now they are linked to corporate interests.[29] From that moment on, the duty of universities became the training of students whose foremost concerns are their chances of finding a job in a highly competitive labour market, at the expense of an emphasis on the value of scientific knowledge *per se*, and the importance it has for them to evolve as persons, for pursuing their own interests and flourishing.

These influences present a difficult outlook for public universities in Spain for two key reasons. Firstly, universities, traditionally the centres of the production of knowledge, and free, critical and non-conformist thinking,[30] are suffering from a

22 For a general overview see Emrullah Tan, 'Human Capital Theory: A Holistic Criticism' (2014) 84 (3) Review of Education Research 411.

23 Gustavo Toledo Lara, 'La universidad española y el proceso de Bolonia: consideraciones para su análisis' (2015) 15–2 Actualidades Investigativas en educación 1; Richard Sennett, *The Culture of New Capitalism* (Yale University Press 2006) 12. Cf. Juan Jesús Garza Onofre 'Sobre la función social de la abogacía ante el actual panorama de globalización' in Manuel Calvo, Fernando Alrlettaz and Jorge García Ibáñez, *Derecho y Sociedad. Reflexiones sobre sociología jurídica, filosofía del derecho y derechos humanos* (Universidad de Zaragoza 2014).

24 Olaniyan and Okemakinde (n 21).

25 Baptiste (n 21) 197.

26 Arturo Campos Langa, 'Universidad y mercado: una reflexión acerca del actual proceso de convergencia europea' (2006) 2 Youkali 87.

27 Previous investigations proved that HCT does not offer a consistent explanation to justify this affirmation: Steven Shulman, 'Discrimination, Human Capital, and Black-White Unemployment: Evidence from Cities' (1987) 22 (3) The Journal of Human Resources 361; Hillary M Lips, 'The Gender Pay Gap: Challenging the Rationalizations. Perceived Equality, Discrimination, and the Limits of the Human Capital Models' (2013) 68 Sex Roles 169; Philip Broyles and Weston Fenner, 'Race, human capital, and wage discrimination in STEM professions in the United States' (2010) 30 (5/6) International Journal of Sociology 251.

28 HCT implies to bring into university curricula the education and training needs of globalisation and capitalism. Cf. Patrick Fitzsimons, 'Human Capital and Theory and Education' (2015) Encyclopedia of Educational Philosophy and Theory 1.

29 Juan Antonio García Amado, 'Bolonia y la enseñanza del derecho' (2009) 5 El Cronista del Estado Social y democrático de derecho 42, 46.

30 Cf. Philip G Altbach, 'Academic freedom: International realities and freedoms' (2001) 41 Higher Education 205; cf. Niall McCrae, 'Nurturing Critical Thinking and

'tendency to transform the truth value of scientific knowledge into the "market truth" value of knowledge'.[31] This reality generates a difficult situation for university educators who refuse to adapt themselves to it, and who think that their duties as lecturers are not compatible with the idea that knowledge is a public good and not a commodity.[32] Secondly, university autonomy and academic freedom are at stake.[33] According to the argument presented above, curricula were modified following market demands and impositions, so the contents of the different subjects were evaluated from the perspective of employability, incorporating a cost-benefit analysis. This has undermined the integrity of law curricula by reducing the opportunity to develop understanding of important holistic issues such as human rights, fundamental freedoms, discrimination, migration and unethical behaviours, all of which are essential for the formation of lawyers who are able to protect and defend the rule of law in a democracy.

To summarise, even though the harmonisation and the streamlining of the university degrees to foster the exchange of expertise and professionals among EU states might be seen as a laudable objective of the Bologna Process, its development and its specific application to the legal studies has had a negative systemic impact. The reduction of the curricula from five to four years was done without sufficient debate about the substantive skills legal experts must have to perform their duties. The use of technical rationality and a normative framework based on Human Capital Theory allowed private corporations to unduly influence the training objectives of law curricula, incorporating neoliberal ideas and promoting the idea of education as a commodity. Judges, public prosecutors, court-appointed lawyers and other legal experts have, like physicians, a duty to serve their communities by assuring the best protection of the fundamental rights stated by our constitutions and welfare systems. Educating professionals who can perform this essential public service is a core duty of the public university[34] but one which has been significantly impeded by the implementation of the Bologna Process in Spain.

## Constitutional democracy and Luigi Ferrajoli's theory of fundamental rights and validity of the law

The impact on the law curricula resulting from the implementation of the Bologna Process in Spain has not affected all areas of legal knowledge equally.[35]

Academic Freedom in the 21st Century University' (2011) 1 International Journal of Teaching and Learning in Higher Education 128.

31 de Sosa Santos (n 4) 297.

32 Ibid.; Moreno (n 20) 24.

33 Clara Serrano García, 'El fin de la universidad pública' in L Alegre and V Moreno (eds), *Bolonia no existe. La destrucción de la universidad europea* (Hiru 2009), 67–72.

34 Cf. John J Salinas and Johnny Tamayo, 'El Rol de la Universidad Estatal como un Bien Público. Retos en el Caso Colombiano' (2018) 29–2 Información Tecnológica 19.

35 See n 14.

The use of HCT and Technical Rationality in the design of the new four-year degrees benefited subjects that private enterprises find valuable (such as business administration, tort law, international commercial law and others), over the ones that foreground reflexivity and critique of the current legal system (such as philosophy, theory of law, human rights, antidiscrimination law, migration law, deontological ethics and others). This change in emphasis in legal education has important implications for the future operation of the Spanish legal system. Currently, the classical hierarchical structure of legal systems that place at the apex of the normative pyramid constitutional or fundamental texts that, on one hand, establish and protect fundamental rights, and on the other hand, recognise structural values and principles that must influence, not only the rest of the legal system, but also the activity of governments and lawmakers, is being challenged. An example of this is the answer given by governments and international institutions to the financial crisis of 2008. Specifically, the Spanish government, influenced by the European Union, International Monetary Fund, stock markets and others, introduced important budget cuts to the protection of fundamental rights. Meanwhile banks were rescued, health rights were curtailed, tuition fees were raised, the welfare system was severely affected, housing rights were limited, among many other areas.

Due to the changes introduced by the Bologna Process in the law curricula, students are less prone to identify, discuss and criticise the decisions that prioritised the protection of private interests over social ones. This shakes the structural scaffolding of constitutional democracies and is one of the reasons of what Professor Luigi Ferrajoli identifies as a crisis for constitutional democracies. To introduce law students to Ferrajoli's ideas on the concept of validity of law can help them to acquire cognitive skills to identify, critique and contest the normative framework which threatens to undermine constitutional democracy. Thus, the scope of this section is to briefly introduce Ferrajoli's conception of the validity of the law before, in the final section, exploring how this can inform an enriched approach to Clinical Legal Education which can counter the degradation in the quality of legal studies.

Ferrajoli developed a full axiomatic theory of law in his main work *Principia Iuris*. In it he arranges his theory in four different blocks:[36] the first on deontics, meaning the relations that exist in every legal system between subjects, rules and its deontic category; the second concentrates on positive law; the third investigates the rule of law; and the last presents a comprehensive account of constitutional democracy. An in-depth analysis of his work falls far beyond the scope of this chapter, so it will focus on examining his arguments regarding the paradigmatic change that his theory introduces on the ontology of basic concepts of constitutional democracies like legal validity law and the important differences he identifies between fundamental rights and their guarantees, which are most relevant to the discussion of CLE provided in part IV.

36 Luigi Ferrajoli, *Principia iuris: teoría del derecho y de la democracia* (v.1, Trotta 2011) VII–XII.

## *The validity of the law and the relevance of fundamental rights*

One of the major ideas introduced by Ferrajoli is the identification of the paradigm shift[37] that constitutional democracies introduced by their recognition of legal validity within continental legal orders.[38] Traditionally, legal positivism is considered as a nomodynamic system[39] that includes norms regulating the diverse ways of producing laws. If lawmakers follow the formal procedure to pass a law, it is valid, so it exists. This is what Ferrajoli defines as formal democracy or formal validity. He argues constitutional democracies introduced a change of paradigm and now this nomodynamic system[40] not only includes formal requirements for the production of laws, but also substantive ones (substantial validity).[41] The validity of the law not only depends on formal democracy, but also on the principle of *substantial legality*, [42] or *strict legality*, whereby 'a norm is valid, in addition to being in force, only if its contents do not clash with the principles and the fundamental rights establish by the constitution'.[43] Ferrajoli holds that for a legal

37 Because of the significance of Ferrajoli's theory, I affirm that it supposes a change of paradigm in the conception of juspositivism. However, other authors state that Ferrajoli's positions should be described as a 'critique within and an (important) improvement of (the paradigm of) Kelsenian juspositivism, rather than a change of it'. Mario Jori, 'Ferrajoli on Rights' (2001) 14 International Journal for the Semiotics of Law 41, 42; Mario Jori, 'Ferrajoli sobre los derechos' in Luigi Ferrajoli, *Los fundamentos de los derechos fundamentales* (Trotta 2001) 106.

38 Paolo Sandro, 'An Axiomatic Theory of Law' (2011) 17 Res Publica 343.

39 The differentiation between nomodstatic and nomodynamic systems has been stated by Hans Kelsen, one of the most influential philosophers of contemporary legal positivism. He defines these two terms to describe his concept of the validity of the norms. In nomosystatic systems 'norms are "valid" [...] by virtue of their contents: Their contents has [sic] an immediately evident quality that guarantees their validity, or in other terms: the norms are valid because of their inherent appeal'. In nomodynamic systems, a norm to be valid has to be created following the mandate of 'the fundamental rule according to which the norms of the system are to be created'; thus, 'a norm forms part of a dynamic system if it has been created in a way that –in the last analysis– determined by the basic norm'. Hans Kelsen, *General Theory of Law and State* (HUP, vol. 1, 1949) 112–113.

40 This is an important shift in the positivist vision of the legal system. According to Sandro 'this is how the *nomostatics* of a constitutional legal system are subordinated to its *nomodynamics*. In other words, *coherence* is here sacrificed to *certainty*. Sandro (n 38) 348.

41 According to Sandro, Ferrajoli's theory introduced 'substantive constraints upon the activity of law-makers themselves'. Sandro (n 38) 357.

42 Luigi Ferrajoli, *Democracia y garantismo* (Trotta 2008) 35.

43 Ferrajoli, *Principia Iuris* (n 36) 37; Luigi Ferrajoli, 'Democracia constitucional y derechos fundamentales. La rigidez de la constitución y sus garantías' in Juan José Moreso and Manuel Atienza, *Luigi Ferrajoli. La teoría del derecho en el paradigma constitucional* (Fundación Coloquio Jurídico Europeo 2008) 90–96; cf. Ferrajoli, *Democracia y garantismo* (n 42) 65–68; Sandro (n 38) 348. Ferrajoli as iuspositivist stands for the complete separation of law and morals. He affirms that his definition of fundamental rights holds an ideological neutrality because every society is free to decide the content of the rights they retain as fundamental as long as they are recognised by everybody. However, if the validity of a statue depends on substantive legality, it is open to

decision to be valid, it should not contradict fundamental rights and principles as they are conceived as limits, firstly, to the free-market economy, and secondly, to the possible abuses that the majority of the population might commit against minorities in the protection of their rights. Therefore, to protect fundamental rights means to safeguard them from the influence of the market or the undue influence of the majority.[44] Thus, laws are not only subjected to formal regulations about their production, but also to a substantial scrutiny about their content to be fully valid.[45] This means that pieces of legislation that conflict with constitutional regulations cannot be considered as fully valid. Whereas the recognition that a statute is in force follows the classic principle of legality that only affects the way it has been produced, the rule that acknowledges the validity of a legal disposition is more complex, as it also entails the principle of substantial legality by recognising the importance of evaluating its content.[46]

Moreover, Ferrajoli affirms that when fundamental rights are constitutionally established, they are norms hierarchically located above other norms and have two distinctive characteristics. Firstly, 'fundamental rights are thetic norms that differentiate themselves from the hypothetical ones as the former are identified with the rules that establish them'.[47] For instance, the right to freedom of thought is nothing more than the constitutional norm by which such right is conferred, in contrast to property rights, which are never norms by themselves as they only have legal implications if the hypothesis they entail is met (being a property owner).[48] Secondly, fundamental rights are norms that deal with the production

a critical evaluation by the appropriate authority (supreme or constitutional court, parliament, etc.). Does this mean that fundamental rights are open to a moral evaluation? This is one of the major doubts about Ferrajoli's definition of substantive equality. Ermanno Vitale, 'A general theory of law or the foundation of the ideal republic? Five doubts about Luigi Ferrajoli's theory of fundamental rights' (2001) 14 International Journal for the Semiotics of Law 97, 103; Ermanno Vitale, '¿Teoría general del derecho o Fundación de una república óptima? Cinco dudas sobre la teoría de los derechos fundamentales de Luigi Ferrajoli' in Luigi Ferrajoli, *Los fundamentos de los Derechos Funadmentales* (Trotta 2001) 68–73; Javier Ansuátegui Roig, *Razón y voluntad en el Estado de Derecho. Un enfoque filosófico-jurídico* (Dykinson 2013) 201; Danilo Zolo, 'Libertad, propiedad e igualdad en la teoría de los "derechos fundamentals". A propósito de un ensayo de Luigi Ferraoli' in Luigi Ferrajoli, *Los fundamentos de los derechos fundamentales* (Trotta 2001) 79–80. Vega suggests that post-positivistic conceptions, such as constitutionalism, transcend this neutral-value component of positivism. Jesús Vega, 'Legal philosophy as practical philosophy' (2018) 34 Revus 1, 18.

44 Ferrajoli, *Democracia y garantismo* (n 42) 23.

45 Sandro (n 38) 348.

46 Ferrajoli, *Democracia y garantismo* (n 42) 51–52.

47 Luigi Ferrajoli, *Principia iuris: teoría del derecho y de la democracia* (v.2, Trotta 2011) 22.

48 Ferrajoli states that one of the differences between fundamental rights and property rights is that the former are non-disposable, meanwhile the latter are. This idea presents an important problem. It holds the vision that fundamental rights can operate paternalistically, so in specific circumstances choices made by individuals might be disregarded. This might be seen as a contradiction on Ferrajoli's theory as paternalism may limit fundamental rights themselves. For example, in a legal system that considers the right to life as a fundamental one (so non-disposable), should laws

of other norms, usually located in the constitution, that regulate substantive aspects for legislation to be produced.

Finally, Ferrajoli asserts that the old paradigm where the judge limits his concern to the formal validity of the law and not its substance has been shifted by the advent of constitutional democracies. In this new paradigm, judges are essentially committed to the constitution, and can uphold the law only if it is constitutionally valid.[49]

## *Fundamental rights and their protection as the* law of the weakest

Continuing the discussion of Ferrajoli's concept of constitutional democracy, this section will focus on the relevance of differentiating between rights and their guarantees, and on the importance of understanding fundamental rights as the *law of the weakest* people;[50] securing basic rights for all and protecting them from the tyranny of the majority.

According to the contemporary formulation of legal positivism developed by Kelsen, rights (even constitutional ones), when they are not correctly guaranteed cannot be considered as proper rights.[51] Ferrajoli opposes this formulation by asserting the need to differentiate between rights and their guarantees. If we confuse these two characteristics, we will be dismissing two of the most important successes the constitutionalism of this century achieved, namely: 'the internalization of fundamental rights, and the constitutionalising of social rights'.[52]

Ferrajoli states that fundamental rights have primary and secondary guarantees.[53] Primary guarantees consist in the prohibition to revoke and the obligation to fulfil all principles and rights created by the constitution, which can only be modified by following the reinforced constitutional procedure to do so, or it cannot be modified at all.[54] Thus, primary guarantees are divided in two:

protecting assisted suicide or voluntary euthanasia be outruled? This is an important debate as paternalism shapes the contents of fundamental rights. Cf. Jori, 'Ferrajoli on Rights' (n 37) 50; cf. Jori, 'Ferrajoli sobre los derechos' (n 37) 121–125; Riccardo Guastini, 'Tres problemas para Luigi Ferrajoli' in Luigi Ferrajoli, *Los fundamentos de los derechos fundamentales* (Trotta 2001) 61–62.

49 Sandro (n 38) 348.

50 Ferrajoli (n 6).

51 Kelsen (n 39) 75–89. Jori, 'Ferrajoli on Rights' (n 37) 42.

52 Ferrajoli, *Derechos y Garantías* (n 6) 59. Cf. Jori, 'Ferrajoli sobre los derechos' (n 37) 106–110.

53 Ferrajoli, *Derechos y Garantías* (n 6) 59; Ferrajoli, *Democracia y garantismo* (n 42) 60–67; Ferrajoli, 'Democracia constitucional' (n 43) 97–104.

54 Luigi Ferrajoli, *Poderes Salvajes: la crisis de la democracia constitucional* (Trotta, 2011) 40. Generally, constitutions protect a list of fundamental rights. This is an essential area of this texts. Depending on the constitution, the modification of the fundamental rights section must be done: 1) following the regular procedure to pass a modification on any law (this is the case of United Kingdom); 2) following a reinforced procedure that requires a different majority regime in the Parliament to be adopted, or/and the obligation for the modification to be endorsed in a referendum (this is the case of the Spanish constitution); 3) or this fundamental rights section cannot be modified at all

negative and positive.[55] Primary negative guarantees limit the actions legislative power can perform when modifying or repealing constitutionally established rights. Primary positive guarantees are related to the obligation appointed to the legislative power to create pieces of legislation that develop all rights detailed in the constitutional body. Secondary guarantees involve the control of unconstitutionality performed by the jurisdictional power to ordinary pieces of legislation and their invalidation when such circumstance is demonstrated.[56]

As a consequence, when the primary negative guarantees are not satisfied, we find *antinomies*, [57] 'invalid laws which can be revoked by the action of secondary guarantees',[58] and which can only be resolved by a ruling in the appropriated court.[59] When we recognise a violation of a primary positive guarantee, we are before a *legal-gap*, [60] the wrongful absence of a law developing a specific right; this can only be solved by the action of the legislative power and not by the courts.

The obligation to secure and to protect fundamental rights and to impose sanctions on those who harm them is a logical duty of the constitutional state. However, it is also a reality that, on one hand, this does not always happen, and on the other hand, occasionally fundamental rights cannot be guaranteed because of state inaction, as they do not develop some rights (like rights to housing) into specific norms that set the framework for them to be enforced. Nevertheless, antinomies and legal-gaps[61] cannot be used to diminish the importance of fundamental rights or the duty the state has to fulfil them; so that, when we encounter a legal-gap in the implementation of a fundamental right, we have to strongly affirm the obligation the state has in providing a remedy.[62]

(this is the case of the German constitution). This is the difference between militant and non-militant democracies. See: Karl Loewenstein, 'Militant Democracy and Fundamental Rights, I' (1937) 31 American Political Science Review 417; Karl Loewenstein, 'Militant Democracy and Fundamental Rights, II' (1937) 31 American Political Science Review 638.

55 Jori, 'Ferrajoli on Rights' (n 37) 42.

56 Ferrajoli, *Poderes Salvajes* (n 54) 43. However, the legitimisation of the traditional judicial-centric system for the protection of fundamental rights is now discussed by scholars that affirm that the Parliamentary Rights Model better represents society in the debates about the definition of the substantial contents of constitutional rights. Janet L Hiebert, 'Parliamentary Bills of Rights: An Alternative Model? (2006) 69–1 The Modern Law Review 7; Alon Harel and Adam Shinar, 'Between judicial and legislative supremacy: A cautious defense of constrained judicial review' (2012) 10–4 ICON 950.

57 Ferrajoli, 'Democracia constitucional' (n 43) 105–115.

58 Ibid. 41.

59 Sandro (n 38) 349.

60 Ferrajoli, 'Democracia constitucional' (n 43) 105–115; cf. Jori, 'Ferrajoli on Rights' (n 37) 45.

61 Primary legal-gaps are the defective stipulation of the deontic modalities to the primary guarantees, and secondary legal-gaps are the defective functioning of the judicial authorities that are compelled to sanction or overrule behaviours that harm fundamental rights.

62 Jori, 'Ferrajoli on Rights' (n 37) 45.

For Ferrajoli this distinction between fundamental rights and their guarantees is necessary for their protection.[63] From the theoretical standpoint, it means that the nexus that exists between individual expectations and their satisfaction is a normative one, so when there is no correlation between them a legal-gap exists, which the state is required to fill.[64] From the legal education perspective, this differentiation gives students the conceptual framework to critique and challenge the action (or inaction) of legal authorities and to connect the legal system with its outcomes. Moreover, it serves us to point out the defective protection of some rights compared to others. The development of the welfare state and the constitutionalising of social rights over the last decades has not been followed by a set of adequate positive guarantees that protect them. This makes visible the inaction of the legislative power before constitutional mandates to fully protect all constitutional rights, and it should never be used to diminish the importance of social rights over other fundamental ones.

For Ferrajoli, the constitutional protection of fundamental rights is the crowning achievement of a centuries long battle against social inequality. These constitutional protections can counteract the asymmetrical relations of power which has so often been used to control and subjugate the powerless. Because of this, the erosion of fundamental rights must not be accepted as they serve to protect the weakest groups of the society. They imply a number of limitations and obligations imposed by the constitutional state on public and political powers to prevent them to act arbitrarily and unfairly. Thus, Ferrajoli defines fundamental rights as belonging to the sphere of the *undecidable.* [65] This means that the protection constitutions set to fundamental rights abstract them from being negotiated and bargained. Political powers have a direct constitutional mandate to fully protect and guarantee all fundamental rights, assuring the threshold defined by the constitution. This averts fundamental rights from being distorted by public and private actors.[66] These protections are one of the fundamental constitutional tasks

63 Ferrajoli, *Derechos y Garantías* (n 6) 59–64; Ferrajoli, *Democracia y garantismo* (n 42) 71–76.

64 Nevertheless, this is not an easy task to do. The *effective implementation* of a given right will be always open to discussion, as many constitutional rights are worded in a very generic and vague way. However, as affirmed by Jori, the task of legal theorists is to raise 'general problems of how law is produced and applied'. Jori, 'Ferrajoli on Rights' (n 37) 46; cf. Jori, 'Ferrajoli sobre los derechos' (n 37) 110.

65 *Sfera dell'indecidibile.* Ferrajoli, *Poderes Salvajes* (n 54) 3–19. See also n 42 and 46.

66 Ferrajoli, *Principia iuris* (n 47) 774. Precisely because fundamental rights are abstracted to public and private bargain about their content, they belong to the sphere of the *undecidable.* Their threshold is defined by the constitution, so political actors have to follow the constitutional mandated to fully develop them. Nussbaum (n 16) 16 also defines fundamental rights in this way: 'both nations [USA and India], however, have written constitutions, and in both, the constitution protects from majority whim a group of fundamental rights that cannot be abrogated even to achieve a large economic benefit. Both nations protect a range of political and civil rights, and both guarantee all citizens the equal protection of the laws regardless of racial, gender, or religious group membership'.

assigned to governments, as the satisfaction of which 'is the condition for social coexistence and the presence of the state itself'.[67]

To understand fundamental rights as norms created to protect the vulnerable is central to Ferrajoli's conception of the constitutional state. Rights, whether social, political, civil, economic or cultural have as their objective the protection from abuses and violence and the fight for the recognition of human dignity and formal and substantial equality. This is precisely why this dialectic must underpin the debates students have at the faculties of law. Reflection on how positive law corresponds with constitutional values and outcomes should be an essential part of their legal education as future legal experts. Clinical Legal Education offers the opportunity for students to debate and discuss these legal issues through learning-by-doing. In the following section, this chapter will show how CLE can engage students with the social problems that can facilitate the critical engagement with the legal system that is necessary for their holistic legal training.[68]

## Clinical Legal Education and the study of fundamental rights

The modifications of the curricula introduced by the Bologna Process did not have a uniform effect on all areas of the law curricula. Subjects deemed to have little direct relevance to commercial concerns such as human rights,[69] philosophy, legal theory, legal ethics, among others, were sidelined or eliminated from the curricula in Spain. This reality negatively shapes the approach students have to cases related to human rights, conflict of interests, discrimination, and other areas of legal knowledge deemed unproductive by private interests. Within this general layout, university professors opposed to this process began to look for new teaching methodologies that enabled them to maintain a focus on the more holistic issues marginalised by the Bologna Process.[70]

Clinical Legal Education (CLE) has a long tradition in North American universities. However, in Spain we cannot acknowledge any training programme of such a type until 2002.[71] A legal clinic, as defined by Wilson[72] and the European

67 Ibid.

68 Richard J Wilson, 'Training for Justice: The Global Reach of Clinical Legal Education' (2004) 22 Penn St Int'l L Rev 421; Frank S Bloch, 'The Andragogical Basis of Clinical Legal Education' (1982) 35 Vand L Rev 321.

69 Pedro López López, 'La enseñanza de los derechos humanos en la universidad' (2011) 14–4 REIFOP; Peter Rosenblum, 'Teaching Human Rights: Ambivalent Activism, Multiple Discourses, and Lingering Dilemas' (2002) 15 Harvard Human Rights Journal 301; Deena R Hurwitz, 'Lawyering for Justice and the Inevitability of International Human Rights Clinics' (2008) 28 Yale J Int'l L 505, 525.

70 Jose García-Añón, 'Teaching and learning legal ethics and professional responsibility under the civil law' in Richard Grimes (ed), *Re-thinking legal education under the civil and common law* (Routledge 2017).

71 See n 76.

72 Wilson defines law school clinical programmes as having six components: 'First, it is created through a law school with the intent that the program be integrally linked to the academic program of the institution. Second, law students, usually in their final

Network for Legal Clinical Education (ENCLE),[73] offers an appropriate training layout[74] for law students to experientially study and work on cases related to social justice, vulnerability and disadvantaged groups. By incorporating CLE into the law curricula, students and professors are able to work, study and debate about 'substantive doctrine, skills, ethics, and values of law practice'.[75] Since 2002, CLE continued to strengthen its presence in Spain,[76] and several universities have now incorporated this teaching model.[77]

years of law school, learn experientially by providing legal services or advice to real clients who qualify for representation by the law school's clinic. Third, those students are closely supervised by an attorney admitted to practice in the relevant jurisdiction, preferably by a member of the law school faculty or a private practitioner, who shares the pedagogical objectives of the clinical experience. Fourth, the clients served by the clinical program generally are not able to afford the cost of hiring private counsel, and they usually come from traditionally disadvantaged, underserved or marginal sectors of the community. Fifth, supervised case representation by students is preceded or accompanied by a pedagogical program that prepares students in what might be called theories of the practice of law. This would include components of substantive doctrine, skills, ethics, and values of law practice, and would be taught by a professor who knows the students' cases well enough to integrate that experience into the clinic classroom. Sixth, the students would receive academic credit toward graduation, hopefully for both the case and class-work they undertake as part of their participation in a clinic.' Wilson (n 68) 423.

73 Clinical Legal Education is a legal teaching method based on experiential learning, which fosters the growth of knowledge, personal skills and values as well as promoting social justice at the same time. As a broad term, it encompasses varieties of formal, non-formal and informal educational programmes and projects, which use practical-orientated, student-centred, problem-based, interactive learning methods, including but not limited to the practical work of students on real cases and social issues supervised by academics and professionals. These educational activities aim to develop professional attitudes and foster the growth of the practical skills of students with regard to the modern understanding of the role of the socially oriented professional in promoting the rule of law, providing access to justice and peaceful conflict resolutions, and solving social problems. ENCLE <encle.org> accessed 12 May 2020.

74 On one hand, Wilson's description of the structural components that a law faculty clinical programme must have is a great resource to design and incorporate it in the law curricula. On the other hand, the definition provided by ENCLE includes the key values that CLE programs foster. Thus, the definition that emerges as the combination of both perfectly depicts what should be understood as a law faculty clinical programme.

75 Wilson (n 68) 423; cf. Susan L Brooks and Robert G Madden, 'Epistemology and Ethics in Relationship-Centered Legal Education and Practice' (2011–2012) 56 New York Law School Law Review 331.

76 The first legal clinic in Spain was at the University Rovira i Virgili of Tarragona. Diego Blázquez Martín and Jose García Añón, 'Las Clínicas jurídicas españolas en el Movimiento Clínico Global. Introducción a la traducción castellana', in F S Bloch (ed.), *El Movimiento Global de Clínicas Jurídicas. Formando juristas en la Justicia Social* (Tirant lo Blanch Valencia 2013) 11–24.

77 Diego Blázquez Martín, 'Las Clínicas jurídicas españolas en el Movimiento Clínico Global. Introducción a la traducción castellana', in Frank Bloch (ed.), *El Movimiento Global de Clínicas Jurídicas. Formando juristas en la Justicia Social* (Tirant lo Blanch 2013).

Among the different CLE models, the Legal Clinic for Social Justice of the University of Valencia[78] (LCSJUV) has implemented the human rights one as defined by Blázquez.[79] The LCSJUV is organised into five branches: live client, international human rights, penitentiary law, migration law and public interest.[80] The kind of projects we develop, altogether with international organisations such as Open Society, CESIDA,[81] CERMI,[82] among others, have always been linked with the deficiencies in the protection of human and fundamental rights. In the training students receive before starting their work at the clinic, we deconstruct the objectivism and formalism[83] students are used to when approaching legal problems elsewhere in their studies. According to my experience, a majority of first-year students arrive at the university thinking that being a lawyer is 'something more socially constructive than just doing a respectable job',[84] so the study of law will empower them to construct a society based on fundamental rights and principles like equality, human dignity and fairness. Nevertheless, they soon realise that the intellectual activity law curricula require from them is learning and uncritically memorising positive rules, without questioning how they interconnect with wider social concerns. As a result, enthusiastic and idealistic law students become passive towards their experience in the classroom and uncritical of the contents of the legal system.[85]

This being so, one of the training outcomes our CLE programme has is to reignite that commitment to social justice students had when they first began their study of law by introducing them to them Ferrajoli's theory about the essential characteristics of constitutional legal systems. In particular we explore the notion that when discussing the validity of a law, we should acknowledge the positive and negative obligations government have to fulfil the formal and substantial aspects of fundamental rights constitutions are meant to protect.[86] Moreover, another

78 Andrés Gascón-Cuenca, 'Clínica Internacional de Derechos Humanos' in Ruth Maria Mestre-i-Mestre (ed.) *Guía práctica para la enseñanza del Derecho a través de las Clínica Jurídicas* (Valencia 2018).

79 Diego Blázquez Martín, 'Clínicas de derechos humanos: causas y ventajas del éxito de un modelo de educación jurídica del siglo XXI' (2015) 11 *Revista Educación y Derecho* 1.

80 My work as clinic supervisor was linked with the international human rights area until 2018. From that moment on, I have been the codirector of the clinic and a mentor in the live client branch.

81 Federal Association of People Living with HIV: <www.cesida.org>.

82 Spanish Committee of Representatives of People with Disabilities: <www.cermi.es>.

83 Roberto Mangabeira Unger, 'The Critical Legal Studies Movement' (1983) 96 Harv L Rev 561, 567–575.

84 Duncan Kennedy, 'Legal Education and the Reproduction of Hierarchy' (1982) 32 J. Legal Educ. 591, 592.

85 Ibid. 594.

86 Jose García-Añon, 'Acceder a la justicia y hacer justiciar: la función de las universidades, las clínicas jurídicas y las ong, y su impacto construyento los límites del derecho' in Cristina García-Pascual (ed.), *Acceso a la justiciar y garantía de los derechos en tiempos de crisis* (Valencia 2018); Andrés Gascón-Cuenca, 'The Crisis of the Welfare State and the Worsening of Access to Justice: The Role of the University and of the

training goal is to develop a clinical programme focused on fostering in students a critical thinking approach, as suggested by Dewey,[87] to the legal system itself. In doing so, students realise that legal experts have to thoroughly research the causes of legal problems before being able to develop a legal solution.[88]

An example of this process is a project focused on racial discrimination of Roma children in schools.[89] The student training was centred in two areas. The first was about the study of the international and national standards of protection of human rights (especially the right to education) and how the political decisions that shape this right do not automatically agree with its complete fulfilment. Ferrajoli's theory is useful to make students understand that the way government interpret decisions, legal objectives and norms does not always support fundamental and human rights standards of protections stated in international covenants and national constitutions. The second area was focused on the deconstruction of biased thoughts students had towards the Roma community as an essential activity for them to critically identify the real cause of the legal problem; that is, as suggested by Dewey, to painstakingly research the true essence of the problem before jumping into a solution, because this 'transforms mere inference into tested inference, suggested conclusions into proof'.[90] To perform this task, students have to study and evaluate all aspects of the given situation. They have to reflect on the substantial contents of the right to education, what is indirect discrimination, why minority students are not mixed with other students from different ethnicities, why the Department of Education of the Council is allowing the situation (relations of power), among other essential questions.[91]

Clinical Legal Movement in Spain and Italy', in Cecilia Blegino and Andrés Gascón-Cuenca (eds) *Epistemic Communities at the Boundaries of Law: Clinics as a Paradigm in the Revolution of Legal Education in the European Mediterranean Context* (Turin 2019).

87 Dewey (n 15) 74.

88 When legal experts look for a legal solution to a case, it is essential to acknowledge all the circumstances that played a role in it. For instance, a case of a woman who has been justifiably dismissed might hide that the real cause for her firing had been her pregnancy. Thus, if legal experts do not conduct a conscientious research of a legal case, they might be failing in fulfilling their legal obligations towards their clients or the society.

89 *DH and others v Czech Republic* ECHR 2007. This case is regarding a systemic racial discrimination in education where Roma children were 27 times more likely to be placed in *special schools* meant to be for students who are mentally disabled. The ECHR ruled that this was a discriminatory application of the Czech education policies which resulted in substantial denial of the right to education. The report done by the LCSJUV had as a purpose to re-evaluate the conditions of Roma students after the judgment. This mentoring was done altogether with Prof. María José Añón Roig, and the report is accessible at: <cjjs.uv.es>.

90 Dewey (n 15) 74.

91 Examples like this one have been well documented by scholars. See; Jean Anyon, *Ghetto Schooling: A Political Economy of Urban Education Reform* (Teachers College Press 1997) 6–9; Iván Parra Toro; Arturo Alvarez-Roldan; Juan F Gamella, 'A Silenced Conflict: Segregation Processes, Curricular Gaps and Dropout among Spanish Gitanos or Calé' (2017) 10–1 Revista de Paz y Conflictos 35; Ana Giménez Adelantado, 'The Education of Gypsy Children within Europe' (2003) 46 New Perspectives for

From the pedagogical perspective, the multidisciplinary approach to real problems that CLE offers to law students is unique to have these debates and to achieve their holistic legal training. At the end of the project, the students realised that without this critical thinking approach to legal issues, the result of their work might end up fostering and supporting hierarchical patterns of discrimination and social control instead of being a factor for social change.[92]

As seen in this example, the learning objectives within CLE require students not only to focus their attention on the interests of potential clients, but also in the need to develop their work around the critical study of the legal system. This involves the specific investigation of the application of a certain regulation and its results, the identification of the content of some standards of protection that help in the formulation of a subsequent strategic litigation process, the collaboration in the suggestion of legislative improvements, discussions about the concept of justice, meaningful relationships between students, clients and the community, or helping in the documentation of discriminatory situations described in respect of minority groups, among others. CLE is constantly evolving, as a dynamic ecosystem[93] constituted by formal norms and customs, complicated procedures, and actors that relate to very different levels, with the objective of promoting, developing and preserving human rights. CLE pedagogy is a useful methodology to counteract the distortions introduced by the Bologna Process in the design of learning outcomes of law curricula. It raises consciousness in areas such as human rights, social justice, discrimination law, legal ethics and deontology, or the legal representation of vulnerable groups or individuals. Combining the legal ontology suggested by Ferrajoli with the legal epistemology encouraged by CLE has proved an important resource to foster alternative ways of learning and understanding positive law, introducing an alternative vision of law practice, values and legal culture.

## Some conclusions

Public universities[94] have an important role in promoting a sense of social responsibility, a defence of fundamental rights and a commitment to constitutional values and principles. This task is jeopardised by the way learning outcomes were identified

Learning 1 <http://learning.pjb.co.uk/wp-content/uploads/2016/09/BP-46-Final-OPRE-ROMA-GYPSIES-UP.pdf> accessed 13 May 2020.

92 Kennedy (n 84) 608; Jose García-Añón, 'El aprendizaje cooperativo y colaborativo en la formación de los jueces y juristas' (2011) 4 *Revista de Educación y Derecho. Education and Law Review* 8–10; Ajay Pandey and Sheena Shukkur, 'Legal Literacy Projects: Clinical Experience of Empowering the Poor in India' in F S Block (ed.) *The Global Clinical Movement. Educating Lawyers for Social Justice* (Oxford University Press 2010) 241–243; cf. Lloredo (n 19).

93 Arturo J Carrillo, 'Bringing International Law Home: The Innovative Role of Human Rights Clinics in the Transnational Legal Process' (2004) 35 Colum Hum Rts L Rev 527, 533.

94 This commitment might be embraced by private institutions as well. Nevertheless, public universities, as funded by public taxes, have an explicit compromise with society, in the defence of the democratic rule of law and the fundamental rights and

after the implementation of the Bologna Process. It opened the door to private corporations to decide which are the relevant skills for students to be trained, and contributed to the commodification of university knowledge. As a result, the study of non-market valued contents such as human and fundamental rights, philosophy, legal ethics and deontology are marginalised in the law curricula and risk being seen as irrelevant by students. This poses a great risk for the constitutional system itself, as legal experts are trained in a strongly positivistic way, which limits their abilities to adopt a critical vision of the legal system in order to contest political decisions and norms that compromise constitutional rights and values. It is the argument of this chapter that the development of a human rights legal clinic where Ferrajoli's concept of fundamental rights is taught has been a successful tool to allow students to realise the problems that exist between the protection of rights and the development of their safeguards made by lawmakers and government authorities. Law graduates have a central role in the protection and application of fundamental constitutional freedoms and civil protections which a Ferrajolian analysis shows are vulnerable to the unchecked influence of private interests on governments and policymakers. To achieve this goal, law professors have to encourage and inspire their students to embrace their public role as defenders of fundamental rights and freedoms and in doing so work to promote social justice.

# 6 Applying Rawls' theory of justice to Clinical Legal Education in the Republic of Croatia

*Omar Madhloom and Barbara Preložnjak*

## Introduction

One of Clinical Legal Education's ('CLE') primary objectives is to provide professional education in the interests of justice.[1] Law clinics are, thus, in a unique position to provide students with a vantage point from which to examine social and economic injustices in society.[2] Pro bono legal assistance allows the poorest and most vulnerable people to assert their rights in various legal matters such as marital and custody cases, employment disputes, and landlord and tenant issues.[3] Without legal aid many individuals would be unable to navigate the justice system, make informed decisions, and obtain remedies.[4] Thus, legal aid plays a key role in facilitating access to justice for individuals who lack the financial means to instruct a fee-charging lawyer. However, without an adequately funded legal aid system, law clinics in Croatia face financial challenges regarding the provision of pro bono legal services. Lack of legal aid funding also impacts on CLE because without adequate funding university law clinics will be unable to equip students with the requisite skills to practise law and provide legal aid.[5]

This chapter seeks to develop CLE beyond the traditional client-centric lawyering model, where the lawyer views their main role as achieving their client's objectives. This model leaves little room for considering wider social issues such as justice and morality. The aim of this chapter is to develop student reflection in relation to social institutions in the Republic of Croatia ('Croatia'), namely the Ministry of Justice ('MoJ'), and the distribution of primary social goods. John Rawls' principles of justice will be applied to CLE as an analytical tool to critique social institutions involved in the provision of legal aid.

1 Stephen Wizner, 'The Law School Clinic: Legal Education in the Interests of Justice' (2002) 70 Fordham Law Review 1929, 1935.
2 Ibid., 1936.
3 Barbara Preložnjak and Juraj Brozović, 'The financial challenges of clinical legal education: an example from a Zagreb law clinic' (2016) 23(4) International Journal of Clinical Legal Education 136.
4 United Nations Office on Drug and Crime, *Global Study on Legal Aid Global* (United Nations 2016), 8.
5 Preložnjak and Brozović (n3) 136.

DOI: 10.4324/9780429299247-7

This chapter is divided into six parts. Part one covers the limitations of legal education in Croatia and importance of funding of university law clinics. This is followed by a discussion on the value of social justice education in CLE. Part three outlines the key elements of Rawls' theory of justice that will be applied to CLE in Croatia. Part four deals with the regulation and funding of university clinics in order to examine their contribution in relation to access to justice. Part five applies Rawls' theory to CLE. The final part outlines some of the limitations of Rawls' theory of justice.

## Clinical Legal Education

Although CLE lacks a universally accepted definition, it has been defined by the European Network of Clinical Legal Education as:

> [A] legal teaching method based on experiential learning, which fosters the growth of knowledge, personal skills and values as well as promoting social justice at the same time. As a broad term, it encompasses varieties of formal, non-formal and informal educational programs and projects, which use practical-oriented, student-centered, problem-based, interactive learning methods, including, but not limited to, the practical work of students on real cases and social issues supervised by academics and professionals. These educational activities aim to develop professional attitudes and foster the growth of the practical skills of students with regard to the modern understanding of the role of the socially oriented professional in promoting the rule of law, providing access to justice and peaceful conflict resolutions, and solving social problems.[6]

In addition to teaching practical skills such as interviewing and drafting legal documents, CLE also promotes social justice. Developing a sense of social justice allows students to identify and challenge injustice and pursue social justice in society. Through CLE, students are made aware of the fact that for some of their clients the law clinic is the only means of access to the justice system. This realisation has the potential to make the student more aware of their responsibility to their client. This heightened sense of responsibility can develop into a feeling of social responsibility for the provision of legal services for socially and financially vulnerable clients.[7] Legal assistance provided through university law clinics not only empowers individuals and communities but also promotes the protection of human rights. Therefore, CLE is a suitable vehicle for promoting social justice values.

As a teaching method, CLE can be contrasted with the dominant doctrinal approach in legal education in Central and Eastern Europe ('CEE'). Legal

6 European Network of Clinical Legal Education, 'Definition of a legal clinic' <http://encle.org/about-encle/definition-of-a-legal-clinic> accessed 06 February 2021.

7 Wizner (n1) 1935.

education in CCE, which includes Croatia, is criticised for its inefficiency and outdated models of teaching which are focused on memorisation rather than on critical analysis.[8] As a result, Croatian law schools promote the illusion that law is value-free and detached from legal order. However, law is more than simply stating the rules of just conduct. Law is also the means of pursuing government policies and for allocating materials to different groups, usually at the expense of other groups.[9] Excluding any necessary reference to values, such as justice and morality, risks limiting the scope of legal analysis to a purely positivist approach. The question, therefore, is how to develop CLE so that students are able to reflect on social justice during their clinical experience. The clinic addresses this question by incorporating Rawls' theory of justice. This methodology allows students to reflect on the distribution of legal aid funds and the extent to which the Free Legal Aid Act 2013 ('FLAA 2013') allows clinics to facilitate access to justice. According to Preložnjak:

> By providing general legal information, legal advice and by assisting in the preparation of documents in various types of procedures for individuals with low income, students for the first time during their studies take responsibility for the resolution of actual cases.[10]

Despite the numerous advantages of CLE, such as the acquisition of lawyering skills and applying theory to real-life cases, a major challenge faced by law clinics in Croatia is that of sustainability, namely funding and resources. The debate over the costs of experiential education is not new nor is it exclusive to Croatia. Swords and Walwer note that:

> Money issues, circa 1980, dominate the American scene. Legal education is no exception, and within legal education any discussion regarding the pros and cons of clinical programs is apt to precipitate anxious concern about relative costs and financing.[11]

Croatia faces a similar 'anxious concern' due to the fact that primary legal aid has been underfunded since 2010.[12] The main financial source for the clinic is the law school.[13]

8 Antal Szerletics and Lidia Rodak, 'Introduction: Legal Education in Central and Eastern Europe. Challenges and Prospects' (2017) 7(8) Oñati Socio-legal Series 1581, 1585 <http://ssrn.com/abstract=3087206> accessed 06 February 2021.
9 Suri Ratnapala, *Jurisprudence* (CUP 2017), 390.
10 Barbara Preložnjak, 'Clinical legal education in Croatia – from providing legal assistance to the poor to practical education of students' (2013) 19 International Journal of Clinical Legal Education 373, 376.
11 Peter de Lancy Swords and Frank K Walwer, *Cost Aspects of Clinical Education, in Clinical Legal Education: Report of the Association of American Law Schools – American Bar Association Committee on Guidelines for Clinical Legal Education* (1980)133, 133.
12 Preložnjak and Brozović (n3) 157.
13 The law school's financial assistance includes office space, postage utilities, and student administrators.

Other costs[14] are funded from the state budget, namely the MoJ and the local community budget (City of Zagreb Grant). Law clinics are permitted to request compensation from the state budget due to their status as providers of legal aid.[15] However, the annual value of budgetary funds allocated for legal aid providers has been constantly decreasing.[16] Consequently, financial challenges directly impact on the quality of work the clinic is able to offer.[17] Resources are essential not only for the establishment of a clinic but also for its sustainability and the number of clients is can assist. The clinic has received positive feedback from both students and clients and yet it faces several financial challenges to its future development, as a provider of legal aid. This 'dysfunctional financing' system of legal aid has led to the inability to finance 70 per cent of the clinic's projects.[18] The issue of the lack of funding and its impact on providing legal aid will be explored through the lens of Rawls' theory of social justice.

## Social justice and CLE

An assumption exists in CLE that exposing students to social problems leads to them learning about social justice.[19] Simply engaging with clients with social and legal issues does not necessarily facilitate a critical understanding of the cause of these issues or their impact on clients' lives.[20] It is imperative that students are provided with a framework that promotes consideration of social justice issues such access to justice, legal aid funding, and the extent to which the regulatory framework promotes access to justice.

Although social justice is a contested term, it is typically taken to denote distributive justice. According to David Miller:

> When we talk and argue about social justice … we are discussing how the good and bad things in life should be distributed among the members of a human society. When … we attack some policy or some state of affairs as socially unjust, we are claiming that a person, or more usually a category of persons, enjoys fewer advantages than the person or group of persons ought to enjoy (or bears more of

14 These costs include the costs for equipment, promotional materials, field activities, and external outreach projects.

15 Article 36, paragraph 1, of the Croatian Legal Aid Act (Official Gazette 143/13; CLAA).

16 Preložnjak and Brozović (n3) 152; European judicial systems Efficiency and quality of justice CEPEJ Studies No. 26 2018 Edition (2016 data), 71 <https://www.coe.int/web/cepej/special-file-publication-2018-edition-of-the-cepej-report-european-judicial-systems-efficiency-and-quality-of-justice-> accessed 06 February 2021.

17 Preložnjak and Brozović (n3) 152.

18 Ibid. 158.

19 Lucy Yeatman, 'Law in the Community and Access to Justice: Linking Theory and Practice' in Chris Ashford and Paul McKeown (eds), *Social Justice and Legal Education* (Scholars Publisher 2018), 133.

20 Ibid.

> the burdens than they ought to bear), given how other members of the society in question are faring.[21]

Similarly, Rawls equates social justice with distributive justice.[22] In his seminal work, *A Theory of Justice*, [23] Rawls refers on several occasions to the 'principles of social justice' when articulating his two 'principles of justice'.[24] The value of incorporating Rawls' theory of justice into CLE is that he considers 'justice' to be a set of principles that 'provide a way of assigning rights and duties in the basic institutions of society and they define the appropriate distribution of the benefits and burdens of social co-operation'.[25] Justice is placed above all other virtues; the 'right' comes before the 'good'.[26] Incorporating considerations of social justice issues allows students to adopt a political dimension[27] into their reflective practice that goes beyond individual justice; justice between wrongdoer and claimant is only a partial form of justice.[28]

## Rawls' theory of justice

Rawls is considered one of the most important political theorists of the latter half of the twentieth century. The significance of Rawls' theory of justice is best highlighted by Robert Nozick, one of Rawls' critics: 'Political philosophers now must either work within Rawls' theory or explain why not'.[29] After the publication of *A Theory of Justice*, utilitarianism, which holds that morality is based on striving to increase the aggregate level of happiness, could no longer be taken for granted.[30] Rawls' theory of justice falls within the social contract tradition. His two principles of justice[31] and his conception of distributive fairness are rooted in fairness to all citizens of the United States:

> My aim is to present a conception of justice which generalises and carries to a higher level of abstraction the familiar theory of the social contract … In order to do this we are not to think of the original contract as one to enter a particular society or to set up a particular form of government. Rather, the guiding idea is that the principles of justice for the basic structure of society

21 David Miller, *The Principles of Social Justice* (HUP1999), 1.
22 John Rawls, *A Theory of Justice* (OUP1971).
23 Ibid.
24 Ibid. 54.
25 Ibid. 4.
26 John Rawls, 'The Priority of Right and Ideas of the Good' (1988) 17(4) Philosophy & Public Affairs 251.
27 Peter Joy, 'Political Interference in Clinical Programs: Lessons from the U.S Experience' (2005) 8 International Journal of Clinical Legal Education 82.
28 A M Honore, 'Social Justice' (1962) 8(2) McGill Law Journal 77, 77.
29 Robert Nozick, *Anarchy, State, and Utopia* (Basic Books 1974), 183.
30 Jon Mandle, *Rawls's A Theory of Justice: An Introduction* (CUP 2009), 3.
31 Rawls' principles of justice will be discussed in detail under the sub-heading 'The two principles of justice'.

> are the object of the original agreement. They are the principles that free and rational persons concerned to further their own interests would accept in an initial position of equality as defining the fundamental terms of their association. These principles are to regulate all further agreements; they specify the kinds of social cooperation that can be entered into and the forms of government that can be established. This way of regarding the principles of justice I shall call justice as fairness.[32]

The above passage, namely 'justice as fairness', captures the spirit of Rawls' theory of justice. For Rawls, justice regulates the distribution of goods throughout society. He considers justice to be 'the first virtue of social institutions, as truth is of systems of thought'.[33] Therefore, the realisation of justice must take priority over any other moral values a society seeks to achieve.[34] This suggests that while there may be other virtues of social institutions, they may not be realised at the expense of justice.[35]

The focus on social institutions, such as the MoJ and universities,[36] adds an additional dimension to CLE that goes beyond the lawyer–client model, which considers the main role of the lawyer is to zealously pursue their client's goals.[37] Thus, zealous advocacy, which focuses on achieving the desired aims of the client, falls under consequentialism. Utilitarianism is the most influential of the consequentialist theories.

Rawls' theory provides CLE students with a theoretical framework to reflect on the distribution of goods and the effect social institutions have on clients' lives. Distributive justice, or social justice, focuses attention on sharing of benefits and burdens.[38] It is important to note, however, that Rawls' theory is not a theory of distributive justice based on needs and wants of individuals or groups:

> [T]he principles of justice do not select specific distributions of desired things as just, given the wants of particular persons. This task is abandoned as mistaken in principle, and it is in any case, not capable of a determinate answer.[39]

32 John Rawls *A Theory of Justice* (22) 11. Emphasis added.
33 Ibid. 3.
34 Tom Campbell, *Justice* (Macmillan Education Ltd 1988), 7.
35 Mandle (n30) 35.
36 University law clinics in Croatia are not separate legal entities. They operate as part of their respective university.
37 See Charles Fried, 'The Lawyer as Friend: The Moral Foundations of the Lawyer-Client Relation' (1976) 85(8) The Yale Law Journal 1060; David Luban, *The Ethics of Lawyering* (Dartmouth 1994); Michael I Krauss, 'The Lawyer as Limo: A Brief History of the Hired Gun' (2001) 8(2) The University of Chicago Law School Roundtable 325; Douglas O Linder and Nancy Levit, *The Good Lawyer: Seeking Quality in the Practice of Law* (OUP 2014), 188.
38 Ratnapala (n9) 407.
39 John Rawls, 'Constitutional liberty and the concept of justice' in Carl J Friedrich and John W Chapman (eds), *Nomos VI Justice* (Atherton Press 1963), 102.

His theory of justice allows students to analyse 'the basic structure of society, or more exactly, the way in which the major social institutions distribute fundamental rights and duties and determine the division of advantages from social cooperation'.[40] The basic structure includes 'the political constitution, the legally recognized forms of property, and the organization of the economy, and the nature of the family'.[41] The basic structure, which is the 'primary subject of justice',[42] is concerned with inequalities in people's life chances and not on the ultimate outcomes. In other words, by arguing for the basic structure as the appropriate subject for a theory of social justice, Rawls is focusing on the inequalities that affect people's chances in life.[43] He writes about people 'born into different positions' and that major social institutions 'favour certain starting places over others'.[44] According to Rawls, 'deep inequalities' are not only pervasive but also impact on people's 'initial chances in life'.[45] By focusing on the basic social structure, CLE students are encouraged to identify the inadequacies of the notions of justice and desert, and reflect on the inequalities, which impact on a client's life chances, caused by social institutions.

Rawls' assertion that laws and institutions must be reformed or abolished, if they are unjust, is predicated on the assumption that individuals possess 'an inviolability on justice that even the welfare of society as a whole cannot override'.[46] This criticism of utilitarianism suggests that the overall utility, which social institutions seek to achieve, must not disregard a commitment to justice to the individual. Rawls rejects utilitarianism because 'it does not take seriously the distinction between persons'.[47] Utilitarianism fails to consider the distinction between persons who are autonomous individuals.[48] Unlike utilitarianism which is concerned with maximising average utility, Rawls writes, 'the principles of justice manifest in the basic structure of society men's desire to treat one another not as means but only as ends in themselves'.[49] Rawls' aim was to offer an alternative view to classical utilitarianism, which, in his opinion, dominated discussions of social institutions and policies to such an extent that serious considerations of alternative approaches were excluded.[50] In relation to CLE, students should be provided with a framework that would not only allow them to reflect on the distribution of wealth and assets but also social goods such as self-respect and

40 Rawls *A Theory of Justice* (n22) 7.
41 Ibid.
42 John Rawls, *Political Liberalism* (Columbia University Press 1993), 258.
43 Rawls *A Theory of Justice* (n22) 7.
44 Ibid.
45 Ibid.
46 Rawls, *A Theory of Justice* (n22) 3.
47 Ibid. 27.
48 Klaus Mathis and Deborah Shannon, 'John Rawls's Theory of Justice' in Klaus Mathis and Deborah Shannon (eds), *Efficiency Instead of Justice? Searching for the Philosophical Foundations of the Economic Analysis of Law* (Springer 2009), 123.
49 Rawls, *A Theory of Justice* (n22) 179.
50 Ibid. 22.

freedom of movement. To achieve this aim, the key elements of Rawls' theory of justice will be outlined.

### *The 'original position' and the 'veil of ignorance'*

For Rawls, the principles of justice are those which provide a way of assigning rights and duties in the basic institutions of society and determine the appropriate distribution of the benefits and burdens of social cooperation.[51] The difficulty lies in formulating the principles of justice which should be adopted in society. A measure of agreement in relation to conceptions of justice is necessary for 'a viable human community'.[52] To arrive at these principles of justice, Rawls draws on social contract theories of John Locke, Immanuel Kant, and Jean-Jacques Rousseau.[53] These theorists were working from the starting point that a government can legitimately govern its citizens, provided those citizens granted the government powers.[54] Unlike previous social contract theorists, Rawls is not concerned with how to legitimise power but with shaping political institutions in accordance with principle of justice.[55]

Rawls distinguishes between people's conceptions about justice and their subjective, self-interested views.[56] What he is seeking to achieve through his social contract theory are mutually agreeable principles of justice.[57] He asks us to imagine a hypothetical 'original position' to determine the principles of justice.[58] The original position is used as a method of representation to establish how best to 'realize the values of liberty and equality'.[59] Rational and mutually disinterested[60] people in the 'original position' debate the principles of justice behind a 'veil of ignorance'.[61] The 'veil of ignorance' creates a forum whereby the deliberators are prevented from knowing certain facts about themselves such as:

1 Their place in society
2 Social status
3 Fortune in the distribution of natural assets and abilities
4 Intelligence and strength
5 Gender[62]

51 Ibid. 4.
52 Ibid. 6.
53 Ibid. 11.
54 Brian H Bix, *Jurisprudence: Theory and Context* (17th edn, Sweet & Maxwell 2015), 96.
55 Mathis and Shannon (n48) 121.
56 Raymond Wacks, *Understanding Jurisprudence: An Introduction to Legal Theory* (5th edn, OUP 2017), 269.
57 Michael Freeman, *Lloyd's Introduction to Jurisprudence* (9th edn, Sweet & Maxwell 2014), 483.
58 Rawls *A Theory of Justice* (n22) 12.
59 Rawls *Political Liberalism* (n42) 5.
60 Rawls *A Theory of Justice* (n22) 17–22.
61 Ibid. 136.
62 Wacks (n56) 269.

6 Religion,[63] and
7 In what time or place they were living.[64]

The aim is for the deliberators to avoid the worst conditions they might find themselves in when the veil of ignorance is lifted, and instead choose Rawls' principles of justice. Therefore, they are motivated by rational self-interest to select principles that will allow them the best chance to realise their conception of the good life. By removing the individuality of the deliberators in the original position they will choose a 'maximin' principle. The reasoning behind this term is 'maximum minimorum' or the maximisation of the minimum position.[65] As rational agents, the deliberators in the original position would choose principles that would guarantee that the worst condition they might find themselves in, when the veil is removed, is the least desirable of the available options. Such deliberation will lead to Rawls' principles of justice. When the principles of justice are determined, social institutions will be formed to distribute social primary goods in accordance with these principles.[66] The next step is to examine the meaning of 'primary goods'.

### *Primary goods*

Rawls distinguishes between two types of 'primary goods': social primary goods and natural primary goods. The former is part of his general conception of justice:

> All social primary goods – liberty and opportunity, income and wealth, and the basis of self-respect – are to be distributed equally unless an unequal distribution of any or all of these good is to the advantage of the least favoured.[67]

Injustice, therefore, equates to any inequalities which are not beneficial to all.[68] Natural primary goods, on the other hand, include health, intelligence, and imagination.[69] Although the acquisition of natural primary goods is influenced by the basic structure, they do not directly fall under its control because natural primary goods are due to the natural lottery rather than the distribution by social institutions. Aspirations for certain goals do not give individuals a claim on social

63 Ibid.
64 Freeman (n57) 483.
65 Rawls, *A Theory of Justice* (n22) 154.
66 Perihan Elif Ekmeci and Bena Arda, 'Enhancing John Rawls's Theory of Justice to Cover Health and Social Determinants of Health' (2015) 21(2) Acta Bioethica 227, 228.
67 Rawls *A Theory of Justice* (n22) 303.
68 Ibid. 62.
69 Ibid.

resources.[70] Thus, for example, an individual's preference for luxury cars does not entitle them to claim additional primary goods to realise their ambition.

### *The two principles of justice*

In the original position and behind the veil of ignorance, the deliberators decide upon the two principles of justice:

> First principle
> Each person is to have an equal right to the most extensive total system of the equal basic liberties compatible with a similar system of liberty for all.
> Second principle
> Social and economic inequalities are to be arranged so that they are both:
> to the greatest benefit of the least advantaged, consistent with the just savings principle; and
> attached to offices and positions open to all under conditions of fair equality of opportunity.[71]

Rawls refers to his first principle as the Principle of Equal Liberty and to his second as the Difference Principle. The first of these principles is to be applied in 'lexical'[72] priority over the second, and the first part of the second principle has lexical priority over its second part. In other words, the deliberators in the original position place liberty above equality because they would not wish to risk their liberty when the veil is 'lifted' and it is revealed that they are among the worst off in society.[73] For the same reasons, the deliberators would choose the first part of the second principle.

According to the Principle of Equal Liberty, basic liberties can be constrained for the sake of liberty in two cases:[74]

1 A less extensive liberty strengthens the overall system of liberties shared by all;
2 A less extensive system of equal liberty is accepted by those with reduced liberty.

Basic liberties are:

1 Political liberty (the right to vote and to hold public office);
2 Freedom of speech and assembly;

70 John Rawls, 'Social unity and primary goods' in Amartya Sen and Bernard Williams (eds), *Utilitarianism and Beyond* (CUP 1982), 171.
71 Rawls, *A Theory of Justice* (n22) 302. Emphasis in the original.
72 Short for 'lexicographical ordering'. A system that completely satisfies a first principle before applying a second principle.
73 Wacks (n56) 271.
74 Rawls, *A Theory of Justice* (n22) 302.

3 Liberty of conscience and freedom of thought;
4 Personal liberty, which includes freedom from psychological oppression and physical assault and dismemberment;
5 The right to personal property; and
6 Freedom from arbitrary arrest and imprisonment.[75]

These liberties are equal to all because individuals in a just society ought to have the same basic rights.[76] The Difference Principle, on the other hand, is concerned with distribution of income and assets and the arrangement of institutions in which differences in power and responsibility take place. Inequalities are permissible provided they improve the circumstances of the least advantaged in society. As far as funding of clinics is concerned, Rawls would argue that we should distribute our benefits and burdens in accordance with the Difference Principle. In relation to the allocation of resources for education the following passage in *A Theory of Justice* illustrates the significance of the Difference Principle to education:

> Now the difference principle is not of course the principle of redress. It does not require society to try to even out handicaps as if all were expected to compete on a fair basis in the same race. But the difference principle would allocate resources in education, say, so as to improve the long-term expectations of the least favored.[77]

Rawls argues that 'resources for education are not to be allotted solely or necessarily mainly according to their return as estimated in productive trained abilities, but also according to their worth in enriching the personal and social life of citizens, including here the less favoured'.[78] Although this passage relates to the distribution of educational resources for the benefit of students, it is equally applicable to CLE for two reasons. Firstly, CLE is not simply a teaching method; it facilitates access to justice for clients who lack the financial means to instruct a lawyer. Resources are, therefore, essential to ensure that clinics can continue to represent clients. Secondly, the Principle of Equal Liberty is applicable to both students and clients. It requires that students receive an education that allows them to pursue their own conception of the good. This can be realised through CLE through the acquisition of legal skills gained through the provision of legal aid services to the local community.[79] In relation to clients, the Principle of Equal Liberty offers an opportunity for individuals to access the justice system and the protection of liberties. To apply Rawls' principles of justice to the basic structure of Croatian society, namely the MoJ and the funding of university law clinics, the next section will outline the regulation and funding of university law clinics.

75 Ibid. 61.
76 Ibid.
77 Ibid. 101.
78 Ibid. 107.
79 Preložnjak and Brozović (n3) 139.

## The regulation of law clinics in Croatia

University legal clinics in Croatia are primarily regulated by the Act on Scientific Activity and Higher Education[80] and the FLAA 2013.[81] The former provides the framework for the implementation of the Bologna Process[82] and modernisation of the organisational scheme in science and higher education. The latter regulates the type of activities, universities law clinics are permitted to carry out, namely 'secondary legal aid', and provides for university law clinics to apply for public funds from the MoJ.

The first FLAA came into force in 2008.[83] The enactment of the FLAA 2008 and the legal standardisation of clinics,[84] facilitated the establishment of clinics at the University of Split and the University of Zagreb.[85] Despite reforming access to justice, the shortcomings of the FLAA 2008 came to light after its implementation.[86] The limitations related to issues concerning practicality and functionality.[87] As a result, it was modified on two separate occasions. The first took place in 2011 by the Constitutional Court, which annulled several of the provisions of the FLAA 2008. The second revision was the result of the enactment of the FLAA 2013.[88] The European Commission against racism and Intolerance ('ECCRI'), in 2015, recognised that one of the most significant improvements in the FLAA 2013 was in relation to widening access to 'primary legal aid'.[89] Reforms to primary legal aid included lowering the means test, and simplifying the overall procedure for obtaining legal aid.[90] However, the criticisms aimed at FLAA 2008 are also applicable to the FLAA 2013, namely in relation to the funding of legal aid. Without continuous and increased financial support to those institutions providing free legal aid, such as law clinics, the scheme would not function adequately.[91] According to the Report on the European Commission for

80 Official Gazette 123/03, 198/03, 105/04, 174/04, 02/07, 46/07, 45/09, 63/11.

81 Official Gazette 143/2013 and came into force on 1 January 2014.

82 Under the Bologna Process, European governments engage in discussions regarding higher education policy reforms and strive to overcome obstacles to create a European Higher Education Area. For further details see <https://ec.europa.eu/education/policies/higher-education/bologna-process-and-european-higher-education-area_en> accessed 06 February 2021.

83 FLAA (Official Gazette no. 62/2008).

84 'Higher education institutions that conduct university studies in the scientific field of law may, through legal clinics, and in accordance with its regulations, can provide primary legal aid'. See čl. 14. ZBPP'08.

85 Preložnjak (n10) 374.

86 Zvonimir Jelinic, 'Legal Clinics and Access to Justice in Croatia: Perspectives and Challenges' (2017) 5(1) Asian Journal of Legal Education 99–108, 101.

87 Ibid.

88 (Official Gazette no. 143/2013). The FLAA 2013 came into force on 1 January 2014.

89 ECRI Conclusions on the Implementation of the Recommendations in respect of Croatia Subject to Interim Follow-up adopted on 18 March 2015 6 (CRI/2015/22).

90 ECRI Conclusions on the Implementation of the Recommendations in respect of Croatia Subject to Interim Follow-up adopted on 18 March 2015 6 (CRI/2015/22).

91 ECRI Conclusions on the Implementation of the Recommendations in respect of Croatia Subject to Interim Follow-up adopted on 18 March 2015 6 (CRI/2015/22).

the Efficiency of Justice ('the Report'), funds spent per capita on legal aid in Croatia were far below that of other European countries.[92] The Report also raises concerns regarding the decrease in approved public funding applications in relation to legal aid.[93]

Lack of legal aid funding impacts on the ability of clients to exercise their life choices and to protect their rights. Under European Union and Council of Europe, member states, such as Croatia, are required to take steps to ensure equal access to legal proceedings. This can be facilitated through appropriate legal aid systems.[94] The right to legal aid ensures effective access to justice for individuals who have insufficient financial means to cover the cost of court fees or costs of legal representation.[95] Thus, legal aid is more than simply the financial ability to access the justice system. Legal aid allows clients to protect themselves against infringement of their rights, to hold executive and judicial powers accountable, and to defend themselves in civil and criminal proceedings. Without legal aid, injustice may be left un-remedied.[96] Therefore, legal aid funding is crucial to supporting clients who lack the means to afford a lawyer. However, member states, such as Croatia, are free to decide how to meet their legal aid obligations.[97] This means that there is no obligation on the Croatian government to provide legal aid in all proceedings.[98] Croatia is permitted to establish selection procedures to determine whether legal aid will be granted in civil cases, on the condition that the selection procedure must not be carried out arbitrarily.[99] This selection procedure, however, might prohibit certain clients from accessing the justice system.

92 European Commission for the Efficiency of Justice, European Judicial Systems: Efficiency and Quality of Justice 66–80 (CEPEJ Studies no. 23, Edition 2016, 2014 data). The report is available at <http://www.coe.int/t/dghl/cooperation/cepej/evaluation/2016/publication/CEPEJ%20Study%2023%20report%20EN%20web.pdf> accessed 06 February 2021.

93 European Commission for the Efficiency of Justice, European Judicial Systems: Efficiency and Quality of Justice 66–80 (CEPEJ Studies no. 23, Edition 2016, 2014 data). The report is available at <http://www.coe.int/t/dghl/cooperation/cepej/evaluation/2016/publication/CEPEJ%20Study%2023%20report%20EN%20web.pdf> 78 also see Eurostat, Europe 2020 Indicators: Poverty and Social Exclusion (data from March 2016) <http://ec.europa.eu/eurostat/statistics-explained/index.php/Europe_2020_indicators_-_poverty_and_social_exclusion> accessed 06 February 2021.

94 Council of Europe, Committee of Ministers *Resolution 78(8) on legal aid and advice* (1978) 2 March 1978.

95 European Union Agency for Fundamental Rights and Council of Europe, *Handbook on European law relating to access to justice* (Publications Office of the European Union 2016), 58.

96 Jonathan Herring, *Legal Ethics* (2nd edn, OUP 2016), 233.

97 European Union Agency for Fundamental Rights and Council of Europe, *Handbook on European law relating to access to justice* (Publications Office of the European Union 2016), 58.

98 ECtHR, *A v the United Kingdom*, No. 35373/97, 17 December 2002 [97].

99 European Union Agency for Fundamental Rights and Council of Europe, *Handbook on European law relating to access to justice* (Publications Office of the European Union 2016), 60.

### *The Free Legal Aid Act 2013*

The status of clinics as providers of legal assistance is recognised by the FLAA 2013 which defines a clinic as 'an organizational unit of a higher education institution conducting university studies in the scientific field of law which, in accordance with its general acts, provides primary legal assistance'.[100] Although clinics in Croatia do not possess separate legal personalities, they do operate within law schools as separate units whose primary function is to provide clients with 'primary legal aid'.[101] As of 2017, three out of a total of four law schools offer legal assistance to clients from low socio-economic backgrounds: Zagreb, Split, and Osijek.[102] In these clinics, students provide clients with general legal information, legal advice, and prepare written legal opinions. Students are not permitted to directly represent clients in court proceedings; however, they are permitted to attend court and assist persons who are authorised to represent clients in court.[103]

A key feature of the FLAA 2013 is the availability of public funds to law clinics.[104] The FLAA 2013 provides that '[f]unds for organizing and providing legal assistance shall be provided in the state budget ... and from the funds of bodies of local and regional self-government units, as donations and other revenues in accordance with the law'.[105] Croatian law schools, as public institutions of higher education, receive funding from the state budget. However, the amount of funds allocated for the provision of legal aid appears to decrease every year.[106] This is problematic in terms of individuals being able to protect their rights and pursuing their life choices.

FLAA 2013 consolidates various provisions relating to the form and scope of the provision of legal aid.[107] The purpose of legal assistance is 'the effective realization of legal protection and access to court and other public bodies under equal consideration'.[108] The FLAA regulates, inter alia, the types and scope of free legal aid ('legal aid'), beneficiaries of legal aid, procedure and conditions for obtaining legal aid, and legal aid providers.[109] Article 4 paragraph 5 defines a 'legal aid provider' to be 'an office, a licensed association, a higher education institution and a lawyer who provide[s] legal assistance in accordance with this Law'. The FLAA 2013 distinguishes between two types of legal aid: primary and secondary.[110] The latter includes:

100 Article 4, para 8, FLAA 2013.
101 Jelinic (n86) 105.
102 Ibid. 106.
103 Art 16 Para 2 of the Ordinance of study. See: <https://www.pravo.unizg.hr/oldwww2018/fakultet/propisi/pravilnik_o_studiju>.
104 Article 36, para 1, FLAA 2013.
105 Articles 35, FLAA 2013.
106 Ministry of Justice Free Legal Aid: <https://pravosudje.gov.hr/besplatna-pravna-pomoc/6184> accessed 26 January 2021.
107 Jelinic (n86) 103.
108 Article 3, FLAA 2013.
109 Article 1, FLAA 2013.
110 Article 8, FLA 2013.

a general legal information
b legal advice
c filing submissions before public authorities, the European Court of Human Rights and international organizations in accordance with international treaties and rules of procedure for those bodies
d representation in proceedings before public bodies
e legal assistance in out-of-court amicable settlement of the dispute.[111]

Primary legal aid can be provided in any legal matter:

a if the applicant himself does not have sufficient knowledge and ability to exercise his right
b if the applicant is not provided with legal aid under specific rules
c if the application is not manifestly ill-founded and
d if the applicant's material circumstances are such that the payment of professional legal assistance could jeopardize the dependency of the applicant and the household members.[112]

Secondary legal aid, on the other hand, focuses on representation in judicial proceedings and includes the following:

a legal advice
b making submissions in the process of protecting the rights of workers before the employer
c making submissions in court proceedings
d representation in court proceedings
e legal assistance in the amicable settlement of the dispute.

Secondary legal assistance also includes:

a exemption from court costs
b exemption from court fees.[113]

The distinction between the two forms of legal aid places a restriction on the level of assistance clinics are permitted to offer. It is difficult to justify this distinction particularly in circumstances where CLE students are supervised by lawyers.

## Applying Rawls' theory of justice to CLE

CLE can be enhanced by incorporating analysis of the issues surrounding the funding of legal aid and law clinics. The application of Rawls' theory of justice to social institutions, such as the MoJ and universities, involves the following steps:

111 Article 9, FLAA 2013.
112 Article 10, FLAA 2013.
113 Article 12, FLAA 2013.

1 Reflecting on whether legal aid should be a primary social good;
2 In the 'original position' and behind the 'veil of ignorance' students consider the principles of justice; and
3 Critique the FLAA using the principles of justice.

### *Legal aid as a primary social good*

Rawls did not include access to legal aid as a social primary good and, thus, a subject of fair distribution. However, there are three reasons for including legal aid as a primary social good. Firstly, in relation to Rawls' theory of justice, legal aid provides an opportunity for individuals to access the justice system to protect their primary goods and facilitates the realisation of the fundamental rights and freedoms listed in the Principle of Equal Liberty. Secondly, including legal aid protects clients who are unable to afford legal representation from the negative consequences of natural lottery and the vicissitudes of life. Thirdly, the Difference Principle commands that goods are distributed for the benefit of the less fortunate members of society. Therefore, resources ought to be allocated to ensure that university clinics are able to provide legal assistance to clients with limited financial means.

### *The original position and the veil of ignorance*

The next step in relation to applying Rawls' theory to CLE is for students to imagine themselves in the 'original position' behind the 'veil of ignorance'. The latter serves as an analytical tool to reflect on the role of social institutions such as the MoJ. The Difference Principle provides that any inequalities which emerge, in terms of legal aid funding, should only be tolerated in so far as they benefit the least advantaged.[114] Thus, Rawls' theory promotes an egalitarian approach to CLE and prioritises the well-being of those clients who are worse off in terms of their financial ability to access justice.

### *Rawls' theory of justice and the FLAA 2013*

The final stage involves students reflecting on the adequacy of the FLAA 2013 in terms of the scope of statutory legal assistance clinics are permitted to offer. This raises the question of whether clinics should be allowed to offer secondary legal aid to their clients. Individuals who do not have the financial means to engage a fee-paid lawyer are limited in their options in terms of accessing the justice system. The scope of primary legal aid restricts the level of assistance clinics are able to provide to their clients. A further issue is that the means-based eligibility criteria may cause difficulties for clients who do not pass the eligibility test under the FLAA 2013, but at the same time these clients may not have the financial means to meet the anticipated costs of resolving their legal

114 Campbell (n34) 87.

issue(s).[115] As a result, individuals may not be able to protect their primary social goods or realise their life choices. The problems caused by distinguishing between primary and secondary legal aid are further compounded by the reduction of state funds available to clinics. It is, therefore, not difficult to conclude that the FLAA 2013 fails to promote access to justice.

## Limitations of Rawls' theory of justice

While Rawls' theory of justice, as formulated in the book of that name, continues to have significant impact, it has attracted a number of criticisms.[116] Firstly, Michael Sandel argues that Rawls' account of the original position and its descriptive premises suffer from ambiguity.[117] For example, it is not clear why those who are not in the 'original position' should accept and adopt principles chosen by those who were.[118] Rawls' assertion that the conditions and constraints of the 'original position' provide a model of procedural fairness, which renders it acceptable by everyone, does not provide an adequate justification. The 'original position' also fails to address the issue of bias in relation to the fair selection of the principles. Milton Fisk states that it is impossible to separate individuals from their material circumstances:

> The thoughts one takes an interest in defending are one's own rarely in more than the sense that one is willing to defend them … They are … inculcated by institutions. And these institutions are strengthened by people defending these very thoughts.[119]

Similarly, GA Cohen criticises Rawls' reliance on the 'original position' on the grounds that it renders the principles of justice dependent on non-moral factors which are themselves misguided.[120]

Secondly, Rawls' Difference Principle is insufficiently egalitarian. For Marxists such as Cohen, equality has a prominent place in their conception of social justice and, therefore, the income and wealth enjoyed by members of a society should be equal. Socialist egalitarians, on the other hand, do not believe in strict equality

115 Jelinic (n86) 104.
116 Brian Barry, *The Liberal Theory of Justice: A Critical Examination of the Principal Doctrines in A Theory of Justice by John Rawls* (OUP1973); Thomas W Pogge, *Realizing Rawls* (Cornell University Press 1989); Amartya Sen, 'Human Rights and Capabilities' (2005) 6 (2) Journal of Human Development 151; Nussbaum, Martha, *Frontiers of Justice: Disability, Nationality, Species Membership* (Belknap Press 2006).
117 Michael Sandel, *Liberalism and the Limits of Justice* (Cambridge University Press 1982), 24–46.
118 Thomas Nagel, 'Rawls on Justice' in Norman Daniels (ed.), *Reading Rawls: Critical Studies on Rawls' 'Theory of Justice'* (SUP 1975), 1; Ronald Dworkin, 'The Original Position' in Norman Daniels (ed.), *Reading Rawls: Critical Studies on Rawls' 'Theory of Justice'* (SUP 1975), 16.
119 Milton Fisk, 'History and Reason in Rawls' Moral Theory' in Norman Daniels (ed.), *Reading Rawls: Critical Studies on Rawls' 'Theory of Justice'* (SUP 1975), 53.
120 G A Cohen, *Rescuing Justice and Equality* (2008).

but follow Rawls' Difference Principle, which states that social and economic inequalities are 'the greatest benefit of the least advantaged'. For Rawls, the Difference Principle is 'an agreement to regard the distribution of natural talents as a common asset and to share in the benefits of this distribution whatever it turns out to be'.[121] Cohen doubts whether the Difference Principle 'justifies *any* significant inequality'.[122] He contends that the Difference Principle should be based on equality, because social inequalities harm the worse off.[123]

Thirdly, Rawls views natural talents as a 'collective asset' to be distributed in a manner whereby 'the more fortunate are to benefit only in ways that help those that have lost out'.[124] Nozick, in his book *Anarchy, State, and Utopia*, which offers a libertarian alternative to Rawls' theory, writes, 'individuals have rights, and there are things no person or group may do to them (without violating the rights)'.[125] Thus, to regard a person's natural assets as common property is contrary to deontological liberalism's defence of the inviolability of the individual.[126]

Fourthly, Rawls' theory, which views primary social goods as 'metrics of justice',[127] is faulted on the grounds that it fails to take into account individuals with disabilities. The parties in the 'original position' imagine themselves to be free and equal and measure well-being in terms of an index of primary social goods. Due to the fact that relative well-being is measured in terms of income and wealth,[128] 'natural disability is no basis for any sort of compensation in the Original Position'.[129] This suggests that the needs of people with disabilities will be not be provided for. An alternative approach, advanced by Amartya Sen and Martha Nussbaum, is known as the capabilities approach. According to Sen:

> [T]he primary goods approach seems to take little note of the diversity of human beings … If people were basically very similar, then an index of primary goods might be quite a good way of judging advantage. But, in fact, people seem to have very different needs varying with health, longevity, climatic conditions, location, work conditions, temperament, and even body size … So what is involved is not merely ignoring a few hard cases, but overlooking very widespread and real differences.[130]

121 Rawls *A Theory of Justice* (n22) 101.
122 G A Cohen, 'Incentives, Inequality, and Community' in Grethe B Peterson (ed.), *The Tanner Lectures on Human Values* (UUP 1992), 178–179. Emphasis in original.
123 Ibid.
124 Rawls, *A Theory of Justice* (n22) 179.
125 Nozick (n29), ix.
126 Ibid. 228.
127 Ingrid Robeyns and Harry Brighouse, 'Introduction: Social primary goods and capabilities as metrics of justice' in Ingrid Robeyns and Harry Brighouse (eds), *Measuring Justice Primary Goods and Capabilities* (CUP 2012), 6.
128 Other primary social goods having been distributed equally.
129 Harry Brighouse, 'Can Justice as Fairness Accommodate the Disabled?' (2001) 27(4) Social Theory and Practice 537, 537.
130 Amartya Sen, 'Equality of What? in S McMurrin (ed.), *The Tanner Lectures on Human Values* (UUP and CUP 1980), 215–216.

Thus, an individual with a disability would not have a claim to additional resources, no matter how severe their disability, under Rawls' two principles of justice. Sen argues that the focus should be on individuals' capability to function.[131] When outlining the type of society to which the Difference Principle applies, Rawls states that he:

> [S]hall assume that everyone has physical needs and psychological capacities within the normal range, so that questions of health care and mental capacity do not arise. … The first problem of justice concerns the relations among those who in the everyday course of things are full and active participants in society and directly or indirectly associated together over the whole span of their life. Thus the difference principle is to apply to citizens engaged in social cooperation; if the principle fails for this case, it would seem to fail in general.[132]

The physical and mental capabilities of each individual in society (to which Rawls intends is theory to apply) are all 'within the normal range' which permits each individual to become an active participant in society. Thus, Rawls' theory is unable to accommodate individuals with severe mental and physical disabilities.[133] To address this limitation in Rawls' theory, Nussbaum's capabilities approach focuses on fundamental human entitlements which should be respected and implemented by all governments 'as a bare minimum of what respects for human dignity requires'.[134] Thus, Nussbaum is able to extend her theory of justice to those with physical and mental disabilities because the starting point of the capabilities approach is the conception of the individual as a social animal 'whose dignity does not derive entirely from an idealized rationality'.[135]

## Conclusion

The pedagogic objectives of CLE are to teach students to employ legal skills and legal theory, to meet individual and social needs, as well as revealing how law either subverts or enhances public welfare and social justice.[136] However, without the relevant conceptual analytical tools, students are unable to convincingly critique whether a certain law promotes or hinders welfare and social justice. Unlike utilitarianism, Rawls' theory of justice aims to constitute a system to ensure the fair distribution of primary social goods.

131 Amartya Sen, 'Justice: Means Versus Freedoms' (1990) 19 Philosophy and Public Affairs 111, 112.
132 John Rawls, *A Theory of Justice* (revised edition) (HUP1971/1999), 83–84.
133 Robeyns and Brighouse (n127) 4.
134 Nussbaum, *Frontiers of Justice Disability, Nationality, Species Membership* (n116) 70.
135 Martha Nussbaum, 'Capabilities and Disabilities: Justice for Mentally Disabled Citizens' (2002) 30(2) Philosophical Topics 133, 135.
136 Wizner (n1) 1935.

By incorporating Rawls' theory of justice into CLE, students are able to analyse issues beyond the lawyer–client model. These issues include commercial acumen in terms of the importance of funding of pro bono services, the significance of pro bono services to low-income clients with regards to protecting their rights and bringing claims, and the relationship between legal aid and access to justice. Thus, Rawls' principles of justice provide a useful analytical tool for enhancing reflective practice. The value of applying Rawls' theory to CLE is three-fold. Firstly, students, as rational individuals, are able to reflect on the principles of justice and apply these principles to the legal aid system in Croatia or any other jurisdiction. Secondly, examining social institutions enhances reflective practice beyond the lawyer–client model; students are able to assess whether the current system of legal aid protects the primary goods of their clients. Thirdly, Rawls' theory of justice combines the entitlement of human choice with a concern for clients who are worse off.

# 7 Towards a capability approach to Clinical Legal Education

*Hugh McFaul*

## Introduction

This chapter will explore how recent work on utilising the capability approach on human development and social justice to develop a theory of civic professionalism can illuminate the practice of Clinical Legal Education. It will argue that the developing literature on civic virtue within the professions is of relevance to legal education in general, but has particular resonance for experiential, or clinical, approaches to professional legal education. Part I will outline the capability approach to social justice and human development pioneered by Amartya Sen and Martha Nussbaum. Part II will consider the relevance of the capability approach to education in general before a review of recent work applying the insights of the capability approach to university level education of professionals in Part III. Finally, Part IV will present a preliminary analysis of how these insights could be applied to enrich and illuminate the practice of Clinical Legal Education.

## Part I. The capability approach

The capability approach provides a theoretical framework for social justice and human development. With origins that can be traced to Aristotle, Adam Smith and Karl Marx, it has been formulated by Amartya Sen and developed by Martha Nussbaum and has had a significant influence on social science and humanities literature.[1] Sen's conception of justice is resolutely at odds with ideal or transcendent or ideal philosophical approaches which have as their primary aim the identification of a perfectly just social order. Sen's bottom-up, comparative approach favours pragmatism over idealism, and seeks to argue for a conception of justice which allows us to rationally discriminate between competing, but reliasable social goods and thus work to alleviate existing injustices.

1 Ingrid Robeyns, 'The Capability Approach' in Edward N Zalta (ed.), *The Stanford Encyclopedia of Philosophy* (Winter 2016, Metaphysics Research Lab, Stanford University 2016) <https://plato.stanford.edu/archives/win2016/entries/capability-approach/> accessed 23 April 2019.

DOI: 10.4324/9780429299247-8

> What is presented here is a theory of justice in a very broad sense. Its aim is to clarify how we can proceed to address questions of enhancing justice and removing injustice, rather than to offer resolutions of questions about the nature of perfect justice.[2]

The effect is to refocus discussion not on ideal state of affairs, but on concrete and achievable ways for making social arrangements *more* just rather than *perfectly* just. This presupposes the need to be able to engage in discussion and practical reason for the comparative work of determining how social improvements can be made and to discriminate between competing claims. The capability approach provides a framework for these normative exercises which serve to evaluate social justice including:

> (1) the assessment of individual well-being; (2) the evaluation and assessment of social arrangements; and (3) the design of policies and proposals about social change in society.[3]

In each of these, priority is given to individuals' capability to realise certain fundamental beings and doings, or functionings such as participating in political life, being healthy, playing, opportunities to travel, benefiting from supportive relationships or having the opportunity to be educated, etc. Within this developing literature the term 'capabilities' is used synonymously with related terms such as 'abilities and skills', 'competencies' and 'capacities'.[4] An open-ended, developing and multi-purpose framework, it is most often referred to as an 'approach' rather than a 'theory'.[5] As such it functions as an interdisciplinary framework that seeks to promote social justice by focusing on expanding individual capabilities that will provide genuine opportunities for the pursuit of a good life. The good life is conceived pluralistically in that individuals should be afforded the opportunity and freedom to be and do what they have reason to value.[6]

A key aspect of capability theory is that it does not mandate how individuals should lead a good life but different formulations of the approach outline certain fundamental capabilities which are central for affording individuals the freedom to do and be what they have reason to value. Martha Nussbaum[7] proposes ten key capabilities that afford this freedom and which are therefore foundational for a life of human dignity and for social justice, paraphrased below:

1 **Life**, including the ability to live a life of normal length;
2 **Bodily health** including nourishment, reproductive health and shelter;

2 A Sen, *The Idea of Justice* (Allen Lane 2009) ix.
3 Robeyns (n 1).
4 Carolin Kreber, *Educating for Civic-Mindedness: Nurturing Authentic Professional Identities through Transformative Higher Education* (Routledge 2016).
5 Robeyns (n 1).
6 Kreber, *Educating for Civic-Mindedness* (n 4); M Nussbaum and A Sen, *The Quality of Life* (Clarendon Press 1993).
7 M Nussbaum, *Creating Capabilities* (Harvard University Press 2011) 34.

3 **Bodily integrity**, including the ability to move freely and be secure from assault;
4 Ability to use **senses, imagination,** and **thought** in a way informed and cultivated by an adequate education and including religious freedom;
5 **Emotions**, being able to have attachments to things and people outside ourselves;
6 **Practical reason**, being able to form a conception of the good and to engage in critical reflection about the planning of one's life;
7 **Affiliation** includes being able to live with and toward others, having the social bases of self-respect;
8 **Other species.** Being able to live with concern for and in relation to nature;
9 **Play**, being able to enjoy recreational activities;
10 **Control over one's environment** including on a political level by being able to participate in political processes and in the material sense of being able to hold property and to seek employment on an equal basis.

If an individual is afforded these fundamental capabilities, they are conceived of having the opportunity to choose their functioning and live a life that they have reason to value. The distinction between functionings and capabilities is central to this approach; capabilities being the opportunities to be or do in particular ways and functionings are particular ways of being and doing.

> A person who is starving and a person who is fasting have the same kind of functioning where nutrition is concerned, but they do not have the same capability, because the person who fasts is able not to fast, and the starving person has no choice … To promote capabilities is to promote areas of freedom, and this is not the same as making people function in a certain way.[8]

Therefore, the capability approach seeks the promotion of key capabilities which affords individuals the opportunity to choose a dignified life.[9] As such the emphasis is not on determining what would be a perfectly just set of social arrangements but on performing pragmatic comparative judgments that help to remedy substantive injustices and promoting the capabilities of individuals to lead a life that they have reason to value.

## Part II. The capability approach and education

The capability approach has been the subject of research across the humanities and social sciences and has also begun to be applied to education research,

8 Nussbaum (n 7) 25.
9 M McLean and M Walker, 'The Possibilities for University-Based Public-Good Professional Education: A Case-Study from South Africa Based on the Capability Approach' (2012) 37 Studies in Higher Education 585, 587.

recognising the role that education can perform in the achievement of dignity: a life that one has reason to value.[10] Sen's work has had more influence on policy and theories relating to education and economy, whereas scholars have utilised Nussbaum's contribution to research the process of education, as her work on education and capability is more directly focused on the content of education.[11]

Education research using the capability approach recognises that it has intrinsic, instrumental and positional value. Education is intrinsically valuable in that it facilitates engagement with fulfilling activities but also provides instrumental value by facilitating the performance of a job. Related to this is its positional value as the location of study and level of qualification has social status implications.[12] The capability approach emphasises the intrinsic value of education and has been used by scholars to challenge the hegemonic status of the human capital approach to education.[13] The human capital approach emphasises the correlation between education and economic growth resulting in policies focusing on labour market needs, rather than on individual aspirations,[14] an approach seen as reductionist from the capability perspective.[15] A capability approach to education emphasises the fundamental aim of education is to promote human flourishing, which requires the development of practical reason and not just the acquisition of economically relevant skills. The literature in this field seeks to consider how different pedagogies could foster capabilities for a variety of audiences and has been applied to a diverse range of issues including social exclusion, lifelong learning, employability and curriculum development.[16] This chapter will now examine how the capability approach has been applied to professional education in particular.

10 Robeyns (n 1); Ana Sofia Ribeiro, 'A Normative Framework or an Emerging Theory? The Capability Approach in Higher Education Research', *Theory and method in higher education research* (Emerald Group Publishing Limited 2015).

11 Sofia Ribeiro (n 10); Walker Unterhalter and Vaughan, 'The Capability Approach and Education' (2007) 13 Prospero 13.

12 Sofia Ribeiro (n 10); E Unterhalter and H Brighouse, 'Distribution of What for Social Justice in Education? The Case of Education for All by 205' in M Walker and E Unterhalter (eds), *Amartya Sen's Capability Approach and Social Justice in Education* (1st ed, Palgrave Macmillan 2007).

13 A Wilson and others, 'Making Professionalism Meaningful to Students in Higher Education' (2013) 38 Studies in Higher Education 1222; B Keeley, *Human Capital: How What You Know Shapes Your Life* (OECD Publishing 2007); Becker, *Human Capital: A Theoretical and Empirical Analysis, with Special Reference to Education* (3rd ed, University of Chicago Press 1993).

14 George Psacharopoulos and Harry Anthony Patrinos, 'Returns to Investment in Education: A Further Update' (2004) 12 Education Economics 111.

15 M Nussbaum, *Not for Profit: Why Democracy Needs the Humanities* (Princeton University Press 2010).

16 Boni and Walker, *Human Development and Capabilities: Re-Imagining the University of the Twenty-First Century* (A Boni and M Walker eds, Routledge 2013); Walker, *Higher Education Pedagogies* (Open University Press 2006).

## Part III. The capability approach and the civic professional

The capability approach has been used as a way of approaching the ethical development of professionals. For the purpose of this paper the term 'professions' can be defined as referring to:

> a changing range of occupations characterised by a knowledge base of abstract theories and complex skills acquired through higher education, relative self-regulation supported by professional bodies and associations, the need to exercise personal judgement, and, perhaps importantly, a commitment to public service.[17]

Concerns regarding the ethical standards of professionals is a recurrent theme within the academic literature on professions and professional education in general. The literature related to the legal professions echoes these wider concerns. Academic discourse on legal education and the legal professions recognises that, in common with other professions, ethical decision making is central to professional legal practice.[18] However, it also points to anxieties around failures within the profession to meet the ethical standards expected of it.[19] Concerns with impact of neo-liberal policies on the ethos of the legal profession have focused on how the promotion of commercial values can serve to undermine public service-orientated ones.[20]

Examples of ethically compromised professional practice are plentiful. The decline in the ethical standing of legal and related professions is starkly illustrated by their role in facilitating the financial dealing that helped lead to the 2007–2008 global financial crash. A failure compounded by recurring scandals concerning the facilitation of complex tax avoidance schemes which teeter on the point of illegality but remain sufficiently within the letter of the law to allow wealthy individuals and corporations to drastically limit their tax bill. These practices have been the subject of stinging, but seemingly ineffectual, criticism by elected politicians[21] and have led senior public figures and academics alike to

17 Carolin Kreber, 'The Idea of a Decent Profession: Implications for Professional Education' (2019) 44 Studies in Higher Education 696, 696.

18 Richard Moorhead and others, 'The Ethical Identity of Law Students' (2016) 23 International Journal of the Legal Profession 235.

19 Richard Moorhead, 'Precarious Professionalism: Some Empirical and Behavioural Perspectives on Lawyers' (2014) 67 Current Legal Problems 447.

20 Moorhead and others (n 18); Donald Nicolson, 'Making Lawyers Moral? Ethical Codes and Moral Character' (2005) 25 Legal Studies 601; John Flood, 'Mega-lawyering in the Global Order: The Cultural, Social and Economic Transformation of Global Legal Practice' (1996) 3 International Journal of the Legal Profession 169; Anthony T Kronman, *The Lost Lawyer: Failing Ideals of the Legal Profession* (Harvard University Press 1995).

21 House of Commons, 'House of Commons – Tax Avoidance: The Role of Large Accountancy Firms – Public Accounts Committee' (2013) <https://publications.parliament.uk/pa/cm201213/cmselect/cmpubacc/870/87002.htm> accessed 13 May 2019.

lament the decline in the public service ideals of the professions. For example, senior UK judge, Lord Justice Jackson, summed up this anxiety by arguing that:

> Professional persons are no longer generally seen as a class of individuals superior to other workers, driven by higher ideals. Most sociologists now characterise the professions as special interest groups which exploit their skills in an endeavour to achieve greater income and higher status in society. Many laymen take a similar view.[22]

Academic literature has looked to possible deficiencies in the ethical formation of professionals to account for this loss of trust arguing that 'the moral and ethical dimension of human life, rather than the quantity and level of education which has let us down so badly'.[23] The critique of ethical standards within the professions has led to a developing literature exploring the role universities could play in working to educate civic-minded professionals. This literature suggests that universities have a moral obligation to educate professionals who not only have the requisite technical knowledge and skills to provide a publicly valuable service, but are also able to make ethically sound choices in how they apply and use that knowledge and skill.[24] In this way, it seeks to reimagine how the 'ideal-type' professional theorised by Parsons, Durkheim and Dewey might be re-orientated to focus their specialised skills and knowledge on contributing to the common good by helping civil society to meet contemporary environmental and social justice challenges.[25]

Educational theorists progressing this agenda, including Melanie Walker and Monica McLean[26] and Carolin Kreber,[27] have drawn inspiration from the

22 'Jackson: Professional Negligence Could Disappear as Attitudes Change' (*Legal Futures*, 27 April 2015) <https://www.legalfutures.co.uk/latest-news/jackson-professional-negligence-could-disappear-as-attitudes-change> accessed 1 July 2019.

23 M Walker, 'A Capital or Capabilities Education Narrative in a World of Staggering Inequalities' (2012) 32 International Journal of Educational Development 384, 387.

24 Kreber, *Educating for Civic-Mindedness* (n 4); M Walker and M McLean, *Professional Education, Capabilities and Contributions to the Public Good: The Role of Universities in Promoting Human Development* (Routledge 2013); A Dzur, *Democratic Professionalism: Citizen Participation and the Reconstruction of Professional Ethics, Identity, and Practice* (University Park, PA: Penn State University Press 2008); J Nixon and others, 'Towards a New Academic Professionalism: A Manifesto for Hope' (2001) 22 British Journal of Sociology of Education 227.

25 T Parsons, *Professions and Social Structure. In Essays in Sociological Theory* (The Free Press 1954); E Durkheim, *Professional Ethics and Civic Morals* (Routledge 1957); J Dewey, *The Public and Its Problems* (H Holt and Company 1927).

26 Walker and McLean, *Professional Education, Capabilities and Contributions to the Public Good: The Role of Universities in Promoting Human Development* (n 24); Monica McLean and Melanie Walker, 'A Capabilities Approach to Educating the Deliberate Professional: Theory and Practice' in Franziska Trede and Celina McEwen (eds), *Educating the Deliberate Professional: Preparing for future practices* (Springer International Publishing 2016) <https://doi.org/10.1007/978-3-319-32958-1_10> accessed 25 April 2019.

27 Kreber, *Educating for Civic-Mindedness* (n 4); Kreber, 'The Idea of a Decent Profession' (n 17).

capability approach to human development to provide a theory-based rationale for the development of public good, or civic professionals.[28] This literature has emphasised the potential for professionals to contribute to building the capabilities which facilitate the genuine and substantive freedom for individuals to pursue a life that they have reason to value. These so-called public good, civic or decent professionals can, it is argued, have a direct impact on social justice.[29] These authors make a connection between Nussbaum's communitarian and relational conception of the capabilities to argue that 'obligations to others directs this maximizing calculus to take into account the improvement of the well-being of others as a means to my own well-being. What I have reason to value as significant to my own good life then includes advancing the well-being of others.'[30]

From this perspective higher education has a moral obligation to develop students' capabilities, and also to develop particular context-specific professional capabilities which will serve both to support future professionals' ability to contribute to social justice and facilitate their personal flourishing. Which particular capabilities each profession should contribute to the public good will vary,[31] so the application of the capability approach to professional education will also be context dependent.

Walker and Mclean map Nussabaum's capabilities against professional roles and argue for a number of professional capabilities which can facilitate a career that can contribute to social justice. These included practical and public reasoning; integrity; emotional awareness; imagination; empathy; having confidence to act for change; and communicating professional knowledge in an accessible way, which Kreber has argued could be conceived collectively as the capability of civic professionalism,[32] or indeed civic virtue. A civic, or decent, professional is, Kreber argues, therefore one which respects diversity (given the pluralistic approach to

28 Melanie Walker and Monica McLean, *Professional Education, Capabilities and the Public Good: The Role of Universities in Promoting Human Development* (Routledge 2013); Carolin Kreber, 'The Civic-Minded Professional? An Exploration through Hannah Arendt's Vita Activa' (2016) 48 Educational Philosophy and Theory 123; Kreber, 'The Idea of a Decent Profession' (n 17); M Walker and M McLean, 'Making Lives Go Better: University Education and Professional Capabilities' (2011) 24 South African Journal of Higher Education 847; M Walker and M McLean, 'A Public Good Professional Capability Index for University-Based Professional Education in South Africa'. Paper Presented at the Annual Meeting of the Society for Research into Higher Education (2009).

29 Kreber, 'The Idea of a Decent Profession' (n 17); Walker and McLean, *Professional Education, Capabilities and the Public Good* (n 28); W Sullivan, *Work and Integrity: The Crisis and Promise of Professionalism in America* (2nd edn, Jossey-Bass 2005).

30 Walker and McLean, *Professional Education, Capabilities and the Public Good* (n 28) 31.

31 Kreber, 'The Civic-Minded Professional?' (n 28).

32 Kreber, 'The Civic-Minded Professional?' (n 28); Walker and McLean, 'A Public Good Professional Capability Index for University-Based Professional Education in South Africa'. Paper Presented at the Annual Meeting of the Society for Research into Higher Education (n 28); Walker and McLean, 'Making Lives Go Better: University Education and Professional Capabilities' (n 28); Walker and McLean, *Professional Education, Capabilities and the Public Good* (n 28).

value inherent within the capability approach) and one where the privileges associated with professional status is justified by a commitment to improving the capacity of individuals to exercise their agency and live a life that they have reason to value.[33] The capability of civic professionalism also entails that the professional is able to build a career that contributes to, rather than diminishes, their own flourishing.

Developing a pedagogy which fully utilises the capability approach to facilitate the development of civic professionalism in the context of Clinical Legal Education is an exciting prospect but one which will require a considerable amount of research, debate and reflection. The following part of this chapter aims to begin this process by identifying three overlapping features of Clinical Legal Education which have the potential to provide a suitable focus to begin this work.

## IV. Towards a capability approach to CLE

To fully address the implications of the capability approach for legal education is the work of a much larger study, or series of studies; therefore, this section will be confined to sketching out three aspects of CLE pedagogy where the synergies with the capability approach to developing civic professionalism are particularly apparent, and which may point the way to further research. It will ground this discussion in the context of UK Clinical Legal Education. This contextual information is intended to illustrate the breadth and variety of contemporary CLE within undergraduate legal education and highlight the common themes that resonate with the capability approach.

### *CLE in the UK*

CLE is an increasingly significant feature of law school practice in the UK.[34] A recent study of Clinical Legal Education in UK law schools found that 70 per cent used some form of CLE in their undergraduate provision,[35] which equates to approximately 10,000 law students taking part in CLE activities across the UK. The types of activity included under the umbrella of CLE in the UK context are varied and it is impossible to provide neat definitional parameters. Kemp et al. argue that 'CLE can mean different things in different contexts'.[36] However, Drummond and McKeever point out that the predominant type of activity is for students to provide legal advice to members of the public under

33 Kreber, 'The Civic-Minded Professional?' (n 28); Kreber, 'The Idea of a Decent Profession' (n 17).

34 Frank S Bloch, *The Global Clinical Movement: Educating Lawyers for Social Justice* (Oxford University Press 2010).

35 Damian Carney and others, *Lawworks Law Schools pro Bono and Clinic Report 2014* (LexisNexis UK 2014) 4.

36 Vicky Kemp, Tine Munk and Suzanne Gower, 'Clinical Legal Education and Experiential Learning: Looking to the Future' (University of Manchester Law School, Manchester 2016) 2.

supervision.[37] Yet even here the range of activities is considerably varied. Kerrigan and Murray show that legal advice clinics can range from in-house advice and representation clinics which can provide a similar service to the client that they would expect if they went to a law firm for advice to advice only services which assist the client in identifying the legal issue and provide a referral service to other agencies.[38] In addition to in-house activities students may take part in placements or externships or specialist projects to provide free legal advice, guidance or representation.

A unifying feature of the pedagogy behind this variety of clinical activity is the value placed on situating theoretical understanding in a real-world context. The term clinical illustrates the inspiration Clinical Legal Education has taken from medical education, which emphasises the importance of applying theoretical knowledge in practical settings. Giddings emphasises the key pedagogical principle that CLE involves learning from experience where students are active in the learning process and have the opportunity to reflect and learn from their experience.[39] It therefore goes beyond skills training and calls on students to engage with the law as an open-ended subject and to scrutinise wide-ranging social and legal issues which, it is hoped, will facilitate professional ethical development in a practical context.[40]

Thus, despite the rich variety of clinical activity within UK law schools there is a commonality in its pedagogical approach which gives primacy to active participation and reflective learning in addition to a foregrounding of social justice issues. Therefore, it is apparent that there are three overlapping features of clinical methodologies which resonate strongly with the capabilities approach and thereby have potential to provide the foundation for the development of civic professionalism within law schools. These areas are: the pervasiveness of a practice-based reflective approach, the exposure of students to real-world social justice issues through interaction with the public through the provision of legal advice, information and guidance, and through providing students with an opportunity to situate the ethical aspects of professional legal practice within a wider philosophical framework.

### *Reflective practice*

The combination of active participation and reflection provides a foundation to encourage the development of a civic minded legal profession in the way advocated for in Part III above. As Kreber argues, reflectivity can help to foster a moral commitment to social justice:

37 Orla Drummond and Gráinne McKeever, *Access to Justice through University Law Clinics* (Ulster University 2015) 15.

38 Kevin Kerrigan, and Victoria Murray. *A Student Guide to Legal Education and Pro Bono* (Palgrave Macmillan 2011).

39 Jeffrey Michael Giddings, *Promoting Justice through Clinical Legal Education* (Justice Press 2013).

40 Drummond and McKeever (n 37) 12.

> A moral commitment to contributing to a fairer world develops, at least partially, through critical reflectivity. Critical reflectivity involves, on the one hand, the testing of validity claims and questioning of presuppositions through abstract or analytical; but it also involves, on the other hand, learning to recognise how relations of power can distort experiences and how hegemonic forces can make us collude in our own oppression. It thereby helps to reveal structural forms of power that serve to sustain social injustices.[41]

The type of reflective activity that Kreber calls for is embedded in CLE pedagogy and therefore strongly resonates with this approach to the development of civic professionalism. Many CLE programmes, including my own institution's,[42] formalise this process as part of the assessment regime to facilitate the award of academic credit and require students to write a critical reflection of their clinical work, often engaging in wider academic discourse on professional identity, social justice and legal ethics. Thus there is a clear synergy between this aspect of CLE and the type of reflection that a capability based approach to civic professionalism calls for.

### *Social justice issues and capability development*

Closely related to the emphasis on reflexivity is the connection between CLE and wider issues of social justice, which is at the heart of the capability approach, most clearly exemplified in the capability of affiliation; the ability to live with and for others.[43] Many CLE programmes include a focus on providing free legal advice and education to the community. Consequently, clinical activity provides a tangible connection to the social justice tradition of pro bono activity within the legal profession. That CLE can provide real insights for students into social justice is relatively uncontroversial, although there remains disagreement about the extent to which the focus of CLE should be on social justice issues rather than providing an educationally rich student experience.[44] Nicolson and Wizner both argue that the educative and public service aims of CLE are not intrinsically incompatible.[45] Given the current social justice orientation of contemporary CLE practice, it is a fertile ground for the implementation of a capability approach to professionalism; resonating particularly with Nussbaum's formulation of the key capabilities of

41 Kreber, *Educating for Civic-Mindedness* (n 4) 51.

42 Hugh McFaul, 'Taking Legal Outreach Online: How Law Students Can Help Bridge the Justice Gap during Lockdown' (*Centre for Innovation in Legal and Business Education (SCiLAB)*, 13 May 2020) <http://www.open.ac.uk/blogs/scilab/index.php/2020/05/13/taking-legal-outreach-online-how-law-students-can-help-bridge-the-justice-gap-during-lockdown/> accessed 19 August 2020.

43 Nussbaum (n 7) 34.

44 Drummond and McKeever (n 37).

45 D Nicolson, *Legal Education, Ethics and Access to Justice: Forging Warriors for Justice* (2015); Stephen Wizner, 'The Law School Clinic: Legal Education in the Interests of Justice' (2001) 70 Fordham L. Rev. 1929.

affiliation (the ability to live with and toward others) and practical reason (able to form a conception of the good and to engage in critical reflection about the planning of one's life) outlined above.

Walker and McLean's mapping of Nussbaum's capabilities list against professional roles (discussed in Part III) offers a more granular conception of the link between professional capabilities and social justice, highlighting capabilities such as practical and public reasoning; integrity; emotional awareness; imagination; empathy; having confidence to act for change; and communicating professional knowledge in an accessible way. Many of these capabilities are developed and foregrounded in the activities undertaken in clinical programmes. For example, students' exposure to the real-world legal problems of marginalised social groups allows for the development of empathy and emotional awareness and many activities, such as advice clinics and public legal education interventions, require students to develop the ability to communicate knowledge in an accessible way. More research is needed to provide a comprehensive mapping of the capabilities developed both by students and the communities they serve in CLE programmes, but the capabilities framework provides an exciting opportunity to link the skills and capacities students develop during their CLE studies with the social justice impacts of the work they engage in.

### *Ethical dimension of legal practice*

The use of this reflective approach to participation in social justice-focused legal activities therefore provides the opportunity for the clinical experience of the ethical dimension of legal practice to be placed in a broader philosophical context. The practical application of theoretical knowledge allows students to interrogate and explore the philosophical principles that underpin legal professional codes of practice in a meaningful way. This provides the opportunity for clinical educators to facilitate the development of the capability of practical reason, operationalised as civic virtue in the professional sphere, for which developed ethical judgement, in addition to technical competency, is required. The capability approach offers a framework that can reinvigorate the ethical dimension of Clinical Legal Education in at least two overlapping ways: firstly, by providing the means to provide a substantive foundation for the political or communitarian aspects of professional ethics which can ground the social justice orientation of contemporary clinical legal education; secondly, by providing a framework which connects a concern with professional ethics with individual flourishing as well as social justice.

Professional ethics education has been critiqued for its apparently apolitical stance where the teaching of ethical codes or professional ethical judgement is confined to training students to function well in a narrow professional domain. Such an approach routinely ignores the democratic potential of professional education by ignoring the communitarian or political dimension.[46] The capability

46 Dzur (n 24).

approach is essentially communitarian in that to enable individuals to build the capabilities necessary for them to choose a life that they have reason to value depends upon the support of others in the community. The capability approach provides those engaged in Clinical Legal Education activities with a framework to reflect on the social justice potential of their professional activities. In this way it can provide a theoretical basis to contextualise the ethical obligations involved in professional practice against the needs and aspirations of the wider community. This approach can be facilitated by engaging with the questions of the following kind:

> What are my clients or the communities I work with actually able to do and be? What opportunities do they have to be and do what they value? How do social arrangements have an influence on expanding people's capabilities? How do we build a profession that values creating capabilities for all? These professionals would be oriented to thinking about opportunities for clients to choose to live in meaningful, productive and rewarding ways. Where they found a failure of capabilities and valuable achievements for individuals, groups and communities they would ask what changes in structures, institutions, policies and practices might enhance people's flourishing.[47]

Further, the capability approach provides a focus on the flourishing of students and professionals. It argues that the civic, or public good professional will be supportive of the common good by seeking to develop the capabilities of the community. This civic orientation occurs not out of an abstract sense of duty, but in the knowledge, based on practical wisdom, that doing so will facilitate a professional career that they have reason to value as it will become 'a life-enriching feature of human identity'.[48] In this way the capability approach provides a framework for Clinical Legal Education which provides a theoretical grounding both for the existing communitarian orientation of CLE pedagogies and for foregrounding the personal flourishing of law students.[49]

## Conclusion

This chapter has explored how the capability approach to the development of civic professionalism can provide an enriched theoretical foundation for Clinical Legal Education pedagogy. It has argued that Clinical Legal Education provides a potentially fruitful environment for fostering civic virtue amongst aspiring legal professionals. It has outlined three features of CLE practice which have particular resonance to the capability approach and which would benefit from further

47 Walker and McLean, *Professional Education, Capabilities and the Public Good* (n 28) 32.
48 Kreber, 'The Civic-Minded Professional?' (n 28) 132.
49 For a broader discussion of the role of theory in Clinical Legal Education see Hugh McFaul, 'Does Clinical Legal Education Need Theory?' (2020) Asian Journal of Legal Education 152; and Mutaz M Qafisheh, 'Clinicalism: An Emerging Theory in Legal Pedagogy' (2020) 11 Transnational Legal Theory 549.

research from a capability perspective; the focus on reflective pedagogy, its social justice orientation and its capacity to provide a practice-based method for a broad exploration of the ethical aspects of legal practice. It has argued that there is potential for the capability approach to provide a framework for Clinical Legal Education that will support law students in pursuing a career that supports social justice by seeking to develop capabilities in the communities they will serve and also to contribute to their own flourishing by providing them with the means to pursue a career that they have reason to value.

# 8 Neoliberalism and Street Law: Examining the success of a communitarian initiative in a neoliberal higher education system

*Ben Perdue*

In *The End of History?*[1] Francis Fukuyama argues that nothing – not fascism, communism, religiosity, nationalism, nor anything else – can overthrow liberal capitalism as the dominant global economic system. He concludes that in the post-history era, economic interests have taken precedence over all other interests and 'the ability to build up material wealth at an accelerated rate … and to distribute it fairly … acquires decisive importance'.[2] According to Fukuyama, liberal economic theory currently enjoys unrivalled global influence and will do so indefinitely. Though he does not use the exact term, Fukuyama is largely talking about the dominance of the economic and political ideology known as neoliberalism. Neoliberal thought, which touts the benefits of economic liberalism, free market authority, and limited government, has become hegemonic, 'suffus[ing] our social norms, our civic institutions, and our political life'.[3] The dominance of the neoliberal mind-set from the early 1980s to today has had wide implications on nearly every aspect of society, and higher education is no exception. Higher education institutions have largely accepted the individual- and market-oriented approach of the neoliberal ideology to guide their curricula, teaching, and programme offerings.[4]

In these four decades of neoliberal dominance, Street Law, community-oriented law school-based initiatives in which law students teach interactive practical law lessons in schools, has also flourished. From its humble beginnings as a post-civil rights era community programme at Georgetown University in the United States,[5] Street Law has become a global movement. Street Law is now mainstream and is found in law schools throughout the world, and a global community of practitioners, academics, and community leaders are propelling it to new universities, communities, and countries.[6] With

1 Francis Fukuyama, 'The End of History?' (1989) 16 The National Interest, 3.
2 Ibid., 17.
3 Michael Goodhart, *Injustice: Political Theory for the Real World* (Oxford Scholarship Online 2018) 12.
4 Malcolm Tight, 'The neoliberal turn in Higher Education' (2019) 73 Higher Education Quarterly 273.
5 Lee Arbetman, 'Street Law, Inc.: Context, History and Future' (2018) 2 International Journal of Public Legal Education 3.
6 David McQuoid-Mason, *Street Law and Public Legal Education: A Collection of Best Practices from Around the World in Honor of Ed O'Brian* (Juta & Company Ltd. 2020); Global

DOI: 10.4324/9780429299247-9

the widespread growth of the initiative, it is now widely accepted by universities, legal regulatory bodies and associations, and even governments, as an important aspect of legal education.

How is it that a communitarian and socially focused educational initiative has grown and thrived in a higher education system that has increasingly become individualistic and market-oriented? In this chapter, I present an explanation for this apparent contradiction. First, to establish a common understanding of the term 'neoliberalism', I describe the ways in which neoliberal thought has come to dominate our economic and political landscape and examine the arguments voiced by its supporters as well as its critics. Next, I explain how neoliberal ideals have permeated higher education (and specifically legal education) and have shaped the standard educational approach in those institutions. Finally, I show how Street Law simultaneously subverts neoliberal ideals in its community-centred approach while still achieving outcomes that fit within the neoliberal value system. These market-oriented and individualistic outcomes have allowed Street Law not only to be accepted, but to flourish within a neoliberal higher education system.

One important caveat should be noted at the outset of this chapter. In describing Street Law's place in a neoliberal higher education system, I offer no positive or negative judgement on the value of neoliberalism, either as a set of economic and political policies or as an education approach. In academic conversations about innovative educational practices, neoliberalism is often viewed as a deleterious barrier to educational success.[7] There is a wide array of thinkers who critique the neoliberal approach and others in this volume have presented arguments for why higher education and legal education specifically should consider different theoretical alignments. This chapter does not present a defence or a critique of neoliberalism in higher education – it simply accepts the practical reality that most universities currently operate with a neoliberal paradigm. With pragmatism as the starting point, I examine the strengths of Street Law within the neoliberal system, delving specifically into the areas where Street Law's outcomes overlap with the desired outcomes of a neoliberal educational approach. Through this lens, we can understand not only how Street Law has managed to survive and flourish over the past four decades but also how proponents of Street Law can advocate for institutional support of the initiative.

## Neoliberalism: an introduction

Neoliberalism has come to dominate the political, economic, and social landscape over the past four decades. Though widely used by both advocates and critics, the term is perhaps murkier than conventional wisdom or even academic scholarship

Alliance for Justice Education, 'Home' <www.gaje.org> accessed 11 November 2020; The International Journal of Public Legal Education, 'Home' (*Northumbria Journals*) <https://www.northumbriajournals.co.uk/index.php/ijple> accessed 11 Nov 2020.

7 Tight (n 4).

might suggest.[8] In modern social science literature, the term 'neoliberalism' is often employed rhetorically as opposed to analytically, referring to a general (and often negative) idea without a substantive and clearly defined meaning attached to it.[9] In an effort to clarify the use of the term in this chapter, George Ritzer's explanation that neoliberalism posits a 'liberal commitment to individual liberty, a belief in the free market, and opposition to state intervention in it' is useful.[10]

At its root, neoliberalism is an economic philosophy drawn from the liberal traditions of Adam Smith.[11] Like all aspects of the ideology, the economic rationale for neoliberalism is centred around the idea of freedom. Neoliberals argue that freedom – and in particular economic freedom – is the impetus for economic success and prominent neoliberal voices have long called for economic freedom to be resolutely protected.[12] Faith in the free market represents one of the most central principles of neoliberal economic theory. Proponents argue that the free market promotes competition between suppliers which increases efficiency and drives up the quality of products.[13] In order to protect the free market, the state must assume a significantly different role than it did in the post-WWII welfare state. As Harvey explains, the role of the state in the neoliberal mind-set is to create institutional frameworks which will 'secure private property rights and to guarantee, by force if need be, the proper functionings of markets'.[14] Beyond that, state involvement in markets should be minimal as the free market itself will determine the optimal supply and prices of products. The role of the state thus is to regulate rather than to provide, and the freedom of the market is elevated above all else.

This altered role of government marks a definitive decision on the part of neoliberals to move away from a centralised planning model and instead rely on marketisation to guide decision making. Central government planning, they argue, has been unsuccessful at generating economic progress and a more marketised mentality is more effective at driving growth.[15] There are strong practical reasons behind this assertion. First, the removal of central planning allows multiple ideas to be tested and implemented simultaneously. The free market fosters competition between those ideas and products and, it is argued, efficiently picks

8 Taylor C Boas and Jordan Gans-Morse, 'Neoliberalism: From New Liberal Philosophy to Anti-Liberal Slogan' (2009) 44 Studies in Comparative International Development 137.

9 Ibid.

10 George Ritzer, 'Neo-Liberalism: Roots, principles, criticisms and new-Marxian alternatives' in George Ritzer (ed.) *Globalization: a basic text* (Wiley-Blackwell 2010), 110.

11 Adam Smith, *The Wealth of Nations* (first published 1776, Modern Library Paperback Edition, Modern Library 2000).

12 Milton Friedman, *Capitalism and Freedom* (first published 1962, Fortieth Anniversary edn. University of Chicago Press 2002).

13 Friedrich Hayek, 'The meaning of competition' (first published 1948, 2016) 13(2) Econ Journal Watch 360.

14 David Harvey, *A Brief History of Neoliberalism* (Oxford University Press 2007), 2.

15 Owen Barder, 'Beyond Planning: Markets and Networks for Better Aid' (2009) Center for Global Development Working Paper No. 185.

winner and losers. Furthermore, marketisation permits the rapid scaling of good ideas that would be bogged down in a central planning bureaucracy. Finally, whereas central planners are often hesitant to take risks and thus are stifled from implementing innovative concepts, marketisation promotes high-risk-high-reward ideas by rewarding successful entrepreneurs.[16]

Despite the apparent benefits, there are strong counterarguments to the economic rationale of neoliberalism. In the wake of the 2008 global economic crisis – arguably an outcome of high-risk-high-reward practices in the financial sector – 'the critics [of neoliberalism] have gained the upper hand, at least for the moment'.[17] Problematically, critics argue, neoliberal ideology assumes that everyone defines success and wellbeing in terms of economic success. This narrow assessment fails to account for cultures and individuals who may choose to define their freedoms and their wellbeing on very different terms.[18] On a more practical level, there are real issues associated with a dogmatic adherence to neoliberal principles. As Harvey points out, neoliberal policies pave the way for not only economic collapses through the upward redistribution of wealth but can also lead to environmental degradation and human rights abuses.[19]

The economic logic of neoliberalism is implemented in the political sphere through a set of specific policies. As Klees explains:

> neoliberal economic policies call for a series of interrelated reforms: macroeconomic stability; cutting back government budgets; privatisation of government operations; ending of tariffs and other forms of protection; facilitating movement of foreign capital; emphasising exports; charging user fees for many public services; and lowering worker protections through flexible labour markets.[20]

These policies were not only implemented in the West but were actively pushed on developing countries as well. In a series of policies that have become known as the Washington Consensus, large multi-national organisations such as the World Bank and the International Monetary Fund pressured developing countries to adopt this set of policies. By providing international aid on the condition that such policies were enacted, the West was able to effectively strong-arm developing countries into accepting the neoliberal agenda, for better or worse.[21]

16 Ritzer (n 10).
17 Ibid., 110.
18 Ibid.
19 Harvey (n 14).
20 Steven Klees, 'A quarter century of neoliberal thinking in education: Misleading analyses and failed policies' (2008) 6(4) Globalisation, Societies and Education 311, 312.
21 Steven Hobden and Richard Wyn Jones, 'Marxist theories of international relations' in John Baylis, Steve Smith, and Patricia Owens (eds) *The globalization of world politics: An introduction to international relations* (4th edn, Oxford University Press 2008) 142.

This economic mind-set and the policies underpinning them attracted hyper-polarised reactions. Neoliberal thinkers like Fukuyama[22] and Thomas Friedman contend that neoliberal policies are the best way to ensure economic growth and suggest that countries have no choice but to don the 'golden straightjacket' of neoliberal policies which tie them to the open world market.[23] Critics of neoliberalism, however, dispute this.[24] With an eye to the origins of political neoliberalism, Naomi Klein argues that Chile is a prime example of neoliberalism's faults. Following the country's 1973 coup, the newly empowered Augusto Pinochet adopted a set of market-oriented neoliberal economic policies. These policies sent inflation rates soaring and set the country on a path to becoming one of the most unequal countries in the world.[25] More recently, the decline of the world economy in 2008 showed a dramatic rift in the supposed faultlessness of neoliberal policies and prompted scholars, academics, and even politicians to critically re-examine the assumption that neoliberalism is the only solution.[26] As Nicolas Sarkozy, then President of France, explained in 2008, 'the idea of the absolute power of the markets that should not be constrained by any rule, by any political intervention, was a mad idea. The idea that markets are always right was a mad idea.'[27]

Beyond its economic and political implications, neoliberalism dictates the relationships that individuals ought to have with the government, other people, and even their own subjectivity. Succinctly, the policies of neoliberalism have shifted choice and responsibility from the state to the individual and have promoted a culture of meritocracy.[28] The self-interested individual becomes the building block of a stable and thriving economy,[29] and by promoting individual freedoms and allowing them to make these self-interested choices in free markets, human wellbeing will advance.[30] While this framing is ostensibly positive (centring individuals' decisions as the impetus for wellbeing), there are some more sinister or even dehumanising consequences of this approach. As neoliberal principles continue to expand throughout the world, more and more services are being treated

22 Francis Fukuyama, *The End of History and the Last Man* (Hamilton 1992).

23 Thomas Friedman, *The Lexus and the Olive Tree: Understanding globalisation* (Farrar, Straus and Giroux 1999).

24 Klees (n 20), 189.

25 Naomi Klein, *The Shock Doctrine: The Rise of Disaster Capitalism* (1st edition, Penguin 2008).

26 Ritzer (n 10).

27 Henry Samuel, 'Nicolas Sarkozy calls for overhaul of capitalism'. *The Telegraph* (Paris, 26 September 2008) <http://www.telegraph.co.uk/news/worldnews/europe/france/3082611/Nicolas-Sarkozy-calls-for-overhaul-of-capitalism.html> accessed 11 November 2020.

28 Government of the United Kingdom, 'Britain, the great meritocracy: Prime Minister's speech' (2016) <https://www.gov.uk/government/speeches/britain-the-great-meritocracy-prime-ministers-speech> accessed 11 November 2020.

29 Mark Olssen and Michael A Peters, 'Neoliberalism, higher education and the knowledge economy: From the free market to knowledge capitalism' (2005) 20(3) Journal of Education Policy 313.

30 Harvey (n 14).

as products and are being commodified. Perhaps more alarmingly, individuals themselves have now been commodified. This over-commodification demeans individuals by characterising them simply as factors of production and ignoring the fact that they are 'living beings endowed with dreams, desires, ambitions, hopes, doubts, and fears'.[31] This concern illustrates how the growing influence of neoliberalism not only affects the economy and policies but also impacts the way that people interact.

## Neoliberalism and higher education

Higher education has not been immune to the growth of neoliberalism. In fact, higher education took to the neoliberal mind-set quickly and strongly.[32] Despite being an area of human activity that is not traditionally associated with markets, education and its focus on measurable achievement easily aligned itself with neoliberal thought. By embracing the neoliberal philosophy, higher education institutions reshaped their core mission from a pursuit of knowledge to a more specific preparation for professional careers. Changes in everything from the structure and management of school systems to the specific content and pedagogy of classes can be traced to this 'neoliberalisation' of education. With this new mind-set, universities turned their attention to outcomes that focus less on the critical examination of information and orthodoxy (arguably the 'traditional' rationale or purpose of education) and more on measurable, systematic indicators like student performance on exams, job placement, and academic audits.[33]

Neoliberal policies in education are diverse, ranging from the vocationalisation of education to the privatisation and marketisation of the education sector. In law schools (as well as other higher education institutions), neoliberalism manifests itself in the way that schools demonstrate the value of the degree that they award. The value of the advanced degree in a neoliberal world is measured not on how well it can educate the whole person but rather on the degree to which graduates can demonstrate the skills necessary to gain entry into the labour market.[34] For this reason, increasing focus has been put on specialised technical knowledge and the immediate practical application of the education in the job market.[35]

Take US law schools as an example. Every year, *U.S. News and World Report* publishes a list that ranks nearly every law school in the nation from best to worst. The rankings, which come out annually, are critically important for schools,

31 Ibid. 167.

32 Tight (n 4).

33 Olssen and Peters (n 29); Frank Gaffikin and David C Perry, 'Discourses and strategic vision: The US research university as an institutional manifestation of neoliberalism in a global era' (2009) 46(1) American Educational Research Journal, 115.

34 Henry A Giroux, 'Bare Pedagogy and the Scourge of Neoliberalism: Rethinking Higher Education as a Democratic Public Sphere' (2010) 74(3) The Educational Forum 184.

35 Mark William Roche, *Why Choose the Liberal Arts?* (2010 University of Notre Dame Press).

impacting nearly every aspect of the institution from student enrolment and later employment to faculty hiring and scholarly publication. With the importance of these rankings, law schools are strongly incentivised to tailor their educational offerings to maximise their rank.[36] These rankings heavily weight items like bar passage and employment at graduation and ten months after graduation.[37] These factors, however, are arguably poor indicators of the quality of the legal education. The bar exam mostly tests students on their ability to memorise thousands of legal rules and facts, and the closed book nature of the exam is far removed from the actual practice of law.[38] Employment is perhaps a better measure, but while employment in the first year after graduation may indicate how well a law school can prepare students for entry into the labour market, it does not show how well they progress or succeed in the labour market. By focusing on the first ten months of a 30+ year career, the ranking misses key factors such as whether or not the graduate advances in their field or contributes to their organisation, not to mention other factors such as their job satisfaction or happiness.

## Street Law – communitarian origins and values

Street Law is a seemingly anti-neoliberal initiative that has thrived in the neoliberal higher education system. The term 'Street Law' originated in the early 1970s when a group of law students from Georgetown University in Washington, DC developed a set of practical law-related lessons to teach to area high school students. This original law school-based programme came to be known as Street Law, referring to the practical nature of the lessons or the law that young people needed to know on the streets. The programme was immediately popular among the high school students who participated, particularly the culminating mock trial competition in which students played the roles of attorneys and witnesses.[39]

From the outset, Street Law was a unique initiative. The content of the classes was specifically chosen to cover issues that were not already included in the school curriculum. The lessons delved deep into topics that the students were likely to encounter in their daily lives as young adults – employment law and the rights and responsibilities of workers and employers, housing laws and what it means to sign a lease, police procedures and the rights of the accused, and much more. The lessons were designed with the students in mind to ensure that they were relevant and applicable to their lives. By centring the student experience, Street Law was an explicitly community-oriented initiative that was wholly different

36 Paul J Heald and Ted M Sichelman, 'Ranking the Academic Impact of 100 American Law Schools' (2019) 60 Jurimetrics 1.

37 Robert Morse, Ari Castonguay, and Juan Vega-Rodriguez, 'Methodology: 2021 Best Law Schools Rankings' (2020) *U.S. News & World Report* <https://www.usnews.com/education/best-graduate-schools/articles/law-schools-methodology> accessed 11 November 2020.

38 Andrea A Curcio, Carol L Chomsky, and Eileen Kaufman, 'How to Build a Better Bar Exam' (2018) 37 New York State Bar Association Journal 37.

39 Arbetman (n 5), 3.

from more traditional legal education. Beyond simply explaining the law or even giving legal advice, Street Law encouraged meaningful discussions about the law. The high school students were encouraged to explore not only what the law was, but also issues around why laws and systems were set up the way they were, whether it was fair, and how they could both operate within the boundaries of the law and push for changes if necessary. The classroom environment was rich, participatory, and democratic.

Street Law fostered this democratic learning environment through its signature interactive teaching methodology. While there is a legal content element to each Street Law class (e.g., family law, housing law, rights and liberties, etc.), the students learn this content through the process of physical interaction rather than through listening alone. Throughout the class, they actively participate in learning scenarios such as role plays, mock trials and legislative hearings, small group discussions, and simulations. As Arthurs and others explain:

> Street Law introduces learners to the law and legal systems while remaining grounded in the best practices in civic education that research shows help learners develop their cognitive, expressive, academic, and critical thinking abilities through the exploration of a variety of civic and law-related situations.[40]

This interactive teaching methodology is a foundational element of Street Law programmes and is precisely this approach that differentiates Street Law from both traditional law school classes and more basic know-your-rights public information campaigns. Through student-centred learning in which students actively participate in the learning process, 'program participants build their understanding of practical legal matters and develop the skills and attitudes they need to effectively engage in the democratic processes of their communities'.[41]

With the explicit focus not only on the acquisition of legal knowledge but also on the improvement of critical thinking (e.g. argument analysis, examination of underlying assumptions, judgements of fairness, etc.), the development of democratic skills (e.g. persuasive argument, building of consensus, public speaking, etc.) and the promotion of civic attitudes (e.g. commitment to the rule of law, understanding of the rights and responsibilities of citizens, belief in the power of civic action, etc.), the goals and intended outcomes of Street Law are different from those of traditional legal education in law schools. Street Law is not recreation of law school for young people, but rather provides an opportunity for them to distil relevant legal topics into practical lessons which build their legal knowledge, democratic skills, and civic attitudes. Success is not measured on academic success

40 Sean Arthurs et al., 'From Zero to 60: Building Belief, Capacity and Community in Street Law Instructors in One Weekend' (2017) 24(2) International Journal of Clinical Legal Education 118, 125.

41 Street Law, Inc., 'Law School Programs' (*Street Law, Inc.*) <https://www.streetlaw.org/programs/law-school-programs> accessed 11 November 2020.

and the passing of exams (or, for that matter, entry into the job market) but rather on personal growth and civic development. The empirical data on the impact of Street Law on high school students, albeit limited, shows that the initiative is highly beneficial to the students. One study found that high school participants improved their critical thinking skills by nearly 25 per cent, showing increased ability to 'articulate and support their opinions, consider multiple perspectives on an issue, evaluate evidence, and formulate a conclusion based on their analysis of a complicated fact pattern'.[42]

## Street Law in a neoliberal higher education system

At a glance, nothing about Street Law is neoliberal. The value proposition at the heart of Street Law is that democratic societies need engaged and critical individuals to be successful. It does not see the self-interested individual as the fundamental building block of the economy but rather sees civically interested individual as the building block of democratic society. Street Law focuses on the enrichment of communities and on how individuals can engage in their community to improve the wellbeing of those around them. While Street Law certainly hopes to improve the knowledge and skills of the individual students, the purpose of that education is not primarily to facilitate students' personal advancement and their development of marketable skills, but rather to support them in to become more engaged, involved, and participatory members of their communities. With this communitarian tinge, neoliberal higher education institutions should have no apparent use for Street Law. While perhaps altruistic, an initiative that aims to build high school students' civic skills does not advance the mission of preparing future lawyers for the market. While other community-oriented programmes like live client clinics at least allow lawyers to practise the skills that they will use in their jobs, no law school explicitly aims for its graduates to be high school teachers. As such, the neoliberal law school should have no use for Street Law.

Yet despite its apparent subversion of the neoliberal mind-set, Street Law has thrived and grown. Over the past four decades – the same time frame that neoliberal policies have become commonplace in both society at large and in higher education – Street Law has grown and expanded and law schools around the world are now actively supporting Street Law programmes at their institutions. Today, by conservative estimates, Street Law now exists in more than 70 law schools in the United States where it began and in hundreds more in at least 40 countries around the world.[43] Robust networks of Street Law programmes and practitioners in Western Europe, Eastern Europe, Asia, and elsewhere now meet and share best practices,[44] international journals dedicated to studying the

42 Sean G Arthurs, 'Street Law: Creating Tomorrow's Citizens Today' (2015) 19 Lewis & Clark Law Review 925, 953.

43 Arbetman (n 5).

44 Association of Legal Clinics of Ukraine, 'Home' <legalclinics.in.ua> accessed 11 November 2020; Center of Development of Legal Clinics, 'Home' <codolc.org>

initiative regularly publish academic examinations of programmes,[45] and global, well-financed organisations now exist to support the further growth and expansion of Street Law.[46]

With an educational approach that is community-centred, not focused on individual advancement, and decidedly differentiated from the values of neoliberalism, how has Street Law managed to not only survive but truly thrive? An explanation lies in an examination of the beneficiaries of Street Law. While the initiative was started specifically with the community (i.e. high school students) as the primary beneficiary, law students (and by association the neoliberal law school institutions that serve those students) also benefit from Street Law. In addition to being a communitarian initiative that focuses on improving wellbeing in the wider community, Street Law is also a valuable educational experience that provides a positive impact for the law student – the self-interested individual at the heart of a neoliberal law school. Though the starting point, rationale, and value orientation of Street Law may be contrary to neoliberal ideals, the outcomes for the law students align with the neoliberal educational approach. Street Law, therefore, is a valuable initiative within the neoliberal higher education system.

It is worth exploring in depth the ways in which Street Law provides benefits to the law students in the context of their legal education. As higher education is expensive, and time and resources are limited, many students (and parents) prefer classes that directly and explicitly tied to knowledge and skills needed for the intended job market. As Roche points out, those that pay for higher education 'want to know that their financial investment will help [them] secure a livelihood'.[47] However, contrary to the implicit argument that more general and less technical educational pursuits are a bad investment, soft skill-focused initiatives may in fact be a more efficient training ground for a lifetime in the labour market. The number and type of jobs in Western economies today are drastically different than they were in the industrial boom after WWII. While there are certainly still factories which require low-skill assembly line labourers, the new knowledge economy means that more and more employers are seeking workers who have a diverse set of skills. Technical or pre-professional training initiatives are only able to train students for the jobs or technology that currently exist. With the rapid pace of social, economic, and technical change that happens within today's society, the pre-professional training that a student receives may be out of date soon after she enters the labour market. More generic and cross-disciplinary skills are not only more enduring but are also more transferrable across the job market. It may actually be more efficient to teach skills such as critical thinking,

accessed 11 November 2020; BABSEACLE, 'Home' <www.babseacle.org> accessed 11 November 2020.

45 The International Journal of Public Legal Education (n 6); The International Journal of Clinical Legal Education, 'Home' (*Northumbria Journals*) <https://www.northumbriajournals.co.uk/index.php/ijcle> accessed 11 November 2020.

46 Global Alliance for Justice Education (n 6); Street Law, Inc., 'Home' <www.streetlaw.org> accessed 11 November 2020.

47 Roche (n 35), 1.

problem solving, and self-teaching skills than to focus solely on pre-professional skills.

There is evidence that the job market, even the with the current neoliberal tinge, does appreciate these 'soft' skills. As Harland notes:

> governments and markets recognize value in liberal education, and certain liberal forms of knowledge are seen to have economic utility. Critical thought and action are required to handle knowledge in the new knowledge economies, and graduates are also recruited on the basis of their critical capacities.[48]

Furthermore, The World Bank recognises that competencies such as problem solving and self-learning are critical skills that every student should learn.[49] Several studies have suggested that when making hiring decisions, employers rate competencies such as communication and problem solving as more important than technical or work experience skills.[50] It is worth noting that while the market may value a soft skills-focused education, that does not mean that the goal of a soft skill education is to provide valuable labour for the market. Rather, the market is rightly discovering that education which celebrates criticality and the building of interpersonal skills in fact turns out superior workers.

Street Law programmes are not designed to be professional training for future lawyers. Few lawyers spend their legal careers teaching young people practical lessons about how their lives and the law are intertwined. However, legal employers and the clients that they serve – like others in the labour market – are increasing valuing the soft skills and relationship building approach that students learn and hone through participating in Street Law. Results from a variety of empirical studies on the competencies that both organisational and individual clients want from their lawyers suggest that an overly technical approach to lawyering and legal education is not always best. As Hamilton notes:

> Technical legal skills are considered a given by clients, and, to stand out, an attorney must demonstrate strong client relationship skills. Whether serving individual or corporate clients, attorneys need to understand the client context and develop the ability to relate to their clients.[51]

48 Tony Harland, 'The university, neoliberal reform and the liberal educational ideal' in Malcolm Tight (ed.) *The Routledge international handbook of higher education* (Routledge 2009) 511, 518.

49 The World Bank, *Building Knowledge Economies: Advanced Strategies for Development* (The World Bank 2007).

50 OECD, *Education Policy Analysis 2001. Paris: Organisation for Economic Co-operation and Development* (OECD 2001) <http://www.oecd-ilibrary.org/content/book/epa-2001-en>.

51 Neil W Hamilton, 'Connecting Prospective Law Students' Goals to the Competencies that Clients and Legal Employers Need to Achieve More Competent Graduates and Stronger Applicant Pools and Employment Outcomes' (2019) 9(2) St. Mary's Journal on Legal Malpractice & Ethics 260, 275.

Not surprisingly, legal employers who are driven by the need to secure clients are also seeing the value of the soft skills emphasised in Street Law programmes. Recognising the need for their employees to have more than simple technical knowledge of the law, many law firms, governments, and other legal employers are moving towards a competency-based hiring approach in which candidates are assessed on their demonstrated interpersonal and legal skills. Among the most important competencies identified are teamwork, communication, and project management.

Law students hone their abilities at these exact competencies through participation in Street Law programs:

- Teamwork – most Street Law programmes operate through a team-teaching approach in which sets of two law students co-teach classes. This collaborative approach requires close collaboration between the students. However, even when students teach alone, they work closely with the partner teacher to ensure that their lessons meet the needs of the school or organisation. They also collaborate with their fellow law students and their professors to debrief and reflect on their work.
- Communication – Street Law students learn to clearly communicate with their students. Specifically, they must explain complex legal topics in language that is understandable to young people and individuals without formal legal training. As young people are curious and ask questions, the law students learn to be prepared to think on their feet and respond appropriately to questions.
- Project management – with a classroom full of students and a teacher relying on the law students to teach, the Street Law students learn to be exceptionally prepared. They must take the time to research legal topics, prepare lesson plans, and execute a dynamic and interactive lesson in the allotted time.

These interpersonal skills align with the human capital theory roots of the neoliberal ideology in education. Brought to popularity in the mid-20th century, human capital theory posits that education or training increases an individual's skills and productivity which in turn allows them to earn higher wages.[52] Though the theory is often associated with a narrow view of education focused solely on job training, the theory does acknowledge the value of more general skills and interpersonal competencies as they relate to economic success.[53] From the purely economic position through which the human capital theory views the world (which, admittedly, has been critiqued as an artificially narrow lens[54]), Street Law

52 Tristan McCowan, 'Theories of Development' in Tristan McCowan and Elaine Unterhalter (eds) *Education and International Development: An Introduction* (Bloomsbury 2015).

53 Donald Gillies, 'Human Capital Theory in Education' in Michael Adrian Peters (ed.) *Encyclopedia of Educational Philosophy and Theory* (2017 Springer).

54 Steven Klees, 'Human Capital and Rates of Return: Brilliant Ideas of Ideological Dead Ends?' (2016) 60(4) Comparative Education Review 644.

builds students valuable human capital which results in a higher individual economic return for them. Neoliberal law schools are thus incentivised to offer these programmes to their consumers, the students. Street Law prepares law students for the job market and does so through a unique and interesting educational experience for them. In the highly competitive market of law schools in which schools compete for students by highlighting not only their job placements but also the rich and diverse learning environment it offers, a neoliberal law school can hardly afford not to offer Street Law.

Though Street Law was conceived as a communitarian programme intended to benefit the community, the initiative has tangible benefits to the law student participants as well. While these benefits for law students are primarily on soft skill growth and the development of strong lawyer–community bonds, the evidence suggests that the labour market is beginning to value these competencies perhaps even more than a technical understanding of the law. From a neoliberal perspective, Street Law programmes are therefore efficient initiatives that provide value for students that in the form of preparing them for their careers and making them attractive on the labour market. Furthermore, the skills law students hone during their participation in Street Law programmes will likely serve students throughout their careers (i.e. beyond the first ten months that law schools are incentivised to care about) and may propel them to become leaders in the field. The marketable skill development of the programmes offers an explanation as to how a seemingly anti-neoliberal initiative like Street Law has been able to grow and flourish in increasingly neoliberal-leaning institutions of higher education. Setting aside the community orientation of Street Law's origin and mission, the outcomes of Street Law as they pertain to the law student participants fit squarely within the neoliberal law school's incentives.

## Conclusion

From its origins, Street Law presented a different educational approach to the traditional neoliberal legal educational model. Its focus on building the knowledge and skills of others, enhancing community connection, and developing of active and engaged citizen does not naturally fit into the individual- and market-oriented mindset of the neoliberal higher education institution. However, Street Law also achieves many of the desired goals of neoliberalism through the benefits that it provides to the law student participants. It prepares them with the marketable soft skills that legal employers are looking for in new hires, helps them hone their critical thinking skills which will serve them throughout their long careers, and ultimately helps develop their human capital. This is not to say that Street Law has somehow been corrupted by neoliberal educational policies – Street Law is simultaneously communitarian and neoliberal, civic and individual. As such, it is perhaps one of the most beneficial initiatives a law school can invest in.

This chapter examined a real-world example of how unique and communitarian educational initiatives can exist within the context of neoliberal thought. The implications of this analysis are not limited to Street Law but can be applied to a wide variety of unique, entrepreneurial, or even subversive initiatives in the higher education setting. Despite its hegemonic status in higher education, neoliberalism can allow for and even value seemingly disruptive ideas and initiatives. The value of unique education programmes like Street Law can cut across the political and ideological spectrum and the benefits of it can appreciated from seemingly disparate viewpoints. As Harland points out:

> liberal educational values may have found a new ally, because neoliberalism has also latched onto the economic benefits of such an education. If these liberal educational attributes do prove their worth in the knowledge economy, recovery of older aims and purposes may be rapid.[55]

Even within the seemingly most rigid and uncompromising political ideologies, forward thinking pragmatism, both in policy and in viewpoint, can support and nurture initiatives of value.

55 Harland (n 48), 520.

# 9 Using institutional theory in legal education

*Peter Čuroš*

The institutional approach utilises Pierre Bourdieu's conception of habitus and contends that the legal profession does not operate solely on formal rules but also on informal knowledge. This chapter demonstrates how students can be familiarised with this knowledge through the lens of institutional analysis, which is holistic; using historical, organisational, and structural features to understand social phenomena. In the case of the institution of the legal profession, it uses its overlapping methods of jurisprudence, legal history, and sociology as it perceives institutions as social facts created by human action to explore and understand how they relate to individuals. Providing students with this contextual understanding aims to help them become aware of their autonomy and to develop personal and professional independence of mind.

The chapter will conclude with some practical suggestions for how this approach could be included in a legal ethics programme, including example materials, exercises, and case law, which will allow students to apply the institutional approach to the concept of the legal profession's independence.

## Introduction

This chapter argues that the institutional approach can provide a way of helping students to identify the influences, normative systems, and biases that are present in the legal profession. Developing an awareness of the legal profession as a socially constructed institution will help students develop and maintain their personal and professional autonomy and independence. It aims to encourage students to identify and become aware of how broader social forces can determine their profession's values and norms. This approach draws on the work of Pierre Bourdieu and seeks to analyse the legal profession as an institution in a diachronic[1] and synchronic[2] way.

1 A method, which focuses on the change – becoming, of the meaning and position of a phenomena in social system in the past. The reader may observe this approach later in the chapter, as pointing on the evolution of the concept of political independence in the past.

2 A method, in which we consider the meaning of a phenomenon in no connection to the past. We focus strictly on the placement of this phenomenon and relations to

DOI: 10.4324/9780429299247-10

This chapter builds on the author's experience of teaching legal ethics in Slovakia. It draws on examples of legal education and the legal system in the related context of Central and Eastern Europe. It aims to help promote an approach to legal education which will support the development of socially responsible lawyers who are accountable for their actions and have a nuanced understanding of their position in society. Although this discussion does not address Clinical Legal Education directly, partly due to the limited use of this pedagogy in Slovakia, nevertheless it is anticipated that readers will find the insights developed in relation to legal ethics are relevant to Clinical Legal Education.

Part I will provide an overview of the legal education system in Slovakia and Part II will summarise the institutional approach, before showing how this can be applied to legal education in Part III. Part IV will explore how these insights can be applied to legal ethics education.

## Part I. Legal education in Slovakia

Slovakia has a civil law legal system and lawyers can serve as judges, prosecutors and procurators, advocates, in-house lawyers, or notaries, and they may serve in legislative or administrative bodies. There are two key threads connecting all of them: they are all required to ensure the proper functioning of the legal system and they are required to act with the independence necessary to maintain fairness and the rule of law.[3] Understanding the institutions of the Slovakian legal system needs to be put in the context of its recent political history following the Velvet Revolution.[4] While the transition of the economy in a country that experienced a half-century of an authoritarian political regime[5] happened quickly, the transition of the legal system remains an ongoing process. It has become evident that changing the formal rules of institutions is not sufficient to ensure the rule of law. There remains a lack of confidence in legal institutions and a concern over

other phenomena in the social system. The reader may observe this approach in chapter on the conceptual analysis of the political independence of the lawyer and relation to other kinds of independence of the lawyer. This method is typical for linguistic analysis. See Ferdinand de Saussure, *Course in General Linguistics* (Philosophical Library 1959) 96.

3 What all legal systems have in common, including the civil and common law traditions, is that 'fundamental to any study of lawyer ethics is an appreciation of the lawyer's role with respect to clients, the profession itself, the state and the public interest generally', James Moliterno and Paul Paton, *Global Issues in Legal Ethics 2d* (2nd edition, West Academic Publishing 2014) 181.

4 Velvet Revolution was a non-violent transition of political power from the rule of the Communist Party of Czechoslovakia to the parliamentary republic in Czechoslovakia in 1989.

5 We may talk about period 1939–1989, as the area was under influence of Nazi Germany form 1939–1945 and the Communist Party came to power in 1948. The period between 1945–1948 was also a time of the rise of the authoritative policies due to the post-war conditions.

corruption.[6] According to the results of a 2020 Eurobarometer survey, 64 per cent of the general public ranked the justice system's independence as bad, while 26 per cent ranked it as good.[7] In the spring of 2020, 13 judges were arrested by the police under accusations of corruption. In the summer and autumn, six others joined them. The ongoing investigation has uncovered the inappropriate relations that these judges held with business leaders, politicians, and advocates; sometimes delivering judicial decisions on request. These investigations have caused the Slovak judiciary to experience a voluntary exodus of judges, which has not been seen since 1989.[8] In sum, nearly 20 judges were accused of corruption, and several advocates are facing charges for corruption and obstruction of justice.[9]

The thesis of this chapter is that these issues are made worse by a narrow conception of law being limited to formal regulation, a conception which is currently being perpetuated by the current Slovak legal education system.[10] The institutional approach to legal education can challenge a narrow and formalistic approach to law, an approach which emphasises textualism and limited grammatical interpretation, rather than the socially nuanced and critically aware understanding that is necessary for the independence of the profession and the operation of the rule of law.

6 See more James E Moliterno and others, 'Independence Without Accountability: The Harmful Consequences of EU Policy Toward Central and Eastern European Entrants (Regulation of Legal and Judicial Services: Comparative and International Perspectives)' (2018) 42 Fordham International Law Journal 551.

7 'PublicOpinion-EuropeanCommission' <https://ec.europa.eu/commfrontoffice/publicopinion/index.cfm/survey/getsurveydetail/instruments/flash/surveyky/2258> accessed 6 December 2020.

According to Eurobarometer results in 2017, only 25 per cent of people in Slovakia tend to trust, and 66 per cent tend not to trust, the judicial system. According to Eurobarometer results in 2013, while in the EU an average of 53 per cent tend to trust the national justice system, and 43 per cent tend not to trust, in Slovakia 25 per cent tend to trust and 66 per cent distrust, there is still 9 per cent of those who did not know whether they trust or not. Overall, Slovakia ended up last but one. In 2009 it was not much different; trust in the Slovak judicial system was on 28 per cent, and the judicial system ended up as least trustworthy among the national parliament and government. In the same issue, it cannot be said that inhabitants of Slovakia would consider this phenomenon to be natural, when 58 per cent considered the situation to be worse than in other systems, while 25 per cent considered it to be similar, and only 6 per cent considered it to be better than in other systems of the EU, 'Flash Eurobarometer 461: Perceived Independence of the National Justice Systems in the EU among the General Public – Ecodp.Common.Ckan.Site_title' <https://data.europa.eu/euodp/en/data/dataset/S2168_461_ENG> accessed 5 May 2020.

8 'Dissimilar Similarities' (*Verfassungsblog*, 26 November 2020) <https://verfassungsblog.de/dissimilar-similarities/> accessed 7 December 2020.

9 <https://spectator.sme.sk/c/22355425/kocners-judges-charged-and-detained.html?ref=av-left>.

10 For more on critique of the textualist approach see Michal Bobek, 'The Fortress of Judicial Independence and the Mental Transitions of the Central European Judiciaries' (2008) 14 European Public Law 99.

## Part II. The institutional approach to social phenomena

The institutional approach seeks to understand the historical, organisational, and structural features of social phenomena. This approach is used in legal theory,[11] history, and sociology and[12] is also used in economics,[13] psychology,[14] and organisational analysis.[15] The origins of the institutional approach can be traced to a range of thinkers, but for reasons of space, this chapter will focus on the contribution made by Pierre Bourdieu, which will be discussed further below.

Institution has been defined in various ways; by content 'they are made up of norms and knowledge, which can be formal or informal and which can persist over time'[16] or by its role in society, 'Institutions are the rules of the game in a society, or, more formally, are the humanly devised constraints that shape human interaction'.[17] Our social life is conducted within social institutions, which are stable structures within society and which shape our understanding of social reality. Institutions provide a map for the individual to communicate and achieve their goals through socially recognised forms of action. As an individual is born and raised within a structure of social institutions, it can be difficult for her to identify them, leading to the assumption that these institutions are natural and eternal, not constructed and temporary.[18]

This chapter proposes the institutional approach can be used as an instrument in legal education to promote a critical understanding of the habitus of the legal profession, which will be discussed further below in relation to the work of Pierre Bourdieu.

### *II.I Bourdieu's conception of habitus*

Pierre Bourdieu's[19] theory of habitus made an essential contribution to the institutional approach and explained the motivation for an individual's action in their

11 See Ota Weinberger, *Law, Institution and Legal Politics: Fundamental Problems of Legal Theory and Social Philosophy*, vol. 14 (Kluwer Academic Publishers 1991). N MacCormick and Ota Weinberger, *An Institutional Theory of Law: New Approaches to Legal Positivism*, vol. 3 (1st ed., Springer Netherlands 1986).

12 As Emile Durkheim calls sociology to be the science of institutions.

13 See Douglass Cecil North, Understanding the Process of Economic Change (Princeton University Press 2005).

14 See Serge Moscovici, 'The Origin of Social Representations: A Response to Michael' (1990) 8 New Ideas in Psychology 383.

15 Ronald L Jepperson 'Institutions, Institutional Effects and Institutionalism'. In Paul J DiMaggio and Walter W Powell, *The New Institutionalism in Organizational Analysis* (University of Chicago Press 1991) 143.

16 Hans Petter Graver, 'Judicial Independence Under Authoritarian Rule: An Institutional Approach to the Legal Tradition of the West' (2018) 10 Hague Journal on the Rule of Law 317, 323.

17 Douglass C North, *Institutions, Institutional Change and Economic Performance* (University Press 1990) 3.

18 John Searle, *Making the Social World: The Structure of Human Civilization* (Oxford University Press 2010).

19 Pierre Bourdieu (1930–2002) – French sociologist, anthropologist, philosopher, and public intellectual.

social framework. His approach is helpful in explaining the structure of the legal profession and professional ethics. In his relational approach, the role of elites, such as legal professionals, is studied as part of 'making' law and the legal field through their competing strategies and practices. As Bourdieu explains, habitus is the underlying structure of social life, the way that we enter the range of objective possibilities[20] with knowledge about ourselves:

> The structures constitutive of a particular type of environment (e.g. the material conditions of existence characteristic of a class condition) produce habitus, systems of durable, transposable dispositions/structured structures predisposed to function as structuring structures that is, as principles of the generation and structuring of practices and representations which can be objectively 'regulated' and 'regular' without in any way being the product of obedience to rules, objectively adapted to their goals without presupposing a conscious aiming at ends or an express mastery of the operations necessary to attain them and, being all this, collectively orchestrated without being the product of the orchestrating action of a conductor.[21]

The habitus builds on shared values and the responses to these values. Our surroundings inform our thoughts, preferences, and values, meaning that we are not as autonomous as we might feel that we are. This structuralist insight of Bourdieu tells us that the aspect of how we look at the world is limited by our habitus or the underlying structure of our social group. A person is usually not aware of the habitus. It is a socially ingrained disposition internalised through our life, primarily in childhood, especially at school and in the family and secondarily at university and in practice. It shapes the individual's perception of social reality and her reaction to it. It is a result of both past events that an individual experienced and of objective social facts characteristic of the individual's position in society. As Bourdieu claims:

> in each of us, in varying proportions, there is part of yesterday's man, it is yesterday's man who inevitably predominates in us since the present amounts to little compared with the long past in the course of which we were formed and from which we result.[22]

The habitus is therefore a socially acquired predisposition to perceive, think, and act in a particular way, and this predisposition results from exposure to the particular events a person encounters. When the individual's position within the group becomes stable, the habitus becomes unconscious: 'Yet we do not sense this

20 This range of objective possibilities is called a field in Bourdieu's theory. A field a is social and professional context in which agents act subject to a hierarchy.
21 Pierre Bourdieu, *Outline of a Theory of Practice*, vol. 16 (University Press 1977) 72.
22 Ibid., 79.

man of the past, because he is inveterate in us; he makes up the unconscious part of ourselves'.[23]

While a habit is the particular mechanical action of an individual, habitus is the way of action in the context of the social conditions and individual experiences. Habitus works on the practical level as a way of categorising perceptions, assessments, and principles of action.[24] It resides in an unconscious adherence to the tastes and distastes, sympathies and aversions, fantasies and phobias, which forge the unconscious unity of a class.[25] All these preferences grow in the individual throughout her life and form attitudes for decision-making. Habitus exists in doxa: while habitus is a system of durable, transposable dispositions among individuals, doxa presents underlying opinions commonly held in a field. It is a socially constructed state, yet often accepted as the natural order.[26]

The habitus works on the principle of regularities and patterns, and it helps the individual to cope with the unpredictable.[27] These regularities and patterns define the reactions of the members of the field, in our case the legal profession, toward situations they face. Therefore, it is possible to expect a similar outcome in similar situations. Thanks to habitus, social practice is reproduced. Bourdieu's habitus explains why lawyers, even from various generations, maintain the processes and ways of action in a particular way, despite the change of the institution of the legal profession and institutions connected to it. A part of the Slovakian legal profession's habitus (discussed above) is mechanical prima facie positivism. The institutional approach is proposed as a means to shift this habitus toward a more socially responsible legal profession which champions the rule of law. The applicability of this approach to legal education will be outlined further below.

## Part III. Institutional approach and legal education

The institutional approach to legal education should give students a clearer picture of the social reality, or habitus, in which they will act as lawyers. It can show them that what they considered to be natural, according to the particular place, time, and environment in which they lived, is mostly a social creation that they take part in, largely unconsciously.

Lawyers are required to gain 'a full understanding of the mode of operation of the social institutions which are charged with the tasks of making, sustaining, interpreting, applying, and enforcing the law'.[28] To understand the law, we must also understand its normative structure; the informal practices, attitudes, beliefs, and values that guide its application, enforcement, and the development of formal

23 Ibid., 79.
24 Ibid., 17.
25 Ibid., 82.
26 Ibid., 164.
27 Ibid., 72.
28 Hans Graver, 'Judicial Independence Under Authoritarian Rule: An Institutional Approach to the Legal Tradition of the West' (2018) 10 Hague Journal on the Rule of Law 317, 321.

rules. An institution is always bound 'to the context of and for the purposes of norms and rules which (in complex sets) variously give sense to, justify, regulate or even authorize human conduct in social settings'.[29]

For example, consider the common question posed by a layperson for a student of law: 'Would you be able to defend a murderer?' This provides an opportunity for students to question the doxa of the legal profession and in contrast to the perspective of the layperson. A layperson is likely to see a lawyer using all the instruments to acquit the client, including misinforming the court or disqualifying a relevant witness. Lawyers know that this is not what lawyers do. Neither rules of a lawyer's duties nor the institution of the judiciary expect the lawyer to represent a defendant in a way that allows misleading the court. Criminal justice expects a lawyer to provide the client with legal advice and representation to protect her rights in case the state could threaten those. No duty can demand that a lawyer mislead the court to help her client.[30] On the other hand, the line of questioning may go: the client is the one who pays the lawyer. If not her, another lawyer may easily agree to the client's strategy; who will know and who will prove that the lawyer offered misleading information to the court?

The answer should be that the lawyer knows. She knows about the rule in the code of conduct for lawyers. Crossing the limits of a lawyer's role in criminal defence is, therefore, breaking the rule on false or misleading information.[31] However, where in the statute is the clear border of how zealous the lawyer can be in defence of her client? Can the lawyer have knowledge of the defendant committing a crime and still support the defendant's declaration of innocence? Can the lawyer use the strategy in the witness's testimony aiming to disqualify the trustworthy witness? The relation between the lawyer and her client, the court, and the opposing party is hard to deduce solely from the content of the professional code. Perhaps that is why, especially on the matter of the lawyer's role in the criminal proceeding, there are many varying opinions of how a lawyer is supposed to act.[32] It is helpful to have these matters solved in case law, which serves as an answer for the lawyer. On the other hand, the civil law system does not consider case law to be a relevant source of law and neither in professional conduct. Memorising the code with vague provisions on the lawyer's duty to the

29 Neil MacCormick, *An Institutional Theory of Law* 14.

30 In reaction to opinion of Monroe H. Freedman, Lawyers' Ethics in an Adversary System (Bobbs-Merrill 1975).

31 CCBE code of conduct, rule 4.4 <https://www.ccbe.eu/NTCdocument/EN_CCBE_CoCpdf1_1382973057.pdf> accessed 20 December 2020.

32 See for instance Carrie Menkel-Meadow, 'The Trouble with the Adversary System in a Postmodern, Multicultural World' (1996) 38 William and Mary Law Review 5, David Luban, 'Legal Ideals and Moral Obligations: A Comment on Simon (Response to Article by William H Simon in this issue, p. 217) (Symposium: W M Keck Foundation Forum on the Teaching of Legal Ethics)' (1996) 38 William and Mary Law Review 25, William H Simon, 'Should Lawyers Obey the Law? (Symposium: W.M. Keck Foundation Forum on the Teaching of Legal Ethics)' (1996) 38 William and Mary Law Review 217.

court without understanding the lawyer's role is not helpful, neither for students nor for lawyers.

Therefore, the institutional approach may give students and practitioners of law a better perspective to view these issues and provide a way of understanding that lawyers' professional responsibility is more than acting prudently enough not to be sanctioned. Students may see the bigger picture regarding the criminal procedure's aims, the history of advocacy, and the role of advocacy or accountability in individual action. Using the concept of Bourdieu, the issue arises of how we can break the never-ending cycle of performing habitus within doxa. The answer is not beating the habitus or getting rid of doxa, but acknowledging their existence and promoting a slow shift through practice and education.

University education needs to provide students with a space for broadening their views and opening them to critical thinking; thinking where the analysis goes beyond the surface level. Thinking critically, a person may doubt how straightforward a concept like independence is, for example, as independence is not as clear-cut as its provision may at first seem. The aim is to challenge the image that the students have towards the legal profession and to encourage them to consider how institutions have impacted on their thinking. When we focus only on the legal provision and leave everything else out of the analysis, we might view some principles or doctrines as simpler than they are. Focusing on this mechanical and formalistic approach in practice not only harms the chances of maintaining the rule of law but also harms the lawyer as an individual, for she becomes just an instrument for the action of another. A brief summary of how this approach can be used in relation to teaching legal ethics will be provided below.

## Part IV. Teaching legal ethics using the institutional approach

Space doesn't allow for a full description of the course, but a summary of the approach taken to teaching the independence of the legal profession will be provided below. The institutional approach to legal education was used for the course of Legal Ethics at the Pavol Jozef Šafarik University in Košice between 2016 and 2019.

The concept of the independence of the lawyer was introduced to students and explored from a variety of perspectives, including financial, personal and political. The approach used to introduce students to the concept of political independence will be explained here. This form of independence was contextualised in two ways. Firstly, it was contextualised in relation to the previous communist political regime. Here the aim was to explore the response to unjust laws and how lawyers became powerless under totalitarianism. Secondly, students were encouraged to compare how the concept of lawyers' independence and accountability functioned in a democratic regime. We started with the question: how did legal professions fail to protect rule of law in history?[33] This task aimed to encourage students to

33 See Gustav Radbruch, 'Five Minutes of Legal Philosophy (1945)' (2006) Oxford Journal of Legal Studies 13. 'An order is an order', the soldier is told. 'A law is a law',

reflect on their role in protecting the rule of law and the importance of learning how to approach the problem of an unjust law.

The 1946 essay 'Gesetzliches Unrecht und Übergesetzliches Recht'[34] by German legal philosopher Gustav Rabdruch provides an excellent starting point for this exploration. The essay presents a topic that is tightly knitted to recent issues facing Slovakia. The first of these is the importance of knowledge of legal institutions in a country that has faced the authoritarianism of Nazism and Communism over the course of 50 years. Providing students with this historical context helps them understand the contemporary situation. Analysing the historical continuities and discontinuities with the past is an essential part of the institutional approach. This analysis can introduce the fundamental question of retroactive law, which has become a contemporary issue in Slovakia since a recent controversial decision of the Constitutional Court.[35] This not only provides an opportunity for students to discuss the decisions of the Constitutional Court,[36] but it also serves as an introduction to the main question that is the central focus of subsequent seminars: the independence and accountability of lawyers and judges.

Using the institutional approach also allows students to engage with the question of how legislative and judicial powers should solve conflicts that exist between two different political regimes, totalitarian and democratic, existing one after the other. In learning how to handle the conflict of the 'unjust law' of the previous regime, students can be referred to various opinions across particular cases from the second half of the 20th century. For example, students can be introduced to the facts regarding the case study of the Grudge Informer[37] case, trying to find a solution on their own, before being introduced to Lon Fuller's arguments. In this way students are able to explore the various ways that courts have resolved the conflict of opposing political regimes.[38] Additionally, they are asked to engage

says the jurist. The soldier, however, is required neither by duty nor by law to obey an order whose object he knows to be a felony or a misdemeanour, while the jurist – since the last of the natural lawyers died out a hundred years ago – recognises no such exceptions to the validity of a law or to the requirement of obedience by those subject to it. A law is valid because it is a law, and it is a law if, in the general run of cases, it has the power to prevail. This view of a law and of its validity (we call it the positivistic theory) has rendered jurists and the people alike defenceless against arbitrary, cruel, or criminal laws, however extreme they might be. In the end, the positivistic theory equates law with power; there is law only where there is power.

34 Gustav Radbruch, 'Gesetzliches Unrecht und übergesetzliches Recht' (1946)1 Süddeutsche Juristen-Zeitung 105.

35 Decision of the Constitutional Court of the Slovak Republic, PL.US 7/2017 on an annulment of amnesty and a presidential pardon.

36 For example, when reading a 127-page-long decision, it might be helpful for undergraduate students to be shown how to go through the decision of the Constitutional Court, distinguish arguments, evaluate position of dissenting opinions, arguing for both sides of the argument, etc.

37 Lon L Fuller, *The Morality of Law*, vol. 1963 (Rev. ed., Yale University Press 1969) 245–253.

38 For example by: a) amendment of the law – new law with no retroactive effects, b) 'This "law" was not a law at all. It was a perversion of law, and therefore it has

with relevant decisions of the Slovakian Constitutional Court and compare them with academic commentary including the Nordhausen court decision,[39] the Bamberg case,[40] and Mauerschutzer,[41] as well as theoretical works on the topic.[42]

Building on this foundation, students are provided with a summary of the development of laws regulating lawyers since 1939. These laws begin with the period of the Slovak Republic under the influence of Nazi Germany (1939–1945).[43] Following that is the period of the rule of the Communist Party in Czechoslovakia (1948–1989),[44] and, finally, the period of democratic transition after 1989.[45] Students are asked to look for provisions on duties that form the cornerstone of the legal profession. These include the duty of confidentiality and management of waivers, remuneration of lawyers, and professional discipline, including the reporting of disciplinary wrongdoings.

A final case study completes the course on the concept of political independence. Students are invited to study the Mešencová's case,[46] a complicated case

always lacked validity', c) the possibility of accepting moral arguments as a priority of one positive prior to other positive law, breaking the standard legal principles such as legal certainty or prohibition of retroactivity, d) interpretation of the law valid in times of the authoritarian regime.

39 Gustav Radbruch, Bonnie Litschewski Paulson, and Stanley L Paulson, 'Statutory Lawlessness and Supra-Statutory Law (1946)' (2006) 26 Oxford Journal of Legal Studies 1.2.

40 H L A Hart, 'Positivism and the Separation of Law and Morals' (1958) 71 Harvard Law Review 593, 617.

41 Case of Streletz, Kessler, and Krenz v. Germany, Applications Nos. 34044/96, 35532/97 and 44801/98 (Strasbourg 22 March 2001).

42 For example, Gustav Radbruch, 'Gesetzliches Unrecht und übergesetzliches Recht' (1946) 1 Süddeutsche Juristen-Zeitung 105. H L A Hart, 'Positivism and the Separation of Law and Morals' (1958) 71 Harvard Law Review 593. Lon L Fuller, 'Positivism and Fidelity to Law: A Reply to Professor Hart' (1958) 71 Harvard Law Review 630.

43 Government regulation no.6/1939 Coll. – on the service of civil servants, judges, and lawyers.

Attorneys following the registration in the Chamber of Lawyers make this oath: 'I swear to the living God that I will always be faithful to the Slovak state and obedient to the government, I swear that we will keep all laws and regulations in force, and that I will fulfill all my duties conscientiously'.

44 Act no. 322/1948 Coll. – Zákon o advokácii (Law on advocacy), Oath: Attorneys are required to contribute to the maintenance and consolidation of the people-democratic regime and to assist state authorities in the implementation of law … Act no. 57/1963 Coll. on Advocacy: The role of the advocacy: § 2 'Advocacy assists with all its activities in educating citizens to preserve laws, to protect socialist property, to observe labor discipline, to respect the rights, honor and honor of fellow citizens, to honor all obligations towards the state and society, and to adhere to the rules of socialist coexistence'.

45 Act no. 132/1990 Coll. on Advocacy: §1 A Duty of the Advocacy (1) Advocacy helps to establish constitutional citizens' right of defence and to protect other rights and interests of citizens and legal entities in accordance with the Constitution and the laws. Advocacy is an independent profession, which could be carried out only by this statute.

46 Decision of the Supreme Court of the Slovak Republic no. 3Sž 36/2006.

in which a lawyer became an agent in service of the police to convict a fellow lawyer of bribery. Students need to sort through several decisions[47] to understand the nature of this case. The final discussion can then be examined to uncover the myriad questions posed, with the students' understanding of the political independence of lawyers informing the educational process.[48]

The primary goal of the institutional theory in education is to give students the bigger picture to understand the institution of the profession itself. The institutional approach may be more demanding and time-consuming for a student. However, it also allows the student to evolve as a leader and an autonomous, socially responsible lawyer. It gives a teacher hope that in her work, she is producing not only rule-obeying servants of the legal system, but independent thinkers who are able to discharge the duty of the institutional duty of the legal profession to promote and defend the rule of law.

The application of the institutional approach to the concept of political independence is just one example. Other aspects of the independence of the lawyer elaborated in the course include financial issues such as the dangers of contingency fees and the financial dependence of the lawyer on the client. Another form is economic independence, which covers the issues of multi-discipline practice and alternative business structures, as well as legal options on how to practice law in Slovakia and other countries. Finally, independence of competence, including issues related to confidentiality and conflicts of interest, are also explored in this course.

Students are encouraged to understand that institutions are a system of norms, rules, and beliefs that both are concerned with, and form the connecting phenomena of social practices.[49] A lawyer is not a machine for legal services, who can possibly be used as a tool for any aim. Lawyers are supposed to be leaders, and, therefore, must be trained as such. Lawyers must not obey rules simply because of the fear of a sanction, for if the sanctions are lacking, then this motivation disappears. Students need the information to understand their role as

47 Decisions of the Special Criminal Court where he was found guilty for attempt of bribery PK- 2Tš/15/2015. Decisions of the appellate court – Supreme Court of Slovak Republic – that confirmed the previous decision of the Special Criminal Court no. 2 Toš 2/2007 and no. 2 To 2/2015, which was the final decision in this case. Decision of the Constitutional Court of the Slovak Republic no. I. ÚS 129/ 2010/33, which revoked the decision. Final decision of the Supreme Court of Slovak Republic no. 2 Toš 2/2007 – the lawyer accused of bribery was acquitted according to the decision no. 2 Toš 2/2015.

48 The questions necessary to be discussed are:

Is it wrong for the lawyer to cooperate with the police department?

Is it different when the lawyer enters the position of a police agent to convict the colleague of bribery?

What is the lawyer supposed to do in Mešencova's position according to national law?

What ought the lawyer to do in your opinion?

49 Ota Weinberger and Alexander Bröstl, 'Inštitucionalizmus: nová teória konania, práva a demokracie' (Institutionalism: New Theory of Behaviour, Law and Democracy) (Bratislava Kalligram, 2010) 70.

lawyers and how they will serve society. Hence, it is crucial to provide for them a picture that is as comprehensive as possible.

Moreover, to foster this autonomy in students it is important to provide them with a space for discussion; a teacher's role becomes more of a moderator than a lecturer. When the teacher finishes the introduction of the arguments, she may follow with the Socratic method and a formal questioning of the details of her students' arguments. The goal is not to come to one single right answer, as often in discursive questions there is none. The goal is to show students how to find and apply arguments and to be accountable to those arguments. In this way the institutional approach echoes Aristotelian conceptions of educational practice: 'virtues we get by first exercising them. … For the things we have to learn before we can do them, we learn by doing them.'[50] Studying previous and hypothetical cases is essential preparation for eventually approaching real clients' cases.

Another helpful method is a comparison to show that the regulative solution of their system is neither the only possibility nor necessarily the best. It is essential to show students how difficult it is to step out of their 'social box' and how instructive it is to have an opportunity to leave it for an alternative view. Another useful method is confronting students with the mirroring of social reality in art. As Herbert Marcuse says, 'only art and the great refusal are ways how to disrupt the social reality we are living',[51] and therefore it is helpful to use cinematography, literature, philosophy, or painting not only as a teaching analogy but for disruption of what we might take as a given.

## Conclusion

Lawyers are essential for the functioning of the rule of law in a democratic society and are symbols of the institution of law itself. Their actions help inform the public's perception of the effectiveness of the law; whether it can protect the rights of the weak and regulate the power of the strong. Using the institutional approach to understand the role of law as a normative concept helps student to appreciate that the role of the lawyer is vital in securing equal rights for the powerless and the powerful.

Teaching legal ethics using the institutional approach is an example of how to show students that they are no longer applying rules in another person's interests.[52] In the case of so-called positive law, in the context of Central and Eastern Europe, the typical legal ethics course is supposed to give an aspiring lawyer all the necessary tools for handling another person's agenda, to decide over another party's case, or to defend another person's rights. Alternatively, in the approach argued for in this chapter, the student is helped to learn how to act with

50 Aristotle, *The Nicomachean Ethics of Aristotle* (Dancing Unicorn Books 2016) 1003a.

51 Herbert Marcuse, *Eros and Civilization: A Philosophical Inquiry into Freud* (Beacon Press 1966) 118.

52 James E Moliterno, 'An Analysis of Ethics Teaching in Law Schools: Replacing Lost Benefits of the Apprentice System in the Academic Atmosphere' (1991) 60 University of Cincinnati Law Review 83, 98–99.

independence. In other words, students in this course do not enjoy the detachment that helps a lawyer maintain her distance in order to gain objectivity in understanding the case of another person. In legal ethics, the question does not stand as, 'How would you solve this issue for your client?' or 'How would you decide such a dispute?' Just the opposite – this course asks a student, 'How would you act in such a situation?' Instead of holding the aspect of an observer, the lawyer is taking upon herself the role of a participant.

> Unlike in other areas, in the law governing lawyers, the lawyer is the client. When a lawyer interacts with the law generally, she does so as a once-removed expert. The client who comes to the lawyer has direct contact with the law; the client has the tort problem or the contract problem. The lawyer's experience with the law is vicarious, through its application to the client. Not so the law governing lawyers.[53]

This approach attempts to help students understand not only the law itself but also its development and implications for society. Therefore, it is necessary to look at the history of the institution and understand the changes that the concept has undergone. Using these methods might help students leave 'the bubble' in which they live. Knowing only of a particular culture at a particular time would unavoidably lead to the so-called mechanical jurisprudence.[54] As lawyers broaden their scope of interest, we might get closer to the primary goal of applying the law: to solve conflicts in society.

We expect a lawyer to be autonomous in her actions, understanding the duties of representing a client, practising candour towards the court, and maintaining the well-being of society. It might be an unreachable goal to obtain these outcomes through a paternalistic education system based on the approach that says, 'Listen, you will be told how the practice ought to be done'. On the other hand, letting students enter the practice without a proper understanding of the role of their profession in society may lead them to understand lawyering as another form of a lucrative business, one that allows a person after legal training to enter the higher levels of society and gain large amounts of wealth.[55] One of the most important outcomes of a student's legal education should be that personal financial gain is not at the core of the attention of the lawyer.

Students need a space to find out that there are no truths of grand narratives and no right answers for discursive concepts. The notion of what they consider to be their subjectivity is formed by the culture, society, and community in which they live. External influences determine personal views and knowledge. It would

53 James E Moliterno, 'Experience and Legal Ethics Teaching' (2001) 12 Legal Education Review 3, 6.

54 Zdeněk Kühn, *The Judiciary in Central and Eastern Europe: Mechanical Jurisprudence in Transformation?* vol. 61 (Martinus Nijhoff Publishers 2011) 191 and following.

55 Aaron Benavot, 'Institutional approach applied on the institution of education'. In Lawrence J Saha, *International Encyclopedia of the Sociology of Education* (Pergamon 1997) 340–345.

make no sense to tell students these sentences at the beginning of the course and continue lecturing as if this information is taken for fact. The role of the institutional approach is to help students of law understand that the moment and place in which they live is part of a flow. Particular human actions of the past are influencing the present and will shape the future. Our views are just a minimal window, determined by our place in the environment in which we presently belong.

# 10 Legal pluralism and Clinical Legal Education in Ethiopia: The contribution of legal aid clinics in realising access to justice

*Getachew Assefa Woldemariam*

## Introduction

In common with other African jurisdictions, Ethiopia's legal system comprises a mix of legal principles of Western origin and its peoples' customary laws. Although the intention of the 'modernising' statesmen of the country was to root out customary laws and institutions of the people and replace them with a single legal system modelled on Western principles, this could not be realised. As this chapter will show, despite the Ethiopian government's derecognition of customary law in criminal law and most civil law areas, de facto, customary legal systems of the various communities still operate in these fields. The Ethiopian legal system therefore comprises of legal norms that originate from both formal and informal sources. Informed by the theoretical conception of 'legal pluralism', legal education in Ethiopia pays attention to the customary legal system alongside the modern state-based laws. The legal aid clinics run by the law schools in Ethiopia utilise customary laws to settle disputes that their clients are involved in.

This chapter analyses the pluralistic nature of Ethiopian laws and legal institutions in relation to Clinical Legal Education and the free legal aid services that law schools in the country give to members of the community who cannot pay legal service fees. The chapter also considers the Clinical Legal Education (CLE) component of the LL.B. curriculum of Ethiopian law schools. It describes the endeavours that law schools are making to ensure access to justice through their legal aid clinics or centres. The chapter closes with concluding remarks that call attention to challenges law schools are facing preventing them from establishing high quality Clinical Legal Education programmes and running more impactful legal aid services. It will also point out the implication of the research for further study.

## Legal pluralism in Ethiopia

The parallel existence and application of religious, customary and formal state laws characterise the Ethiopian legal system throughout its existence dating back to around 1000 BC.[1] Until the last quarter of the 20th century, it had a

1 Harold Marcus, *A History of Ethiopia* (University of California Press 2002) 3.

DOI: 10.4324/9780429299247-11

monarchical form of government. Christianity remained a state religion from AD 331 until 1974 when the communist military government that toppled Emperor Haile Selassie disbanded this arrangement and started promoting an anti-religious policy. Owing to this fact, up until 1930, the normative order of most of the Christian highland of the country consisted of monarchical edicts, canonical laws[2] and of course the people's own folk laws. In the case of communities in far-flung areas that had only tribute-paying relationship with the monarchs, the predominant normative orderings at work were their own indigenous (folk) laws, because they were not under the direct control of the monarchs.[3] In 1930, Ethiopia had its first penal code, with a purported nationwide application, often cited as the pioneering state-enacted modern law.

Although Ethiopia was never colonised and, therefore, Western laws were not imposed on it through colonial administration, Ethiopian monarchical governments became predisposed to receiving Western legal institutions and styles of public administration, at the turn of the 20th century. This emanated from their strong belief that the Western legal and institutional modes of governance would usher in what in Amharic is known as 'ስልጣኔ' (pronounced as *silitane,* roughly meaning modernisation). Thus, in 1907, for the first time in the country's history, ministerial departments based on a Western government model were established by Emperor Menelik II (r. 1889–1913). As noted above, the Emperor's decision to create various departments was motivated by his desire to 'modernise' the governance and justice system of the country for the benefit of all its inhabitants.[4] This was followed by the creation of divisions of courts, under the Minister of Justice, that were to preside over different segmented parts of the country. Western-style substantive and procedural laws were enacted starting from the 1930s.[5] Between 1957 and 1965, Emperor Haile Selassie (r. 1930–1974) oversaw the enactment of six codified laws.[6] Five of the six codes were drafted by foreign comparative law experts.[7]

Emperor Haile Selassie's policy was to create a legal system that was modelled on the Western laws by completely displacing the customary laws and institutions of the society. This same policy continued under the military

2 Abba Paulos Tzadua (transl.), *The Fetha Negast: The law of the kings* (Carolina Academic Press 2009) xvii.
3 Bililign Mandefro, 'Agricultural Communities and the Civil Code' (1969) 6(1) Journal of Ethiopian Law 145, 152; Norman Singer, 'Modernization of law in Ethiopia: A study in process and personal values' (1970) 11 Harv Intl LJ 73, 74.
4 Mahteme-Selassie Woldemeskel, Zikre Neger (in Amharic) (2nd edn, Addis Ababa: n. p., 1970), 53.
5 See Getachew Assefa, 'Towards widening the constitutional space for customary justice systems in Ethiopia' in Susanne Epple and Getachew Assefa (eds), *Legal Pluralism in Ethiopia: Actors, Challenges and Solutions* (Transcript, 2020) 43.
6 The legal codes were: the 1957 Penal Code; 1960 Civil Code; Commercial Code (also of 1960); 1961 Criminal Procedure Code; 1961 Maritime Code; and 1965 Civil Procedure Code.
7 Peter Sand, 'Current trends in African legal geography: The interfusion of legal systems' (1971) 5 Afr LS 1, 12, 14.

government.[8] The policy of total displacement of customary legal institutions was changed to some degree with the coming to power of the Ethiopian Peoples' Revolutionary Democratic Front (EPRDF) – a front of guerrilla movements that turned into a ruling coalition – defeating the military government. Through a Constitution it adopted in 1995, the EPRDF established a federal state structure with nine state members to the federation and two city governments designated as federal territories. In an unusual way, the Constitution bestows sovereignty on entities within the country it calls 'nations, nationalities and peoples'[9] and gives each and every one of them an unconditional right to self-determination, including secession. In this chapter, these entities are collectively referred to as 'ethno-linguistic communities' or 'cultural communities'.

The 1995 Constitution carried EPRDF's policy position into effect by embracing customary and religious laws and courts. According to the Constitution, thus, 'the adjudication of disputes relating to personal and family laws in accordance with religious or customary laws through religious and customary courts, with the consent of the parties to the dispute' is not precluded.[10] Accordingly, litigants may opt to have their disputes in the area of family and personal matters settled by customary (and religious) laws and courts even when the standards in these laws and courts may not live up to the ones provided by the Constitution itself or other state-enacted laws. The constitutions of the member states of the federation have made analogous arrangements with regard to customary and religious laws and courts.

The constitutional dispensation just described imparts a significant message, yet in another respect. The explicit carving out of family and personal matters as areas serviceable through customary and religious laws and courts gives the meaning that all other areas of dispute, and law and order, are under the monopoly of the formal state-enacted laws and state-created institutions. Although this may be the intention of the framers of the Constitution, in reality, the state laws and institutions have never fully and completely displaced the customary laws and institutions in areas such as criminal law or other civil matters. As noted earlier, Emperor Haile Selassie's revolutionary scale attempt to uproot the customary legal system could not be realised. This is because the people continued to use their customary laws in rural areas far away from the reaches of the central state which account for most of the population. Although over the years the state apparatus has increasingly spread out to the rural areas, the way of life of the people remained deeply cultural. Thus, the reality has always been that most disputes – from the simplest to the most complex, such as homicide cases[11] – especially outside urban locations – get resolved through customary systems. Each

8 Getachew (n 5).
9 Art 39(5).
10 Constitution of Ethiopia, articles 34(5) and 78(5).
11 See, generally, Dolores A Donovan and Getachew Assefa, 'Homicide in Ethiopia: Human rights, federalism, and legal pluralism' (2003) 51(3) Am J Comp L 505; Alula Pankhurst and Getachew Assefa (eds), *Grass-roots justice in Ethiopia: The contribution of customary dispute resolution* (United Printers, 2008).

of the more than 80 cultural communities in the country has its own customary legal institution which has its own rules and procedures as well as institutional structures to settle just about any kind of dispute arising within the geographical scope of the concerned community.

As it should be clear by now, the legal systems in operation in Ethiopia can be categorised into three broad types. The first one is the formal state-sponsored legal system controlled and enforced by the state. Applying Brian Tamanaha's exposition of legal pluralism,[12] one can say that the state-enacted legal system is itself very richly plural, comprising federal law, state law, local government law, the customary laws of various cultural communities incorporated into the formal laws, applicable international law and other normative orders that are directly sanctioned by the state. The second legal system consists of the customary and religious laws and courts allowed by the Constitution to function in the areas of family and personal matters. This component of the legal system is different from the first one mainly because its normative contents are not created by the state but are sourced from the customs and religious rules of the concerned communities. The third legal system comprises the composite of de facto vibrant customary legal institutions of the more than 80 ethno-linguistic communities which handle all kinds of disputes that arise in the communities. Its difference with the second one is its non-recognition by the state. It lies outside the de jure recognition of the state. But despite the state policy towards them, the customary institutions of the ethno-linguistic communities have continued to function in these areas unaffected by the lack of state recognition giving rise to a de facto situation of legal pluralism.

The existence in Ethiopia of the three types of normative orderings described above could be analysed within the context of the theory of legal pluralism. One of the foremost theorists of the field, John Griffiths, notes that legal pluralism is 'the presence in the social field of more than one legal order'.[13] He says, 'when in a social field more than one source of law, more than one legal order is observable that the social order of that field is said to exhibit legal pluralism'.[14] All the social fields in a given political society identifiable as a modern state are acted upon by various sources of regulation for the multitudes of activities taking place in them. These multiple sources of regulation are what is called legal pluralism.[15]

Griffiths identifies two regimes of legal pluralism: strong and weak. By strong legal pluralism is meant the reality of existence of different legal systems and institutions in a society without one being superior to or the other being

12 See Brian Z Tamanaha, 'Understanding Legal Pluralism: Past to Present, Local to Global' (2008) 30 Sydney L Rev 375; Brian Z Tamanaha, 'The Promise and Conundrums of Pluralist Jurisprudence' (2019) 82(1) MLR 159.

13 John Griffiths, 'What is Legal Pluralism' (1981) 24 J Leg Plur 1, 1.

14 Ibid., 38.

15 As it is well known, this view of sources of law is to be contrasted with the 19th century proposition by legal positivists that law is the command of the sovereign. See John Austin, *The Province of Jurisprudence Determined* (first published 1832, W E Rumble, ed., CUP 1995).

dependent on the first, while weak legal pluralism is the admission that a legal system is pluralistic when the state validates or recognises different bodies of law for groups within the population differentiated on account of religion, ethnicity and the like.[16] Weak form of legal pluralism, Griffiths observes, is a compromise by the ideology of legal centralism until the heterogeneous and less advanced societies of former colonies have grown into a homogeneous population of a modern nation-state.[17] This colonial ideological relic has been taken over by the post-colonial governments of ex-colonies nourished by the desire to aid economic and social development. The weak form of legal pluralism has theoretical support beyond it being the darling of political practitioners in post-colonial societies.[18]

Griffiths' seminal work is widely credited for shattering the myth constructed around the pre-eminence of state-enacted laws vis-à-vis all other normative orders in a society. Even critics of Griffiths such as Brian Tamanaha[19] acknowledge the path-breaking contribution of Griffiths' 'What is Legal Pluralism?' As Sally Merry observes, 'legal pluralism is a central theme in the reconceptualization of the law/society relations'.[20] It therefore is fair to say that Griffiths brought to the limelight the theoretical discourse on the relationship between state, law and society. This does not mean, however, that all the questions on and about the notion of legal pluralism have been settled. As Sally Merry notes, there are debates on the very meaning of the notion, on its components, on whether all normative orders in society can be properly called law, and on the terminology or proper name for the non-state normative orderings.[21] One terminological saga, for example, relates to the term 'customary law'. Theorists in the field such as Hooker and Snyder argue that the term 'customary law' is a colonial creation that should not be applied to the true indigenous laws of the people in the colonised world, including Africa.[22]

Nonetheless, there is also a wide concurrence on certain important aspects of the notion of plural normative orderings in a society. The idea of legal centralism is discredited. It is widely accepted that in today's complex societies, there are other 'multiple systems of ordering'[23] in addition to the state-sponsored legal order. Some of these normative orderings may or may not be recognised by the state. But they regulate the social fields to which they apply and by which they

16 Griffiths (n 13), 7.
17 Ibid.
18 See, eg., M B Hooker, *Legal Pluralism – An Introduction to Colonial and Neo-Colonial laws* (OUP, 1975).
19 In the two works cited above (n 12), Tamanaha objected to Griffiths' classification of legal pluralism into 'weak and strong', arguing that the idea of 'weak' legal pluralism has undermined the rich diversity and pluralist features of what comes under the rubric of formal (state-enacted) law; see ibid.
20 Sally E Merry, 'Legal Pluralism' (1988) 22 LS Rev 869.
21 Ibid., 875–879.
22 See Hooker (n 18); Francis G Snyder, 'Colonialism and Legal form: The Creation of "Customary Law" in Senegal' (1981) 19 J Leg Plur 49.
23 See Sally Falk Moore, 'Law and social change: The semi-autonomous social field as an appropriate subject of study' (1973) 7 LS Rev 719, 720.

are given effect. The most important such non-state legal field is the indigenous or customary legal regime that is still vibrant in most of the African societies, including Ethiopia. Empirical studies also consistently show that there are interactions, cooperation and even hybridity between state law and non-state law.[24]

In Ethiopia, the state has recognised customary as well as religious laws and courts in the areas of family and personal matters. But in all other areas, customary law does not have formal state recognition. But the reality is that the customary laws of the ethno-linguistic communities have not been abandoned and are indeed being applied consistently to regulate the affairs of the communities to which they apply. It needs to be noted in this connection that though the formal legal system has not recognised customary systems of the people in fields other than family and personal, the former no longer posits itself as incompatible with the latter.[25] There have developed different ways of cooperation and complementarity between the two. Moreover, in some fields such as land disputes, the laws of the federating units have identified customary institutions as first instance avenues for the settlement of such disputes.[26]

Legal education in Ethiopia takes a broader or pluralistic approach to normative orderings. This is evidenced by the fact that in the harmonised national LLB curriculum the following courses are offered: *Customary Law, Legal History and Traditions, Islamic Law* and *Alternative Dispute Resolution.* Moreover, one of the clinical courses in the LLB curriculum is called *Restorative Justice.* These courses look at various aspects of the non-state legal fields and their interactions with state-enacted laws and institutional structures. Through these courses, the law students are equipped with the necessary knowledge about the de facto and de jure positions of the non-state normative orderings and their relationship with the state (formal) legal system. After taking the courses, the students appreciate the importance and continued relevance of the customary (non-state) justice institutions of the more than 80 cultural communities inhabiting Ethiopia. The CLE programmes of Ethiopian law schools translate the theoretical legal education offered through the earlier noted courses into reality via live client clinics and externships. As discussed below, based on the nature of the legal disputes to which the clinic's clients are parties, the legal aid staff advise them to follow either state or non-state justice platforms.

## Clinical Legal Education in Ethiopia

CLE is an American creation. It started in the US law schools in the 1960s with Ford Foundation grants to promote practical legal education and instil

24 Merry (n 20), 881; see also Kairedin Tezera, 'Legal Pluralism and Emerging Legal Hybridity: Interactions between the customary, state and religious law among the Siltie of southern Ethiopia' in Susanne Epple and Getachew Assefa (eds), *Legal Pluralism in Ethiopia: Actors, Challenges and Solutions* (transcript, 2020) 263.

25 Kairedin Tezera, ibid.

26 Getachew (n 5).

professional responsibility in the graduates.[27] Geraghty and Quansah observe in this connection that:

> the clinical movement in American legal education has evolved to the extent that clinical education is now evident in every law school in the country. Almost every American law student is exposed to the 'real world' of lawyering through clinical legal education.[28]

Since then, CLE methodology migrated to different parts of the globe in different shapes and forms. In Africa, for example, CLE is part of the law curricula in Botswana, Ghana, Kenya, Malawi, Nigeria, Sierra Leone, South Africa, Tanzania and Uganda.[29] As this chapter discusses, Ethiopia has also offered CLE in its law schools since 2006.

CLE has been characterised as an effective interactive methodology for the teaching of law. Legal education in Africa, like education in many other disciplines, is dominated by uncritical receptive learning by students.[30] A clinical method of teaching can be used to change this approach to one in which students actively take part in the teaching–learning process. Clinical methodology involves a variety of models, including participation in live-client clinics, 'carefully supervised student externships in government agencies, non-governmental organizations (NGOs), and human rights organizations'.[31] During their clinical activities, students are brought in contact with the reality of legal practice; observe the good performances and shortcomings of the justice system in its treatment of the poor and marginalised, as well as the responses of government and non-governmental bodies to these needs.[32] If properly implemented, clinical education effectively responds to the real legal practice issues and social needs. By so doing it can resolve the longstanding criticism about African legal education that it is dominated by abstract legal theory of Western origin unrelated to the African reality.[33]

## The law curriculum in Ethiopia

Formal legal education in Ethiopia began as part of the then University College of Addis Ababa, the predecessor of Haile Selassie I University, in February 1951.

27 See Thomas F Geraghty, 'Legal Clinics and the Better Trained Lawyer (Redux): A History of Clinical
Education at Northwestern' (2006) 100 NW UL Rev 231.

28 Thomas F Geraghty and Emmanuel K Quansah, 'Reform of Legal Education in Ethiopia: the Ethiopian Experience in the Context of History, the Present, and the Future' (2008) 22(1) Journal of Ethiopian Law 49, 65.

29 Ibid., 63.

30 Muna Ndulo, *Legal Education in Africa in the Era of Globalization and Structural Adjustment* (2002) 20 Penn St Intl L Rev 487.

31 Geraghty and Quansah (n 28), 63.

32 Ibid.

33 Richard J Wilson, *Training for Justice: The Global Reach of Clinical Legal Education* (2004) 22 Penn
St Intl L Rev 421, 424.

In the 1950s, legal education at the University College was offered only in the evening programme at sub-degree level.[34] The first law school in the country was formally established as part of the current Addis Ababa University (then known as Haile Selassie I University) in 1963.[35] For more than 30 years, this Law School remained the only centre of legal education. It was only from the 1990s onwards that new university law schools were opened. At present, there are about 28 law schools which are all part of publicly owned and funded universities. The total number of undergraduate law students in all years (from 1–5) in all law schools in the regular programme is about 8,000. Each law school's annual intake of law students is about 60.

Legal education is an undergraduate education in Ethiopia. Students are admitted to law school after completing academic studies of 12 years culminating in the national school leaving examination. Before the early 2000s, university education was divided up into two phases: a general education[36] during the first (freshman) year and three years (four years for legal education, engineering and pharmacy, and six years for medical studies) of disciplinary studies. From around 2002 onwards, however, new education policy kicked in whereby the freshman year was removed from university curricula reducing the overall duration of university education by one year. Although this change is generally maintained in most disciplines of study, since 2006, fields of study like law, engineering, pharmacy and medicine readjusted the duration to what it used to be previously, i.e., five years and six years as noted earlier, without reintroducing the freshman year. As explained below, in the case of legal education, the readjustment of the duration was one of the recommendations of a report produced by the Legal Education Reform Programme initiated by the government. It is interesting to report here also that the freshman year has been reintroduced across all universities starting from the 2020/2021 academic year, thereby increasing by one year the duration of university education of those disciplines reduced to three years since 2002. The duration of legal education which has been five years shall remain the same with adjustments to accommodate the reintroduced freshman year.

Legal education in Ethiopia is being conducted based on a harmonised national curriculum introduced in 2006. Since 2013, the delivery mode for most of the courses has become modular with the 'European Credit Transfer System' (ECTS) for accumulation of required academic credits, by changing the hitherto 'credit hour' system. Accordingly, depending on the relative length of the materials for study, the modules of the LLB curriculum are made to have 3, 5, 7, 8 or 10 ECTS.

34 See, n.a., 'A short history of the Faculty of Law' (2000) 20 Journal of Ethiopian Law 161. The students at the time were judges, parliamentarians and other legal practitioners who hadn't had full-fledged legal studies before they assumed their various jobs.

35 Ibid., 164.

36 The freshman courses comprised of freshman English, liberal arts, life science and quantitative methods.

As earlier noted, since 2006, CLE has been part of the curriculum of legal education in Ethiopia. Before 2006, although there were practical courses of some sort in the curriculum through which law students obtained hands-on training, those courses were not delivered as clinical courses in the real sense of the term. The curriculum revision that resulted in the inclusion of the CLE component was preceded by a diagnostic study undertaken from 2003–2004 by an initiative dubbed the 'Comprehensive Justice Reform Programme' conducted under the auspices of the now defunct Ministry of Capacity Building. The reform programme assessed the state of legal education at the time and made some recommendations.[37] It suggested, inter alia, that law schools should be encouraged to introduce participatory and practice-oriented methods of teaching such as moot courts, legal clinics, practical attachments, exercises in legal drafting and legal interpretation, field research, problem-based assignments, and tutoring by legal professionals.[38] It in particular emphasised that legal clinics should be established and strengthened in all law schools.

The comprehensive justice reform programme was followed by a more focused 'Legal Education Reform Programme' under the same ministry which aimed at making a complete study of legal education in the country and coming up with suggestions that could be implemented. The report of the study that became public in 2006 notes, inter alia, that:

> The [law] curriculums in place [in Ethiopia] have failed to incorporate new demands and developments such as … alternative dispute resolution studies. The curriculum's failure to focus on skills-oriented courses and its inclination towards theory based courses stand out as a major problem of the curriculum. There is serious shortage of human and material resources needed for achievement of goals set by the curriculum. Another downside of the curriculum is its failure to clearly indicate mechanisms for quality assurance.[39]

The study conducted as part of the legal education reform programme led to two important outcomes: the revision of the law curriculum and the development of a five-year strategic plan (2007/08–2012/13). Although most of the planned activities of the strategic plan remained unfulfilled, the revised curriculum came into effect starting from the 2006/07 academic year. The 2006 curriculum was designed in such a way that it remedies the defects inherent in previous law curricula implemented at different times, chief among which were rigidity, focus on theoretical study and being divorced from the world of legal practice as well as current societal problems. The 2006 harmonised curriculum thus introduced many elective courses and skills-oriented courses.[40] It also incorporated courses of

37 See Federal Democratic Republic of Ethiopia, *Comprehensive Justice System Reform Program: Baseline study report* (PrimaveraQuint, 2005).

38 Ibid., 43.

39 Cited in Geraghty and Quansah (n 28), 67.

40 See Abdi Jibril Ali, 'The Need to Harmonise Ethiopian Legal Education and Training Curricula' (2011) 4(1) Ethiopian Journal of Legal Education 50.

study that cater for the new times that we are in. The elective courses were meant to allow students to have a broad spectrum of choices to plan their intellectual and career development. Skills-oriented courses introduced in the curriculum include Legal Research Method, Legal Writing, Pre-Trial Skills and Trial Advocacy, Appellate Advocacy and Appellate Moot Court, Judgment Writing, Externship and Clinical Programme.[41] The clinical programmes of the law schools that have become the harbingers of the legal aid clinics serving as points of access to justice will be elaborated on in the subsequent sections of this chapter.

## Access to justice and legal aid clinics in Ethiopia

### *Access to justice*

This chapter addressed the contribution of CLE to the realisation of access to justice. It is therefore necessary to briefly discuss the concept of access to justice.

Access to justice is a very broad notion and this chapter does not attempt to provide a comprehensive definition of the term but adopts a meaning given to it by scholars who have the same purpose for it as the one this chapter endeavours to achieve. Professor Marc Galanter's definition is one such definition. He notes that since the 1970s, the notion of 'access to justice' has come to mean 'the ability to avail oneself of the various institutions, governmental and non-governmental, judicial and non-judicial, in which a claimant might pursue justice'.[42] Another definition by Cappelletti and Garth is very relevant as well:

> The words 'access to justice' … serve to focus on two basic purposes of the legal system, the system by which people may vindicate their rights and/or resolve their disputes under the general auspices of the state. First, the system must be equally accessible to all; second, it must lead to results that are individually and socially just.[43]

In Galanter's definition, the fact that all avenues of dispensation of justice that meet the needs of those seeking settlement to their disputes satisfy the trust of the notion is noteworthy while the message Cappelletti and Garth's definition emphasises has to do with the accessibility to all of the justice system with the provision of just disposition of disputes. This is the meaning that the access to

41 National Harmonised Curriculum of the LLB Program (Ethiopia) (2006) (copy on file with the author).

42 Marc Galanter, 'Access to Justice in a World of Expanding Social Capability' (2010) 37 Fordham Urb LJ 115,116. See also M Drew and D Morris, 'Clinical Legal Education and Access to Justice: Conflicts, Interests, and Evolution' in S Estreicher and J Radice (eds), *Beyond Elite Law: Access to Civil Justice in America* (Cambridge University Press, 2016) 194–217.

43 Mauro Cappelletti and Bryant Garth, 'Access to Justice: The Newest Wave in the Worldwide Movement to Make Rights Effective' (1978) 27 Buff L Rev 181, 182.

justice we aim to make possible through the legal aid component of Clinical Legal Education in Ethiopian law schools has adopted.

Access to justice is a human right. Reference is made to this notion in the Ethiopian Constitution's Bill of Rights as well as in most of the major international and regional human rights instruments. Article 37 of the Ethiopian Constitution states in part that '[e]veryone has the right to bring a justiciable matter to, and to obtain a decision or judgement by, a court of law or any other competent body with judicial power'. Likewise, the Universal Declaration of Human Rights stipulates that 'everyone has the right to an effective remedy by competent national tribunals for acts violating the fundamental rights'.[44] The International Covenant on Civil and Political Rights[45] also guarantees, among others, the right to an effective remedy.[46]

In the context of the poor and the socially marginalised sections of the society, the main concern of the access to justice endeavour is to enable individuals to have a meaningful access to avenues of dispute settlement and make sure that their rights and interests are protected before these institutions by providing the support the particular persons ask for. In the legal aid sphere of the CLE programmes run by Ethiopian law schools, access to justice in no way is equated with access to formal institutions of justice alone. It rather has its meaning as access to all avenues of justice and dispute settlement, whether formal or informal. This understanding of access to justice bodes well not only for the theoretical frame of legal pluralism adopted by this chapter but also is a widely accepted meaning of the notion of access to justice.[47]

## *Legal aid providers other than the law school clinics*

There is a high demand for legal aid services in Ethiopia owing to the financial hardship most people face. The Ethiopian government has established a Public Defenders' Office (PDO) through which it provides representation to persons accused of crimes entailing loss of liberty. The Ethiopian Constitution provides that 'accused persons have the right to be represented by legal counsel of their choice, and, if they do not have sufficient means to pay for it and miscarriage of justice would result, to be provided with legal representation at state expense'.[48] Although the PDO preceded the Constitution in its establishment,[49] the main

44 Adopted 10 December 1948 UNGA Res 217 A(III) (UDHR), art 8.
45 Adopted 16 December 1966, entered into force 23 March 1976, 999 UNTS 171 (ICCPR), art 2(3).
46 See Mizanie Abate et al., 'Advancing Access to Justice for the Poor and Vulnerable through Legal Clinics in Ethiopia: Constraints and Opportunities' (2017) 11(1) Mizan Law Review 1, 4–5.
47 Lawrence M Friedman, 'Access to Justice: Some Historical Comments' (2010) 37 Fordham Urb LJ 3, 3.
48 Art 20(5).
49 The PDO was originally established in 1994 with the main purpose of representing the members of the toppled military government, known as 'Derg' that ruled the country from 1974–1991, in the criminal charges that were brought against them;

reason for its maintenance is the constitutional obligation on the government just noted. But as the statement quoted shows, the Constitution speaks only of persons accused of crimes that may entail miscarriage of justice to be the beneficiaries of the right. In other words, those who need legal assistance in their civil cases and, arguably, in simple criminal cases cannot claim to have such a constitutional right. But, in any case, the PDO in reality is extremely understaffed and its practical contribution in ensuring access to justice remained insignificant.

Through a sub-constitutional law, the government is also obliged to provide or oversee the provision of free legal aid services to indigents in civil matters. Proclamation No. 943 (establishing the federal Attorney General's Office) provides that the Attorney General has the duty to conduct litigation by representing citizens, especially women, children, disabled and the elderly, who do not have financial capacity to institute their civil action in federal courts. It is also given the mandate to represent victims of crime who do not have financial means in litigations or negotiations for their compensation, reinstitution and protection of their civil interests arising in relation to the crimes committed against them.

The other government-facilitated legal aid service is the one provided by licensed attorneys based on a legal requirement to render pro bono services of at least 50 hours per annum.[50]

The law says that free legal service (or service upon minimum payment) should be rendered to, among others, persons who cannot afford to pay or persons on whose behalf a court of law requests legal service. In reality, the enforcement of this mandatory pro bono service remained very minimal. Of late, the Attorney General's Office, the governmental organ in charge of the enforcement of this requirement, developed a practice of assigning one case to every attorney. An attorney who is assigned a case gets another case only after the case assigned to him or her has been disposed.

Although these legal requirements to support the litigation of those with financial hardship are commendable and display a pro-poor policy of the Ethiopian government, the fact of the matter is that due to the limited human resource capacity of the Attorney General's Office and the overall shortage of legal practitioners in the country, the number of poor and needy who face the justice system without any legal representation or counsel is enormous.[51] In this regard, therefore, especially when it comes to the human resource component, law school

Julie V Mayfield, 'The Prosecution of War Crimes and Respect for Human Rights: Ethiopia's Balancing Act' (1995) 9 Emory Intl L Rev 553, 555.

50 Federal Court Advocates' Code of Conduct Council of Ministers Regulations No. 57/1999 (Ethiopia), Article 49.

51 See Abera Hailemariam, *Needs Assessment Report on the State of Legal Aid Services: Assessments in Addis Ababa, Adama, Assosa, Bahir Dar, Hawassa, Jigjiga and Mekelle* (Addis Ababa, 2015). The existence of efforts by other institutions like the Ethiopian Lawyers' Association and civil society associations to provide free legal aid services in Addis Ababa and some regional cities is noteworthy as well. But due to the limited financial and human resources available to them, their impacts are insignificant. See ibid.; Mizanie (n 46), 11–13.

clinics fare very well compared to the Attorney General's Office and other individual efforts by civil society organisations. The law school clinics have the potential to engage generations of law students in the provision of the free legal aid services by opening legal aid centres. As the following sections attempt to demonstrate, the positive impacts, and potentials for more, of legal aid programmes of law schools are already felt strongly.

## *Law school clinical programme*

As earlier noted, the CLE programme was introduced in 2006 as part of the national harmonised LLB curriculum. In the curriculum, four courses (modules since 2013) have been designated as clinical modules. These are modules on Restorative Justice, Domestic Violence, Child Rights and the Rights of Prisoners. Among these four elective modules, a student is required to take only one. Each of the modules is given as a 3 ECTS module during the first Semester of the final (fifth) year of the LLB programme. The externship module is given during the second semester of the final year of the LLB degree studies at 20 ECTS as a required module to be taken by all students. The clinical module is said to require about 81 hours of work which should be spent on it by a student in the form of lecture sessions, tutorials, problem-solving sessions, project/clinic work, presentation and independent study.

Of the 81 hours of work, 18 hours (normally at the beginning of the module's delivery) are spent in the classroom y reviewing theoretical issues, and the relevant statutory and case laws applicable to the module. The classroom interactions also cover discussion on various tools such as interviewing, counselling, negotiation and mediation skills. The students are helped to acquire these skills through lecture and role plays or simulations.

Once the classroom component is completed, the students taking the clinical module embark upon the practical component, which is taken mostly in the legal aid clinics but in limited cases may be completed with other organisations. Students are expected to spend more than 30 hours of the total allotted time on their projects or cases which they happen to work on, working with their clinical pro fessors, and legal aid supervisors, and the clients of the legal aid centres. As explained below, this objective of the school's CLE programme was bolstered by the funding obtained from donors that helped create legal aid centres through which the students carried out the practical component of their clinical modules. In some legal aid centres, like those of Addis Ababa University Law School, each legal aid centre has a legal aid provider, a junior lawyer, who works full-time in the centre. The workings of the major legal aid clinics of the law schools in Ethiopia are described below.

## *Law school legal aid clinics*

As earlier noted, the harmonised LLB curriculum has introduced four elective clinical courses out of which a student has to take at least one. Thus, all the 28 law schools run some form of clinical programme. But the strengths (in human and material resources) of the law schools are dramatically different. Most of the law schools are less than ten years old. Their clinical programmes are just taking off and leave much to be desired. If anything, what should be said here is that they require support in terms of experienced faculty and resources in order for them to be able to produce competent and ethical legal professionals. In what follows, I shall limit my discussion to only the clinical legal aid programme of Addis Ababa University (AAU) Law School due to space limitations.

When the AAU Law School was established in the 1960s, it started out with a strong leaning on skills courses such as legal analysis, trial advocacy and legal drafting in order to address the immediate needs of trained legal professionals in the judiciary, prosecution, other governmental bureaucracies and private legal practice.[52] The graduates were supposed to take up their respective jobs in these institutions without any further skills-oriented, post-law school training because there was no institution to provide that. The students of the law school also in the early years took part in outreach services and practical education activities. The legal awareness creation exercise through dedicated radio programmes, and a student service programme[53] through which law students were attached to government offices were such noteworthy practical engagements.

But what can be properly called a clinical legal aid programme started at the AAU Law School in 2004 and even then only in a rudimentary way. It was initiated by this author's personal endeavour, supported by the then Dean of the Law School. A local NGO, known as the Organization for Social Justice in Ethiopia (OSJE) signed a memorandum of understanding with the law school in which it agreed to financially support the opening and upkeep of one legal aid centre in Addis Ababa. I became a faculty supervisor of the legal aid centre and some senior students participated in the rendition of legal aid services to the needy who sought the services. Students were not receiving any academic credits for their involvement with the legal aid centre because CLE was not part of the law curriculum back then. The legal aid centre which was opened off campus within walking distance of the law school operated for a little over a year and was suspended due to the troubles OSJE got into following the 2005 elections in Ethiopia because of the government's targeting and imprisonment of its highly talented and energetic human rights activist director, Mr Netsanet Demissie.[54]

52 James C N Paul, '"In the Beginning": Reflections on the Early Years of the Addis Law School' (2008) 22(1) Journal of Ethiopian Law 145, 147. James C N Paul (d. 2013) was the founding Dean of the Law School.

53 This programme was called 'Ethiopian University Service' and was launched in 1967 and required students to spend one year before their graduation on giving different services to the society related to their disciplines. See ibid., 150

54 Mr Netsanet Demissie, and also the current Commissioner of the Ethiopian Human Rights Commission, Dr Daniel Bekele, leaders of the Ethiopian Teachers' and Journalists' Associations, were thrown into prison along with leaders of the political opposition in November 2005 and later released after languishing in prison for more than two years.

As mentioned above, the CLE programme found its niche in the 2006 national harmonised LLB curriculum, giving its existence a curricular grounding. But due to financial and other organisational problems, the legal aid clinics as the most important platforms for the conduct of CLE were not operationalised until 2015. In 2015, the law school developed a project called 'Addis Ababa University Clinical Legal Education Public Interest Project'. This project was funded by the Royal Danish Government for two years (February 2015–March 2017). During its tenure, four legal aid clinics were operationalised in different locations of Addis Ababa (one on campus and the other three in premises of courts in Addis Ababa). With the expiry of this project in 2017, the law school approached the US State Department's Bureau of Democracy, Human Rights and Labor (DRL) by developing the 'Widening Access to Justice in Addis Ababa and its Environs' project. In September 2017, the project funding was granted by DRL initially for two years and has been renewed for another two years. Under the new project, two more legal aid centres were opened. The two additional centres were meant to serve as access to justice for the population (Affan Oromo speakers as well as non-Affan Oromo speakers) who seek justice in the justice institutions of the Oromia regional state of Ethiopia surrounding Addis Ababa, the working language of which is Affan Oromo.[55]

The stated goals of the project are: '[T]o improve students' practical lawyering skills and instil a strong sense of social responsibility and professional ethics, and to promote access to justice through the provision of legal aid service to indigent, at risk and vulnerable sections of the society in the target areas'. In respect of the access to justice component of the project's goals, attempts are being made to use the six legal aid clinics to reach those clients who have financial hardships to obtain paid legal counsel or representation. Over the last four and half years, the law school through, in the first two years four and from the third year on six legal aid centres, has been able to render different kinds of legal aid services to more than 7,000 needy clients. The legal services rendered at the legal aid centres include legal information/advice, writing statements of claim, defence, memorandum of appeal and court representation. There are also legal awareness programmes undertaken under the auspices of the project, including through radio broadcast by which over the last four years more than 150 radio programmes on different topics relevant to the lives of the majority of the population of Addis Ababa and its environs have been aired. These legal awareness programmes have created legal sensitisation of the public, thereby facilitating access to justice.

The legal aid clinics at AAU Law School (and indeed many other law schools in Ethiopia) are not specialised. All available legal aid centres accept all kinds of cases and provide the sought services. AAU Law School's legal aid centres are

55 This brings the number of such centres to three (one of the four previously opened centres – located in the premises of the Oromia Supreme Court in Addis Ababa – also renders service in Affan Oromo. In fact, the clinics working in Affan Oromo handled cases for needy clients in as far as Adama city of the Oromia region, 100 km away from Addis Ababa.

each staffed by a lawyer – legal aid provider – who works full-time in the centre. This lawyer handles all day-to-day legal services given by the centre where she/he works. Each centre is also supervised by a law faculty – legal aid clinic supervisor – who is in charge of the administrative as well as technical issues of the centre she/he is put in charge of. Ideally, the legal aid clinic supervisor would review the performance of the centre at least once every week, normally at the end of the week in review. But she/he also avails herself/himself physically and otherwise whenever she/he is needed for consultation on clients' cases or for guidance of students attached to the centre.

The students taking part in the legal aid clinics are those taking the elective clinical course noted earlier in this paper. In addition to these students, the project also involves volunteer students, usually those who have completed their third year of legal studies, to help in giving legal services under supervision of the faculty supervisor of the centre and the legal aid provider. In this way, each year, more than 200 law students have taken part in the provision of legal services as volunteers since the centres were opened.

## *The corpus of laws used at the legal aid centres*

One of the central aims of this chapter is to inform the reader that at the legal aid centres of AAU Law School (which is the case in all other law schools in the country as well) the laws utilised for catering for the needy clients that come to the centres are not only the various state-enacted laws. The corpus of laws used for entertaining the cases of clients contains both formal, state-enacted laws, and the informal (customary) laws of the people. This in fact is more so with the other law schools located outside Addis Ababa and far out in the peripheries of the country where, as discussed earlier in the chapter, customary laws and institutions of the various cultural communities of the country that live around the law schools are still vibrant.[56] Thus, the understanding that undergirds the conduct of CLE in Ethiopia is that the 'normative pluralism'[57] in the Ethiopian legal system is to be cherished and utilised to realise access to justice. As discussed earlier in this chapter, the legal education prepares the students to consider non-state legal orderings as effective for ensuring access to justice in most cases. At the legal aid centres, therefore, careful 'forum shopping'[58] takes place by the legal aid providers between state and non-state justice platforms in pursuit of the best interests

56 For the status of customary laws and institutions of the more than 70 various cultural communities of Ethiopia, see Pankhurst and Getachew (n 11); Gebre Yntiso, Fekade Azeze and Assefa Fiseha (eds), *Customary dispute resolution in Ethiopia* (Ethiopian Arbitration and Conciliation Centre, 2011).

57 John Griffiths, 'The Idea of Sociology of Law and its Relations to Law and to Sociology' (2005) 8 Curr Leg Iss 49, 64.

58 For the discussion on how forum shopping becomes a regular phenomenon in African legal systems where both formal and informal orderings exist side by side, see Keebet von Benda-Beckmann, 'Forum Shopping and Shopping Forums-Dispute Settlement in a Minangkabau Village in West Sumatra' (1981) 19 J Leg Plur 117.

of the clients. In the process of selecting a forum, we pay attention to the cases in which women and minorities may not be treated fairly in some non-state forums in which clients are advised to get access to the state justice platforms.[59]

The majority of the cases that come to the clinics relate to property issues (of which land-related disputes are the dominant ones), family and successions, and criminal matters. All of these disputes can potentially be resolved by the customary institutions based on customary laws.[60] Thus, at the legal aid clinics, when a client walks in with his/her case, after having listened to the presentation of the case, the first thing the student, the law professor or the legal aid provider at the centre does is to inquire about attempts, if any, that were made to settle the case through traditional dispute settlement means. If attempts were made but the disputants could not agree on the solutions proposed by the traditional institution, the centre proposes to make its own fresh attempt at mediating between the two sides. If the client becomes adamantly against any further attempt at the out-of-court settlement, then the centre advises the client of the possibilities about his/her case based on the formal (state-enacted) laws of the country.

Likewise, if the client's case is such that it is brought to the centre without passing through a customary forum, the centre would advise the client if he/she is willing to settle the case with his/her adversary through customary dispute settlement institution. If the client is willing to do so, the centre itself plays the role of mediator or refers the matter to traditional institutions for settlement based on the consent of the client. If the mediation (known in Amharic as *shimgilina* and in Affan Oromo *arrara*) by the centre or the traditional institution becomes successful, the agreement will be reduced to writing and signed copies issued to the parties. The legal bases for the settlement of the dispute at hand by the traditional institution are the customary norms of the society. But if the centre itself brokers the settlement, it does so by considering all matters, including the formal law. But the most important consideration for the centre is fairness and satisfaction in and agreements to the settlement by the parties.

The parties are expected to execute the settlement of disputes brokered by the centre in the way elaborated above. But it needs to be noted that one of the parties might change its mind down the line and comes back to the centre and seeks assistance for the case to be taken to a court of law. There is thus this lack of the binding nature of the out-of-court settlement of disputes of clients by the legal aid clinics. In the event that the client comes back (citing any hurdle that prevented the deal earlier made from being implemented) for the case to be entertained de novo, the court to which the case is taken may again advise the parties to try to settle it out of court through traditional avenues. In such instances, the

59 The unequal normative dispensations in some African non-state normative orderings are well known. See, for example, Ann Griffiths, 'Legal Pluralism in Botswana: Women's Access to Law' (1998) 30 J Leg Plur and Unoff L 123.

60 Each cultural community has at least one traditional institution that resolves disputes among members of the community. The institutions of some societies have hierarchical levels or jurisdictional strata while in others a given traditional institution has jurisdiction to settle any kind of dispute; see ibid.

fact that the case at hand had been subjected to mediation attempts weighs strongly against the court's decision to divert it to out-of-court settlement. But in cases that were not previously subjected to *shimgilina* or *arrara*, in most cases, the court would advise settlement out of court before it goes about settling it on the basis of the applicable formal law.[61]

The advantages of settlement of disputes by using traditional institutions have been well noted.[62] Among the most relevant advantages to our discussion here is its ability to both provide access to a friendly justice to the disputants and to ensure post-dispute settlement peace and harmony among the disputants and the whole community of which the disputants are members. Traditional institutions of dispute settlement do not stop at passing decisions on the cases brought before them. That is just one stage of their services. The next and most important step in the dispute settlement continuum is overseeing reconciliation (*erq* in Amharic or *arrarsa* in Affan Oromo) among the disputants and the people (relatives, neighbours, etc.) on the sides of the disputants. The latter one often involves an elaborate ceremony accompanied by feasts and mixing of the disputants and the people around them with each other.[63] This remains important in Ethiopia for a long time to come because of the strong traditional way of life of the people in which community plays a pivotal role. The legal aid clinics of the law schools are aware of this reality and are trying to utilise it as a tool in their attempts to help the realisation of access to justice in ways that sit perfectly well with the norms and ways of life of the communities which they are part of.

## Concluding remarks

This chapter has highlighted the attempts of CLE programmes in Ethiopian law schools to ensure quality and practical legal education while at the same time helping members of the community around them have an opportunity to access justice. The chapter has also outlined the pluralistic nature of the Ethiopian legal system and how the legal aid clinics are taking advantages of the various sources of law to settle disputes and bring about lasting social harmony among the disputants and the community at large. In this regard, the CLE programmes have taken the lead to educate law students about and to take advantage of the various normative orders to ensure access to justice of members of the society getting service from the legal aid clinics of the law schools. The CLE programmes of the law schools are contributing their fair share in making the policymakers recognise the vitality of the customary justice systems of the cultural communities. It has become clear to the government that the policy of Austinian legal positivism religiously pursued for most of the 20th century has never worked.

61 In my capacity as legal aid clinic supervisor of one of the legal aid centres of AAU Law School, I took part in several mediation attempts that were initiated by the centre and those that the courts of law before which we represented our clients had directed or advised.

62 See, e.g., Pankhurst and Getachew (n 11).

63 Ibid.

To conclude, this chapter will discuss two pivotal matters. The first relates to the challenges that law schools are facing: the bottlenecks preventing the law schools from doing better.

The first challenge has to do with the overall lack of experience by the law school faculties to teach or supervise clinical modules. The same faculty inexperience is also standing in the way of meaningfully delivering other skills-oriented courses introduced by the 2006 national harmonised curriculum. This is a fundamental problem that undermines the efforts of law schools, which needs to be addressed. The second challenge has to do with lack of funding to ensure the sustainability of the legal aid programmes that are serving thousands of needy people every year. Most of the legal aid services in all of the law schools are being provided through donors' financial supports. The sustainability of the legal aid services cannot be ensured unless the universities embrace the law schools' legal aid services and include them in their annual budgetary plans. The point of effectively turning the legal aid centres currently put in service by the law schools into the conventional legal clinics which Mizanie and colleagues discussed as lacking needs to be given a serious thought as well.[64] Finally, it is important to note that in all the law schools providing legal aid services, there is no meaningful cooperation between the legal practice and the law schools through which the judiciary and the practising attorneys support the practical components of CLE programmes. Concerted efforts therefore need to be made to institutionalise such relations to boost the resources the law schools.

The implications of the discussion in this chapter are manifold. I will mention two important ones here. The first one is the significance of a legal pluralist approach in the settlement of disputes and ensuring access to justice. The adoption of this approach by the CLE programme of Ethiopian law schools has tremendously contributed to increasing access to justice of members of society. Further research should be undertaken to broaden this approach and make it part of the practice of other legal aid providers as well. Second, now that increased use of non-formal legal norms is called for, it is necessary to put in place guidelines for CLE programmes and other legal aid service providers to, in a consistent manner, properly navigate through the plural normative orders to realise access to justice that protects the interests of all members of the society, including women, children, minorities and persons with disability or special needs.

64 See Mizanie et al. (n 46), 18–25.

# 11 The University of The Gambia Law Clinic: The role of a university law clinic in securing access to justice from the perspective of human rights and duties

*Christopher F Gray*

## Introduction

The Gambia is a small Commonwealth state in West Africa which has only had domestic legal education over the past 15 years, with Clinical Legal Education ('CLE') beginning even more recently still. The Gambia emerged from a 22-year dictatorship in 2017 with a democratically elected government,[1] and since transitioning to a freer and more democratic society there has been opportunity and political will for increasing concern for human rights and the rule of law.[2] This chapter will explore the opportunity of doing CLE in this political context, by looking at the activities of a law clinic through the lens of human rights in politics, philosophy and law. It will reflect on the goal of promoting access to justice through the framework of liberal human rights discourse and considers alternative approaches to understanding human rights and the obligations they create. Three activities of the University of The Gambia ('UTG') Law Clinic ('the Clinic') – casework, Street Law, and specialised clinics – will then be examined through these perspectives, reflecting particularly on the teaching implications of each of those activities.

This chapter will seek to evaluate the Clinic as a means of improving access to justice in the context of The Gambia. This will be done in three stages: firstly, examining how the Clinic articulates a goal of improving access to justice; secondly by considering how improving access to justice can be conceived of as a human rights obligation, and to whom that falls; and thirdly, how the Clinic's activities work towards this goal, and the extent of the Clinic's capacity to fulfil a duty to improve access to justice, which would be implicit under a human rights approach.

1 Al-Jazeera, 'Barrow to be officially sworn in as Gambia's president' *Al-Jazeera* (18 February 2017) <https://www.aljazeera.com/news/2017/2/18/barrow-to-be-officially-sworn-in-as-gambias-president> accessed 26 November 2020.

2 Madi Jobarteh, 'Civil and Political Rights in The Gambia' *Law Hub Gambia* (5 July 2018) <https://www.lawhubgambia.com/lawhug-net/civil-political-rights-gambia> accessed 26 November 2020.

DOI: 10.4324/9780429299247-12

The thesis of this chapter is that a liberal human rights approach to access to justice does not capture the value added by CLE because liberal human rights see their corresponding duties vested solely in the state. Viewing access to justice through a solidarity-community approach to human rights sees a duty to promote access to justice decentralised and vested in a range of actors in the local, national, and international community. Through this framework, the value of CLE as a tool for furthering access to justice can be seen more clearly. This framework will be used to analyse the three activities of the Clinic, outlined above, and it will be seen how the aim of the Clinic in inculcating students with social consciousness helps to fulfil human rights by promoting a commitment to improve access to justice as a duty. This framework will also expose the limits in CLE in promoting access to justice in The Gambia, as a solidarity-community approach to human rights also envisages duties owed by others in the international community in fulfilling human rights in The Gambia.

It is important to note that this chapter cannot claim to present the philosophical orientation which influenced the development of the Clinic. The author's involvement was brief and cannot be said to have shaped drastically the activities, which were developed prior to his involvement. The approach taken by the Clinic is a reflection of the values and hard work of staff and students at the University of The Gambia past and present. The purpose of the chapter is to articulate how CLE can be thought of as working to fulfil human rights obligations, rather than thinking of it as secondary to, or some charitable extra to, state activity to improve access to justice. The Gambia makes a particularly interesting case study for this as human rights has emerged as an increasingly important theme in political discourse, with the state's recent transition to a more free and democratic government.

## The UTG Law Clinic

The Clinic was established in 2012, the first instance of CLE offered to undergraduate students in the country. Over the period since its creation, the Clinic has had flurries of activity, offering a range of different activities to students, although its consistency has wavered due to resource issues.[3] There have been many successful projects: students have engaged in casework under the supervision of practitioners on issues relating to property, inheritance, and contractual disputes; they have built and implemented Street Law programmes for delivery in local communities; the Clinic has created specialist clinics through collaboration with other organisations, for example by undertaking research and policy work for agencies such as the Gambian Commission for Refugees.

The first constitution of the Clinic posits two objectives:

> 1.1 The objectives of the Law Clinic shall be:
>
> (i) To further the education of student members by exposing them to law in practice, providing comprehensive training and supervision in

3 For example: Report of Fulbright Specialist, Professor David Tushaus, to the University of The Gambia (9 June 2017) (on file with author).

practical skills and legal judgment and to foster in them a sense of social responsibility.

(ii) To provide accessible legal services to the local and wider community, strengthen the capacity and complement the work of other legal service providers and legally empower inhabitants of The Gambia.[4]

The first aspect of this provision, its educational aim, looks inwards at the pedagogical function of a law clinic. These include a practical pedagogy, exposing student members to 'law in practice': the processes and interactions which constitute the reality of the legal profession beyond that taught in doctrinal legal education; and a value-based pedagogy: 'a sense of social responsibility'. The second aspect of this provision, its legal aid aim, looks outwardly at the provision of services by the Clinic to the community. It suggests a direct provision of service, in 'providing accessible legal services to the [...] community'; and a support function, in 'strengthening the capacity [...] of other legal service providers'.

The work of the Clinic as a direct provider of legal services and in a supportive function creates a role within the Gambian legal system as a provider of legal services and a place for it within a broader scheme of access to justice. The activities which it undertakes all serve some function with respect to this aim, while also serving some educational benefit to the student members. As a legal aid provider, the Clinic fits into a broader ecosystem within the Gambian system, seeking to further a goal of access to justice. However, its educational aim also seeks to further access to justice, in that it seeks 'to foster a sense of social responsibility' within student members.[5] As will be explored in more detail below, this promotes access to justice by instilling it as a value among participating students.

## Political situation in The Gambia

After gaining independence in 1965, The Gambia was known for decades as an international leader in human rights.[6] The Prime Minister and later President Dawda K Jawara[7] was an advocate for human rights, democracy, and development, and during his tenure The Gambia had a reputation for stability, multiparty democracy, and the rule of law.[8] Jawara's rule was ended by a coup d'état in 1994, when a young military officer named Yahya Jammeh took power. Jammeh ruled as a military leader until 1997, and then as a civilian president

4 The University of The Gambia Law Clinic Constitution (July 2012) (on file with author).

5 Ibid. para 1.1 (ii).

6 James Kirby, 'African Leadership in Human Rights: The Gambia and The Commonwealth Human Rights Commission, 1977–83' (2020) 56(1) Journal of Contemporary History 191.

7 After a referendum in 1970 The Gambia transitioned from a constitutional monarchy to a republic within the Commonwealth.

8 Kirby (n 6) 196.

until 2017.[9] Jammeh's regime was criticised for its attacks on free speech, rule of law, torturing and disappearing political dissidents, and controlling the judicial system.[10] After a surprise election upset in 2016, Jammeh refused to concede power until military intervention from neighbouring states oversaw transition of power to Adama Barrow: a candidate put forward by a coalition of political parties united in opposition to Jammeh's 22-year rule.[11]

Since the new government in 2017, The Gambia has gone from an authoritarian regime to a liberal multi-party democracy. This transition has not been a simple or straightforward process, but it has been defined by a political discourse of human rights and democratic values: journalists have celebrated steps taken towards protecting freedom of expression;[12] a national human rights commission has been established;[13] and a Truth and Reconciliation Commission has worked towards redressing rights abuses by the previous regime.[14] While much remains to be done,[15] this unique transitional context is an opportunity for The Gambia to focus on activities improving the human rights situation after two decades of authoritarianism.

Doing CLE in this context is one way in which this opportunity can be seized. The two aims discussed above – fostering social responsibility and providing legal services – both capture the mood of the broader political environment. The Interdisciplinary Committee for Civic Education in The Gambia have called for centring of political and civil literacy in the transition period, sensitising the population on rights and citizenship to improve critical engagement with the politics.[16] Access to

9 Ebrima J Ceesay, *The Military and 'Democratisation' in The Gambia: 1994–2003* (Trafford Publishing 2006).

10 See, e.g.: Chidi Odinkalu, 'The Gambia's bloodcurdling threat' *The Guardian* (1 October 2009) <https://www.theguardian.com/commentisfree/2009/oct/01/gambia-jammeh-human-rights> accessed 29 January 2021; Sidi Sanneh, 'Judicial Interference is the problem' *Sidi Sanneh* (5 August 2013) <https://sidisanneh.blogspot.com/2013/08/judicial-interference-is-problem.html> accessed 29 January 2021.

11 Al-Jazeera, 'Barrow to be officially sworn in as Gambia's president' (n 1).

12 Nicolas Leblanc, 'A year after Jammeh: Free press returns to The Gambia' *Al-Jazeera* (Banjul, 6 February 2018) <https://www.aljazeera.com/gallery/2018/2/6/a-year-after-jammeh-free-press-returns-to-the-gambia/> accessed 29 January 2021.

13 The National Human Rights Commission Act, 2017 (No. 8 of 2017).

14 Truth, Reconciliation and Reparations Commission, 'Our Mandate' *TRRC.gm* (undated) <http://www.trrc.gm/our-mandate/> accessed 29 January 2021.

15 For example: Satang Nabaneh, 'The need for an independent Gambian judiciary' *Law Hub Gambia* (14 December 2018) <https://www.lawhubgambia.com/lawhug-net/independent-gambian-judiciary> accessed 29 January 2021; Jarra Cham, 'UN rapporteur urges Gambia to reform judicial system' *The Point* (3 December 2019) <https://thepoint.gm/africa/gambia/article/un-rapporteur-urges-gambia-to-reform-judicial-system> accessed 29 January 2021.

16 Interdisciplinary Committee for Civic Education in The Gambia, 'Leaping forward into the political renaissance of the post-Jammeh regime: the missing instrument in our toolbox' *The Point* (15 June 2017) <https://thepoint.gm/africa/gambia/article/leaping-forward-into-the-political-renaissance-of-the-post-jammeh-regime-the-missing-instrument-in-o> accessed 29 January 2021.

justice rises in importance as the courts entrench their independence from the executive and rule of law is placed in higher regard.[17]

## Access to justice and human rights

Before evaluating the Clinic's activities, the concept of access to justice should be defined, and its connection to human rights considered. The purpose of this chapter is to consider how the Clinic's goal of improving access to justice relates to human rights, and particularly the performance of obligations corresponding to human rights. This section will outline the issues captured by the concept of access to justice, before considering how a human rights approach can conceive of access to justice in terms of rights and duties.

Access to justice is a nebulous concept encompassing a range of different aspects, aimed at providing real and meaningful access to the institutions within a state responsible for ensuring justice or law within society.[18] The term notably grew in its scope through the comparative work of Cappelletti,[19] from referring to systems of legal aid for disputes within a formalised court system, to encompassing the diverse modalities and institutional settings in which 'justice' is pursued by claimants.[20] Improving access to justice may be about procedure (e.g. rules of standing); it may be about improving institutions (e.g. ensuring timely justice); it may be about substance (the norms binding those against whom a claimant seeks justice).[21]

The growth and popularity and change in use of the term 'access to justice' came with expansion in the West of mechanisms for accountability and remedy within society, in the period of reform spurred by the end of the Second World War and the civil rights era.[22] This coincided with the expansion of globalisation, and importantly, the global systems of human rights and the economic and social development. The end of the Second World War saw the creation of a number of international frameworks for human rights protection, aimed at preventing the atrocities seen in the war. The concept of global development emerged alongside, as states like The Gambia obtained their independence from formal colonialism, and the newly independent states and their former colonial powers negotiated a changed

17 For example: Momodou Lamin Yaffa, 'A Litmus test of the Rule of Law by Gambia Supreme Court' *The Standard* (31 January 2020) <https://standard.gm/a-litmus-test-of-the-rule-of-law-by-gambia-supreme-court/> accessed 29 January 2021.

18 Lawrence M Friedman, 'Access to Justice: Some Historical Comments' (2010) 37(1) Fordham Urban Law Journal 3; Marc Galanter, 'Access to Justice in a World of Expanding Social Capability' (2010) 37(1) Fordham Urban Law Journal 115, 115–116; Estelle Hurter, 'Access to Justice: To dream the impossible dream?' (2011) 44(3) Comparative & International Law Journal of Southern Africa 408, 408.

19 Mauro Cappalletti et al. (eds), *Access to Justice, Vols 1–4* (Sijthoff and Noordhoff 1978–1979).

20 Galanter (n 18) 116.

21 Friedman (n 18) 4.

22 Lawrence M Friedman, *Total Justice* (Russell Safe Foundation 1985), chapter 9.

relationship.[23] Both of these approaches to improving the governance of individuals around the world bring with them their own methods and assumptions, both of which will be explored below in more detail.

Access to justice is undoubtedly an issue of human rights. Francioni argues that the right of an individual to access judicial proceedings has a long history of recognition as a principle of customary international law,[24] and that the protection of international human rights has always been premised upon justiciability of, and remedy for, the violation of those rights.[25] However, while many argue its fundamental importance, a right of access to justice has not crystallised into law in the same way as, for example, the right to a fair trial or the right to political participation.[26] As the concept manages to capture so many different aspects of procedure, institutions, and access, so too does it differentiate itself from other comparable values.

To understand this difference, we can consider how access to justice fits into theories of human rights. Two conceptions will be explored here. The first conception, inarguably the dominant, is a liberal conception of rights of individuals correlating to duties of the state. The second, which shall here be called a 'solidarity-community' approach, decentralises duties from the state, so that other actors might also hold responsibilities to fulfil human rights. It is argued here through this second approach that the duty to improve access to justice rests in the individual, the community, the state, and the international community. It is here that CLE's effectiveness as a tool for improving access to justice becomes a fulfilment of human rights obligations – as it fosters a sense of responsibility in students, promotes access to justice as a value, and provides services that allow meaningful access to justice for individuals.

## Liberal approach to human rights

The Preamble to the Universal Declaration of Human Rights ('UDHR') presents a basic assumption on which the contemporary human rights movement is founded: 'recognition of the inherent dignity and of the equal and inalienable rights of all members of the human family is the foundation of freedom, justice and peace in the world'. This presents two key features. First is the 'inherent dignity' from which all rights flow. Human rights discourses are based on a moral claim that humans have rights simply in virtue of being human.[27] Donnelly further claims that human rights protect 'those things needed for a life of dignity, for a life worthy of a human being'.[28] The second feature which follows from that is the

23 Erik Thorbecke, 'The Evolution of the Development Doctrine, 1950–2005' in George Mavrotis and Anthony Sharrocks (eds), *Advancing Development: Core Themes in Global Economics* (Palgrave Macmillan 2007), 3.

24 Francesco Francioni, *Access to Justice as a Human Right* (OUP 2007), chapter 1.

25 Ibid. 30–31.

26 Ibid. 55–56.

27 John Gardner, '"Simply in Virtue of Being Human": The whos and whys of human rights' (2008) 2(2) Journal of Ethics & Social Philosophy 2.

28 Jack Donnelly, *Universal Human Rights in Theory and Practice* (Cornell University Press 1989) 17.

claim to universality. Universal rights find their philosophical origins in Hobbes[29] and Kant,[30] but the development of international law protecting human rights over the last 75 years has sought to provide some version of a practical reality to these philosophical and moral assertions.

The moral assumption of universally held human rights must give rise to corresponding duties.[31] Beitz claims 'human rights are standards for domestic institutions whose satisfaction is a matter of international concern'.[32] The consequence of this thinking in the contemporary human rights movement has been the assignment of these duties to the state, appropriate as it is the 'basic unit of the world's political organization'[33] in a Westphalian system where states have sovereignty and discrete authority of their territory. This connects the claim to universality and the reality of assigning that responsibility as legal duty, and it is in this way that human rights as an idea are translated into international human rights law: states are bound by international law to take such action necessary to realise the human rights held by individuals under their jurisdiction. The enforceability of these rights internationally against the state creates a presumption that official institutions of the state are burdened with the duty to perform the activity necessary to realise those rights. Human rights laws have found some political acceptance, and by the late 20th century could be found protected in the constitutions of the overwhelming majority of states, with the legal potential for enforcement in domestic law.[34]

As previously discussed, access to justice in its broadness of definition has not wholly crystallised into a norm of human rights law; however, there are norms which go towards it. A key provision which could be seen as protecting an individual right of access to justice, taking account of non-judicial justice, is found in the International Covenant on Civil and Political Rights ('ICCPR'). This provides that states must provide remedy for violations of rights: 'by competent judicial, administrative or legislative authorities, or by any other competent authority provided for by the legal system of the State'.[35] This provision serves as a clause to ensure the vindication of the protection of the civil and political rights found in the ICCPR itself;[36] however, it does not provide a duty to allow broader access to the justice system for other rights.

29 Thomas Hobbes, *Leviathan* (1651).
30 Hans Reiss (ed.), *Kant: Political Writings* (2nd edn, Cambridge University Press 1991) 125.
31 Wesley Newcomb Hohfeld, 'Some fundamental legal conceptions as applied in judicial reasoning' (1913) 23 Yale Law Journal 16.
32 Charles R Beitz, *The Idea of Human Rights* (OUP 2009) 128.
33 Ibid. 128.
34 Louis Henkin, 'The Universality of the Concept of Human Rights' (1989) 506 The Annals of the American Academy of Political and Social Science 10, 13.
35 International Covenant on Civil and Political Rights (adopted 16 December 1966, entry into force 23 March 1976) (ICCPR), article 2(3)(b).
36 UN Human Rights Committee, *General Comment No. 131: The Nature of the General Legal Obligation Imposed on States Parties to the Covenant*, 26 May 2004, UN Doc CCPR/C/21/Rev.1/Add.13, paras 15–16.

A more narrow definition of access to justice might see it as synonymous with a right to judicial protection, which can be found protected by various human rights instruments, such as the UDHR,[37] the European Convention on Human Rights,[38] the American Convention on Human Rights,[39] and the African Charter on Human and Peoples' Rights.[40] The various versions of this right provide very similar content: the right to access to a tribunal or court of law, for a hearing in determination of a criminal charge against them, or their civil rights and obligations.

Achieving access to justice is not simply the provision of access, but it requires well-functioning and fair procedures without any barriers to entry. An example of a barrier to meaningful access, which will be considered below in more detail, is the provision of legal aid: if an individual is not able to pay a lawyer to present their case before a justice procedure, then do they have meaningful access to justice? It can be argued that their participation would be less meaningful, and that this is a barrier to having their case heard. In many respects, access to justice is also about the fairness of proceedings and is thus strongly linked with the right to a fair trial. Requirements imposed by international human rights protection of the right to fair trial, including equality of access[41] independence and impartiality of the tribunal,[42] or a requirement for procedures to happen within a reasonable time,[43] are all relevant for access to justice. When these requirements are not met, access to justice is fettered or prevented.

International human rights law provides an individual's right of access to a court system as a right to judicial protection, and some documents, like the ICCPR above, acknowledge that the right to a remedy might not be simply judicial. However, this does not completely capture the full scale of access to justice. A pertinent example in the case of The Gambia[44] is the recognition of legal pluralism in access to justice. While included within the definition of a court procedure,[45] international human rights law can restrain access to justice in

37 Universal Declaration of Human Rights (adopted 10 December 1948) UNGA Res 217 A(III) (UDHR) art 8.

38 Convention for the Protection of Human Rights and Fundamental Freedoms (European Convention on Human Rights, as amended) art 6(1).

39 American Convention on Human Rights (adopted 22 November 1969, entered into force 18 July 1978) art 8.

40 African Charter on Human and Peoples' Rights (adopted 27 June 1981, entered into force 21 October 1986) (1982) 21 ILM 58 (African Charter) art 7(1)(a).

41 For example: ICCPR, article 14(1); UN Human Rights Committee (UNHRC), *General Comment No 32, Article 14: Right to equality before courts and tribunals and to a fair trial*, 27 August 2007, U.N. Doc CCPR/C/GC/32, para 7.

42 For example: ICCPR, article 14(1); UNHRC, *General Comment No 32* (n 41) para 15.

43 For example: ICCPR, article 14(3)(c); UNHRC, *General Comment No 32* (n 41) para 35.

44 The Constitution of The Gambia of 1997 recognises the jurisdiction of Sharia Law and customary law in addition to the common law and Acts of the National Assembly (art 8).

45 Helen Quane, 'Legal Pluralism and International Human Rights Law: Inherently Incompatible, Mutually Reinforcing or Something in Between?' (2013) 33(4) Oxford Journal of Legal Studies 675, 677.

pluralist legal orders, by placing operational hurdles on customary and religious courts which mean that their justice is not enforceable.[46]

The roster of human rights spans a range of different aspects of governance, and it can be useful to consider how human rights have been categorised. The 'first generation' rights are civil and political in nature, with prominent examples being freedom of religion, freedom of expression, freedom of assembly, and right to fair trial. These rights are descended from classical Western political ideas,[47] and they generally protect the freedom of the individual from unnecessary state intervention.[48] The 'second generation' rights are economic, social, and cultural rights. Protections such as the right to education, the right to health, and the right to housing are generally considered to have evolved in the 20th century when European states started to take responsibility for the welfare of its citizens.[49] With the development of modern international human rights law after the Second World War, these first two generations of rights were advocated for by the states of the West and East respectively, as reflective of their liberal and social ideologies.[50]

Approaching access to justice with this categorisation shows that it does not fit easily. It shows many hallmarks of a civil and political right: it is concerned with liberty, democracy, equality, and the rule of law. However, if we consider the right to legal aid, this is a welfare provision for those who are not able to access justice without financial help from the state.[51] Further, legal aid is indispensable in the realisation of all rights, and particularly economic, social, and cultural rights.[52]

## Complicating the liberal human rights approach – third generation rights

Seminal writers on international human rights law Steiner, Alston, and Goodman have stated that:

> Observers from different regions and cultures can agree that the human rights movement … stems principally from the liberal tradition of Western political and legal thought … No characteristic of the liberal tradition is more striking than its emphasis on the individual.[53]

46 Ibid.
47 See, e.g.: Le Déclaration des droits de l'homme et du citoyen de 1789.
48 Christian Tomuschat, *Human Rights: Between Idealism and Realism* (OUP 2014) 71.
49 Ibid. 72.
50 Ibid. 73.
51 Kristel Jüriloo, 'Free Legal Aid – A human right' (2015) 33(3) Nordic Journal of Human Rights 203, 213.
52 Andrea Durbach, 'The Right to Legal Aid in Social Rights Litigation' in Malcolm Langford (ed.), *Social Rights Jurisprudence: Emerging trends in international and comparative law* (CUP 2008) 59.
53 Henry J Steiner, Philip Alston, and Ryan Goodman, *International Human Rights in Context: Law, Politics, Morals: Texts and Materials* (OUP 2008) 512.

The focus on the individualism inherent in these rights ties them with a broader ideology. This creates problems for their claim to universality, when applied in different cultures and ideologies.

The philosophical, moral, and legal position we have set out thus far presents the individual as the holder of a right, universally and on the basis of their dignity. While we have also discussed the obligations which these rights create, these are legal derivations more than inherent in the philosophy. Even with respect to the socio-economic rights, classically associated with socialist states in the classification system, the focus is on individual protection of access to basic goods such as health. For example, although we can infer a duty to fulfil the right to health, this duty is only considered not performed where the law would see an individual unable to access healthcare, and the right itself is violated.[54] To complicate the theory of liberal human rights discourse we have set out so far, we can consider human rights that challenge this traditional paradigm, known as the third generation of rights.

The third generation of human rights, sometimes called the solidarity rights, emerged around 1980 as a group of rights which did not fit into the first and second generations.[55] These are rights which are distinguished by solidarity among humanity to be realised, for example, the right to development, the right to a healthy environment, the right to peace, and the right to intergenerational equity.[56] These rights have not seen so much express protection at the international level. Although a third international covenant was discussed, and a preliminary draft tabled in 1981,[57] this did not culminate in any international agreement. The most progressive agreement with reference to these rights, notably to our current discussion, is the African Charter on Human and Peoples' Rights ('ACHPR'). Adopted in 1981, this regional human rights instrument recognised the rights of all person to development (art 22), to national and international peace and security (art 23), and to a 'satisfactory environment favourable to their development' (art 24). The African Commission on Human and Peoples' Rights, responsible for monitoring enforcement of the Charter, has even held that third generation rights can be justiciable.[58]

These third generation rights have been criticised by some for the difficulty in fitting them within the existing conceptual framework of individual rights. Donnelly, for example, has said that the right to development adds nothing to

54 Many socio-economic rights even present near-impossible burdens to be considered justiciable, or for violations to be found. See, e.g.: Aoife Nolan, Bruce Porter, and Malcolm Langford, 'The Justiciability of Social and Economic Rights: An Updated Appraisal', *CHRGJ Working Paper No. 15*, July 2009.

55 Susan P Marks, 'Emerging Human Rights: A new generation for the 1980s?' (1981) 33(2) Rutgers Law Review 435.

56 Philip Alston, 'A third generation of solidarity rights: progressive development or obfuscation of international human rights law' (1982) 29(3) Netherlands International Law Review 307, 307–308.

57 Ibid. 313.

58 Communication No 155/96 *SERAC v Nigeria* [2001] AHRLR 60 (15th Annual Activity Report), para 52.

individual rights, as it combines existing individual rights and turns the emphasis away from the state and the individual, instead creating obligation between richer and poorer countries.[59] This emphasis on solidarity poses a problem for the liberal philosophical approach discussed above, where the individual right and state duty are foundational.

In a lecture at the International Human Rights Institute in Strasbourg in 1979, one of the first instances of the solidarity rights entering Western human rights discourse, Karel Vasek explained that solidarity rights 'can be realised only through the concerted efforts of all the actors on the social scene: the individual, the State, public and private bodies and the international community'.[60] This further complicates the liberal approach discussed above, particularly as human rights are enshrined in law, whereby the state is the duty-bearer, and is responsible for realising the rights of individuals. International human rights law is not easily able to conceive of the responsibility of individuals, private bodies, or the international community as a duty-bearer. In the context of furthering access to justice, it is argued here that individuals and the international community might both play an important role; however, our understanding of human rights and duties needs to be able to accommodate this.

One difficulty is the absence of responsibilities for the individual within the liberal conception of human rights. Saul highlights that rights advocates have treated duties placed on the individual in international human rights with 'deep and well-justified suspicion',[61] as duties to state, church, lords, and monarchy were part of a system of European domination for many centuries. The contemporary human rights movement sees individual duty to run counter to struggles for freedom from domination. Duties placed on individuals have generally been excluded from international human rights law,[62] until, notably, the ACHPR. The ACHPR entitles its list of rights as 'Rights and Duties', and at articles 27–29 lists duties of the individual towards the family, society, and state. Examples include the duty to respect and not to discriminate (art 28); the duty to preserve the family (art 29(1)); and the duty to preserve social and national solidarity (art 29(4)).

Morgan-Foster suggests that the emphasis on a paradigm of individual rights presents a limitation for liberal human rights discourse, which prevents it from understanding the role played by members of the community, such as family

59 Malcolm Freeman, *Human Rights* (Polity Press 2017) 136, citing Jack Donnelly, 'In search of the unicorn: the jurisprudence and politics of the right to development' (1985) 15(3) California Western International Law Journal 473.

60 Karel Vasek, 'Pour une troisième generation des droits de l'homme' in Christophe Swinarski (ed.), *Studies and Essays on International Humanitarian Law and Red Cross Principles* (Kluwer Law International 1985) 839.

61 Ben Saul, 'In the Shadow of Human Rights: Human Duties, Obligations, and Responsibilities' (2001) 32 Columbia Human Rights Law Review 565, 616.

62 Jason Morgan-Foster, 'Third Generation Rights: What Islamic Law Can Teach the International Human Rights Movement' (2005) 8 Yale Human Rights & Development Law Journal 67, 79–80.

members, teachers, and in turn guaranteeing the sorts of goods that can only be achieved by social communal governance.[63] Baderin notably compares the approach to rights and duties in liberal human rights discourse with that from Islamic law, and concludes that although the two share very similar aims and purposes, they take contrasting approaches with respect to rights and duties: with Islamic law placing the positive obligations on the individual to promote human welfare and to prevent harm.[64] Morgan-Foster's argument suggests that the liberal conception of human rights, defined by the culture of the West, might be challenged by the notion of individual duty inherent in solidarity rights.[65]

A second difficulty that poses a problem for liberal conceptions of human rights is recognising the role of the international community in realising these third generation rights. The right to development is a good case study of this. The right to development through a liberal lens would still see the individual as the rightsholder,[66] and that individual's state as having the duty. The concept of holding a third state accountable for human rights violations in international law is very limited. While this might be possible, for example, where a state enters another state to kill the injured state's population, the idea that a rich state would be held accountable for failing to fulfil a right to development of the population of another state goes against traditional conceptions of international law and human rights law.

Third World approaches to international law ('TWAIL') present a different understanding of the right to development, however, wherein the responsibility of colonising states to fulfil that right is immediately apparent. TWAIL scholarship looks at international law as the continuation of the colonial disempowerment by the West over the 'Third World',[67] and therefore seeks to 'defang international law of its imperialist and exploitative biases against the global south'.[68] Gothii traces the origins of the right to development to Africa, and finds a more radical claim than the right found in international human rights law today.[69] Thiam, a Senegalese Foreign Minister in the 1960s, proposed a right to development

63 Ibid. 73.

64 Mashood A Baderin, *International Human Rights and Islamic Law* (OUP 2003) 43.

65 Morgan-Foster (n 62).

66 See: Declaration on the Right to Development, UNGA Res 41/128 (4 Dec 1986) (adopted by 146 votes to 1 (USA voting against); 8 abstentions: Denmark, Finland, Germany, Iceland, Israel, Japan, Sweden, United Kingdom), art 2(1). The declaration does recognise that the right can be held collectively (art 2(2)), but with the UN adjudicating bodies of international human rights law not accepting complaints by groups, only by individuals, the system generally still focuses on the individual's right. See: Markus G Schmidt, 'Individual Human Rights Complaints Procedures Based on United Nations Treaties and the Need for Reform' (1992) 41(3) International and Comparative Law Quarterly 645.

67 Makau Mutua, 'What is TWAIL?' (2000) 94 Proceedings of the Annual Meeting (American Society of International Law) 31.

68 Makau Mutua, 'Review' (2010) 104(3) The American Journal of International Law 532, 533.

69 James Thuo Gathii, 'Africa and the Radical Origins of the Right to Development' (2020) 1 TWAIL Review 28.

collectively held by the former colonies, correlating with duties on their colonisers to right the wrongs of colonial rule.[70] The right to development in these origins implicates the international community, and particularly the West, in realising the right to development of communities in the Third World.

Bedjaoui, also writing in the 1960s, argued that the right to development was about 'the right to an equitable share in the economic and social well-being of the world'.[71] This logic applies to many others of the third generation solidarity rights discussed above: the right to intergenerational equity; and the right to a healthy and sustainable environment. These solidarity rights place duties on the international community to promote the well-being and development of other parts of the world. Realising this in practice, however, is very difficult in international human rights law and a liberal conception of human rights. Although the interpretation of third generation rights has occasionally been able to extend obligation to other states in the international community, for example, protecting other states against transboundary environmental harm,[72] the extension of radical positive duties to improve other states cannot be conceived of in liberal conceptions of international human rights law.

## A solidarity-community approach to a right to access to justice

The central argument here is that, although not generally included in lists of such rights, access to justice can be usefully thought of within the third generation rights. It has been shown above that a liberal approach to human rights fails to capture the breadth of issues that access to justice is concerned with. A liberal approach to human rights fails to imagine duty-holders beyond the state itself, and therefore is not easily able to conceive that the responsibility to improve access to justice is decentralised, and vested in individuals, communities and the international community. The Clinic, in engaging student members in a variety of ways to promote and improve access to justice and fostering a sense of responsibility for access to justice, achieves this and this can be understood through the solidarity-community obligations on which its philosophy rests.

There are two main aspects to this argument: firstly, the proximity of access to justice to the right to development; and secondly, in the importance of solidarity to access to justice: the range of actors who must be responsible if a system is to realise good access to justice. On the first point, access to justice is tied to the right to development. Access to justice has been co-opted as a key element on the agenda for development. It is included on the UN's 2030 Sustainable Development Goals at Goal 16, which includes the goal to 'provide access to justice for all

70 Ibid. 38 citing Doudou Thiam, 'L'Afrique demande un droit international d'un nouveau' (1968) 1(1) Verfassung und Recht in Ubersee 52.

71 Mohammed Bedjaoui, 'The Right to Development' in Mohammed Bedjaoui (ed.), *International Law: Achievements and Prospects* (Martinus Nijhoff 1991).

72 *The Environment and Human Rights*, Advisory Opinion OC-23/17, Inter-American Court of Human Rights Series A No 23 (15 November 2017).

and build effective, accountable and inclusive institutions at all levels'.[73] Issues with access to justice are inevitably linked to poverty and underdevelopment: poverty takes away the resource needed at an individual level to vindicate rights and access justice processes; underdevelopment and less economic resource at state level means that there cannot be good provision of legal aid and proper functioning and staffing of systems. On the second point and relatedly, realising access to justice requires activity from more than just the state. Certainly, making provision for legal aid and the proper functioning of judicial processes are political and fiscal choices; the state needs to create fair procedures and ensure the impartiality and independence of its processes. However, ensuring and promoting access to justice particularly in a country without excessive financial resource, such as The Gambia,[74] relies on a strong civil society, assistance and aid from other states and intergovernmental organisations, and voluntary and pro bono work. This decentralisation of obligation, which can see it placed on individuals, private bodies, and other states, rather than simply the state itself, is very challenging to the liberal conception of a human right of access to justice. However, as we have seen above, a solidarity-community approach engages other actors as necessary to realise human rights, in a way more fitting for access to justice.

If access to justice is viewed as a human right in a solidarity-community perspective, then we can see that efforts to improve access to justice are the responsibility of a range of different actors. The responsibility does not fall solely on the state, but may be vested in individuals, private organisations, and in other states and intergovernmental organisations to provide aid and assistance. It is here that the value of CLE as a tool for realising human rights becomes clear: no longer do we see human rights as being improved through state activity, but that responsibility might be more widely dispersed. We have already seen that one of the Clinic's central aims – to 'foster a sense of social responsibility' – engages students with responsibility for improving access to justice in their community and The Gambia more generally. Furthermore, the specific activities that have been adopted to pursue this aim support this.

## Clinic projects

There are difficulties of analysing access to justice through a liberal conception of human rights represented by human rights law, which we have shown to be limited to rights held by individuals enforceable against the state. If we are to construe access to justice as an issue of human rights, then a solidarity-community approach is more successful, decentralising responsibility away from the state and

73 Transforming our world: the 2030 Agenda for Sustainable Development, UNGA Res 70/1 (21 October 2015).

74 The Gambia has a GDP of $1.8 billion, making it the 170th largest economy. See *The Gambia Economic Factsheet* (UK Foreign Commonwealth and Development Office Economics Unit – October 2020) <https://assets.publishing.service.gov.uk/government/uploads/system/uploads/attachment_data/file/931114/Economic_Factsheets_October2020_The_Gambia.pdf> accessed 22 November 2020.

conceptualising the roles played by other actors in improving access to justice. This section of the chapter will now return to the Clinic and consider its mission within this framework. As discussed above, the Clinic's aims are three: firstly, its practical pedagogy, exposing student members to the law in practice; secondly, its value-based pedagogy, seeking 'to foster in [student members] a sense of social responsibility';[75] and thirdly, to provide and support legal aid services. By considering these aims, and three examples of activities performed by the Clinic, the Clinic will be evaluated through a human rights lens, looking at how it serves the realisation of human rights and the performance of the duty to realise those rights. Both the liberal and solidarity-community approaches will be reflected here, thinking particularly about how they envision improving access to justice.

### *'Live client' casework*

The first activity which will be discussed with reference to the realisation of human rights is the performance of legal services to the community in the form of casework with clients. Compared with states such as the United Kingdom[76] and South Africa,[77] where there is a well-established system of in-house live client clinics, building a walk-in live client clinic has proven difficult with few resources and without many structures already in place. That said, there have been successes throughout the period since the establishment of the Clinic in doing casework. Student members have taken cases and written advice for members of their community in areas such as land disputes, inheritance, and employment disputes. They have been supervised by lawyers practising in The Gambia and law school faculty. Student members engaging in such casework have gone on to qualify and then returned to supervise other students over the years.

As with most university law clinics, this activity is central to the Clinic's purpose, and directly contributes to its aims. The pedagogical benefits of this casework are clear and have been well-documented:[78] students get to experience the law in action rather than the law in books;[79] developing practical skills needed for

75 UTG Law Clinic Constitution (n 4) para 1.1 (ii).

76 Irene Antonopoulos and Omar Madhloom, 'Promoting international human rights values through reflective practice in clinical legal education: a perspective in England and Wales', University of Bristol Law Research Paper Series #001 (2020) <http://www.bristol.ac.uk/media-library/sites/law/research/Madhloom%20et%20al%20BLRP%20No.%201%202020%20-merged.pdf> accessed 26 November 2020, 5–6.

77 M A du Plessis, 'Closing the gaps between the needs of the students and the community they serve' (2008) 33(2) Journal for Juridical Science 1, 2.

78 For example: Hugh Brayne et al., *Clinical Legal Education: Active Learning in Your Law School* (Blackstone Press 1998); David McQuoid-Mason, Ernest Ojukwu, and George Mukundi Wachiri, 'Clinical Legal Education in Africa: Legal Education and Community Service' in Frank S Bloch (ed.), *The Global Clinical Movement: Educating Lawyers for Social Justice* (OUP 2010) 23.

79 Roscoe Pound, 'Law in books and law in action' (1910) American Law Review 12.

lawyering; and introducing ethics to a usually doctrinal curriculum.[80] Casework also addresses precisely the legal aid aim of the Clinic. The Clinic is able to provide free legal advice, assistance, and in some cases representation to the local community, making itself a provider and potentially have great impact on the accessibility of justice procedures.

### *A human rights duty to improve legal aid*

In evaluating the role of the Clinic as an actor in performing human rights duties, we need to consider whether its legal aid aim, discussed above, is in fulfilment of human rights obligations. A good metric for this in the liberal conception of human rights can be quickly achieved by considering the status of a 'right to legal aid' in international human rights law, and whether The Gambia holds any obligations in that regard.

The UN Principles and Guidelines on Access to Legal Aid in Criminal Justice Systems ('the UN Principles') derives a right to legal aid in criminal proceedings from the standards of fair trial granted in the UDHR, the ICCPR, and soft law documents of international human rights law.[81] Principle 2 outlines the responsibilities of the state with respect to that right, stating:

> States should consider the provision of legal aid their duty and responsibility. To that end, they should consider, where appropriate, enacting specific legislation and regulations and ensure that a comprehensive legal aid system is in place that is accessible, effective, sustainable and credible. States should allocate the necessary human and financial resources to the legal aid system.[82]

Other responsibilities are mentioned, such as protecting the independence of legal aid providers, and ensuring that communities are made aware about their rights within the justice system.[83]

Although those UN Principles are a soft law document, they suggest UN human rights interpretation of access to justice as a human right. While the right to legal aid it discusses is derived from rights protected by the ICCPR, it is debatable whether the UN Principles themselves can be said to confer rights to individuals. This might also have implications for the 'responsibilities' outlined in the Principles, and whether they create legal obligations for states.

A right to legal aid outside of criminal justice, which might be capable of providing free legal assistance for civil claims, is also difficult. The importance of civil

80 Donald Nicolson, 'Legal Education or Community Service? The Extra-Curricular Student Law Clinic' (2006) 3 Web JCLI <http://www.bailii.org/uk/other/journals/WebJCLI/2006/issue3/nicolson3.html> accessed 26 November 2020.

81 UNGA Res 67/187, 'United Nations Principles and Guidelines on Access to Legal Aid in Criminal Justice Systems' (28 March 2013) UN Doc. A/Res/67/187, Annex, Introduction, and Principle 1.

82 Ibid. para 15.

83 Ibid. paras 16–18.

legal aid is recognised across the UN human rights system. The UN Special Rapporteur on the Independence of Judges and Lawyers in 2013 said of legal aid that it is: 'a right in itself and an essential precondition for the enjoyment of a number of human rights, including the right to a fair trial and the right to an effective remedy'.[84] The right to an effective remedy is found within various international human rights documents as a clause to ensure reparation for the violations of other rights. Sedley suggests that the right to effective remedy is essential as it upholds other rights.[85] If the obstruction of other freedoms could not be challenged in a justice system then those rights cannot be vindicated and are therefore worthless.

### *Legal aid providers in The Gambia and the Clinic*

The situation of state legal aid in The Gambia is one characterised by progressive and human rights-compliant legislation that is insufficiently implemented.[86] The state funds the National Agency for Legal Aid ('NALA') which is authorised to provide legal aid according to criteria set out in the Legal Aid Act ('LAA').[87] The LAA was enacted in 2008, and expanded upon a constitutional guarantee that state legal aid should be provided in situations where a defendant faced a criminal charge which carries a penalty of death or life imprisonment.[88] It importantly added that legal aid should be provided in 'any criminal or civil matter [where a litigant] earns not more than such minimum wage as the Government may specify'.[89] This provision has significant potential for improving access to justice: allowing indigent criminal defendants to be represented in court; and providing legal advice and representation to those with civil claims who might not otherwise have the means to vindicate their rights or settle their disputes.

There are, however, important issues affecting the implementation of the LAA. The minimum wage to qualify for legal aid has not been specified by the Government, and therefore extension of rights to criminal defendants not facing death or life imprisonment, and to those with civil claims, are rendered unenforceable. Despite good efforts by the lawyers working at NALA to address the need for legal aid, there is still a gap in access to legal aid in the state, which is entrenched by operational and financial difficulties.[90]

84 UN Human Rights Council, Report of the UN Special Rapporteur on the Independence of Judges and Lawyers (15 March 2013) UN Doc A/HRC/23/43, para 20.
85 Stephen Sedley, *Freedom, Law and Justice* (Sweet & Maxwell, 1999), 3.
86 For more on this, see: Christopher F Gray, 'Legal Aid and Access to Justice in The "New Gambia": A case for strengthening the implementation of the Legal Aid Act' (2018) 1(1) The Gambia Law Review 33.
87 Legal Aid Act (Act No. 16 of 2008) in *Laws of The Gambia* (2009), Cap 6:07.
88 The Constitution of the Republic of The Gambia of 1997, section 24(3)(d). Additionally, since 2005, the Children's Act had also provided for legal aid to be supplied by the state to juvenile defendants. See: Children's Act (Act No. 5 of 2005) in *Laws of The Gambia* (2009), Cap 45:01, section 72(1).
89 LAA (n 87) section 30(2).
90 Ahmed Kemo Ceesay, 'Opinion: The Need to Constitutionalise Access to Justice and Legal Aid in the Draft Constitution' *The Point* (6 January 2020) <https://thepoint.

This legal aid gap is met by efforts from civil society, and there are a range of organisations who provide pro bono advice and representation to individuals across a variety of legal claims. Examples of these include Gambia Legal Support, who provide a volunteer-run legal advice service.[91] Other examples include the Female Lawyers Association of The Gambia ('FLAG') and the Institute for the Advancement of Children's Rights ('IACR'), which provide free legal advice and representation to children and women where they have the capacity to do so.

The Clinic also seeks to contribute to this framework, as it articulates in its constitution. As discussed above, the legal aid aim of the Clinic seeks to provide services and to contribute and complement the work done by other providers. The Preamble to the constitution elaborates on this further:

> Commending both governmental and non-governmental institutions for their work towards making legal aid accessible,
>
> Supplementing legal aid work done by existing institutions such as the National Agency for Legal Aid ('NALA')

While a right to legal aid would entail an obligation on the state, it is important to note that international human rights bodies expressly consider the role of civil society, and even law clinics, in realising such a right. The UN Principles mention expressly the role of non-state legal aid providers and provide that states should engage in partnerships with non-government organisations ('NGOs') and other providers where appropriate.[92] The Principles expressly provide recommendations to state to 'encourage and support the establishment of legal aid clinics in law departments within universities [and] encourage and provide incentives to law students to participate'.[93]

In providing the grounds for the Clinic to exist, the state has in some way worked towards its obligations to provide legal aid. The University is established as a public institution by an act of the National Assembly.[94] Although the Clinic is independent from the government and in practical terms, it acts as a civil society,[95] its creation by a public institution means that it is in some sense an object of the state's fulfilment of its responsibility to realise a human right to legal

gm/africa/gambia/article/opinion-the-need-to-constitutionalise-access-to-justice-and-legal-aid-in-the-draft-constitution> accessed 20 November 2020.

91 See: Gambia Legal Support – Pro Bono Lawyers in The Gambia (undated) <https://gambialegalsupport.org/> accessed 20 November 2020.

92 UN Principles (n 81) para 70.

93 Ibid. para 72.

94 University of The Gambia Act (Act No 2 of 1999), section 3.

95 Although a university itself would be considered a public sector institution, the Clinic operates through voluntary labour in pursuit of a charitable goal, making it more akin to a civil society organisation than a public body. For more on the historical connection between CLE and charitable sector organisations, see: Frank S Bloch and Mary Anne Noone, 'Legal Aid Origins of Clinical Legal Education' in Frank S Bloch, *The Global Clinic Movement: Educating Lawyers for Social Justice* (OUP 2010) 153.

aid. The Clinic itself is an example of the implementation of the responsibilities placed on the state by the UN Principles.

The question then becomes how the Clinic's live client casework might contribute towards a broader duty held by the individual to the community, and it is here that the Clinic's aims ought to be revisited. As mentioned above, the Clinic's constitution includes in its educational aim that it intends: 'to foster in [student members] a sense of social responsibility'.[96] For students, playing a part in the Clinic has the effect of contributing towards the broader realisation of a human right to legal aid. Although the human rights obligation does not itself fall on the student members or the Clinic, the early experience of participating in the realisation of this right might have a positive impact on the development and learning of the law student, and their responsibility to provide and improve access to justice in their community.[97] An approach to CLE which places this responsibility at the forefront, and is supplemented by teaching about legal aid and its role within the legal system, is argued here to have a strong human rights relevance particularly when thinking about solidarity-community approaches to realising human rights.

The organisations mentioned above are testament to the social duty performed by lawyers in The Gambia in promoting access to justice and realising a right to legal aid. The role which the Clinic plays as a provider of legal advice, assistance, or representation impacts on its teaching function in instilling the values of access to justice and social equity through its interaction with human rights duties held by the state, the individual, and the community.

### *Street Law*

Street Law is a programme whereby students are enlisted to develop and deliver training on basic rights awareness into their local communities. Since being developed in the United States in the 1970s as an initiative for NGOs, various versions of Street Law programmes are now found in countries throughout the world,[98] and these programmes are regularly conducted by student law clinics.

Developing a Street Law project in a student law clinic requires little resource, as many of the training materials are available free online and can be tailored according to the context and time in which it is found. In 2017 at the Clinic, students developed a course in children's rights in The Gambia. The students developed a training module and manual over the course of a semester, which culminated in days spent at two high schools in the local community delivering the teaching material.

96 UTG Law Clinic Constitution (n 4) para 1.1 (ii).

97 Donald Nicolson, '"Education, Education, Education": Legal, Moral and Clinical' (2008) 42(2) The Law Teacher 145, 159–160.

98 Lee Arbetman and Edward O'Brien, *Street Law: Understanding Law and Legal Issues* (McGraw-Hill Education 2011) iv; David McQuoid-Mason, 'Street Law as a Clinical Program: The South African Experience with Particular Reference to the University of KwaZulu-Natal' (2008) 17(1) Griffith Law Review 27, 28.

The benefit of this activity mirrors the aims of the Clinic: it serves a pedagogical function with respect to the student members of the Clinic, and it plays a role in access to justice through rights education. With respect to the pedagogical benefits to the students, developing a Street Law programme, like many other CLE activities, is an experiential teaching methodology. This technique presents a different form of learning from those traditional forms of law school teaching such as lecturing and small-group discussions. McQuoid-Mason suggests that this can lead to better retention and improvement in performance of students who participate in such programmes.[99]

The relevance of the Street Law programme to the Clinic's legal aid aim can then be considered. Education about rights can be seen as an integral part of access to justice and the provision of legal aid. The UN Principles (discussed above) state that responsibilities of the state include:

> States should enhance the knowledge of the people about their rights and obligations under the law … States should endeavour to enhance the knowledge of their communities about their justice system and its function, the way to file complaints before the courts and alternative dispute resolution mechanisms.[100]

The relevance of Street Law programmes as a provider of rights education to communities can be clearly seen, and the UN Principles highlight that this education is integral to access to justice. Education is also recognised in the International Covenant on Economic, Social and Cultural Rights,[101] the Convention on the Elimination of All Forms of Racial Discrimination,[102] and the Convention on the Rights of the Child[103] as essential for the development of respect for human rights. A right to education places obligations on the state to fulfil that right, which the Committee on Economic, Social and Cultural Rights have further stated is composed of an obligation to facilitate, and to provide, the right to education.[104]

Although Street Law is relevant to the realisation of human rights, it would be a stretch to say that there is an obligation on the state through human rights law to provide rights education. It is once again imposed through the soft law UN Principles, and while it may rhetorically come within the right to education, placing an obligation on the state to provide this would not capture the reality of providing rights education. Mubangizi examines the situation of rights education in South Africa and highlights three main levels of provision: government-

99 McQuoid-Mason (n 98) 31.
100 UN Principles (n 81) para 17.
101 Adopted 16 December 1966, entry into force 3 January 1976, article 13(1).
102 Adopted 21 December 1965, entry into force 4 January 1969, article 7.
103 Adopted 20 November 1989, entry into force 2 September 1990, article 29(1)(b).
104 UN Committee on Economic, Social and Cultural Rights, *General Comment No. 13: The Right to Education (Art. 13 of the Covenant)*, 8 December 1999, UN Doc E/C.12/1999/10, paras 46–47.

supported formal education; national human rights institution ('NHRI'); and civil society.[105] The obligation from human rights, in theory and law, lies with the state as we have determined above. The role of civil society is usually essential in supplementing the activities of government in rights education. Mubangizi notes that government may fail to take its human rights education responsibility seriously 'as the more successful they become, the more the public will demand redress and retribution for human rights violations'.[106] In light of this reality, civil society have 'an irreplaceable responsibility in the creation of a culture of human rights'.[107]

Returning to the Clinic's aim to 'foster in [students] a sense of social responsibility', it is here that this activity might serve a useful function both in terms of pedagogy and in furthering access to justice: instilling in student members of the Clinic the importance of rights education in improving access to justice is an important part of the goal in the state.[108] Certainly, the performance of the activity itself might not be sufficient to perform this pedagogical function; however, combining Street Law activities with curriculum integration with a focus on social justice values,[109] and encouraging reflective practice as a teaching methodology, can ensure that this is achieved.[110] In our experience in The Gambia, we required classes before engaging in the Street Law activity to discuss its value, and required submission of a reflective piece.[111]

Rights education is recognised by human rights bodies as centrally important to access to justice, and as discussed earlier, civic and rights education has been highlighted by the Interdisciplinary Committee for Civic Education in The Gambia as an important activity to support improvements in human rights and the rule of law in the state. However, a liberal human rights approach stops short of forming a right to rights education, and as Mubangizi suggests, the state may not be the most reliable body to ensure that provision. CLE here goes above a liberal human rights approach: it provides a service to the local community which improves access to justice, and crucially it fosters a social responsibility and an understanding by the student members of the importance of rights education to improving the society in which they live.

105 John C Mubangizi, 'Human Rights Education in South Africa: whose responsibility is it anyway?' (2015) 15 African Human Rights Law Journal 496.

106 Ibid. 512.

107 Ibid. 508.

108 There is a wealth of literature supporting the notion that CLE is the best methodology for teaching social justice values. See, e.g.: Nicolson, 'Legal Education or Community Service?' (n 80); D Singo and A Raymond, 'Clinical Legal Education and social justice – a perspective from the Wits Law Clinic' (2018) 29(2) Stellenbosch Law Review 295.

109 Nicolson, 'Legal Education or Community Service?' (n 80)

110 Omar Madhloom, 'A normative approach to developing reflective legal practitioners: Kant and clinical legal education' (2019) 53(4) The Law Teacher 416.

111 M A du Plessis and Neels Swanepoel, 'Reflective journals as an assessment method in Clinical Legal Education' (2014) 47 De Jure 283.

### *Specialised clinics*

In performing its aim as a provider of legal services to the community, the Preamble of the Clinic's constitution also highlights its commitment to supplementing the work done by existing agencies, in the public sphere and civil society. It is in this spirit that the Clinic has sought partnerships with other providers of legal assistance to perform various activities. Examples of this have included a project for the UN High Commissioner for Refugees Office in Senegal: a relationship which involved students being trained on legal issues affecting refugees, providing sensitisation workshops in The Gambia on their legal rights, and doing some casework.

Iya argues that specialised clinics pose a particularly fruitful opportunity for Clinical Legal Education in Africa, and the teaching of human rights on the continent.[112] Iya argues that this is about promoting a culture of human rights in African states, and by including specialised clinics, there can be a greater focus on human rights issues taught in a practical way.[113]

Specialised clinics focus on issues, which provide a greater opportunity for instilling awareness than general casework, which could be seen as having more focus on practical skills than social justice.[114] It is more similar to the working style of human rights NGOs, and therefore could be argued to promote that sort of work and build a stronger civil society. Producing specialised clinics in partnership with civil society organisation instils social consciousness grounded in the knowledge of a specific issue, for example refugees, women's rights, children's rights, which works towards the Clinic's educational aims of promoting social responsibility and issues relating to access to justice.

Connecting human rights NGO activity and the work of student members builds an understanding of their work and the importance of collaboration within civil society. Student members of the Clinic learn about the work of these organisations and may be inspired to work in the civil society sector, but that sense of social responsibility also captures that collaborative spirit, and demonstrates how access to justice is improved by individuals at different levels and in different sectors collaborating to improve services.

## The limitations of the Clinic in promoting access to justice

The Clinic has the potential to educate for social responsibility in its student members through their getting involved in activities contributing to legal aid provision in the state. This educational benefit is vital to promoting access to justice in Gambian society: the lessons that it teaches through practical experience are those which the lawyers being trained in the university will take with them as

112 Philip F Iya, 'Enhancing the Teaching of Human Rights in African Universities: What Role for Law School Clinics?' (2005) 7 International Journal of Clinical Legal Education 20.
113 Ibid. 26.
114 Nicolson, 'Legal Education or Community Service?' (n 80).

they go on to practise law in the state, or as they go into civil society or government. This can have a great impact on the human rights situation through creating that sense of duty, maybe even especially so where that human right is viewed through a solidarity-community lens, which as Vasek said in 1979[115] places responsibility on a wealth of different actors.

Notably, the importance of the international community as a key actor in these solidarity-community rights cannot be addressed by the Clinic's educational focus on responsibility. As TWAIL scholarship showed particularly the responsibility of colonisers for development, this can be applied to other solidarity-community rights, recognising the importance of aid, assistance, and provision in realising rights viewed through this lens, and particularly as we have argued, access to justice. CLE in The Gambia has been shown to play a wide role in instilling duty to improving access to justice, but it can do little in this regard. The responsibility of the West for an under-resourced and disempowered government must be at the forefront of human rights and aid discourses, as Third World approaches have argued for decades.[116]

In this sense, a liberal conception of human rights might miss the true impact of the Clinic, disempowering the Clinic and its members from any duty in realising human rights, where that liberal conception can only conceive of duty subsiding in the state itself, without necessarily recognising the relationship between the state and the students who may go on to positions of power within those structures. On the other hand, international law on human rights is incompatible with a duty on the international community, or previous colonisers, to contribute to and promote development in states such as The Gambia.

There have been some notable aid projects in The Gambia that look at promoting access to justice.[117] The Clinic might in some sense benefit these, serving as a conduit for external financial intervention, as a provider of legal aid and a promoter of access to justice, and as an agent of development. Building a reputation as a legal aid provider might give non-government organisations, inter-government organisations, and other states an actor for funding in furthering economic, social, and cultural development. However, the Clinic is limited in its ability to use education to create this sort of duty and responsibility.

## Conclusion

The Clinic has been shown to provide legal services to its community through its activities, making it an important institution for furthering access to justice, while

115 Vasek (n 60).

116 It is important to note that not all TWAIL scholarship conforms with the critical view discussed here. See, e.g., Gathii (n 69) 46–48.

117 The EU completed a project in 2015–2017 on the themes of access to justice and legal education. See: Abdoulie Nyockeh, 'EU introduces 2.7M Euro project for access to justice, legal education' *The Point* (15 January 2015) <http://thepoint.gm/africa/gambia/article/eu-introduces-27m-euro-project-for-access-to-justice-legal-education> accessed 26 November 2020.

serving an educational function in promoting access to justice as a value, and a responsibility to its student members.

Educating for social responsibility in this broad way can have great effect on the realisation of human rights in a state such as The Gambia. That the UTG is the only provider of a Gambian Bachelor of Laws degree means that good presence and integration of clinical activities into the Faculty of Law's curriculum can impact a huge section of the legal community. This can have great impact on human rights, maybe even especially so where that human right is a solidarity right placing responsibility across different actors. We have here shown that the Clinic can educate student members to promote access to justice as a responsibility for individuals to their community, and with impact on the public and private sector as well. The activities discussed – casework, Street Law, and specialised clinics – all build on this sense of responsibility and encourage student members to think about human rights as the responsibility of the individual within the community, rather than solely the duty of the state.

However, the importance of the international community as a key actor in development and access to justice cannot be addressed by the Clinic's impact on social conscience among its student members. TWAIL scholarship particularly emphasises the role of the international community, and especially richer states which were former colonisers in promoting development, and as has been argued here, access to justice. CLE plays an important role in promoting human rights values, solidarity, and social responsibility around the world; however, to look at how this might promote development and global access to justice we must look at clinics around the world and the duties, perhaps, that they owe to each other.

# 12 Developing reflective practitioners through human rights education in relation to HIV-positive clients

*Miguel A Ramiro Avilés and Omar Madhloom*

## Introduction

Human rights have been defined as:

> [B]asic moral guarantees that people in all countries and cultures allegedly have simply because they are people. Calling these guarantees 'rights' suggests that they attach to particular individuals who can invoke them, that they are of high priority, and that compliance with them is mandatory rather than discretionary. Human rights are frequently held to be universal in the sense that all people have and should enjoy them, and to be independent in the sense that they exist and are available as standards of justification and criticism whether or not they are recognised and implemented by the legal system or officials of the country.[1]

Thus, human rights protect dignity and integrity and are universal in the sense that they apply to persons irrespective of their nationality, citizenship, religion, gender, sexuality, disability, health status, or any other category. Moreover, they are moral rights irrespective of whether or not they are recognised by law.[2] In this sense, human rights can be useful in arguing what the law ought to be.[3]

In relation to Clinical Legal Education ('CLE'), client dignity and integrity are especially significant for women, children, refugees, asylum-seekers, minorities, indigenous peoples, persons with chronic conditions and persons with disabilities, for the simple reason that such clients tend to be in some of the most vulnerable and/or disadvantaged positions due to structural stigma and discrimination.

CLE can act as a vehicle for teaching human rights because law clinics are a form of experiential learning and as such they are 'laboratories' where students engage in reflection on human rights issues and apply theory to real-life cases.[4]

1 Jack W Nickel, *Making Sense of Human Rights: Philosophical Reflections on the Universal Declaration of Human Rights* (University of California Press 1987), 561.
2 Francisco Laporta, 'Sobre el concepto de derechos humanos' (1987) 4 Doxa 23.
3 Gregorio Peces-Barba, *Ética, Poder y Derecho* (Centro de Estudios Constitucionales 1995).
4 Richard Susskind, *Tomorrow's Lawyers* (Oxford University Press 2017), 161.

DOI: 10.4324/9780429299247-13

Thus, students can develop reflective practice by identifying and solving legal and moral issues arising from their clinic work. In other words, human rights education allows students to connect to their clinic work and provides a framework for analysing law and policies.[5] Clinics can, therefore, develop comprehensive legal education that goes beyond mere technical preparation for professional practice.[6] This can be achieved by teaching students the value of rational discussion and critical reflection using human rights as a framework for law reform.

## The Legal Clinic at the University of Alcalá

The Legal Clinic ('the Clinic') of the University of Alcalá ('UAH') was founded in the academic year 2012–2013 as part of a teaching innovation project and an institutional collaboration agreement with CESIDA (which is a nationally based associations platform for HIV and Aids).

One reason for founding the Clinic was to try to address the access to justice gap in relation to Spain's response to HIV-positive persons. A 2005 study measuring the level of HIV-related discrimination faced by people living with HIV[7] and a 2010 study analysing the beliefs and attitudes of the Spanish population towards people living with HIV[8] found that there were still institutional, legal and attitudinal barriers in Spain that prevented people living with HIV from enjoying their rights on an equal basis. The Clinic, which receives client enquiries through CESIDA or healthcare professionals and private individuals, aims to create a tool to facilitate access to justice through the provision of advice and assistance,[9] which in the first instance ensures 'that people are aware of and able to take advantages that the law can confer, even if no problem has arisen'.[10] Additionally, the Clinic complements the legal guidance and free legal aid provisions provided by the Bar Associations.

## The value of human rights in CLE

Adopting Amartya Sen's view, this chapter argues that the value of implementing human rights in CLE, especially in relation to HIV-positive persons, is that they provide clinic students with a moral framework in relation to their duties towards their clients:

5 Manuel Atienza, 'Problemas abiertos en la Filosofía del Derecho' (1984) 1 Doxa, 29.
6 Francisco-Javier Ansuátegui, 'Sobre algunos rasgos caracterizadores de la Filosofía del Derecho' (1995) 12 Anuario de Filosofía del Derecho 175.
7 FIPSE, *Discriminación y VIH/Sida* <https://fipse.es/uploads/publicaciones/discriminacion.pdf> accessed 21 January 2021.
8 FIPSE, *Creencias y actitudes de la población española hacia las personas con VIH* <www.seisida.es/wp-content/uploads/2015/12/informe-seisida-fipse.pdf> accessed 21 January 2021.
9 Miguel A Ramiro and Paulina Ramírez, 'El acceso a la justicia por las personas con VIH: La experiencia de la Clínica Legal de la Universidad de Alcalá como aprendizaje-servicio' (2018) 8(4) Oñati Socio-Legal Series, 464.
10 Susskind (n 4) 94–95.

> Human rights generate reasons for action for agents who are in a position to help in the promoting or safeguarding of the underlying freedoms. The induced obligations primarily involve the duty to give reasonable consideration to the reasons for action and their practical implications, taking into account the relevant parameters of the individual case. The reasons for action can support both 'perfect' obligations as well as 'imperfect' ones, which are less precisely characterized. Even though they differ in content, imperfect obligations are correlative with human rights in much the same way as perfect obligations are. In particular, the acceptance of imperfect obligations goes beyond volunteered charity or elective virtues.[11]

Therefore, human rights allow students to recognise their moral duties towards their clients, irrespective of their clients' citizenship, nationality, disability, health status or any other characteristic. This is an important issue in CLE because some students elect to volunteer in law clinics out of self-interest (ethical egoism) as opposed to altruistic reasons and, therefore, may privilege their own interests over the interests of their clients.

A second advantage of using human rights to develop CLE is that the 'implementation of human rights can go well beyond legislation, and a theory of human rights cannot be sensibly confined within the juridical model in which it is frequently incarcerated'.[12] Human rights, therefore, provide a normative framework for critiquing the law and its impact on clients. Thirdly, the 'universability of human rights relates to the ideas of survivability in unobstructed discussion – open to participation by persons across national boundaries'.[13] Human rights are rights which persons are entitled to by virtue of being human. A human rights framework provides students with conceptual tools to analyse their conduct towards their clients and the impact of the law on their clients' dignity.

Universality makes it possible to analyse the dissociation that exists between the ethical dimension and the legal dimension of human rights. From an ethical point of view, the universal nature of human rights means that they could be attributed to every human being. The translation of that characteristic to the legal arena has always been imperfect because, firstly, there are countries where human rights are not recognised; and, secondly, because in countries where they are recognised, some groups of people are excluded.[14] In this regard, it should be noted that 'the most significant form of exclusion today, at least in terms of its extent and the difficulties it entails, is that which is ensured by the distinction between man and citizen … and which will affect foreigners'.[15] In Spain, for

11 Amartya Sen, 'Elements of a Theory of Human Rights' (2004) 32(4) Philosophy & Public Affairs 315, 319.

12 Ibid. 319.

13 Ibid. 320.

14 Rafael De Asís, *Las paradojas de los derechos fundamentales como límites al poder* (Debate 1992), 112.

15 Javier De Lucas, *El desafío de las fronteras* (Temas de Hoy 1994), 46.

example, in order to qualify for healthcare, persons with HIV must satisfy the residency requirement.[16]

A fourth advantage is that of equality, which is related to access to justice.[17] The discussion of equality requires students to consider:

> [T]he relational nature of the idea of equality, that is, its postulation as a *relation* between people, things or facts ... Such a relation, however, does not establish any kind of comparison between the elements to which it refers, but only, precisely, that of equality (A is worth *as much as* B), and not that of mere similarity (A is *almost like* B) [which] leads to the question of the connection between equality, identity, similarity and difference.[18]

Incorporating the concept of equality assists in analysing various forms of discrimination: direct, indirect or by association. The first type appears in the case of the exclusion of people with HIV from being employed by private security firms.[19] The legal reform that should be undertaken would put an end to direct discrimination, which is discrimination that occurs when a person with HIV is treated less favourably than another person in a similar situation on the grounds of or because of their HIV status.

Indirect discrimination can occur when certain laws disadvantage persons due to their HIV status. This is illustrated by the case of non-EU students who, due to the regulation of the study visa, are excluded from the National Health System. Discrimination by association occurs when HIV-negative persons are treated less favourably than those in a comparable situation. This less favourable treatment is based on an association with persons who are HIV-positive.[20] Discrimination by association occurs where, for example, an HIV-negative person works with someone who is HIV-positive. Consequently, this type of discrimination affects HIV-negative individuals who live with those with HIV, because due to the regularity of the cohabitation, they are excluded from donating blood or bone marrow.[21] The analysis of the concept of equality has to take into account the intersectionality in discrimination, not only as a cumulative phenomenon of causes but also as an expression of the position and situation in which people with

16 Irene Antonopoulos, Paulina Ramírez and Miguel A Ramiro, 'Exploring migration and migrants' rights in clinical legal education: two case studies' in Richard Grimes, Věra Honuskova and Ulrich Stege (eds) *Teaching migration and asylum law: theory and practice* (Routledge 2021) forthcoming.

17 Norberto Bobbio, *Igualdad y Libertad* (Paidos 1993), 56.

18 Alfonso Ruiz-Miguel, 'Sobre el concepto de igualdad' in Miguel Carbonell (ed.) *El principio constitucional de igualdad* (Comisión Nacional de Derechos Humanos 2003), 44. Emphasis in the original.

19 Miguel A Ramiro and Paulina Ramírez, 'La exclusión de las personas con VIH de los cuerpos uniformados de seguridad en España' (2018) 112 Revista Vasca de Administración Pública 209.

20 Case C-303/06 S. *Coleman v Attridge Law and Steve Law* [2008] ECR I-5615, para 56.

21 However, in Case C-528/13 *Léger* [2015] ECR I-288, the Court validated the exclusion of men who had sex with men from donating blood.

HIV find themselves which have been created by social structures.[22] Intersectionality makes it possible to observe that the causes of discriminatory treatment can be multiple, and sometimes it is not possible to point to a single cause, because there are structures and types of discrimination that are not correctly reflected in legal systems. The combination of two or more causes gives rise to a situation of discrimination that is distinct from the sum of its parts.[23]

Fifthly, a critical reflection on the legal norms and public policies that affect the rights of people with HIV must take into consideration the diversity of situations produced by age and gender. Thus, human rights also include children's rights. In the case of minors, the question arises as to the ownership of rights and the capacity to exercise them without the intermediation or representation of parents or people with parental authority.[24] A recurrent query in this field concerns the decision-making capacity of minors to request HIV testing and, where appropriate, to start pre-exposure prophylaxis ('PrEP'), post-exposure prophylaxis or antiretroviral treatment, without informing and obtaining the consent of their parents. In relation to CLE, this provides an opportunity for students to reflect on issues such as the age where a child's consent is deemed valid,[25] and whether or not the holders of parental authority are entitled to access the child's medical record.[26]

In the case of female clients, although HIV in the EU is highly masculinised,[27] it should be analysed how their rights are taken into account when designing legal norms and public policies. One of the consultations where this impact needs to be analysed is the one on voluntary HIV testing during pregnancy. Act 41/2002 states that any health intervention on a person's body must be preceded by a process of information to obtain valid consent but public policy established in Spain to reduce vertical transmission of HIV assumes that all pregnant women must be mandatorily tested for the virus.[28] The question here is whether we are

22 María Ángeles Barrère, 'La interseccionalidad como desafío al *mainstreaming* de género en las políticas públicas' (2010) 87–88 Revista Vasca de Administración Pública 225.

23 María José Añón, 'Principio antidiscriminatorio y determinación de la desventaja' (2013) 39 Isonomía 127.

24 Isabel Fanlo, 'Niños y derechos humanos: Consideraciones sobre una problemática relación' in Miguel A Ramiro and Patricia Cuenca (eds) *Los derechos humanos: la utopía de los excluidos* (Dykinson 2010), 203–227.

25 Federico De Montalvo, Miguel A Ramiro, 'Los derechos fundamentales y libertades públicas en el marco de los dilemas bioéticos' in Fernando Rey (ed.) *Los Derechos Humanos en España: Un Balance Crítico* (Tirant lo Blanch 2015), 559–632.

26 Agencia Española de Protección de Datos, *Informe Jurídico 0114/2008* <https://www.aepd.es/es/documento/2008-0114.pdf> accessed 11 March 2021.

27 European Centre for Disease Prevention and Control, *HIV/AIDS Surveillance in Europe 2020–2019 data* <https://www.ecdc.europa.eu/en/publications-data/hivaids-surveillance-europe-2020-2019-data> accessed 11 March 2021.

28 Grupo de Expertos de la Secretaría del Plan Nacional sobre el Sida, Grupo de Estudio de Sida/Sociedad Española de Ginecología y Obstetricia y Sociedad Española de Infectología Pediátrica. *Documento de consenso para el seguimiento de la infección por el VIH en relación con la reproducción, embarazo, parto y profilaxis de la transmission vertical del niño expuesto* <http://gesida-seimc.org/documento-de-consenso-para-el-seguimiento-de-la

facing a situation in which the subordination of women has been institutionalised as a result of a social construction known as the sex/gender system that defines and constrains the possibilities of action and decision-making.[29]

Sixthly, clinic students working in the Clinic are often required to analyse the legal and moral rights of EU nationals, non-EU nationals, refugees and asylum-seekers. Certain migrants are vulnerable because they are incapable of protecting their interests. This could be due to various factors such as difficulties accessing legal advice, language barriers, or economic resources. Migrants with HIV have been identified as an 'at risk situation' due to a higher prevalence in the number of diagnoses. Epidemiological data also reveals the greater risk to HIV exposure of migrant women.[30]

## Applying human rights in CLE

While it is not controversial to state that the right to health is a basic human right, this does equate to claiming that persons have the right to be healthy. Thus, in Spain, or any other jurisdiction, the state should not be expected to provide protection against every case of ill health or disability. However, migrants who are HIV-positive and denied access to healthcare face additional barriers such as language difficulties, financial constraints and lack of access to legal advice. Therefore, are there any moral duties on the state to provide access to healthcare and legal assistance to persons with HIV?

According to the Universal Declaration of Human Rights ('UDHR'):

> Everyone has a right to a standard of living adequate for the health and well-being of himself and of his family, including food, clothing, housing and medical care and necessary social services, and the right to security in the event of unemployment, sickness, disability, widowhood, old-age or other lack of livelihood in circumstances beyond his control.[31]

The International Covenant on Economic, Social and Cultural Rights ('ICESCR'), which was the first human rights treaty to require state to recognise the right to physical and mental health in the highest attainable standard, also conceives right to health in broad terms that include a standard of living adequate for basic health. While it is true that the right to health is vital to the

-infeccion-por-el-vih-en-relacion-con-la-reproduccion-embarazo-parto-y-profilaxis-de-la-transmision-vertical-del-nino-expuesto/> accessed 11 March 2021.

29 María José Añón, 'Autonomía de las mujeres: una utopía paradójica' in Miguel A Ramiro and Patricia Cuenca (eds) *Los derechos humanos: la utopía de los excluidos* (Dykinson 2010), 127–162.

30 Comunidad de Madrid, *Informe Epidemiológico Semanal* <https://www.comunidad.madrid/sites/default/files/doc/sanidad/epid/informe_epidemiologico_semanal.pdf> accessed 11 March 2021.

31 Article 25.

32 Michael Freeman, *Lloyd's Introduction to Jurisprudence* (9th edn, Sweet & Maxwell 2016), 1296.

exercise of other rights,[32] the same can be said for access to justice. Due to the social stigmatisation, certain persons with HIV in Spain are unable to protect or realise their rights due to their health status or immigration status. In terms of human rights language, it can be said that their dignity is violated.

The concept of human dignity can be traced to the work of Immanuel Kant. According to Kant, human beings, as autonomous agents, are ends in themselves that possess dignity and value.[33] Thus, certain laws or policies that prevent individuals from exercising their autonomy can be said to negatively impact on their human dignity. For present purposes, we mean law and policies that prevent those who are HIV-positive, such as migrants, from accessing legal and medical services or purchasing private health insurances and services.

Although human rights are recognised by international and domestic legal instruments, to enhance reflective practice in CLE, students are required to present persuasive arguments as to what the law ought to be. Moral arguments cannot be settled by appealing to settled law.

Theory of law promotes reflection by allowing students to gain a deeper understanding of their clients, the relevant law, and how the law and political institutions operate in a practical context. Applying human rights discourse in CLE allows students to identify laws which are discriminatory and to suggest legal reforms in cases where human rights are not recognised by law. The type of CLE pedagogy advocated in this chapter also provides students with a framework to confront whether unfair rules should be obeyed.[34]

## Conclusion

Jeremy Bentham, an early critic, dismissed natural rights as 'simple nonsense: natural and imprescriptible rights, rhetorical nonsense – nonsense upon stilts'.[35] However, today human rights extend to children and go beyond social and economic rights. The concept of human rights has been described as: 'one of the greatest inventions of our civilisation [which] can be compared in its impact on human social life to the development of modern technological resources and their application to medicine, communication, and transportation'.[36]

The value of applying human rights to CLE is that it allows students to reflect on issues beyond settled law. To do so, this chapter has argued that a normative framework, based on human rights discourse, is required to challenge the status quo.

Because human rights are inalienable, students gain an appreciation that their clients have rights, irrespective of the clients' gender, sexuality, citizenship,

33 Immanuel Kant, *Groundwork for the Metaphysics of Morals* (Mary Gregor and Jens Timmerman eds, first published 1785, 2nd edn, CUP 1992) [4: 434–435].

34 H L A Hart, 'Problems of the Philosophy of Law' in H L A Hart, *Essays in Jurisprudence and Philosophy* (Clarendon Press 1983), 118–119.

35 Jeremy Bentham, 'Anarchical Fallacies' in Jeremy Waldron (ed), *Nonsense upon Stilts: Bentham, Burke and Marx on the Rights of Man* (Methuen & Coy Limited 1987), 53.

36 Carlos Santiago Nino, *The Ethics of Human Rights* (Clarendon Press 1993), 1.

religious affiliation, health status or any other category. While it is true that not all rights are recognised by law, focusing on client dignity through the lens of human rights provides students with the necessary analytical skills to identity when laws and policies violate a person's rights. Human rights also provide students with a platform to critique the role of the state in relation to both citizens and non-citizens. This last point is succinctly articulated by Hanna Arendt: 'the right to have rights, or the right of every individual to belong to humanity, should be guaranteed by humanity itself'.[37]

37 Hannah Arendt, *The Origins of Totalitarianism* (Brace & World 1968), 297.

# 13 Clinical Legal Education: A paradigm for business entities

*Tobore O Okah-avae*

Utilising the debate on the corporate objective as a backdrop, this chapter argues that Clinical Legal Education could encourage a more progressive form of corporate governance. Business law clinics could help challenge the prevailing orthodoxy on the role of business in society in the following ways: first, they could help instil progressive values in participating student body, who would undoubtedly form the next generation of leaders in business, government, academia and the judiciary; second, by advising businesses in their infancy, clinics are able to encourage companies to formulate policies that prioritise the needs of employees and their host communities as a whole.

## Introduction

In August 2019, the influential Business Roundtable, a conglomeration of CEOs of the largest corporations, released a statement in favour of what it termed 'Stakeholder Capitalism'.[1] This was a major shift from its previous position that the corporation should be run to benefit shareholders mainly and all other competing interests were to be merely ancillary to this overarching objective. This statement represented a tectonic shift in the Anglo-American approach to corporate governance and adds further fuel to the decades-long debate on the corporate objective and the primacy of shareholder interests.[2]

The focus of the corporate objective has oscillated between the current focus on investors and the maximisation of their interests and a more pluralistic view of

1 Business Roundtable, 'Statement on the Purpose of the Corporation' *Business Roundtable* (19 August 2019) <https://www.businessroundtable.org/business-roundtable-redefines-the-purpose-of-a-corporation-to-promote-an-economy-that-serves-all-americans> accessed 16 December 2020.

2 For the stakeholder view of the firm, see: R Edward Freeman, Andrew Wicks and Bidhan Parmar, 'Stakeholder Theory and the Corporate Objective Revisited' (2004) 15(3) Organization Science 369; for discussions on the reasons a shareholder-centric view is justified, see Michael Jensen, 'Value Maximization, Stakeholder Theory and the Corporate Objective Function' (2002) 12(2) Business Ethics Quarterly 235; Anant Sundaram and Andrew Inkpen, 'The Corporate Objective Revisited' (2004) 15(3) Organisation Science 350.

DOI: 10.4324/9780429299247-14

the firm, which pays attention to a host of other constituencies, including employees, customers, the host communities and indeed the physical environment. A society's approach to corporate governance is a natural consequence of its view of the firm and the role of business in society. Therefore, a society which views the firm as a privately ordered vehicle for private wealth enhancement would consequently require the company to do no more than fulfil its core objective. This approach would inevitably differ in societies that view corporation as a means to attain a greater social good.

The focus on the corporate objective, has a lot to do with its proven impact on social outcomes.[3] Qualitative data show that societies which adopt the Anglo-American approach to corporate governance tend to be ultra-capitalistic and rife with sub-par social outcomes in health and education are often marked by extreme wealth inequalities.[4] On the other hand, societies which ascribe the firm with civic responsibilities and adopt a communitarian view of wealth creation are thought to fare better; they have overall better living standards, entrenched worker rights, etc.[5] The question this chapter seeks to explore, therefore, assuming a progressive approach to corporate governance is most desirable, is: can this be adopted within Anglo-American jurisdictions, and if so, what role could Clinical Legal Education ('CLE') play in helping businesses achieve this objective?

CLE is viewed by some commentators as a social good; whose initial conception was a vehicle for attainment of social justice objectives by 'educating students about economic disparities, unequal application of the law, and abuses of power'.[6] As such, a law clinic should service those least able to afford the legal costs and most in need of legal service. Thus, clinics step into a figurative void, left by decades of divestment from a threadbare social welfare infrastructure.[7]

There is the view held by some within CLE that a clinic's social justice function is ultimately undermined when it adopts a superficially neutral function, like

3 Martin Wolf, 'Milton Friedman was wrong on the corporation' *Financial Times* (London, 8 December 2020) <https://www.ft.com/content/e969a756-922e-497b-8550-94bfb1302cdd> accessed 05 January 2021.

4 The US, for instance, where the AA model developed, is said to lag behind similarly developed nations in most standard metrics like income inequality, poverty, access to healthcare, public spending and public infrastructure. Annalisa Merelli, 'The US has a lot of money, but it does not look like a developed country' *Quartz* (New York, 10 March 2017) <https://qz.com/879092/the-us-doesnt-look-like-a-developed-country/ > accessed 16 February 2020.

5 CROWE, 'Socialism, Social Democracy, and Capitalism: A debate on which is right for America' *CROWE* (Wisconsin, 11 March 2020) <https://crowe.wisc.edu/wp-content/uploads/sites/313/2020/03/Updated-CROWE-Debate-Booklet.pdf> accessed 16 February 2021.

6 Praveen Kosuri, 'Losing My Religion: The Place of Social Justice in Clinical Legal' (2012) 32(2) Boston College Journal of Law & Social Justice 331, 342; Donald Nicolson, 'Legal Education, Ethics and Access to Justice: Forging Warriors for Justice in a Neo-liberal World' (2015) 22(1) Intl Journal of the Legal Profession 51, 52.

7 Nicolson (n6) 52.

servicing the business or financial community.[8] However, in this chapter, I argue that business law clinics could perform a social justice function and I highlight some of the ways law clinics could train student participants to work with businesses on the benefits of corporate social responsibility and aid businesses along the path towards full corporate citizenship. The discussions in this chapter are theoretical and are focused on the participants of business law clinics, and how they could support the businesses they engage with over the course of their studies.

The chapter is outlined as follows: the next section will consider the traditional/mainstream Anglo-American view of the firm and whether it should have a social function. Section two will explore the possibility and benefits of a more progressive approach to corporate governance in the UK. Section three will consider the social justice function of law clinics and how business law clinics fit within this agenda, while the fourth section will address the practical ways the latter could be achieved. The chapter concludes thereafter.

## Modern business and corporate social responsibility

Milton Friedman, in considering the concept of corporate responsibility, stated unequivocally that the only responsibility of a business was to increase its profits.[9] It is fair to say that whilst this view might have been slightly outside of the mainstream at the time the article was published in 1970, the pervasion of neo-liberalism in the decades since has ensured its acceptance as the norm.[10] It is, therefore, the popular view that the corporation prioritises profits, and shareholder interests should be at the forefront of the corporate agenda.[11]

Despite its popularity in boardrooms across Anglo-American jurisdictions, the shareholder primacy doctrine[12] has received pushback from those who insist that the corporation should have responsibilities that extend beyond profit

8 Elaine Campbell, 'A Dangerous Method? Defending the Rise of Business Law Clinics in the UK' (2015) 49(2) The Law Teacher 165, 166.

9 Milton Friedman, 'The Social Responsibility of Business is to Increase its Profits' *The New York Times Magazine* (New York, 13 September 1970) <https://www.nytimes.com/1970/09/13/archives/a-friedman-doctrine-the-social-responsibility-of-business-is-to.html> accessed 16 February 2021.

10 Neoliberalism is an extreme form of free market economics, which '[i]t champions economic liberalisation, privatisation, free trade and deregulated markets, and seeks to reduce government spending as far as possible. Neo-liberalists believe that leaving matters to private enterprise is far more efficient than collective action, and consequently seek to replace the state with private enterprise, and notions of social justice and the public good with profit-making and self-interest.' Nicolson (n6) 52.

11 In *Peoples Department Stores v Wise* (2003) 244 DLR, the Canadian court declared that 'the interests of the corporation as coinciding with the interests of all of the shareholders in the pursuit of the objectives of the creation of the corporation'.

12 This is the view that the corporate objective should be the maximisation of shareholder wealth. D Gordon Smith, 'The Shareholder Primacy Norm' (1998) 23 J CORP L, 277.

maximisation.[13] The resistance to this ingrained value system has only intensified in the wake of devastating financial crises, extreme levels of income and wealth inequalities, not to mention the adverse effects of corporate activity on environmental sustainability in the long term. These increased agitations have not been without response, however, as corporations have voluntarily shown an openness to broaden the corporate objective, showing a willingness to countenance the needs of the firm's other stakeholders.[14] Hence, corporate social responsibility has become a fashionable and important weapon in the public relations arsenal of the largest corporations.

Notwithstanding the laudability of this leftward shift – if one were to disregard the patent self-promotive intents – it remains the case that corporate social responsibility ('CSR') continues to be voluntary, in the sense that corporate acts of social responsibility continue under an incentivised self-imposed system, rather than from an innate acceptance of its responsibility to all its stakeholders. However, to fully critique the current position, one must first consider two key questions: do firms have a social responsibility; and is this responsibility grounded in morality?

## *The traditional view of the corporation: the view of the firm as amoral*

As living standards have improved in the developed world, people in the West have begun to consider the 'social cost of their own enrichment'.[15] This has caused us to question our purchasing habits, as well as the environmental and social impact of the industrial and productive processes, which afford our leisured lifestyles. These questions are invariably put towards the corporation, which is the prime vehicle of the technological advancements that have made all these possible. In so doing, we project the burdens of our own moral consciences onto the corporate form; hence: if our individual or collective consternation about the costs of our lifestyle ignites a sense of responsibility towards society at large, there must therefore be a corresponding sense of corporate responsibility.

As mentioned above, until recently the consensus on corporate responsibility was a singular focus on shareholder wealth maximisation.[16] Corporations were focused on the interests of its owners for a myriad of reasons,[17] and were urged to pay some consideration to the interests of its other stakeholders. This is known as

13 Freeman et al., 'Stakeholder Theory and the Corporate Objective Revisited' (n2) 369.

14 Susan McPherson, 'Corporate Responsibility: What to Expect In 2019' *Forbes* (New Jersey, 14 January 2019) <https://www.forbes.com/sites/susanmcpherson/2019/01/14/corporate-responsibility-what-to-expect-in-2019/?sh=507f402690f4> accessed 16 February 2021.

15 Thomas Kempner, Kevin Hawkins and Keith Macmillan, 'The Role of Business in Society' (1970) 2(4) Long Range Planning 3.

16 Michael Jensen echoed this position when he said that 'multiple objectives, was no objective'. Jensen, 'Value Maximization, Stakeholder Theory and the Corporate Objective Function' (n2) 238.

17 Some of the common reasons proffered to justify the maximisation of shareholder interests are: that shareholders are a vulnerable class, a consequence of their position

the enlightened shareholder value approach.[18] There is no evidence to suggest that the drafters chose this approach to corporate governance due to a recognition of the corporation's responsibility to all its stakeholders, as from the need to balance corporate interests effectively.[19]

Corporate social responsibility 'consists not only of engaging in business activities that benefit society but also of avoiding activities that impose significant social costs or harms'.[20] To this point, Friedman believes that the notion of corporate social responsibility was antithetical to the interests of shareholders.[21] He argues that if managers were to undertake policies aimed at advancing social interests, the opportunity costs would be to forgo opportunities to enhance the wealth of his owners. As such, he states:

> What does it mean to say that the corporate executive has a 'social responsibility' in his capacity as businessman? If this statement is not pure rhetoric, it must mean that he is to act in some way that is not in the interest of his employers. For example, that he is to refrain from increasing the price of the product in order to contribute to the social objective of preventing inflation, even though a price increase would be in the best interests of the corporation. Or that he is to make expenditures on reducing pollution beyond the amount that is in the best interests of the corporation.

as residual claimants. This argument ignores that fact that shareholders are entitled to dividend payments and are also able to potentially earn significant returns on their initial investments when there are price increases. Kenneth Goodpaster, 'Business, Ethics and Stakeholder Analysis' (1991) 1(1) Business Ethics Quarterly 69. Furthermore, Jensen, amongst others, argues that prioritising shareholder interests is the most efficient way to govern the corporation and reduce agency costs. Michael Jensen and William Meckling, 'Theory of the Firm: Managerial Behaviour, Agency Costs and Ownership Structure' (1976) 3(4) Journal of Financial Economics 305.

18 Companies Act 2006, s 172 encouraged directors to prioritise the interest of its members, whilst paying consideration to the needs of other stakeholders including employees, customers, suppliers and the environment. This position has been branded the Enhanced Shareholder Value (ESV) one which still subscribes to the notion of shareholder primacy, but still considers the needs of the other stakeholders, albeit as having a secondary status. Andrew Keay, 'Having Regard for Stakeholders in Practising Enlightened Shareholder Value' (2019) 19(1) Oxford University Commonwealth Law Journal 118.

19 The Company Law Reform Steering Group (CLRSG) was tasked with identifying the best approach to corporate governance. The committee was also charged with the codification of director's duties, which was previously grounded in common law. The group's objective was to maintain the common law approach of shareholder primacy, but sought to 'strike a balance' between the competing stake-holding interests, to achieve the stated goal. This approach was deemed necessary to encourage the cultivation of long-term relationships, which would help corporations to avoid being overly focused on the short-term. See John Armour, 'Shareholder Primacy and the Trajectory of UK Corporate Governance' (2003) 41(3) British Journal of Industrial Relations 531, 531.

20 Kempner et al. (n15).

21 Friedman (n9).

It appears that Friedman looks beyond the charade of corporate personality and views the corporation as a legal fiction, meant to facilitate the business activities of the private actor.[22] This view considers the corporation as a mere platform for the transactional, principal–agent relationship between manager and investors, with the former being the only entity capable of exercising responsibility; a responsibility, which is owed – as far as the corporation is concerned – solely to shareholders. Mirroring Friedman's position on CSR is the view which holds the firm as having some responsibility but agrees that focusing the corporate objective on shareholder interests is the most efficient way to govern.[23] Adolf Berle believed that it was to the wider interest that the corporate objective be narrowed sufficiently to enhance the interests of its members,[24] arguing that prioritising investor interests was the best way to curb managerial powers and control for managerial abuse.[25] Although Berle's middling view avoids the ostentation and brashness of Friedman's opinion, he essentially arrives at the same conservative conclusion; at best his views represent a form of progressive conservatism.

It is important to note that in times past, the view within Anglo-America of the role of business was very different. Nineteenth century entrepreneurs took a more active role in the wellbeing of their employees and immediate community, and in many ways were forced to do so.[26] A notable example is Henry Ford of the Ford Motor Company, who believed that paying a good wage to his employees was ultimately to the company's economic benefit.[27] Kemper et al. note, however, that this sense of responsibility began to weaken with the expansion of the welfare state[28] as the government began to play a more active role in the provision of services companies previously undertook.

Some would argue that the firm does in fact owe an unconditioned social responsibility and this responsibility is to all constituencies touched by corporate activity.[29] This responsibility extends to its employees, customers, creditors and the environment. One could argue that the corporation has a responsibility to treat its employees fairly and pay a fair wage, deal with its creditors in an ethical

22 Here Friedman echoed the contractarian view of the firm, which views the latter as a nexus of contracts, basically a platform upon which private actors can contract. Marc Moore, 'Private ordering and Public Policy: The Paradoxical Foundations of Corporate Contractarianism' (2014) 34(4) Oxford Journal of Legal Studies 693.

23 Friedman (n9).

24 Adolf Berle Jr, 'For Whom Corporate Managers Are Trustees: A Note' (1932) 45 Harvard Law Review 1365, 1367.

25 Ibid.

26 Due to the absence of a social safety net. Kempner (n15).

27 Tim Worstall, 'The Story of Henry Ford's $5 a Day Wages: It's Not What You Think' *Forbes* (New Jersey, 14 March 2012) <https://www.forbes.com/sites/timworstall/2012/03/04/the-story-of-henry-fords-5-a-day-wages-its-not-what-you-think/?sh=3d62096a766d> accessed 16 February 2021.

28 Kempner (n15); also see Norman Bowie, 'A Kantian Approach to Business Ethics' in Thomas Donaldson, Patricia Werhane and Margaret Cording, *Ethical Issues in Business: A Philosophical Approach* (Prentice Hall 2002) 61, 69.

29 R Edward Freeman, 'The Politics of Stakeholder Theory: Some Future Directions' (1994) 4(4) Business Ethics Quarterly 409, 419.

manner, provide the best service to its customers and be responsible about its environmental impact.[30] The preceding is not optional, but imperative.

## Towards a more progressive corporation

Friedman decried the costs of corporate social responsibility; he believed that a corporation's engagement with social causes effectively placed costs on its stakeholders.[31] These costs could be in the form of higher rates for customers, as well as lower profits and wages for investors and employees, respectively. He posits that utilising corporate resources for the advancement of social causes is effectively akin to managers spending other people's money; that the decision to utilise firm resources to advance social causes should be left to the people whose resources it was, and people should do good 'at their own expense'.[32]

In a nutshell, Friedman endorsed the rapacious, winner-takes-all, shareholder capitalism we currently bear witness to, the legacy of which has been the unprecedented levels of economic and social inequality, a plethora of corporate scandals – sometimes triggering financial crises – environmental destruction and global political unrest.[33] The widespread dissatisfaction with the status quo, amid widely publicised sustainability concerns in relation to the climate, as well as long-term economic health, has led to increased calls for a rethink of our capitalistic ethos. These calls have reverberated across the globe in the wake of a wave of economic populism, which has swept across large swathes of the global north, inhabiting the agitations of the many who feel left behind by the current system.

That those who have benefited most from the status quo are now calling for a rethink is a signifier of a broad realisation of the detrimental externalities it produces and the need to pursue a more sustainable version of capitalism. The statement by the business roundtable espousing the virtues of stakeholder capitalism[34] is a credible first step, but true change would require a lot more than verbal commitment to egalitarian virtue. It would require tangible action. The issue, however, assuming this commitment to a corporate pluralism is genuine, is do corporations who have been engineered and governed towards the attainment of selfish objectives have the capacity to be any other way? If they do, what should change look like?

To be honest, this author has nothing but pessimism regarding the first point; as for the second, a reengineered stakeholder capitalism would be the opposite of everything we have witnessed in recent decades and to that point, Martin Wolf paints a fair portrait of what that could look like:

30 Bowie (n28) 9.
31 Friedman (n9).
32 Ibid.
33 Martin Wolf, 'There Is a Direct Line from Milton Friedman to Donald Trump's Assault on Democracy' in Luigi Zingales, Jana Kasperkevic and Asher Schecter (eds) *Milton Friedman 50 years Later* (Promarket 2020) 114.
34 Business Roundtable (n1).

> It is one in which companies would not promote junk science on climate and the environment; it is one in which companies would not kill hundreds of thousands of people, by promoting addiction to opiates; it is one in which companies would not lobby for tax systems that let them park vast proportions of their profits in tax havens; it is one in which the financial sector would not lobby for the inadequate capitalisation that causes huge crises; it is one in which copyright would not be extended and extended and extended; it is one in which companies would not seek to neuter an effective competition policy; it is one in which companies would not lobby hard against efforts to limit the adverse social consequences of precarious work; and so on and so forth.[35]

It goes without saying that the above would require a significant amount of divestment from the status quo to facilitate a pivot to a better system. Whether corporations could exercise the requisite willingness and capacity for change remains to be seen. Furthermore, there is little chance that the future would bring with it the political will needful for legislative intervention. Institutions of higher education represent the best options for the reorientation needed to effect the desirable changes. I argue that there could be an opportunity for business law clinics to take on a major role in these efforts.

There is some controversy about law clinics going beyond a social justice function and servicing the business community,[36] even leading to some scepticism about the legitimacy of transactional clinics.[37] In the following sections it will be argued that the idea of social justice and business law clinics are not mutually exclusive and there is a role for business law clinics in redefining the objective of the corporation and steering them on a path towards citizenship.

## Beyond a social justice function? A role for Clinical Legal Education facilitating a wholesome corporation

Law clinics have traditionally been seen as existing to provide access to justice to those who otherwise would be excluded. The pervasive consensus is that the promotion of a socially just cause should steer the activities of the law clinic.[38] The reason for this is that the first law clinics were inextricably linked to the civil rights movement and were established to train future lawyers in 'client-centred lawyering'.[39] There is some debate as to the ultimate purpose of the law clinic, as some have argued that these clinics could and perhaps should have a purpose that transcends a purely social justice function, while others have resisted this view and

35 Wolf, 'There Is a Direct Line from Milton Friedman to Donald Trump's Assault on Democracy' (n33).
36 Campbell (n8) 171.
37 Kosuri (n6) 341.
38 Ibid. 332.
39 Ibid. 333.

maintain that clinics are meant to serve the least in society.[40] What should be the true purpose of the law clinic? CLE is defined as a:

> [T]eaching method based on experiential learning, which fosters the growth of knowledge, personal skills and values as well as promoting social justice at the same time. As a broad term, it encompasses varieties of formal, non-formal and informal educational programs and projects, which use practical-oriented, student-centered, problem-based, interactive learning methods, including, but not limited to, the practical work of students on real cases and social issues.[41]

Clinics aim to provide the students with these skills by exposing them to real clients with real issues and allowing the students to gain the knowledge and skills along with an awareness of the intricacies of legal practice. All of this is done, of course, under the supervision of clinicians, who are usually qualified lawyers.[42] Clinics generally aim to service low-income and indigent clients who typically would be unable to afford legal fees. Kosuri states that clinicians justify the social justice function of law clinics on the grounds that most students might otherwise never encounter these issues over the course of their professional lives.[43]

The bias in favour of social justice stems from the origins of CLE, which came about in response to the inadequacies of the case method of legal education.[44] However, clinics were not meant to replace the case method in its entirety, but to

40 Campbell (n8) 170.

41 The European Network of Clinical Legal Education, 'Definition of a legal clinic' <http://encle.org/about-encle/definition-of-a-legal-clinic> accessed 16 February 2021.

42 Ibijoke Patricia Byron, 'The Relationship between Social Justice and Clinical Legal Education: A Case Study of the Women's Law Clinic, Faculty of Law, University of Ibadan, Nigeria' (2014) 20(2) International Journal of Clinical Legal Education 563, 565.

43 Kosuri (n6) 339.

44 The development of the case method legal education is credited to Christopher Langdell, a former Dean of Harvard Law School. It is the predominant method of teaching in US Law schools and focuses on the analysis of legal and judicial opinions as against the provision of lectures and reading of textbooks. Pioneers of CLE like Karl Llewellyn and Jerome Frank were part of a group of legal realists who decried the emptiness of the case method, with its emphasis on interpretation of legal rules, calling instead for a fact-based educational method which focused on the conversion of legal knowledge into action. Frank likened a rule-based legal education to 'architects who study pictures of buildings and nothing else', and his proposed remedy was the establishment of 'legal clinics' in law schools that would help to deepen the students' understanding of legal theory. With the aim that these clinics would service legal-aid groups, but also government agencies and quasi-public bodies. Accordingly, this method was not meant to replace the case method in its entirety, but to work conjunctionally with the latter in providing a wholesome legal training. Jerome Frank, 'Why Not a Clinical Law School?' (1933) 81 University of Pennsylvania Law Review 907, 908; Karl Llewellyn, 'On What's Wrong with So-called Legal Education' (1935) 35 Columbia Law Review 651, 658.

work conjunctionally with the latter in providing a holistic form of legal training. The function of these clinics began to evolve in the 1960s, with the dawn of the civil rights movement in the United States, when a number of clinics began to take on social justice causes.[45]

The preceding section explains the deep embeddedness of social justice at the core of CLE and elucidates the reluctance to accept the legitimacy of clinics which deviate from this service orientation. To this point, it is therefore easy to understand how the notional business law clinic would seem somewhat counter-intuitive. This might explain the unwillingness of most within the CLE community to subscribe to the legitimacy of these clinics.[46] However, those in favour of business law clinics are quick to outline that the merits of a business-centred CLE exceed the mere provision of legal service to fledgling businesses, but could also meet the social justice ethos at the heart of CLE.

### *Business law clinics as social justice?*

Kosuri[47] and others[48] argue that restricting the scope of law clinics to social justice issues could have the adverse effect of narrowing the experience and exposure of law students. This narrowing of the scope and subsequent mainstreaming of the perceived purpose of law clinics has led to a form of 'intellectual homogeneity'.[49] He mentions that there is a danger of law clinics being managed in such a way as to get the students to see the world through the eyes of clinicians rather than develop their own viewpoint and ideology.[50]

Kosuri highlights the educational value of law clinics with a wider focus, arguing that clinics that move beyond a narrow social justice brief provide students with transferable competencies, which could serve them in whatever field they choose to go into. Business law clinics for instance, could help equip students with skills that serve them well in the commercial sphere, like negotiation, drafting, dispute avoidance and resolution. He contends that although devoid of a social justice function, these clinics still provide the participants with soft skills and a stronger understanding of human motivations and the value cooperation in goal attainment.[51] He further argues that a failure of the clinical establishment to recognise the value of the highlighted skills risks having the legitimacy of business law clinics questioned.[52]

45 Stephen Wizner, 'The Law School Clinic: Legal Education in the Interests of Justice' (2002) 70(5) Fordham Law Review 1929, 1933.
46 Kosuri (n6) 341.
47 Ibid. 335.
48 Campbell (n8) 172; For a view of the implications of the narrowing of the broader approach of legal education within law schools, see Eric J Gouvin, 'Teaching Business Lawyering in Law Schools: A Candid Assessment of the Challenges and Some Suggestions for Moving Ahead' (2009) 78(2) UMKC Law Review 429.
49 Kosuri (n6) 336.
50 Ibid. 340.
51 Ibid. 341.
52 Ibid.

Following on from the above, whilst Eric Gouvin admits that the legal education remit is to provide students with the knowledge and skills that would serve them well over the course of a legal practice career, he does warn that the approach taken appears to be unevenly skewed towards litigation, to the detriment of the students' ability to develop the transactional skills that they would need to be successful outside of a litigation-based practice.[53] These are skills that a business law clinic could provide to the students, in addition to helping prepare them for a possible career outside of the law. The importance of providing law students with transferable skills is highlighted by the fact that fewer students go on to have legal careers.[54]

Considering the preceding discussions on the viability of business law clinics, the important issue is whether business law clinics have or could potentially have a social justice function. It is my argument in this chapter that they could and will proceed to expatiate on this idea in the following section.

## *Business law clinics can fulfil the social justice mandate of law clinics*

As discussed above, one of the major arguments against business law clinics is that they fail to fulfil the social justice mandate – by servicing the needs of the indigent – clinics are thought to have.[55] This view, I believe, stems from a misconception of the nature and scope of transactional law clinics. It is fair to admit that advising clients on intellectual property or investment issues does not appear to have the same weighting on the altruistic scale as the work traditionally done within law clinics. That said, this section aims to highlight the potential of business law clinics from a social justice perspective, and how fulfilling this potential could help alter the current view of the effectiveness of these clinics. In this section I argue that business law clinics could work with fledgling businesses, helping educate the directors of these infant corporations on the values of progressive, socially conscious corporate governance, as well as the wider social benefits this approach could have.

First, and most importantly, business law clinics that have a commitment to progressive values – a commitment to environmental preservation, economic justice and true equality of opportunity – could have the effect of instilling these values within the students. This could have wider benefits in the future as the students go on to careers in business and legal practice. Students who have participated in a business law clinic with social justice at its core, and who imbibe these values in their praxis, could carry these on into careers in business, legal practice, politics and other forms of public service, which could lead to more responsible corporate governance, socially and environmentally friendly public

53 Gouvin (n48) 431.

54 Noam Scheiber, 'An Expensive Law Degree, and No Place to Use It' *The New York Times* (New York, 17 June 2016) <https://www.nytimes.com/2016/06/19/business/dealbook/an-expensive-law-degree-and-no-place-to-use-it.html> accessed 16 February 2021.

55 Kosuri (n6) 341.

policy mandates and possibly a more informed electorate, and spur greater socially conscious activism.

Also, these law clinics could help educate start-up corporations on corporate citizenship, which recognises the firm has responsibilities to its immediate environment, similar to civic duties owed by individuals to the state. These responsibilities are concomitant with its licence to operate within the host community, as is the case with individuals. Corporate citizenship suggests that the company at its core recognises it has a responsibility to other stakeholders beyond its investors, and this recognition could have an effect on the formulation of the corporate objective and enable the company to pivot from the profit-centred mindset discussed earlier in the chapter. This manifests itself in a number of ways.

For a start, a clinic could educate fledgling businesses on employee rights and the right approach to employee management. Companies could be encouraged to view their workers as prime assets and not liabilities to be used and abused. They could be encouraged to set policies in place that ensure the statutory rights for employees are upheld, particularly in the areas of compensation. Companies could be advised to ensure all workers are compensated fairly and not the least allowed by law, refrain from harmful practices like wage theft[56] and the utilisation of casualised, unsecure labour.

The preceding is important for the following reasons: first, it could have a positive impact on employee morale, which translates to better individual and collective performance. Research has shown that firms whose employees believe they are treated fairly tend to outperform their peers.[57] Second, there are also the practical implications of having well-compensated and motivated employees, in the sense that they are more likely to form part of the company's customer base. The latter fact was recognised by the pioneer Henry Ford over a century ago.[58] On a final note, firms should be discouraged from the mainstream perception of employees as expendable and refrain from the knee-jerk reaction of effectuating job losses upon an economic downturn. At an early stage companies could be encouraged to countenance the broader social and economic impact of every lost job and explore other cost-cutting measures, resorting to workforce reduction only as a last resort.

56 Victoria Noble, 'How Britain's Online Retailers are Profiting from Wage Theft' *Open Democracy* (30 September 2020) <https://www.opendemocracy.net/en/oureconomy/how-britains-online-retailers-are-profiting-from-wage-theft/> accessed 16 February 2021.

57 Clement Bellet, Jan-Emmanuel De Neve and George Ward, 'Does Employee Happiness Have an Impact on Productivity? (2019) Saïd Business School WP 2019–13 <https://ssrn.com/abstract=3470734 or http://dx.doi.org/10.2139/ssrn.3470734> accessed 16 February 2021.

58 Henry Ford advocated for higher wages and better working conditions for his workers not out of charity but based on the conviction that this would improve worker productivity and benefit the business in the long-term. See Sarah Cwiek, 'The Middle Class Took Off 100 Years Ago … Thanks To Henry Ford?' *NPR* (27 January 2014) <https://www.npr.org/2014/01/27/267145552/the-middle-class-took-off-100-years-ago-thanks-to-henry-ford?t=1610371465943> accessed 16 February 2021.

Furthermore, law clinics could encourage fledgling corporations to develop an appreciation of the value of situating and maintaining its activities within its local community. Rapid globalisation has made it easier for corporations to situate their core business activities in offshore locations, due to the cost-saving benefits.[59] As such, the last four decades have borne witness to a gradual but sustained erosion of our manufacturing and productive capabilities, with the largest corporations choosing to outsource these to low wage countries, spurred on by the enormous savings on wages and tax liabilities.[60] The consequences to the communities impacted have been devastating. The apparent lack of political will to address these issues has left a vacuum that law clinics could help fill, by helping enlighten founders of these start-ups of the benefits of a community-oriented approach to corporate governance rather than being profit-centred. That harks back to the idea of corporate citizenship discussed previously; if the firm sees itself as part of the community it would be more likely to make decisions to benefit the latter. Furthermore, on a more practical point, the students could be trained to advise entrepreneurs aware of various tax and investment reliefs provided by the central and local governments in the UK. It could be argued that if infant businesses are made aware of the various reliefs available whilst in their infancy and are able to properly take advantage of these, it could help reduce the likelihood that they seek the benefits offered elsewhere.

Business law clinics could further prove useful in advising the businesses they work with on the benefits of being mindful of their environmental impact. Climate change, as we know, is poised to be one of if not the greatest challenge of the twenty-first century and corporate activity has been a major contributor to the phenomenon to date.[61] The reversal of the current trend towards a complete environmental meltdown would depend to a huge extent on whether companies choose to address the way they do business. Business law clinics, I believe, could aid them along those lines: encouraging fledgling corporations/start-ups to consider the environmental impact of their chosen businesses and perhaps persuade them to adopt the least environmentally destructive path towards achieving the corporate objective. Furthermore, they could help these start-ups affirm a commitment to limiting their environmental impact, by having these drafted into the company's articles either at inception or post-formation.

59 Mojtaba Kheryian, 'Where would Globalisation be Without Outsourcing' (2015) CGSRS Research Paper, 4 <http://cgsrs.org/publications/2#:~:text=Globalization%20has%20led%20to%20an,to%20a%20common%20global%20economy> accessed 16 February 2021.

60 Andrew Barber and David Riker, 'The Effect of Outsourcing on Domestic Workers' (2017) USITC Office of Economics Working Paper 2017–10-A, 3 <https://www.usitc.gov/publications/332/working_papers/ecwp-2017-10-a-10-03-17-as-pdf.pdf> accessed 16 February 2021.

61 Elliot Hyman, 'Who's Really Responsible for Climate Change?' *Harvard Political Review* (Cambridge, 2 January 2020) <https://harvardpolitics.com/climate-change-responsibility/> accessed 16 February 2021.

## Conclusion

The preceding discussions are intended to explore a possible role for law clinics in encouraging corporations along a path towards corporate citizenship and highlighting the benefits of a corporate governance model which is inclusive and prioritises the interests of multiple constituencies. The focus has been on fledgling corporations for two reasons: first, more established corporations are less likely to require the services of business law clinics than new start-ups. Furthermore, established corporations would understandably have a more entrenched culture which would be more difficult and take longer to change. On the other hand, clinics could help an infant business position itself as a citizen with corresponding rights and obligations, within its host community, which would invariably impact the culture within the corporation as well as its approach to business.

# 14 Rebellious lawyering theory, sustainability and Clinical Legal Education

*Richard Owen*

As sustainability presents a number of complex and urgent challenges it will consider how rebellious lawyering needs to evolve and adapt in response. In particular it will look at recent developments in human rights litigation and activism in the commercial sphere and asses their implications for rebellious lawyering.

It also examines the role of strategic litigation in a rebellious lawyer's toolkit, and the relationship between strategic litigation, on the one hand, and law and policy reform, on the other.

It considers how students can best be prepared in a Clinical Legal Education setting for the sustainability challenges they will face in their careers. This includes looking at the knowledge they need to acquire, as well as the practical training.

## Introduction

This chapter will explore how rebellious lawyering theory can inform sustainability practice in a Clinical Legal Education setting. As a result, it will look at the intersection of sustainability, the provision of legal services and Clinical Legal Education (CLE). It will argue that rebellious lawyering can be a more effective approach in achieving sustainability aims than more traditional approaches. As sustainability presents a number of complex and urgent challenges it will consider how rebellious lawyering needs to evolve and adapt in response. It also examines the skills and attributes which need to be developed in students if they are to be effective sustainability practitioners.

## Rebellious lawyering theory

Although there have been a number of definitions of rebellious lawyering, what they have in common is their belief in an approach to legal practice which seeks to bring about social change. It has been developing as a theory since the 1990s, although there were forms of legal practice which prefigured it and is based on a rejection of a hierarchical relationship between lawyer and client, so called

DOI: 10.4324/9780429299247-15

'regnant lawyering'.[1] By contrast, rebellious lawyers see themselves in egalitarian collaboration with the communities they serve.

Rebellious lawyers will work with community leaders, community groups, agencies and allies. This heightened awareness of the community dimension to lawyering means they see the client as their community as opposed to companies, individuals or groups of individuals. This resonates with lawyers working in the sustainability space who can also see their client as an abstraction. For example, the environmental law charity, ClientEarth, believes that the Earth is its client rather than any individual or grouping.[2]

Rebellious lawyers are open to different methods of dispute resolution. They seek methods that will be effective in addressing their communities' problems. This means a willingness to explore avenues other than litigation in order to find workable solutions for the community. They will use litigation but are aware that their clients might find it difficult to access and may not result in all the remedies that they most need, as, by itself, it is unlikely to achieve the remedies that are most needed.

Litigation also creates a risk of creating a hierarchy between lawyer and client, as the lawyer in courts and some tribunals will have rights of audience, which will not extend to lay members of the communities they work with, although that risk can be mitigated, for example, by demystifying the process. They will use a range of tactics in addition to litigation, such as working for legislative change, lobbying, public education, media campaigns, political mobilisation and community organisation.[3] They will deploy these tactics in such combinations as the context prescribes.[4]

As rebellious lawyers are working in egalitarian collaboration with community groups, their aim is to demystify the law and legal process. They are open and transparent as to what they want to achieve with the groups with which they work. This, in turn, empowers these groups and they have a more informed idea of the evidence they need to gather in order to assist the lawyer they are working with.

Another characteristic of the rebellious lawyering approach is to be aware of how large structure such as political, economic and political forces affect the ability to bring about change in the communities in which they operate.

The need for self-reflection is strong in rebellious lawyering. Rebellious lawyers experiment with their collaborative work, 'constantly re-evaluating their own institutional and personal efforts'.[5] They have to be self-critical in reflecting on their own performance, so they do not get hemmed in by their own 'tiny habits'.[6]

1 Gerald P López, *Rebellious Lawyering: One Chicano's Vision of Progressive Law Practice* (Westview Press 1992).
2 James Thornton and Martin Goodman, *Client Earth* (Scribe UK 2017) 14.
3 Barbara Bezdek, 'Alinsky's Prescription: Democracy Alongside Law' (2009) 42 John Marshall Law Review 723.
4 Ibid.
5 López (n 1) 48.
6 Ibid. 7.

Rebellious lawyering has been influenced by and has synergies with community organising as propounded by Saul Alinsky. He envisaged democracy working from the bottom up with an active citizenship at the local level.[7] As a result, he advocated a revitalisation of democracy through a People's Organisation, which would be inclusive of all the people and organisations within the communities they serve.[8] As this is organising from the bottom up, 'native or indigenous leadership is of fundamental importance'.[9] The People's Organisation accepts that all problems are related and are the result of certain fundamental causes.[10] If there is a failure to observe the relationship between problems, there will be no understanding of the functional relationship between a local community and the larger social scene, and how a neighbourhood is shaped by forces that transcend the local scene.[11] As a People's Organisation brings different stakeholders together there will be both similarities and differences in opinion. The organiser can set some general principles at the outset after which there will be an interplay of ideas leading to a common agreement as to the Organisation's programme.[12] A People's Organisation is a learning community. It will learn, 'through its own practices, of the functional relationship between the community, the city, the state, the nation, and the world as a whole'.[13]

The main synergies between rebellious lawyering and Alinsky's method of community organising are the bottom-up approach, the importance of community leadership, the need to contextualise the community's challenges within a wider context and the need to learn and develop. Both rebellious lawyering theory and Alinsky's method of community organising talk of the need for lawyers and organisers to have the skills which are needed to communicate effectively with the communities they serve.

Despite these synergies, there are differences too. Many following Alinsky's method are confrontational and have taken on roles 'as provocateurs or angry oppositionists'.[14] Rebellious lawyers, on the other hand, are more likely to use a collaborationist approach.[15] They dislike the tone of a 'rabble rouser' as they think it is less effective, because it implies a lack of spontaneity. They think groupings which appear to come together spontaneously without professional organisation are more likely to be effective.[16]

Rebellious lawyers want the communities they serve to set their own agendas. They think, 'Like the client, the lawyer always teaches and always learns'.[17] This

7 Saul D Alinsky, *Reveille for Radicals* (Vintage Books 1989) 17.
8 Ibid. 202–203.
9 Ibid. 64.
10 Ibid. 59–60.
11 Alinsky (n 7) 60.
12 Ibid. 54.
13 Ibid. 167.
14 Bezdek (n 3).
15 Ibid.
16 López (n 1) 359.
17 Ibid. 53.

reciprocal educative relationship is particularly important in the sustainability space where there can be issues which blight the community, such as air pollution, which cannot be perceived with the senses.

Alinsky rejected litigation as a strategy[18] whereas rebellious lawyers might be sceptical that communities will have access to it, but will be prepared to use it, as it is part of their toolkit. Alinsky said, '[we] the people will work out our own destiny', not, 'leave it to the lawyers'.[19] Rebellious lawyers see themselves as working not only with clients but also with community leaders, community groups, agencies and allies.

This is another difference; this method of working with groups has been called 'co-citizenship',[20] whereas Alinsky sees solutions being generated from within the community – through political as opposed to legal decision making via a revitalised democracy – not working with it in a partnership. Rebellious lawyers will inevitably find that there are conflicts of interest within a community. Alinsky's idea of a common agreement show rebellious lawyers a method for reconciling these conflicts. Therefore, they will work with those drawing on Alinsky's methods even if there may be differences over approach and tactics, as there is also a large overlap between the two approaches.

## Rebellious lawyering theory and sustainability

Sustainable development was defined in the Brundtland report as: 'development that meets the needs of the present without compromising the ability of future generations to meet their own needs'.[21] This is a definition of sustainable development, as opposed to sustainability. The difference between the two is often seen as sustainability being a long-term goal (that is, a more sustainable world) and sustainable development as the pathways and processes to achieve it, for example, sustainable production.[22]

The original conception of rebellious lawyering theory makes no explicit reference to sustainability.[23] This could be more of a reflection of the political, economic and social agenda in the 1990s when it was formulated than of any incompatibility of the theory with sustainability. However, rebellious lawyering requires continuous experimentation, so it has been said that it is not a methodology but 'prescriptively normative' with principles – such as egalitarianism,

18 Gerald Rosenberg, 'Saul Alinsky and the Litigation Campaign to Win the Right to Same-Sex Marriage' (2009) 42 John Marshall Law Review 643.

19 Sandford Horwitt, *Let Them Call Me Rebel: Saul Alinsky – His Life and Legacy* (Vintage Books 1992) xiii, 408 as cited in Rosenberg (n 18).

20 Bezdeck (n 3).

21 World Commission on Environment and Development, Our Common Future 'the Brundtland Report' (1987) Chapter 1, para. 49.

22 'Sustainable Development' (UNESCO undated) <https://en.unesco.org/themes/education-sustainable-development/what-is-esd/sd> accessed 8 August 2019.

23 López (n 1).

contextualisation and self-reflection – guiding rebellious lawyers as they evolve their legal pedagogy and practice.[24]

It is submitted that rebellious lawyers should now evolve their legal pedagogy and practice to consciously embrace a sustainability agenda. There is greater awareness of the sustainability challenges facing us now compared to the 1990s when the theory was first formulated. For example, it was not until 2000 that it was suggested that the impact of human activities has been so significant that it can be regarded as having created a new epoch, the 'Anthropocene'.[25] This means that: 'The human imprint on the global environment has now become so large and active that it rivals some of the great forces of Nature in its impact on the functioning of the Earth system'.[26] The liminality of moving from one epoch to another requires a change in approach. So, rebellious lawyering theory needs to evolve to accommodate a sustainability agenda.

In order to achieve a more sustainable world several environmental challenges need to be tackled, such as anthropogenic climate change, depletion of stratospheric ozone, air and water pollution, soil erosion and degradation, land contamination, waste management and disposal, depletion of natural resources, ocean acidification, disposal of plastics, the acidification of surface waters, deforestation and habitat loss, the depletion and extinction of species, over fishing, melting of polar ice caps and the decline of biodiversity.

Although successfully addressing these environmental challenges is a large part of ensuring a sustainable future, sustainability combines environmental with socio-economic issues. So, sustainability also includes issues such as the development of skills, tackling inequalities, maintaining and improving social quality with concepts such as cohesion, reciprocity and honesty, the importance of relationships amongst people, acting in a globally responsible manner, as well as a sustainable approach to increases in prosperity.

Sustainability therefore encompasses a number of significant, pressing and interconnected challenges. They can be said to be wicked problems, i.e. problems with many interdependent factors making them *seem* impossible to solve. Wicked problems are seen to be different from scientific or engineering problems. Whereas the natural sciences have a findable solution, social problems are ill defined and depend upon political resolution.[27] Therefore, a mathematical problem, such as solving an equation, has a clear mission and it is also clear whether the problem has been solved.[28] It is what can be called a 'tame' problem.[29] However, wicked problems do not have these traits and have ten characteristics.[30]

24 Anthony Alfieri, 'Rebellious Pedagogy and Practice' (2016) 23 Clinical L. Rev. 5, 5.
25 Paul Crutzen and Eugene Stoermer, 'The "Anthropocene"' (2000) 41 Global Change Newsletter, 17.
26 Will Steffen and others, 'The Anthropocene: conceptual and historical perspectives' (2011) 369 (1938) *Philosophical Transactions of the Royal Society*, 842.
27 Horst Rittel and Melvin Webber, 'Dilemmas in a General Theory of Planning' (1973) 4 Policy Sciences 155–169.
28 Ibid.
29 Ibid.
30 Ibid.

### *1. There is no definitive formulation of a wicked problem*

It is difficult to define a wicked problem. Formulating the problem is part of the problem itself as different stakeholders will have different versions of what the problem is.

### *2. Wicked problems have no stopping rule*

The problem solver knows when they have a solution to a mathematical equation. This is not the case with social policy problems where the problem solver can always try to do better because there is no end to the interlinking chains of the open problem. As there is no definitive, stable problem there is often no definitive solution.

### *3. Solutions to wicked problems are not true-or-false, but good-or-bad*

Many stakeholders will be interested, and/or entitled to judge the solutions. However, none of these stakeholders have the power to set formal decision rules to determine whether their solution is the correct one.

### *4. There is no immediate and no ultimate test of a solution to a wicked problem*

With wicked problems, any solution, after being implemented, will generate waves of consequences over an extended period of time. Because wicked policy problems are multi-causal with many interconnections to other issues, it is often the case that measures introduced to address the problem lead to unforeseen – sometimes adverse – consequences elsewhere.

### *5. Every solution to a wicked problem is a one-shot operation; because there is no opportunity to learn by trial-and-error, every attempt counts significantly*

Every implemented solution to a wicked problem is consequential. It leaves traces that cannot be undone. Many people's lives will have been irreversibly influenced by the attempt at a solution to a wicked problem, and a large amount of money will have been spent. Any attempt to reverse any unintended and undesirable consequences will pose another set of wicked problems. As a result, a learning orientation is required, supported by an analysis based on systems thinking.[31]

31 Carl Brønn and Peggy Simcic Brønn, 'Sustainability: A Wicked Problem Needing New Perspectives' in Helen Borland and others (eds) *Business Strategies for Sustainability* (Routledge 2018).

### *6. Wicked problems do not have an enumerable (or an exhaustively describable) set of potential solutions*

It is not possible to know if all possible solutions to the wicked problem have been identified. When looking at sustainability, complex interactions of social, ecological and economic systems result in a high degree of causal ambiguity, which challenges standard perspectives and approaches to decision making.[32]

### *7. Every wicked problem is essentially unique*

Although wicked problems may have many similarities with previous problems, they will also have differences. It is never possible to be certain whether this difference overrides its commonalities with previous problems.

### *8. Every wicked problem can be considered to be a symptom of another problem*

The interdependencies, multiple causes and internally conflicting goals of wicked problems usually involve a range of coordinated and interrelated responses and attempts at resolving them often involve trade-offs between conflicting goals. Wicked problems hardly ever sit conveniently within the responsibility of any one organisation. Solutions to wicked problems usually involve coordinated action by a range of stakeholders, including organisations (different levels of government), non-profit organisations, private businesses and individuals.

### *9. There is always more than one explanation for a wicked problem because the explanations vary greatly depending on the individual perspective*

People choose those explanations which are most plausible to them. The analyst's world view is the strongest factor in their explanation as to the causes of the wicked problem and in advocating the solutions which, in their opinion, will resolve it.

### *10. Planners/designers have no right to be wrong and must be fully responsible for their actions*

It is a principle of science that solutions to problems are only hypotheses offered for refutation. Therefore, the scientific community will not blame a scientist who postulates a hypothesis which is later refuted. As planners attempting to resolve wicked problems, they will be held responsible for the consequences of the actions they generate as a lot of people will be affected by them.

32 Ibid.

Three coping strategies have been identified to cope with wicked problems: authoritative, collaborative and contested.[33]

Authoritative strategies place the problem solving in the hands of a few stakeholders, such as public authorities or experts, who have the authority to define a problem and come up with a solution.[34] The advantage of this is that problem solving can be quicker as fewer stakeholders are involved. The disadvantage is that the problem and potential solutions can be defined too narrowly.[35]

Competitive strategies see stakeholders assuming it's a zero-sum game. If the stakeholder's opponents win the right to define the problem and choose the solution, then that stakeholder loses. If the stakeholder wins the right, then its opponents lose.[36] The advantage is that it can be a spur to innovation. The disadvantage is that pushed to extremes it can lead to violence and warfare.

In collaborative strategies stakeholders join forces with a view to accomplish more as a collective than they can achieve by acting as independent agents. At the core of collaboration is a win-win view of problem solving.[37] The advantage is that costs and benefits can be shared. You get 'the whole system in the room' and a dialogue can commence from which everyone learns. The disadvantage is that as there are more stakeholders, agreement can be harder to reach.[38]

Roberts argues that collaborative strategies are the most effective in dealing with wicked problems. As wicked problems are socially defined, then getting the 'whole system in the room' enables people to learn from one another, which is useful.[39] Social learning – the theory that new behaviours can be acquired by observing and imitating others – is more likely to be successful in a 'self-organizing, complex adaptive system that co-evolves as stakeholders meet, interact, and inform one another's actions'.[40]

Like Roberts, who advocates collaborative strategies to work on wicked problems, there are those operating within the sustainability space who advocate approaching it 'through a "whole systems thinking model", which offers us a profound way to re-orientate our worldview'.[41]

This type of systems thinking has clear affinities with rebellious lawyering and their method of working with community leaders, community groups, agencies and allies in order to bring the 'whole system in the room'. However, the perceived disadvantage of this is how slow it can be to reach agreement when so many stakeholders are involved. It can also get very complicated very quickly if

33 Nancy Roberts, 'Wicked Problems and Network Approaches to Resolution' (2000) 1 (1) International Public Management Review 1–19.
34 Ibid.
35 Ibid.
36 Ibid.
37 Roberts (n 33).
38 Ibid.
39 Ibid.
40 Ibid.
41 Stephen Sterling, *Sustainable Education: Re-visioning Learning and Change* (Green Books for the Schumacher Society) Kindle Edition, 874.

everyone is involved when it will be possible to have discussions but not so easy to agree on the effective action, which is the aim of rebellious lawyering. However, if rebellious lawyers draw on Alinsky's methods, they can initially impose general principles, which in a sustainability context will mean principles like acting in a globally responsible way, living within sustainable limits, etc.

This is the dilemma of the current sustainability debate. It is a wicked problem so requires a whole systems approach to come up with effective solutions. However, it takes time to acquaint stakeholders with the requirements of a whole systems approach, as they get to grips with its complexities and interconnectedness of problems. The challenge is that there is not much time. In 2018, the UN Intergovernmental Panel on Climate Change, which only deals with certain aspects of sustainability, said urgent and unprecedented action would need to be taken over 12 years if climate catastrophe is to be averted.[42]

## Strategic litigation, human rights and sustainability

Although rebellious lawyers have traditionally been sceptical about litigation, there has been increasing creativity with the use of strategic litigation by environmental lawyers often working with communities, which has been effective. Strategic cases often see the 'parties seek to leverage the litigation to instigate broader policy debates and change'.[43] Innovative strategic litigation is starting to be seen by linking human rights issues, climate change and other aspects of sustainability such as public health and equality.

Although the European Convention on Human Rights does not enshrine any right to a healthy environment, it has been argued that the exercise of certain Convention rights may be undermined by the existence of harm to the environment. At the time of writing, six Portuguese young people (ranging from eight to 21 years old) have filed a legal action before the European Court of Human Rights accusing 33 countries of violating their right to life by not aligning their plans with their commitment under the Paris Agreement to limit global temperature rise 'well below 2C' after lethal wildfires in Portugal in 2017.[44] Researchers have linked the intensity of the wildfires to global warming. Amongst other things they argue breaches of the following Convention Articles: Article 2 (right to life), Article 3 (prohibition of inhuman or degrading treatment), Article 8 (right to private and family life and home) and Article 14 (prohibition of discrimination).

42 V Masson-Delmotte and others (eds), *Global Warming of 1.5°C. An IPCC Special Report on the impacts of global warming of 1.5°C above pre-industrial levels and related global greenhouse gas emission pathways, in the context of strengthening the global response to the threat of climate change, sustainable development, and efforts to eradicate poverty* (UN Intergovernmental Panel on Climate Change, 2019).

43 Joana Setzer and Rebecca Byrnes, 'Global trends in climate change litigation: 2020 snapshot' *Grantham Research Institute for Climate Change and Environment, London School of Economics* (2020) 2.

44 Agostinho and Others v. Portugal (no. 39371/20).

The case is being funded following a successful crowdfunding campaign, which shows further new possibilities for activists to bring strategic litigation cases as the associated financial risk is spread widely. The application has satisfied the European Court of Human Rights admissibility requirements without the need to have exhausted the domestic remedies of potentially 33 states.[45]

Strategic litigation may have additional objectives other than winning the case, such as a wider strategy to engage stakeholders into an argument for policy change or law reform and build public awareness of the links between climate change and other issues such as public health. These are rebellious lawyering objectives that underpin coalition building efforts.

The disadvantage of this approach is that it involves an incrementalist change on a case-by-case basis when the urgency of the issues requires a swift response. There is also the risk that judges will be accused of being activist, as they develop provisions which do not explicitly assert the right to a healthy environment, and therefore lack legitimacy. Courts will be drawn into balancing interests and policy, which is arguably best left to the legislature, which has the democratic legitimacy to carry out such tasks.

Even if the case succeeds, it may not give the applicant the remedy they need, as a court may be limited as to its range of remedies. For example, they may receive compensation when what they really need is a change of policy or legislation. This underlines why strategic litigation can only be one tool in the rebellious lawyer's toolkit. It shows the need for rebellious lawyers as co-citizens being in a reciprocal educative relationship with clients, as if the case is pushing, say, anti-discrimination provisions, to achieve wider environmental objectives the case will be very technical. However, it also supports Alinsky's theory that ultimately holistic solutions for communities can only come from the political sphere, although strategic litigation can increase pressure for political settlement.

## New developments in activism and the commercial sector

Sustainability requires change in behaviour not just from government, but also from businesses and individuals. There has been a recent trend for different types of activist, private law litigation directed at companies. Whilst the majority of climate change-related litigation is still directed at government, approximately 10 per cent is now directed at companies.[46] Activists have brought cases against asset managers about holdings in fossil fuel stock and the financial risk in investing too heavily in them as there is a transition away from them.[47]

45 European Court of Human Rights, 'Information Note on Agostinho v. Portugal (no. 39371/20)' 13 November 2020 <http://hudoc.echr.coe.int/eng?i=001-206535> accessed 15 February 2021.

46 Sabin Center for Climate Change Law, 'Climate Change Litigation Databases' <http://climatecasechart.com/> accessed 12 February 2021.

47 'The Wrong Side of the Law' The Economist Sustainability Week, 9 October 2020 <https://app.swapcard.com/event/sustainability-virtual-week/planning/UGxhbm5pbmdfMTY3MTQ3> accessed 29 January 2021 per Nigel Brook.

Activism has also affected investors. In Japan there was a shareholder revolt against Zuohua Bank over its investments in coal. Although the shareholder resolution did not pass, Zuohua essentially was shamed into changing their investment policies. In this case, litigation and investment pressure acted hand in hand.[48] This is a feature of strategic litigation: a credible threat can be as effective as litigation itself.

In Europe, there have been cases brought against companies who burn, or want to burn, coal. The charity, ClientEarth, have been successful in bringing a business risk case against the directors and officers of a company. They bought shares in Enea SA and sued the company for the annulment of a resolution consenting to the construction of a coal-fired power plant on grounds of its climate change-related financial risk. The court ruled that the company resolution was legally invalid.[49]

ClientEarth see legal enforcement, and therefore litigation, as central to their strategy.[50] However, their tactics accord strongly with rebellious lawyering theory. For example, they empowered the work of local groups in Ghana to handle the new legal frameworks placed around forestry issues, demystifying the law for them to facilitate civil society's lobbying of government.[51]

## Rebellious lawyering theory, coalition building and the commercial sector

When engaging in sustainability practice, rebellious lawyers need to be aware that they might be able to look wider for allies than their traditional pool of community groups, government and the not-for-profit sector. This is mainly as a result of what is happening as sectors respond to the results of climate change. One of the normative principles of rebellious lawyering is that they must engage in self-reflection and evolve and experiment with their legal practice. Therefore, they need to take cognisance of what is currently happening in the commercial space.

There is an argument that company law needs to be amended as it ensures that corporate behaviour is unsustainable. Company law requires the interests of shareholders to be put first, which means to put profit first – before all else.[52] The law thereby entrenches a norm in the belief in the value of money over and above the welfare of our wider Earth community.[53] However, in addition to investor activism, which is discussed above, there have been developments in the way companies are constituted, which would make some companies more suitable bedfellows in coalitions in which rebellious lawyers participate.

48 Ibid. per James Thornton.
49 *ClientEarth Prawnicy dla Ziemi v. Enea SA* (IX GC 1118/18) 31 July 2019.
50 Thornton and Goodman (n 2) 13.
51 Ibid. 184.
52 Polly Higgins, *Dare to be Great: Unlock Your Power to Create a Better World* (FLINT 2020) 51.
53 Ibid.

Certified B Corporations (B Corps) seek a cultural shift to redefine success in business and build a more inclusive and sustainable economy. They have standards of verified social and environmental performance, public transparency and legal accountability to balance profit and purpose.[54] In total, 3,790 companies in 74 countries are B Corp certified.[55]

Rebellious lawyers may find that there is more commonality of interest with B Corp companies than with companies who prioritise the need to maximise profits above all else, which has implications for their coalition building. They may find that as they may share objectives with B Corps companies, they will have common interests so will be more likely to be able to work with them as coalition partners than other types of company who prioritise profits over all other considerations.

This comes at a time when companies are starting to come under pressure to collaborate with others. The United Kingdom has passed legislation setting a goal of net zero carbon emissions target by 2050.[56] In order to meet this target there will have to be a cross-sector, private, public and civic societal effort that will require new levels of collaboration that society has never experienced before, which means that rebellious lawyering will have to rethink how it collaborates with the private sector, and the private sector will have to reconsider how it collaborates *inter se* and with other sectors.

## Rebellious lawyering theory, sustainability and Clinical Legal Education

It is submitted that Clinical Legal Education with its use of experiential learning – 'the process whereby knowledge is created through the transformation of experience'[57] – and using rebellious lawyering techniques is the ideal form of teaching delivery when developing students' understanding of sustainability legal practice.

Experiential approaches require students to look at problems in their entirety, which is ideal when systems thinking is needed to address wicked problems.[58] The urgent and daunting challenges of sustainability mean students need to be confronted by the realities of real-life problems, so they learn to be creative and adaptive as sustainability practitioners. As rebellious lawyers work with community leaders, community groups, agencies and allies, and collaborative approaches

54 Certified B Corporation, 'About B Corps' <https://bcorporation.uk/about-b-corps> accessed 4 February 2021.

55 Certified B Corporation, 'A Global Community of Leaders' <https://bcorporation.net/> accessed 4 February 2021.

56 Climate Change Act 2008, s 1, as amended by The Climate Change Act 2008 (2050 Target Amendment) Order 2019, SI 1056, s 2.

57 David Kolb, *Experiential Learning: Experience as the source of learning and development* (Prentice-Hall 1984) 41.

58 Adrian Ely, 'Experiential learning in "innovation for sustainability": An evaluation of teaching and learning activities (TLAs) in an international masters course' (2018) 19 (7) International Journal of Sustainability in Higher Education 1204.

are thought to be best at tackling wicked problems, then it is also an ideal approach to use rebellious lawyering techniques in experiential learning when looking at sustainability issues.

The conditions under which sustainability practice is carried out can vary in different parts of the world. In 2019, 212 land and environmental defenders were murdered when peacefully protesting. Half of all these reported killings occurred in two countries: Colombia and the Philippines.[59] The opportunities to use strategic litigation also vary according to the legal system. For example, rules of standing in judicial review cases and costs rules vary between jurisdictions.

*Askesis* is the word in Ancient Greek to denote any kind of practical training or exercise, and *mathesis* is the word for theoretical knowledge. In Ancient Greece, it was common to learn by a combination of *mathesis* and *askesis*. The *askesis* of the Greeks had a very specific purpose: to have set in place the 'moral equipment that will permit [a person] to fully confront the world in an ethical and rational manner'.[60] Clinical Legal Education with its mix of theory and practice contributes to both the *mathesis* and *askesis* of sustainability legal practice.

As part of students' *mathesis* students need to be made aware that there are a number of different approaches that can be made to sustainability. However, all approaches to reject the dominant idea from the last few hundred years that the environment has been largely seen as external to humanity, and the relationship between people and the environment could be characterised as humanity's dominance over nature.[61] By contrast, all forms of sustainability recognise that humanity is dependent on the environment to meet needs, and rather than dominating the environment the economy and human relations are nested within it.[62]

There are weak and strong conceptions of sustainability. Weak approaches favour technological based solutions to overcome environmental challenges. The spectrum of weak approaches ranges from those who use the status quo to those who use reform approaches.[63] Those favouring the status quo acknowledge that there are problems which need to be addressed but this can be done through technology and market-based approaches. There is no need for a fundamental reorganisation of society, and economic growth will be a necessary part of achieving sustainability.[64]

59 Global Witness, 'Global Witness records the highest number of land and environmental activists murdered in one year – with the link to accelerating climate change of increasing concern' 29 July 2020 <https://www.globalwitness.org/en/press-releases/global-witness-records-the-highest-number-of-land-and-environmental-activists-murdered-in-one-year-with-the-link-to-accelerating-climate-change-of-increasing-concern/> accessed 12 February 2021.

60 Higgins (n 52) 58.

61 Bill Hopwood, Mary Mellor and Geoff O'Brien, 'Sustainable Development: Mapping Different Approaches' (2005) 13 Sustainable Development 38.

62 Ibid.

63 Ibid.

64 Ibid.

Those taking a reform approach do see the need for change, but do not see an imminent environmental or social collapse as being likely or that fundamental change is necessary. However, they are critical of certain government and business policies, as well as certain societal trends such as excessive consumer consumption. They focus on technology, science and information, changes to market regulation and reform of government, as the response to sustainability issues.[65] Transformationists feel that a collapse in ecological or social systems is likely and therefore fundamental socio-economic and political change is a necessity in order to meet sustainability challenges.[66]

Both rebellious lawyering and Alinsky's method of social organisation require awareness of large structure, and therefore the global dimension to sustainability issues. So, in preparing students for sustainability practice using rebellious lawyering techniques, for example, they need to be aware that the costs of climate change are not evenly distributed. Rich countries burn more fossil fuels than poorer countries, which generates more carbon dioxide emissions. Within any country, richer people benefit more from the fossil-fuelled economy by virtue of the fact that they can afford to consume more goods and services. The poorest people live in the areas hardest hit by global warming such, as drought-prone regions of sub-Saharan Africa.[67]

There are also complex geopolitical questions around historic emissions. Currently, China is the largest emitter of $CO_2$ emissions, at 9.8 billion tons in 2017 compared with the United States at 5.3 billion tons, although the United States is still a bigger emitter on a *per capita* basis.[68] However, cumulative emissions from the entire industrial era - roughly from 1800 to the present – have been primarily caused by the US and Western Europe, but these regions are not paying the greatest price for historic cumulative emissions.[69]

There is growing recognition within the field of economics that the emissions of developing countries should not be viewed in the same way as those of countries which have been historic emitters. Raworth propounds a form of sustainable economics called 'doughnut economics' where all human life fits into a 'sweet spot' between the 'social foundation', where everyone has what they need to live a good life, and the 'environmental ceiling'.[70] For low- and middle-income countries to have sufficient social foundation to climb into the 'sweet spot', 'significant [economic] growth is very much needed'.[71] However, this is a means to reach social goals within ecological limits. Raworth's analysis identifies a need for

65 Ibid.
66 Ibid.
67 James K Boyce, *Economics for People and the Planet: Inequality in the Era of Climate Change* (Anthem Press 2019) 7.
68 Noam Chomsky and Robert Pollin, *Climate Crisis and the Global Green New Deal* (Verso 2020) 92.
69 Ibid. 91.
70 Ciara Nugent, 'Amsterdam Is Embracing a Radical New Economic Theory to Help Save the Environment. Could It Also Replace Capitalism?' Time, 1 February 2021.
71 Ibid.

reduction in the consumption levels of high-income people. This shows the need to examine values, particularly in relation to humanity's relationship with nature and materialism, as any part of sustainability education.

Whatever students' stance on sustainability, they should be encouraged to develop a 'personal environmental ethic', as sustainability works on the premise that humanity is part of the environment and not dominant over it.[72] They need to know where they stand on the spectrum of weak and strong sustainability.

In order to develop this ethic students will need an *askesis*, or practical training, in voicing their personal environmental ethic. Research shows the more students practise using their voice when it comes to values, the more skilful they will be in doing so.[73] Values conflicts will inevitably arise in the workplace. Students need to be aware of the need to practise using their voice when it comes to values, as part of their continuous professional development.[74] This practice should commence with 'rehearsals' as part of their induction and training for Clinical Legal Education.[75] People are more effective in voicing their values in the workplace if they are equipped with self-knowledge, which is further reason to explore their personal environmental ethic during their Clinical Legal Education.[76] They are also more likely to be effective in voicing their values if they can anticipate the likely rationalisations they will face when voicing them.[77]

One of these frequently expressed ethical dilemmas in the workplace is when there is a clash of values of whether it is better to obtain a short-term advantage or think whether it would be ultimately more advantageous to think long-term even if results are not immediately apparent.[78] Students need to be aware when developing their personal environment ethic that setting up the short- and long-term in opposition to each other is a false dichotomy. For example, if we moved to zero carbon emissions immediately, we could not function. We would be unable to go to work or get provisions for our sustenance. The short- and long-term need to be in dialogue with each other and voicing our values means before taking a decision its true costs and trade-offs have been assessed and evaluated.[79]

## Conclusion

Rebellious lawyering with its systems thinking approach is an ideal form of legal practice for sustainability. When practised in a Clinical Legal Education setting it enables students to contextualise their studies and think about how lawyers

72 Joy Palmer and Philip Neal, *The Handbook of Environmental Education* (Routledge 1994) 19.
73 Mary C Gentile, *Giving Voice to Values: How to Speak Your Mind When You Know What's Right* (Yale University Press 2010) 168.
74 Ibid. 168.
75 Ibid. 169.
76 Ibid. 108.
77 Ibid. 170.
78 Gentile (n 73) 179.
79 Ibid. 183.

interact with other stakeholders, as well as facilitate practising how they will voice sustainability values in their employment.

As part of the evolution of rebellious lawyering it needs to keep up to date with new forms of activism, particularly in the human rights and commercial spheres, which relate mainly to climate change-related litigation, but also have important implications for other forms of sustainability, such as the protection of health.

This activism also shows the need for a proper appreciation of the role of strategic litigation in a rebellious lawyer's toolkit, and the relationship between strategic litigation, on the one hand, and law and policy reform, on the other. There also needs to be reflection on how current sustainability challenges affect every sector, in particular the implications this has for coalition building between communities and purpose-driven companies.

# 15 Teaching movements

*Scott L Cummings*[1]

## The power of place

As a rule, I am not a fan of the wired classroom. Too many distractions. However, on the 24th of November 2014, I confronted a dilemma. The country was expecting an announcement from the St. Louis County prosecutor about whether a grand jury had decided to return an indictment against white police officer Darren Wilson, who had shot and killed an unarmed black man, Michael Brown.[2] It was the latest in a long and ugly history, in which black people, mostly men, were killed by law enforcement officers with impunity. The case had sparked protest and international outrage, contributing to the rise of the Black Lives Matter movement (BLM). As the day grew longer and no word was issued, I had to consider what to do.

Let me back up. I am a professor at the University of California, Los Angeles (UCLA) School of Law, where I teach courses on the legal profession, local government law, and corporations. Since 2002, I have also taught a Clinic in Community Economic Development, which represents non-profit organisations and coalitions on transnational and policy matters related to affordable housing and economic justice. I have been enormously fortunate to do that work at UCLA, the flagship law school in Los Angeles, which has long been a national leader in the Clinical Legal Education (CLE) movement. Indeed, I joined the UCLA faculty to stand on the shoulders of true giants. My senior colleague, David Binder, had built the UCLA programme from the ground up, joining the faculty in 1972, when he used funding from the Ford Foundation to launch what would become one of the most important centres for CLE in the world. Binder's casebook on client-centred lawyering, written with my other colleague Paul Bergman, set the standard for clinical pedagogy.[3] There were others who taught me the

1 Robert Henigson, Professor of Legal Ethics, UCLA School of Law – cummings@law.ucla.edu.

2 Monica Davey and Julie Bosman, 'What Happened in Ferguson' *New York Times* (New York, 24 November 2014) <www.nytimes.com/interactive/2014/08/13/us/ferguson-missouri-town-under-siege-after-police-shooting.html> accessed 10 February 2021.

3 David A Binder, Paul Bergman, and Susan C Price, *Lawyers as Counselors: A Client-Centered Approach* (West Publishing Company 2001).

DOI: 10.4324/9780429299247-16

theory and craft of clinical teaching, and also showed me how to combine that teaching with ambitious, socially relevant scholarship. I was able to learn from Al Moore, a master teacher, and Gary Blasi, a legendary public interest lawyer turned academic. Although they were no longer there when I started, I also felt the presence of incredible clinical scholars such as Lucie White and Jerry López.[4]

It was a magical place, one enabled by an egalitarian ethos and a commitment to innovation. The UCLA that I arrived at was one of the few in the nation that granted full academic tenure to faculty who taught clinical courses. That meant both that the school valued clinical teaching as an intellectual project and that it expected that clinicians could and should produce scholarship at the highest level. This meant, in turn, that the faculty provided sustained intellectual support, while demanding the highest standards. It also created tensions that, over time, have caused the school to lose some of what was distinctive back then. As all American law schools suffered economic constraint in the post-Great Recession world, financial cutbacks took aim at CLE, deemed 'expensive' due to low student–faculty ratios. This, as well as the general political drift away from progressive social justice values in law schools and broader society, meant that there was less overall support for pedagogy and scholarship that was often overtly normative (and left-leaning). Finally, UCLA over time came to hold a peculiar place in the overall environment of US CLE. Whereas most law schools had developed in-house clinics, with live-client representation on social justice issues the norm, UCLA had pioneered simulated courses, what is now commonplace under the rubric of 'experiential education'. This meant that there was gradually shrinking space for live-client clinical work, which required more time – time that competed with increasingly intense scholarly demands.

Nevertheless, UCLA is special for other reasons that relate to, and in some sense build on (and push beyond), CLE. In particular, it is home to the first programmes in Critical Race Studies and Public Interest Law and Policy in the country. These programmes have permitted the law school to recruit social justice-minded students and faculty, and to become an anchor for innovative and impactful scholarship and activism. From 2008 to 2014, I was the faculty director of our Epstein Program in Public Interest Law and Policy, which is an intensive specialisation designed to recruit and train the public interest leaders of the future. Perhaps unique among American law schools, programme faculty and students get to select incoming 1Ls through an admissions process that seeks to identify applicants with high public interest potential as demonstrated in their past work experience, personal background, extracurricular activities, and affirmative goals.[5] As a result of this process, we typically attract an older, more

4 For seminar works, see Gerald P Lopez, *Rebellious Lawyering: One Chicano's Vision of Progressive Law Practice* (Routledge 1992); Lucie E White, 'Subordination, Rhetorical Survival Skills, and Sunday Shoes: Notes on the Hearing of Mrs. G.' (1990) 38(1) Buff L Rev 1.

5 Richard L Abel, 'Choosing, Nurturing, Training and Placing Public Interest Law Students' (2002) 70(5) Fordham L Rev 1563.

experienced, and more activist programme class each year: 25 of the most passionate, dedicated, and inspirational students that I am privileged to know.

Precisely because these students care so deeply about social justice, the goal of the programme is not to keep the world out of the classroom – like so much of law school – but to bring it in. It is to show how law shapes oppression, inequality, and injustice, and – critically – how law can be used as one tool (in coordination with others) to fight for a more just world. In this sense, it shares core values with the CLE movement.[6] My public interest students are optimists, they are dreamers, and although they could do anything they want in the world, they choose to stand on the side of righteousness and to challenge power.

On the evening of the 24th of November 2014, that commitment to stand with the oppressed presented a pedagogical difficulty. I was scheduled to have class with Epstein Program students in the seminar all second-year students are required to take, 'Problem Solving in the Public Interest'. In fact, that night was to be our final class of the term, a culmination and celebration of all the work that the students had done that semester. During the course, students were asked to develop an advocacy plan combining different tactics (litigation, policy advocacy, organising, and media advocacy) to address an important social problem about which they cared deeply. That term, the projects reflected and engaged with the most pressing issues outside the cloistered law school walls – issues to which many of the students had deeply personal connections. There was a clear theme in the student work with a significant number choosing to pursue projects that responded directly to the massive inequalities and injustices in the criminal justice system. Michael Brown's death and the history and continued reality of police mistreatment of communities of colour was in the background and on the surface. As an example, one student wrote powerfully about police militarisation and its impact on individuals with mental health issues. Others highlighted problems with criminal defence and prisons. Still others focused on the relation between criminal justice and communities of colour, particularly immigrants. Michael Brown, and the countless others whose lives had also been shattered by the criminal justice system but whose names were not remembered, were on our collective minds – which is what made that night a challenge.

As the class was intended to unfold, students were to present analyses and recommendations from their final paper projects. Then, as a celebration, we were to have some food and drink, taking in a breath before the hard, final stretch of examinations. Yet the real world was to intervene to disrupt this pedagogical plan. Midway through the two-hour session, I began to notice students too intently focused on their computer screens. They were not just taking diligent notes or reviewing assignments. As I began to circulate around the room, I realised what was happening: St. Louis County prosecutor Robert McCullouch had begun the news conference in which he was to announce the grand jury decision

6 William M Sullivan, Lloyd Bond, Anne Colby, Lee S Shulman, and Judith Welch Wegner, *Educating Lawyers: Preparation for the Profession of Law* (Jossey-Bass 2007).

in the Michael Brown case.[7] Computer screens were streaming news feeds. The student presentations faltered as a hush came over the room. Normally students would be shamed into closing their computer screens to avoid revealing their covert non-class activity. But not this time. Groups of students began to huddle around the screens of those who were running the newscasts until someone uttered the unthinkable words that smashed the silence: 'no indictment'.

Shock and grief flooded the room. Some students became visibly distraught, eyes welling with tears. What should I do? What should I say? Should we carry on as planned? I quickly tried to recover. After a bit of conferencing, we decided that the final student presentations should go on, that it was only fair to credit all of their hard work, but that we could not – did not want to – proceed in celebration of the end of our class together. Suddenly, celebration felt unseemly, a cruel denial. We needed to do something to mark the moment and think about how we should respond: how we as lawyers and lawyers-to-be could do something to voice our collective demand that violence under cover of law would no longer receive law's protection. That was, after all, why we all were there: to make law live up to its promise.

As the presentations ended, we rallied together. Instead of socialising and unwinding, we went outside into the courtyard in the dark, and formed a silent circle. At this point, the students had taken the lead. I was following. We joined hands. And one by one each of us stepped into the circle to speak one truth about how we felt and what we wanted to do. Some spoke of the searing pain of seeing family and friends harassed by police, who acted with impunity. Others talked about the strength they took from our solidarity. Still others talked about their need to leave the circle and to act. When it was finally my turn, I could find words only to say how much courage and inspiration I took from them all.

Those truths connected our community to the one outside – one of anguish, outrage, but also resistance and mobilisation. When we broke hands, some students left to join that resistance, going to mass rallies and marches that were erupting around the city. In the days that followed, many of those same students, joined by faculty, would be on the front lines of a new movement asserting that BLM, using the force of collective action to change law and social practice. Six months later, Los Angeles became the nation's largest city to mandate that its police officers wear body cameras in an effort to document police–community interaction and, it was hoped, improve police conduct and accountability. Although movement activists continued to fight over the details – whether the police would be able to review the video footage before writing their reports and whether they would be able to withhold footage from the public – it was a step forward for a department infamous for its treatment of black and brown

7 In the United States, prosecutors present evidence to grand juries, which are responsible for deciding whether to issue indictments against defendants based on probable cause. Although in most places grand juries have broad investigatory authority to request and review a wide range of evidence, in practice, prosecutors tend to control what information grand juries get to see and thus have a significant influence on the outcome of the grand jury review process.

residents. It was also precisely what I and my colleagues had, in our public interest and clinical courses, been trying to teach: that it is organised movements of people, allied with lawyers and other activists, speaking truth to power that changes law; that changing law is just one step in the never-ending struggle to shift power in favour of those who lack it.[8]

## A social movement perspective

I have reflected on the Michael Brown moment in my class many times in the past year. And I have thought a great deal about our circle and what it meant to speak truth among ourselves at that moment of hurt and anger. That moment was one of the most profound in my nearly decade and a half of teaching. One – as countless others fade – I will most certainly never forget. As I have reflected, I have tried to understand its lessons for my own teaching: about law as a system of rules which reflects power inequality, but also about law as an aspiration to greater justice and as a tool to be leveraged to hold those in power to their claim to respect law. That aspiration led me to Alabama that summer, where I took my daughters to study and draw inspiration from the history and legacy of the Civil Rights Movement.[9] It was there I was reminded of Martin Luther King Jr's unforgettable speech on the eve of the Montgomery Bus Boycott, given to an

8 James Gray Pope, 'Labor's Constitution of Freedom' (1997) 106 Yale LJ 941; Michael McCann and Helena Silverstein, 'Rethinking Law's "Allurements": A Relational Analysis of Social Movement Lawyers in the United States' in Austin Sarat and Stuart Scheingold (eds), *Cause Lawyering: Political Commitments and Professional Responsibilities* (OUP 1998), 261; William N Eskridge, 'Some Effects of Identity-Based Social Movements on Constitutional Law in the Twentieth Century' (2002) 100 Mich L Rev 2062; Kenneth W Mack, 'Rethinking Civil Rights Lawyering and Politics in the Era Before Brown' (2005) 115 Yale LJ 256; Anthony V Alfieri, 'Faith in Community: Representing "Colored Town"' (2007) 95 Calif L Rev 1829; Jack M Balkin and Reva B Siegel, 'Principles, Practices, and Social Movements' (2006) 154 Univ PA Law Rev 927; Jennifer Gordon, *Suburban Sweatshops: The Fight for Immigrant Rights* (Belknap Press 2007); Michael J Klarman, *From Jim Crow to Civil Rights: The Supreme Court and the Struggle for Racial Equality* (OUP 2006); Austin Sarat and Stuart A Scheingold (eds), *Cause Lawyers and Social Movements* (SUP 2006); Reva B Siegel, 'Constitutional Culture, Social Movement Conflict and the Constitutional Change: The Case of the de facto ERA-2005–06 Brennan Center Symposium Lecture' (2006) 94 Calif L Rev 1323; Douglas NeJaime, 'Winning Through Losing' (2010) 96 Iowa L Rev 941; Catherine Albiston, 'The Dark Side of Litigation as a Social Movement Strategy' (2011) 96 Iowa L Rev Bull 61; Tomiko Brown-Nagin, *Courage to Dissent: Atlanta and the Long History of the Civil Rights Movement* (OUP 2011); Michael E Waterstone, Ashley Stein, and David B Wilkins, 'Disability Cause Lawyers' (2012) 53 Wm & Mary L Rev 1287; Susan D Carle, *Defining the Struggle: National Organizing for Racial Justice, 1880–1915* (OUP USA 2013); Lani Guinier and Gerald Torres, 'Changing the wind: Notes toward a demosprudence of law and social movements' (2013) 123 Yale LJ 2740; Gwendolyn M Leachman, 'From Protest to Perry: How Litigation Shaped the LGBT Movement's Agenda' (2014) 47 UCDL Rev 1667.

9 See Taylor Branch, *Parting the Water: America in the King Years 1954–63* (Simon and Schuster 2007).

overflow crowd of several thousand at the Holt Street Baptist Church, in which he intoned, to explosive applause: 'And we are not wrong, not wrong in what we are doing. If we are wrong, the Supreme Court of this nation is wrong. If we are wrong, the Constitution of the United States is wrong.'[10] Law matters in the fight for equality not because it resolves conflict, but rather because it is a symbol of what is right – a symbol that can be mobilised by people to create hope and demand change.

The aspiration to greater justice had also led me to undertake a sustained scholarly investigation of how social movements shaped law and how law – sometimes – could be a tool to advance social movements. That investigation familiarised me with an interdisciplinary literature and new theoretical perspective on 'law and social movements', which I sought to understand and extend. My research resulted in several important lessons and a deeper theoretical perspective on how law matters in social change.[11] In particular, I learned that law reform builds from bottom-up activism by social movements that make normative claims on democracy; and that those normative claims, voiced by those on the frontline of struggle, are ultimately what gives content to law.[12] I also learned that authentic legal change builds from lawyers who exercise leadership that is accountable to the people lawyers claim to serve and that social change through courts can produce powerful advances but also mobilise powerful backlash.[13] Overall, I learned that there is never one route to transformative social change, particularly on behalf of those who lack power, but that multidimensional advocacy to shift law and politics must proceed on interrelated tracks – and be committed to sustained struggle over multiple cycles of contention.[14] Moreover, this theoretical perspective became the lens through which I came to see my clinical teaching.

As I thought back about applying this theoretical perspective back to my public interest and clinical courses, one lesson was clear: that there was nothing more powerful and enduring than directly confronting the law in action – for good or ill. And if that meant departing from my script, going into a space of discomfort where I did not have a learning goal or even know what might happen, that was necessary to arrive at the truth that we so often obscure in our day-to-day teaching: that for so many in our society, the law does not work. Indeed, I have thought since that genuine learning – confronting the fact that law does not always work but that we nonetheless have to continue to fight to demand that it

10 Clayborne Carson and Kris Shepard, *A Call to Conscience: The Landmark Speeches of Dr. Martin Luther King, Jr* (Grand Central Publishing 2002).

11 Scott L Cummings, *An Equal Place: Lawyers in the Struggle for Los Angeles* (OUP 2020).

12 Scott L Cummings, 'The Social Movement Turn in Law' (2018) 43(2) Law & Soc Inquiry 360.

13 Scott L Cummings, 'Movement Lawyering' (2017) U Illinois L Rev 1654; Scott L Cummings, 'Law and Social Movements: Reimagining the Progressive Canon' (2018) 3 Wis L Rev 441.

14 Scott L Cummings, 'The Puzzle of Social Movements in American Legal Theory' (2017) 64 UCLA L Rev 447.

does – requires walking outside the space of comfort into the dark courtyard of vulnerability.

But, of course, that moment of candour in the face of raw injustice we experienced on the 24th of November 2014 could not be predictably reproduced. So, I have also reflected on how that honesty, that space for speaking truth and for galvanising action, could be recaptured and sustained in a more systematic way as I go forward. This has led me to think of the metaphor of our circle and how it both signified something important about building communities of solidarity within the law school and making it link to circles outside in the real world of movements for social change.

## A pedagogical call to action

What I have come up with is not a path-breaking new programme, but rather a recommitment to the core values that drew me to become a law professor in the first instance – values that are too often neglected in the race for the status goods associated with academic success. How to exist in the Ivory Tower[15] of academia while remaining accountable to those whose voices too often do not carry over its walls has been the central puzzle of my experience as a law professor. I have not solved that puzzle, but I have redoubled my efforts to continue trying by building and deepening the links between my own work and the larger political project of supporting movements of the marginalised to make my city – and my country – better. This involves three choices:

The first is to reinvest in building communities of students who are connected to movements for social change and understand our law school as a space where political engagement is valued and even promoted. This means continuing to bring in social justice-minded students to our Epstein Public Interest programme, to connect them to one another and to faculty, and to ensure that they have the institutional resources and guidance to make it through law school with their dreams of social change solidified and their skills strengthened. It means standing up for the contributions these students make to the law school independently of what it might mean for the *US News* ranking algorithm. It means fighting for students who have non-traditional backgrounds: students like Frankie Guzman, who at the age of 15 was put in juvenile detention for holding up a Kmart clerk at gunpoint and by 24 had already spent six years behind bars.[16] Despite the odds, Frankie fought his own way to college and then to UCLA law school, where he applied in order to become a lawyer for young people like the person he used to be – stuck in the juvenile justice system with no hope for the future. We

15 A metaphorical place where people are happily cut off from the rest of the world in favour of their individual pursuits. For a history of the term, see Steven Shapin, 'The Ivory Tower: The history of a figure of speech and its cultural uses' (2012) 45(1) British Society for the History of Science 1.

16 Meredith May, 'From prison to juvenile justice lawyer' *SFGATE* (San Francisco, 17 February 2013) <www.sfgate.com/crime/article/From-prison-to-juvenile-justice-lawyer-4286757.php> accessed 05 February 2021.

accepted Frankie and he accepted us. He brought his commitment here and we supported him to carry that commitment back to his community: as a Soros Fellow at the National Center for Youth Law, where he fights for juvenile justice sentencing reform to make sure first-time youth offenders are not placed in adult prisons. Although Frankie's story is particularly compelling, his commitment and drive are not unique. The challenge we face as educators who want to support the work of Frankie and other students like him is that law schools have become increasingly inhospitable to their dreams. The economic model of contemporary legal education subsidises those who score high on the metrics that 'count' most in the race for rankings. Too often, this means that students with the background and resources to achieve high scores on the law school admission test (known as the LSAT) pay a substantially discounted tuition rate (and sometimes no tuition at all), while those with LSATs below their law school's average, many from less privileged backgrounds pursuing social justice dreams, pay full freight. This places significant obstacles in the way of those students who overcome incredible odds in the drive to give back to their communities as public interest lawyers – but who confront mountains of debt to do so. Creating communities of social justice in law schools requires ensuring that law school remains financially accessible and that loan assistance actually works to enable graduates to pursue the path of hope and helping. This will be even more important in the post-pandemic era to come.

The second choice is to bring my own resources to bear in supporting movements for change. Leading is by example and not just exhortation. For me, this means redoubling my commitment to teach courses that allow me to connect my students with local struggles – to use our collective capital to challenge poverty and inequality in Los Angeles. In this regard, I have been lucky to be on a faculty that has supported my colleagues and me to teach clinical courses from a position of complete parity. And I have used this to teach clinical courses on community economic development which have over the past decade supported initiatives by local movements for economic justice: helping shape policy around labour standards in the waste and port trucking industries; assisting local organisations in the pursuit of community benefits agreements in connection with downtown development; supporting the creation of worker-owned cooperatives owned by immigrant workers in sectors like landscaping; and helping community-based organisations preserve affordable housing against the forces of gentrification and displacement. Doing this work is an individual choice, but it is one that operates in the context of broader institutional choices by my law school to support this type of clinical work. My law school has long been a leader in Clinical Legal Education: a fount of client-centred, rebellious, and third-dimensional lawyering, and a continued leader in movements to end injustice against immigrants and promote police accountability. But this vision is under stress as law schools confront the intersecting pressures of fiscal austerity and new requirements for experiential learning by the American Bar Association (ABA) and some state bars.[17] Intensive

17 See American Bar Association, Standards and Rules of Procedure for Approval of Law Schools 2014–2015, Standard 303(a)(3) (requiring law schools to offer a curriculum that allows each student to complete 'one or more experiential course(s)

clinical work that trains students through experiences with live clients with real problems and real struggles is costly. There are incentives for deans, which other schools have confronted, to cut back and invest in less costly teachers and approaches. There is no inevitability to the continuation of the social justice mission of CLE that was one of its cornerstones when it was institutionalised nearly a half-century ago. To maintain the ability to connect our work through robust clinical education to the world around us – to enrich our communities as we enrich the experiences of our students – we have to continue to struggle to create that institutional space, or it will shrink and atrophy.

My third choice is to take what I learn about and from social movements for change – in Los Angeles and beyond – and channel it back into my teaching and scholarship. I have tried to do this in multiple ways. I have taught a seminar on 'law and social movements' that asks students to think about how foundational movements of social change – labour, civil rights, LGBT[18] rights, and others – have changed (or failed to change) American society. What lessons can we learn from them? What role do lawyers play in them? A focal point of that class, and my scholarly work on social movement lawyering, has been to challenge students to embrace the positive role that lawyers can play as allies and even leaders in struggles for change. All too often, I have seen law students adopt critical views of lawyers as change agents – views that have been shaped by a half-century's worth of critical commentary that suggests lawyers often do more harm than good to social movements. My teaching and scholarly project has been to reclaim an affirmative role for lawyers and their legal tools – to challenge students to think about how law can support and enlarge the scope of transformative change. Less explicitly, but no less deliberately, I also have sought to reincorporate movements into my doctrinal teaching: using them in my course on the legal profession to highlight how lawyers manage conflicts and in my corporations' class to show how workers' movements have sought to challenge the traditional conception of corporate ownership.[19]

It has now been over seven years since that Michael Brown moment and that circle in my seminar – that moment that changed the country and also changed me. And as I have embarked anew teaching my Community Economic Development course, I have tried to carry the lessons of 2014 forward. This past year, a colleague and I co-taught the course around the very issues that sparked the BLM movement: how public interest lawyers have responded – and should continue to

totalling at least six credit hours'); State Bar of California, Task Force on Admissions Regulation Reform: Phase II Final Report 2 (2014) (stating recommendation that new applicants to the bar should have 'taken at least fifteen units of practice-based, experiential course' work). The American Bar Association sets the accreditation standards for US law schools and, in that role, may impose curricular requirements like those on experiential learning.

18 LGBT is an initialism which stands for lesbian, gay, bisexual, and transgender.

19 In Business Associations, I teach a class on worker-owned cooperatives and another on employee rights to corporate property, using the famous case *Local 1330, United Steel Workers of America v. United States Steel Corporation*, 631 F 2d 1264 (1980).

respond – to injustice at the intersection of local racial and economic inequality in low-income communities of colour. As we now confront a global pandemic that has disproportionately affected African American and Latinx people in the United States, alongside a new eruption of global racial justice protest sparked by the killing of George Floyd,[20] it is imperative to reshape teaching – not just clinical teaching, but all teaching – to meet the moment and to begin devising alternative legal rules and institutions that recognise and fight against systemic racism.

It is all too easy for us to forget about lawlessness and the damage it inflicts as we step each day into our offices and classrooms built as monuments to the rule of law. It should not take senseless death to remind us that law is only an ideal that requires unceasing struggle to achieve. And yet we should also not let that tragedy pass without honouring it with action. As King spoke at the eulogy of the four girls killed in the bombing of Birmingham's 16th Street Baptist Church:

> And so my friends, they did not die in vain. God still has a way of wringing good out of evil. And history has proven over and over again that unmerited suffering is redemptive. The innocent blood of these little girls may well serve as a redemptive force that will bring new light to this dark city.[21]

Let us make it so.

20 BBC, 'George Floyd: What happened in the final moments of his life' *BBC News* (London, 16 July 2020) <www.bbc.co.uk/news/world-us-canada-52861726> accessed 06 February 2021.

21 Carson and Shepard (n 10), 89.

# Index